ORTHODOX DOGMATIC THEOLOGY

The First Ecumenical Council.
*Icon by Monk Theophanes the Cretan, Catholicon of St. Nicholas,
Stavronikita Monastery, Mount Athos, ca. 1546.*

ORTHODOX DOGMATIC THEOLOGY

A CONCISE EXPOSITION

By
PROTOPRESBYTER MICHAEL POMAZANSKY

Translated and edited by
HIEROMONK SERAPHIM ROSE
and the St. Herman of Alaska Brotherhood

Third Edition

ST. HERMAN OF ALASKA BROTHERHOOD
2005

Translated by Hieromonk Seraphim Rose with the blessing of
His Eminence AVERKY, Archbishop of Syracuse and Holy Trinity
Monastery (Russian Orthodox Church Outside of Russia), from the
Russian original (*Pravoslavnoye Dogmaticheskoye Bogosloviye*)
published by Holy Trinity Monastery, Jordanville, New York,
1963, and revised by the author in 1973.

First (English) Edition, 1983
Second Edition, 1994
Second Printing of Second Edition, 1997
Third Edition, 2005

Third Edition printed with the blessing of His Grace LONGIN,
Serbian Orthodox Bishop of the U.S.A. and Canada,
New Gracanica Metropolitanate, and Bishop Administrator of the
Serbian Orthodox Diocese of Western America.

Printed in the United States of America.

Front cover: 19th-century icon of Christ "Not Made with Hands,"
from Valaam Monastery in Russia, now located at the St. Herman
of Alaska Monastery, Platina, California.

Publishers Cataloging-in-Publication

Pomazansky, Protopresbyter Michael, 1888–1988.
  Orthodox dogmatic theology: a concise exposition / by Protopresbyter Michael
Pomazansky; translated and edited by Hieromonk Seraphim Rose and the St.
Herman of Alaska Brotherhood.— 3rd ed.
    p. cm.
  Originally published in Russian as: *Pravoslavnoye Dogmaticheskoye Bogosloviye*.
  Includes bibliographical references and indexes.
  ISBN–13: 978–0–938635–69–7
  ISBN–10: 0–938635–69–7
  1. Theology, Doctrinal. 2. Orthodox Eastern Church—Doctrines. I. Rose,
Seraphim. II. Title.

BX320.3.P66 2005
230/.19—dc22   2005936831

Contents

PART II: GOD MANIFEST IN THE WORLD

Chapter 3: God and the Creation

Chapter 4: The Providence of God

Chapter 5: Concerning Evil and Sin

Chapter 9: Prayer
As the Expression of the Inward Life of the Church

Chapter 10: Christian Eschatology
The Future Fate of the World and Mankind

APPENDICES

Appendix I

On the New Currents in Russian Philosophico-Theological Thought, from the Point of View of the Dogmas of the Orthodox Christian Faith

Appendix II

The Ecumenical Councils and the Heresies That Have Attacked the Church's Teaching

Appendix III

Fathers and Teachers of the Church and Church Writers Mentioned in the Text of *Orthodox Dogmatic Theology*

Editor's Preface to the
Third Edition

PROTOPRESBYTER Michael Pomazansky's *Orthodox Dogmatic Theology* has long been regarded as a standard source of Orthodox theology. After its publication in Russian in 1963, it was used as a textbook at Holy Trinity Orthodox Seminary in Jordanville, New York, at which Fr. Michael taught.

In 1973, Hieromonk Seraphim Rose, an American convert to the Russian Orthodox Church, conceived the idea of translating Fr. Michael's book and publishing it in English. As a missionary-minded monk living at the St. Herman Monastery in the mountains of northern California, Fr. Seraphim was always seeking ways of making the sources of Orthodox Christianity available to his fellow Americans. He believed that *Orthodox Dogmatic Theology* was "important and timely"[1] for the contemporary English-speaking Orthodox world.

Fr. Seraphim chose this book as a vehicle by which to present Orthodox theology in English not only because he found it a clear, concise and Biblically based presentation of Orthodoxy, but also because it was the main dogmatics textbook of Holy Trinity Seminary. The Jordanville seminary/monastery was the chief theological, intellectual and publishing center of the Russian Orthodox Church Outside of Russia, of which Fr. Seraphim was a faithful son. But even more significant to Fr. Seraphim was the fact that the "Jordanville school" of Orthodoxy (as it was called by others) was a continuation of the more traditional streams of theological thought and spiritual life in pre-Communist Russia.

The "Jordanville school" was not without its critics, who accused it primarily of being heir to the "Western influences" that had made their

---

[1] Letter of Fr. Seraphim to Fr. Alexey Young, March 27, 1981. In Fr. Alexey Young, ed., *Letters from Father Seraphim*, p. 224.

Hieromonk Seraphim Rose (1934–1982).

way into the Russian Orthodox Church prior to the Bolshevik Revolution. These influences—so the critics claimed—were more than mere blemishes on an otherwise sound tradition: they were a cancer that affected the whole body of the tradition, and therefore a total overhaul of the tradition was necessary.

Fr. Seraphim was aware of this criticism, but he strongly believed that the Orthodox Patristic theological tradition and way of life had never been lost in Russia, nor had it been lost in its continuation at Jordanville. The "Western influences," he said, only touched upon certain outward modes of expression (which he agreed were unfortunate), but did not touch the heart of the tradition. The Russian theological tradition was firmly established, having been founded on a conscious assimilation by the Russian people of the Orthodoxy of the Byzantine Empire, and of the mind of the Holy Fathers. To dismiss this theological tradition as being hopelessly lost, and to attempt to start over, as it were, was an enterprise fraught with its own dangers. Concerning a would-be contemporary theologian who was writing outside of any such firmly established tradition, Fr. Seraphim wrote: "I have the impression [he] demonstrates quite a bit of rationalism himself; he writes not as from within a tradition himself, but as one who is *striving* to get into that tradition. Our uninterrupted Russian tradition, for all its real and supposed Westernisms, has a strength and resiliency which the 'rediscoverers of tradition' do not have."[2] About other such "rediscoverers of tradition," Fr. Seraphim commented: "They virtually boast that they alone are 'great theologians' who have just now rediscovered a lost theological tradition; but actually their theology is remarkably crude and simplistic, especially when put beside the writings of a truly great theologian in the unbroken Orthodox tradition—our own Fr. Michael Pomazansky of Jordanville—who is subtle, refined, deep—and totally overlooked by the 'bright young theologians.'"[3]

---

[2] Letter of Fr. Seraphim to Alexey Young, March 30, 1976. *Letters from Father Seraphim,* p. 161.

[3] Letter of Fr. Seraphim to Andrew Bond, May 1, 1976. In Hieromonk Damascene, *Father Seraphim Rose: His Life and Works,* p. 524.

Fr. Seraphim highly valued Fr. Michael precisely as one who wrote and taught theology from *within* the Orthodox tradition. Desiring to be "linked up" to the tradition himself, he would write to Fr. Michael asking him theological and historical questions that would arise in the course of his own writing and publishing. "We ourselves," he noted, "follow the Jordanville school, which is in the best Orthodox tradition (and is being much and unjustly slandered today), and we frequently take counsel from Fr. Michael Pomazansky and others, whose judgment we trust and respect, knowing that thus we are in a good tradition and do not have to trust our own faulty judgment for all the answers."[4]

As highly as Fr. Seraphim regarded Fr. Michael, there was one theological writer whom he valued even more: Archbishop Averky of Jordanville, the rector of Holy Trinity Seminary and the abbot of Holy Trinity Monastery. Not long after his conversion to Orthodoxy, Fr. Seraphim's archbishop and spiritual father, St. John (Maximovitch) of Shanghai and San Francisco, had directed him to Archbishop Averky as a reliable guide in theological matters. "Archbishop Averky," Fr. Seraphim wrote later, "is in the genuine Patristic tradition as few other living Orthodox fathers. A disciple of the great 20th-century theologian and holy hierarch, Archbishop Theophan of Poltava,[5] Archbishop Averky is a bearer and transmitter, in a direct and unbroken line of Orthodox theologians, of the genuine Patristic doctrine."[6] Fr. Seraphim's estimation of Archbishop Averky was shared by Fr. Michael. As Fr. Seraphim noted in a letter: "We just asked Fr. Michael Pomazansky: *who* is an authentic theological guide for today? And his reply: Archbishop

---

[4] Letter of Fr. Seraphim to Alexey Young, May 6, 1973. *Letters from Father Seraphim,* p. 93.

[5] Elsewhere Fr. Seraphim wrote that, in the decade following the Russian Revolution, Archbishop Theophan of Poltava "was widely acknowledged as the most Patristically minded of all the Russian theologians abroad" ("The Holy Fathers of Orthodox Spirituality, Part I," *The Orthodox Word,* no. 58 [1974], p. 191). Archbishop Theophan was the disciple of a Holy Father of 19th-century Russia, St. Theophan the Recluse.

[6] [Fr. Seraphim Rose], "Archbishop Averky of Jordanville," *The Orthodox Word,* no. 62 (1975), p. 95.

Averky."[7] Over the years, Fr. Seraphim would write to Archbishop Averky as he did to Fr. Michael, seeking guidance on many issues.

In 1973, when Fr. Seraphim formed the desire to translate Fr. Michael's textbook, he wrote to Archbishop Averky and Fr. Michael, asking their blessings. Soon he received blessings from both of them, together with a number of initial revisions which Fr. Michael asked to be incorporated into the English edition. Later Fr. Michael sent a new introduction and corresponded with the fathers of the St. Herman Monastery about the book's content. As a result of this exchange, he sent new material to be added to the English version, primarily in order to underline yet further the Orthodox teaching on the redemption of mankind. Asking for nothing in return for the rights to his book, he even sent donations to help to fund the book's publication.

Fr. Seraphim translated much of Fr. Michael's book aloud into a tape recorder. He often did this after meals in the monastery refectory, as everyone sat around the table, so that the monastery brothers (most of them American converts) could benefit from the book, which was then being heard for the first time in the English language. Others would transcribe these tapes, and Fr. Seraphim would carefully edit the translation and prepare it for publication.

Fr. Seraphim also wrote numerous footnotes to be incorporated into the book. These were either to provide clarification on certain points or to introduce helpful information not included in the main text. To make the book even more valuable as a reference tool, he also wrote appendices which gave basic information on the Ecumenical Councils, on the main heresies which have attacked the Church, and on the Holy Fathers who have set forth the Church's dogmatic theology.

In 1975, not long after Fr. Seraphim had begun to translate *Orthodox Dogmatic Theology*, Fr. Michael—then eighty-six years old—wrote to the fathers that he would very much like to live to see it completed. Ironically, it was Fr. Michael and not Fr. Seraphim who lived to see it in

---

[7] Letter of Fr. Seraphim to Alexey Young, November 4, 1975. *Letters from Father Seraphim,* p. 146.

published form. Although Fr. Seraphim finished translating and editing Fr. Michael's book, he died in 1982 at the relatively young age of forty-eight, before he was able to have it printed. It was printed in 1984, two years after Fr. Seraphim's repose. In 1988 Fr. Michael reposed in Jordanville, just days short of his hundredth birthday.

FATHER Seraphim especially esteemed Fr. Michael's book because of the simplicity of its presentation. It was accessible not only to students, but to the contemporary layman in general. Avoiding highly academic language, Fr. Michael wrote his book with the mind of a pastor: he wanted it to reach and touch everyone. In a letter, Fr. Seraphim commented: "Fr. Michael avoids the 'academic' pitfall because he understands the whole of Orthodox theology so well that he can present it simply and clearly, and from just the right point of view (it's called the 'Jordanville' ideology ... but it's just plain Orthodoxy, shorn of academic pretensions, down to earth)."[8]

While Fr. Michael's book is strongly Patristic, with references to Patristic teachings and quotations from the Holy Fathers spread throughout, his primary source and primary emphasis is on the Holy Scriptures. In fact, this work can be seen as a reference book of Scriptural passages as they relate to the basic dogmas and practices of the Orthodox Church. Certainly no other English-language book on Orthodox theology has fulfilled this purpose as well as has Fr. Michael's book.

Since its publication over twenty years ago, the English edition of *Orthodox Dogmatic Theology* has received a very positive response, and has come to be regarded as one of the best introductory books on Orthodox theology. Readers comment on how surprised they are to find that this textbook is not only highly informative, but also highly *inspiring*. It is now used not only at the Jordanville seminary, but at other Orthodox seminaries as well.

To this third English edition of *Orthodox Dogmatic Theology*, we have added more substantive footnotes, primarily consisting of quota-

---

[8] Ibid., January 20, 1975. *Letters from Father Seraphim,* pp. 125–26.

tions from the Holy Fathers. Like the footnotes Fr. Seraphim added to the first English edition, these new footnotes are intended to provide further elucidation and clarification of Orthodox doctrines.

In order to preserve the identity of Fr. Michael's original work, and of Fr. Seraphim's material as the original editor, we have made every effort to differentiate these for the reader, and to further differentiate them from our own additions.

The main text of the book belongs entirely to Fr. Michael. All the footnotes belong either to Fr. Seraphim or to us, the editors of the third edition. We have indicated our own footnotes by appending the abbreviation "—3RD ED." at the end of each such note. All the other footnotes in the book (i.e., those having no abbreviation at the end) were written by Fr. Seraphim as the editor of the first edition. In a few places we have added some material to Fr. Seraphim's footnotes; this added material is enclosed in brackets.

It is our hope and prayer that this new edition of Fr. Michael's book will touch many more hearts with the riches and depths of Orthodox theology. Through it may yet more souls enter into the continuous, unbroken stream of Orthodox Patristic tradition, of which Fr. Michael was an authentic carrier.

Hieromonk Damascene
St. Herman of Alaska Monastery
Platina, California
Bright Wednesday, 2005

Protopresbyter Michael Pomazansky (1888–1988).

About the Author

Protopresbyter Michael Pomazansky:
Theology in the Ancient Tradition

[First published in The Orthodox Word, *no. 97 (1981).]*

PROTOPRESBYTER Michael Pomazansky is unique among contemporary Orthodox theologians. At 93 years of age he is surely the oldest of those still writing theological articles; but more important, he received his theological formation not in any of the theological academies of the present day, all of which reflect to some degree the theological uncertainties and divisions of today's Orthodoxy, but in the pre-Revolutionary academies of Russia, when Orthodoxy was still one in spirit, was still rooted in the age-old past of theological tradition, and did not suffer from the "identity crisis" that plagues so much of Orthodox theological literature today.

Some Orthodox writers today seem to have so little awareness of the distinctness of Orthodoxy that they lead people into the false opinion that Orthodoxy is scarcely different from the Western confessions at all, and if only a few more "joint theological committees" will work out a few more "agreed statements" about the faith, we can all be one again and even share the same Holy Mysteries; this is the aim of the various societies and activities of the "ecumenical movement."

The reaction to this movement, on the other hand, even when it goes under the name of a "Patristic revival," sometimes produces a definition of Orthodoxy so narrow that it proclaims all but a small group of today's Orthodox to be without Grace, or breaks off contact with its own Orthodox roots by declaring that only today are a few Orthodox theologians becoming free of the "Western captivity" (dominance by

Roman Catholic or Protestant ideas) in which Orthodoxy has supposedly been held in recent centuries.

Both of these extremes are perilously close to losing their very identity as Orthodox. Perhaps the crucial test for the extremists of either side is that of *continuity:* Are they teaching the same teaching they received from their own fathers in the faith, who in turn received it from their Fathers, and so on in an unbroken line with the past? More often than not, the extremists will have to admit that—no, they themselves are "correcting the mistakes" of their fathers, that 19th-century theology (for example) is too narrow and anti-Western or (in the opposite extreme) too "scholastic" and pro-Western; that some respected Orthodox theologians of earlier centuries are "out of date" and inapplicable to today's "ecumenical" Christianity, or (in the opposite extreme) are "Westernizers" who "didn't understand the real Orthodox teaching" and should be rejected as Orthodox authorities.

Meanwhile, the genuine Orthodox tradition continues as it has always been, trying to preserve its integrity in the midst of these conflicting currents. Fortunately, this tradition has a way—with the help of God, Who looks after His Church—of preserving itself from the extremes that often try to deflect it from its course. This self-preservation and self-continuity of the Orthodox tradition is not something that requires the assistance of "brilliant theologians"; it is the result of the uninterrupted "catholic consciousness" of the Church which has guided the Church from the very beginning of its existence. It is this catholic consciousness which preserved the wholeness of Russian Orthodoxy in the 1920s when the extreme reforms of the "Living Church" seemed to have taken possession of the Church and many of its leading hierarchs and theologians; this same catholic consciousness is at work today and will continue to preserve Christ's Church through all the trials of the present day, just as it has for nearly 2000 years. Those who speak for it are often not the "brilliant theologians," who can be led astray as easily as anyone else, but more often humble laborers in Christ's vineyard who would be surprised and even offended that anyone should make anything of their labors or even call them "theologians."

One of such humble laborers in the Russian Church today is Fr. Michael Pomazansky.

Fr. Michael was born on November 7/19, 1888, in the town of Koryst in the province of Volhynia in the west of Russia. His father's family had been parish priests for generations, and the simple impressions from the churchly way of life of his childhood set their seal on Fr. Michael's whole life, influencing him more—as he himself has said—than all the theological schools he attended.

Fr. Michael's years of attending the theological preparatory school and seminary (1901–1908) coincided with the Russo-Japanese War and the first Russian Revolution of 1905, which threatened the end of the Orthodox way of life in Russia, but also made evident the need for faithfulness to Orthodox tradition in those who, like Fr. Michael, were church-oriented. During these same years a great hierarch of the Russian Church was transferred to the diocese of Volhynia—Bishop (later Metropolitan) Anthony Khrapovitsky, a highly educated churchman, a flaming preacher, a devoted son of the Church and an ardent Russian patriot, but at the same time an enemy of mere routine and "taking for granted" in church life, a man of warm heart who had an especially close contact with and influence on young people, and especially future monks and clergy. Bishop Anthony had a great influence on the soul of the young student Michael.

Fr. Michael entered the Kiev Theological Academy in 1908, graduating from it in 1912. The Kiev Academy had long been a center for the defense of Orthodoxy in Western Russia, especially against the Latins, and had produced five Metropolitans who were numbered among the saints. The emphasis in the Academy in Fr. Michael's time was on solid theological and historical knowledge, and none of the professors was noted for special eloquence or "popularity." Fr. Michael's dissertation was on a technical historical subject: "Particularities of the Divine Services in the Church of Western Russia According to the Printed Service Books of the 17th Century." Here he was able to study in detail the question of "Western influences" in the Russian Church.

After graduation, Fr. Michael spent two years in the south of Russia as a missionary among the sects that flourished there; this experience made him for life a zealous student of the New Testament, which the sectarians distorted for their own ends, but which, rightly understood, contains the profound teaching of the Orthodox Church. In 1914 he was appointed an instructor in the Kaluga seminary not too far from Moscow. Here he remained for three years, until the outbreak of the Revolution. With the closing of the seminary at that time, he returned with his small family to his homeland in the south; he had married the daughter of a priest, Vera Theodorovna Shumskaya, and had several children.

By an agreement between the Polish and Soviet governments, Fr. Michael's native village fell within the boundaries of Poland (only ten miles from the Soviet border). Fr. Michael received a teaching position in a Russian high school in Rovno, where he taught Russian language and literature, philosophy and Latin. In this position he was able to send his children through high school, and once this responsibility was discharged he was able to receive ordination to the priesthood, in 1936.

His first assignment as priest was to the Warsaw cathedral of St. Mary Magdalen, where he served as a diocesan missionary; and when the main church in this cathedral was given over to Ukrainian services, he went with other clergy to the lower church, where Slavonic services were continued. Near the end of the Second World War (1944), he was able to go with his family to Germany, where he entered the clergy of the Russian Church Outside of Russia under Metropolitan Anastassy.

While in Warsaw, Fr. Michael was the unofficial editor of the church newspaper *The Word*, and after its closure he was official editor of the magazine *Sunday Reading*. In these years (1936–1944) he also published articles in the *Messenger of Orthodox Theologians* in Poland.

In Germany he was entrusted with the organization of the official organ of the Russian Church Abroad, *Church Life;* he was in charge of this from 1947 until his departure for America in August 1949. Since that time he has lived at Holy Trinity Monastery at Jordanville, New York, teaching in the seminary there for many years, from the very beginning of its existence in 1950, and writing numerous articles for the monastery's periodicals,[1] in addition to his major work, *Orthodox Dogmatic Theology*, which for long has been the seminary's textbook for its course in dogmatic theology.

Fr. Michael's writings have been on various Church subjects: apologetics, defenses of the faith against modern errors (Bulgakov's "sophiology," the "ecumenical movement," "renovationism" in liturgical theology, etc.), on various feast days and Church services, on aspects of the teachings of the Holy Fathers (in particular, two enlightening comparisons of ancient Fathers with St. John of Kronstadt: St. Basil on the Six Days of Creation, and St. Symeon the New Theologian on Grace), and many other subjects.

Especially helpful to present-day Orthodox Christians who are surrounded by the non-Orthodox are his careful distinctions (especially in *Orthodox Dogmatic Theology*) between Orthodox beliefs and those of Roman Catholicism and Protestantism, even on some points which may seem outwardly identical. This he does without any tone of irritation against the non-Orthodox—something so common in polemical writings today—but, always after describing their views with fairness, he sets forth the Orthodox teaching in an objective manner that helps Orthodox Christians to understand their own faith much better.

In all his writings, Fr. Michael is not trying to discover anything "new" in Orthodox tradition, or to stand out for the sharpness of his criticisms—common faults in today's academic theology. Rather, he attempts to give only his own humble, serene reflections on the wealth of Orthodox teaching which he accepts as already established and experienced by centuries of theologians and simple Christians before him. Even when, for the sake of truth, he does find it necessary to criticize a view, whether inside or outside the Orthodox Church, he does it with such gentleness and good intention that it is impossible for anyone to be offended by him.

Most of all, in Fr. Michael's writings one may see a characteristic of

---

[1] These have been collected into two volumes in Russian: *Life, Faith, and the Church* (Jordanville, N.Y.: Holy Trinity Monastery, 1976). [An English edition, consisting of selections from the Russian edition, has been published under the title *Selected Essays* (Jordanville, N.Y.: Holy Trinity Monastery, 1996).]

genuine Orthodox theology that is so often lost sight of in our cold, rationalistic age. Theology is not primarily a matter of arguments, criticisms, proofs and disproofs; it is first of all men's *word about God*, in accordance with the Divinely revealed teaching of Orthodoxy. Therefore, its first purpose and intent is always to inspire, to warm the heart, to lift one above the petty preoccupations of earth in order to glimpse the Divine beginning and end of all things and so to give one the energy and encouragement to struggle towards God and our heavenly homeland. This is certainly the meaning and spirit of the theology of Orthodoxy's three preeminent "theologians": St. John the Evangelist, St. Gregory Nazianzen, and St. Symeon the New Theologian; they, one may say, have set the tone for Orthodox theology, and this remains the tone and the task of theology even in our cold-hearted and analytic age.

Fr. Michael's theology is in this warm-hearted and inspiring tone. He is not the only one to write Orthodox theology with this intent today, but he is one of the few, in an older generation that is fast vanishing, who can serve as a link between us and the genuine theology of the Holy Fathers. Fr. Michael himself would be offended to hear such words, or even to discover that we have written this much about him; but that itself is only another sign that he is someone totally penetrated with the true spirit of Orthodox theology. May the younger generations learn from him!

Hieromonk Seraphim Rose, 1981

Translator's Preface

[Compiled from the handwritten notes of Fr. Seraphim Rose, who reposed before completing this Preface.]

ORTHODOX *Dogmatic Theology* is Fr. Michael Pomazansky's masterpiece. It is calmly and soberly written. Although it is systematic—as it must be for a school textbook—it is not pedantic.

One of the major advantages of this book is its simplicity of presentation. It was written not for academic theologians, but primarily for pastors, and thus it has a practical approach that is missing in many works of contemporary academic theology. In his theological writings, Fr. Michael remains deeply rooted in the tradition of the Orthodox Church, not trying to supercede with his own private opinions any revelation that the Church has handed down to us. Indeed, he avoids presenting mere "opinions" altogether, since his intent here is to write about exactly *what the Church teaches*—what pastors can give to their flocks as the certain, unchanging teaching of the Church—and not about what is "disputed." There is a distinct *wholeness* in Fr. Michael's approach, which allows for no confusion over the Church's actual teaching. Another advantage of this book, especially for pastors who deal with converts to Orthodoxy from various religious denominations, is that it contrasts the traditional Orthodox teaching with the errors and innovations of Roman Catholicism and Protestantism.

If the works of Fr. Michael can be referred to as "school" theology, this is only in the best sense of the word. Fr. Michael is the last surviving graduate of a pre-revolutionary Russian theological academy (that of Kiev), and is therefore one of the few living contacts we have with the long-standing centers of traditional Russian theology, the direct inheritance of the Byzantine Fathers. Always faithful to the instruction of the Church, his actual "school" is, ultimately, the Church herself.

Hieromonk Seraphim Rose, 1981

Author's Preface to the English Translation

IN the Church of Christ Truth is one, as indeed it should be. Historically it is one, common to all the Church's faithful, and unchanging; it has been such from the great day of the Apostolic Pentecost, when the New Testament Church received its beginning, and after that for the course of two thousand years until our time, and it will remain such until the end of time. This attribute of the Church is splendidly expressed in the Church hymn (the kontakion) for the commemoration of the First Ecumenical Council at Nicaea, which we celebrate on the Sunday before the solemn day of Holy Pentecost. Here are the words of this Church hymn:

The preaching of the Apostles and the dogmas of the Fathers have sealed the one faith of the Church. And wearing the garment of truth, woven of the theology from above, she rightly dispenses and glorifies the great mystery of piety.

Thus, the great mystery of Christian piety, that is, life in Christ, is built on an unchanging unity of faith in the one Truth. Arbitrary attempts to introduce into our faith anything new—even though they do occur, sometimes from the naive desire of private individuals to attract attention to the faith by this means, or to put freshness into church life—are decisively rejected by the Orthodox Church.

The present book—an exposition of Christian dogmas—has for its subject what the Holy Apostles teach us in their epistles, what the great Holy Fathers kept in its power and authenticity in their self-sacrificing ministry against various heretical attacks (Sts. Athanasius the Great, Basil the Great, Gregory the Theologian, John Chrysostom), what the Church has preserved, guarded, defended, and confesses unaltered in our days. There is no Orthodox theology that is in any particular way

26

"Russian" or that belongs to any other nation, as is sometimes supposed by superficial observers. By human nature "imperfection" is something that belongs to each of us and to everything we do.

However, since faith is active in life and is a living thing, the circumstances of various epochs cause dogmatic expositions to devote special attention to those various points of faith which *in that epoch* it is desirable, profitable, important to make firm in the consciousness of readers. Thus, in the present exposition of Orthodox theology a special place is allotted to the truly close and inseparable bond *between the Church on earth and the Heavenly Church*—our spiritual communion in the Church with "the heavenly Jerusalem, and to an innumerable company of angels, to the general assembly and church of the firstborn, which are written in heaven" (Heb. 12:22–23). Here is to be found the authentic *pleroma*—the fullness, the catholicity of the Church. Special attention has been directed in the book to this attribute of the Church. This truth has been forgotten, ignored, or completely rejected in the great part of what is called Christianity.

The fullness of actual life in the Church on earth is manifested in three aspects: (*a*) confession of faith; (*b*) moral life; and (*c*) the Divine services. Therefore, each Christian is called (*a*) to believe; (*b*) to live and act according to faith; and (*c*) to glorify God and to pray. Although dogmatic theology occupies itself only with the one aspect of confession of faith, still it is from faith that the second and third aspects come—life acording to faith, and prayer. And so the present book is called to indicate likewise the principles on which are erected the Christian *moral life* and the Christian life bound up with the *Divine services.*

The present exposition of faith attempts to fulfill this obligation: (*a*) it indicates what kind of moral life is directly dictated by the exploit of Christ on the Cross. This path is our *personal struggle in the name of the Cross of the Lord.* The always expressive visible banner of the Cross serves for our gaze as a constant reminder of this. The very concept of the spiritual Cross contains in itself not only the various forms of personal struggle, but also the involuntary sorrows of life which are accepted in humility before the Providence of God.

Finally, (*b*) the book indicates what forms and kinds of our *prayer and glorification of God* proceed from the fullness of our beliefs. The general character of our worship of God is dictated by the words of the Psalm: "Bless the Lord, O my soul, and *all that is within me* bless His holy name" (Ps. 102:1). "All that is within me" means all the capacities of the soul. Therefore, it is perfectly natural for them to be manifested to our holy feelings in the various forms of noble human activity, the talents given us by God. We call on nature itself to join us in the Church's glorification.

Such is the aim and the content of the present book.

Protopresbyter Michael Pomazansky
June 1981

Introduction

1. THE SOURCES OF CHRISTIAN DOCTRINE

The Concern of the Church for the Purity of Christian Teaching

FROM the first days of her existence, the Holy Church of Christ has ceaselessly been concerned that her children, her members, should stand firm in the pure truth.

I have no greater joy than to hear that my children walk in truth, writes the Holy Apostle, John the Theologian (III John, v. 4).

I have written briefly, exhorting and testifying that this is the true Grace of God wherein ye stand, says the Holy Apostle Peter in concluding his Catholic Epistle (I Peter 5:12).[1]

The Holy Apostle Paul relates concerning himself that, having preached for fourteen years, he went to Jerusalem by revelation with Barnabas and Titus, and there he offered—especially to the most renowned citizens—the gospel which he preached, *lest by any means I should run, or had run, in vain* (Gal. 2:2).

"Instruct us in Thy path, that we may walk *in Thy Truth*"—is the first petition in the priestly prayers (the Prayers at Lamplighting[2]) in the first Divine service of the daily cycle, Vespers.

The true path of faith, which has always been carefully preserved in the history of the Church, from of old was called *straight, right,* in Greek, *orthos*—that is, "orthodoxy." In the Psalter—from which, as we

---

[1] "Catholic," meaning "universal," is the name applied to the New Testament Epistles (those of James, Peter, Jude and John) which were addressed, not to individuals or local churches (as are all the Epistles of St. Paul), but to the whole Church or to believers in general.

[2] The "Prayers at Lamplighting" are the silent prayers read by the priest before the Royal Doors while Psalm 103 is being read aloud by the Reader.

know from the history of the Christian Divine services, the Church has been inseparable from the first moment of her existence—we find such phrases as the following: *my foot hath stood in uprightness* (Ps. 25:10); *from before Thy face let my judgment come forth* (Ps. 16:2); *praise is meet for the upright* (Ps. 32:1); and there are others. The Apostle Paul instructs Timothy to present himself before God *a workman that needeth not to be ashamed, rightly dividing* (that is, rightly cutting with a chisel, from the Greek *orthotomounta*) *the word of truth* (II Tim. 2:15). In early Christian literature there is constant mention of the keeping of "the rule of faith," the "rule of truth." The very term "orthodoxy" was widely used even in the epoch before the Ecumenical Councils, then in the terminology of the Ecumenical Councils themselves, and in the Fathers of the Church both of the East and of the West.

Side by side with the straight, or right, path of faith there have always been those who thought differently (*heterodoxountes*, or "heterodox," in the expression of St. Ignatius the God-bearer[3]), a world of greater or lesser errors among Christians, and sometimes even whole incorrect systems which attempted to burst into the midst of Orthodox Christians. As a result of the quest for truth there occurred divisions among Christians.

Becoming acquainted with the history of the Church, and likewise observing the contemporary world, we see that the errors which war against Orthodox Truth have appeared and do appear (*a*) under the influence of other religions, (*b*) under the influence of philosophy, and (*c*) through the weakness and inclinations of fallen human nature, which seeks the rights and justifications of these weaknesses and inclinations.

Errors take root and become obstinate most frequently because of the pride of those who defend them, because of intellectual pride.

Dogmas

So as to guard the right path of faith, the Church has had to forge strict forms for the expression of the truths of faith: it has had to *build*

---

[3] For biographical information on Fathers and teachers of the Church, see Appendix III at the end of this book.

up the fortresses of truth for the repulsion of influences foreign to the Church. The definitions of truth declared by the Church have been called, since the days of the Apostles, *dogmas*. In the Acts of the Apostles we read of the Apostles Paul and Timothy that *as they went through the cities, they delivered them the decrees (dogmata) for to keep, that were ordained of the apostles and elders which were at Jerusalem* (Acts 16:4; here the reference is to the decrees of the Apostolic Council which is described in the fifteenth chapter of the book of Acts). Among the ancient Greeks and Romans the Greek word *dogma* was used to refer (*a*) to philosophical conceptions, and (*b*) to directives which were to be precisely fulfilled. In the Christian understanding, "dogmas" are the opposite of "opinions," that is, inconstant personal conceptions.

The Sources of Dogmas

On what are dogmas founded? It is clear that dogmas are not founded on the rational conceptions of separate individuals, even though these might be Fathers and teachers of the Church, but, rather, on the teaching of *Sacred Scripture* and on the Apostolic *Sacred Tradition.* The truths of faith which are contained in the Sacred Scripture and the Apostolic Sacred Tradition give the *fullness* of the teaching of faith which was called by the ancient Fathers of the Church the "catholic faith," the "catholic teaching" of the Church.[4] The truths of Scripture and Tradition, harmoniously fused together into a single whole,

---

[4] In such phrases the word "catholic" means "universal" as referring to the Church of all times, peoples, and places, *where there is neither Greek nor Jew, circumcision nor uncircumcision, Barbarian, Scythian, bond nor free: but Christ is all and in all* (Col. 3:11). A celebrated definition of "catholic" in the early Church was given by St. Vincent of Lerins, the 5th-century monastic Father of Gaul, who in his *Commonitorium* says: "Every care should be taken to hold fast to what has been believed everywhere, always, and by all. That is truly and properly 'catholic,' as indicated by the force and etymology of the name itself, which comprises everything truly universal" (chap. 2; FC, p. 270). The *name* of "catholic" has been kept from early times in the "Roman Catholic" church, but the *teaching* of the early Church has been preserved in the Orthodox Church, which even to this day can be and still is

define the "catholic consciousness" of the Church, a consciousness that is guided by the Holy Spirit.

Sacred Scripture

By "Sacred Scripture" are to be understood those books written by the Holy Prophets and Apostles under the action of the Holy Spirit; therefore they are called "Divinely inspired." They are divided into books of the Old Testament and the books of the New Testament.

The Church recognizes thirty-eight books of the Old Testament. After the example of the Old Testament Church,[5] several of these books are joined to form a single book, bringing the number to twenty-two books, according to the number of letters in the Hebrew alphabet.[6] These books, which were entered at some time into the He-

---

called "catholic." In many places in this book Fr. Michael will be contrasting the teaching of Roman Catholicism and the true catholic or Orthodox teaching.

[5] Although the Church in the strict sense was established only at the coming of Christ (see Matt. 16:18), there was in a certain sense a "Church" in the Old Testament also, composed of all those who looked with hope to the coming of the Messiah. After the death of Christ on the Cross, when He descended to hell and *preached unto the spirits in prison* (I Peter 3:19), He brought up the righteous ones of the Old Testament with Him into Paradise, and to this day the Orthodox Church celebrates the feast days of the Old Testament Forefathers, Patriarchs, and Prophets as equal to the Saints of the New Testament. On the Church of Christ in general, see chap. 7 below.

[6] The twenty-two "canonical" books of the Old Testament are: (1) Genesis, (2) Exodus, (3) Leviticus, (4) Numbers, (5) Deuteronomy, (6) Joshua, (7) Judges and Ruth considered as one, (8) First and Second Kings (called First and Second Samuel in the King James Version), (9) Third and Fourth Kings (First and Second Kings in the KJV), (10) First and Second Paralipomena (First and Second Chronicles in the KJV), (11) First Esdras (Ezra) and Nehemiah, (12) Esther, (13) Job, (14) Psalms, (15) Proverbs, (16) Ecclesiastes, (17) the Song of Songs, (18) Isaiah, (19) Jeremiah [including the Lamentations of Jeremiah], (20) Ezekiel, (21) Daniel, (22) the Twelve Prophets (Hosea, Joel, Amos, Obadiah, Jonah, Micah, Nahum, Habakkuk, Zephaniah, Haggai, Zechariah, Malachi). This is the list given by St. John Damascene in the *Exact Exposition of the Orthodox Faith* 4.17; FC, p. 375.

brew canon, are called "canonical."[7] To them are joined a group of "non-canonical" books—that is, those which were not included in the Hebrew canon because they were written after the closing of the canon of the sacred Old Testament books.[8] The Church accepts these latter books also as useful and instructive and in antiquity assigned them for instructive reading not only in homes but also in churches, which is why they have been called "ecclesiastical." The Church includes these books in a single volume of the Bible together with the canonical

---

[7] The word "canonical" here has a specialized meaning with reference to the books of Scripture, and this must be distinguished from the more usual use of the word in the Orthodox Church, where it refers not to the "canon" of Scripture, but to "canons" or laws proclaimed at Church councils. In the latter sense, "canonical" means "in accordance with the Church's canons," and "uncanonical" or "non-canonical" has the quite pejorative meaning of "not in accordance with the Church's canons." But in the former, restricted sense, "canonical" means only "included in the Hebrew canon," and "non-canonical" means only "not included in the Hebrew canon" (but still accepted by the Church as Scripture). In the Protestant world the "non-canonical" books of the Old Testament are commonly called the "Apocrypha," often with a pejorative connotation, even though they were included in the earliest printings of the King James Version, and a law of 1615 in England even forbade the Bible to be printed without these books. In the Roman Catholic Church since the 16th century the "non-canonical" books have been called "Deuterocanonical"—i.e., belonging to a "second" or later canon of Scripture. In most translations of the Bible which include the "non-canonical" books, they are placed together at the end of the canonical books; but in older printings in Orthodox countries there is no distinction made between the canonical and non-canonical books (see for example the Slavonic Bible printed in St. Petersburg, 1904, and approved by the Holy Synod).

[8] The "non-canonical" books of the Old Testament accepted in the Orthodox Church are those of the "Septuagint"—the Greek translation of the Old Testament made by the "Seventy" scholars who, according to tradition, were sent from Jerusalem to Egypt at the request of the Egyptian King Ptolemy II in the 3rd century B.C. to translate the Old Testament into Greek. The Hebrew originals of most of the books have been lost, and most of the books were composed only in the last few centuries before Christ. The "non-canonical" books of the Old Testament are: Second and Third Esdras (usually called First and Second Esdras in the West), Tobit, Judith, the Wisdom of Solomon, Ecclesiasticus or the Wisdom of Joshua the Son of Sirach, Baruch, three books of Maccabees, the Epistle of Jeremiah, Psalm 151, and the additions to the book of Esther, to II Chronicles (The Prayer of Manasseh), and to Daniel (The Song of the Three Youths, Susanna, and Bel and the Dragon).

books. As a source of the teaching of the faith, the Church puts them in a secondary place and looks on them as an appendix to the canonical books. Certain of them are so close in merit to the Divinely inspired books that, for example, in the 85th Apostolic Canon[9] the three books of Maccabees and the book of Joshua the son of Sirach are numbered together with the canonical books, and concerning all of them together it is said that they are "venerable and holy." However, this means only that they were respected in the ancient Church; but a distinction between the canonical and non-canonical books of the Old Testament has always been maintained in the Church.

The Church recognizes twenty-seven canonical books of the New Testament.[10] Since the sacred books of the New Testament were written in various years of the apostolic era and were sent by the Apostles to various points of Europe and Asia, and certain of them did not have a definite designation to any specific place, the gathering of them into a single collection or codex could not be an easy matter; it was necessary to keep strict watch lest among the books of apostolic origin there might be found any of the so-called "apocryphal" books, which for the most part were composed in heretical circles. Therefore, the Fathers

---

[9] The "Apostolic Canons" or "Canons of the Holy Apostles" are a collection of 85 ecclesiastical canons or laws handed down from the Apostles and their successors and given official Church approval at the Quinisext Council (in Trullo) of 692 and in the First Canon of the Seventh Ecumenical Council (787). Some of these canons were cited and approved at the Ecumenical Councils, beginning with the First Council in 325, but the whole collection of them together was made probably not before the 4th century. The name "apostolic" does not necessarily mean that all the canons or the collection of them were made by the Apostles themselves, but only that they are in the tradition handed down from the Apostles (just as not all the "Psalms of David" were actually written by the Prophet David). For their text, see *The Seven Ecumenical Councils*, NPNF, pp. 594–600. The 85th Apostolic Canon lists the canonical books of the Old and New Testaments.

[10] These books are: the Four Gospels of Matthew, Mark, Luke, and John; the Acts of the Apostles; the seven Catholic Epistles (one of James, two of Peter, three of John, one of Jude); fourteen Epistles of the Apostle Paul (Romans, First and Second Corinthians, Galatians, Ephesians, Philippians, Colossians, First and Second Thessalonians, First and Second Timothy, Titus, Philemon, Hebrews); and the Apocalypse (Revelation) of St. John the Theologian and Evangelist.

and teachers of the Church during the first centuries of Christianity preserved a special caution in distinguishing these books, even though they might bear the name of Apostles. The Fathers of the Church frequently entered certain books into their lists with reservations, with uncertainty or doubt, or else gave for this reason an incomplete list of the Sacred Books. This was unavoidable and serves as a memorial to their exceptional caution in this holy matter. They did not trust themselves, but waited for the universal voice of the Church. The local Council of Carthage in 397, in its 33rd Canon, enumerated all of the books of the New Testament without exception.[11] St. Athanasius the Great names all of the books of the New Testament without the least doubt or distinction, and in one of his works he concludes his list with the following words: "Behold the number and names of the canonical books of the New Testament. These are, as it were, the beginnings, the anchors and pillars of our faith, because they were written and transmitted by the very Apostles of Christ the Saviour, who were with Him and were instructed by Him" (from the *Synopsis* of St. Athanasius).[12] Likewise, St. Cyril of Jerusalem also enumerates the books of the New Testament without the slightest remark as to any kind of distinction between them in the Church. The same complete listing is to be found among the Western ecclesiastical writers, for example in Augustine. Thus, the complete canon of the New Testament books of Sacred Scripture was confirmed by the catholic voice of the whole Church. This Sacred Scripture, in the expression of St. John Damascene, is the "Divine Paradise."[13]

Sacred Tradition

In the original precise meaning of the word, Sacred Tradition is the tradition which comes from the ancient Church of Apostolic times. In

---

[11] This list was again ratified at the Seventh Ecumenical Council in Nicaea in 787.—3RD ED.

[12] St. Athanasius listed the books of the New Testament in a letter of 367. See *Letters of Athanasius,* NPNF, pp. 551–52.—3RD ED.

[13] *Exact Exposition of the Orthodox Faith* 4.17; FC, p. 374.

the second to the fourth centuries this was called "the Apostolic Tradition."

One must keep in mind that the ancient Church carefully guarded the inward life of the Church from those outside of her; her Holy Mysteries were secret, being kept from non-Christians. When these Mysteries were performed—Baptism or the Eucharist—those outside the Church were not present; the order of the services was not written down, but was only transmitted orally; and in what was preserved in secret was contained the essential side of the faith. St. Cyril of Jerusalem (4th century) presents this to us especially clearly. In undertaking Christian instruction for those who had not yet expressed a final decision to become Christians, the hierarch precedes his teachings with the following words: "When the catechetical teaching is pronounced, if a catechumen should ask you, 'What did the instructors say?' you are to repeat nothing to those who are without (the church). For we are giving to you the mystery and hope of the future age. Keep the Mystery of Him Who is the Giver of rewards. May no one say to you, 'What harm is it if I shall find out also?' Sick people also ask for wine, but if it is given at the wrong time it produces disorder to the mind, and there are two evil consequences: the sick one dies, and the physician is slandered" (Prologue to the *Catechetical Lectures,* chap. 12).

In one of his further homilies St. Cyril again remarks: "We include the whole teaching of faith in a few lines. And I would wish that you should remember it word for word and should repeat it among yourselves with all fervor, without writing it down on paper, but noting it by memory in the heart. And you should beware, lest during the time of your occupation with this study none of the catechumens should hear what has been handed down to you" (Fifth Catechetical Lecture, chap. 12). In the introductory words which he wrote down for those being "illumined"—that is, those who were already coming to Baptism—and also for those present who were baptized, he gives the following warning: "This instruction for those who are being illumined is offered to be read by those who are coming to Baptism and by the faithful who have already received Baptism; but by no means give it either to the catechumens or to anyone else who has not yet become a Christian, otherwise you will have to give an answer to the Lord. And if you make a copy of these catechetical lectures, then, as before the Lord, write this down also" (that is, this warning) (end of the Prologue to the *Catechetical Lectures*).[14]

In the following words St. Basil the Great gives us a clear understanding of the Sacred Apostolic Tradition: "Of the dogmas and sermons preserved in the Church, certain ones we have from written instruction, and certain ones we have received from the Apostolic Tradition, handed down in secret. Both the one and the other have one and the same authority for piety, and no one who is even the least informed in the decrees of the Church will contradict this. For if we dare to overthrow the unwritten customs as if they did not have great importance, we shall thereby imperceptively do harm to the Gospel in its most important points. And even more, we shall be left with the empty name of the Apostolic preaching without content. For example, let us especially make note of the first and commonest thing: that those who hope in the name of our Lord Jesus Christ should sign themselves with the sign of the Cross. Who taught this in Scripture? Which Scripture

---

14 These three citations may be found in St. Cyril, *Catechetical Lectures*, NPNF, pp. 4, 32, 5. This strictness with regard to the revelation of the Christian Mysteries (Sacraments) to outsiders is no longer preserved to such a degree in the Orthodox Church. The exclamation "Catechumens depart!" before the Liturgy of the Faithful is still proclaimed, it is true, but hardly anywhere in the Orthodox world are catechumens or the non-Orthodox actually told to leave the church at this time. (In some churches they are only asked to stand in the back part of the church, the narthex, but can still observe the service.) The full point of such an action has been lost in our times, when all the "secrets" of the Christian Mysteries are readily available to anyone who can read, and the text of St. Cyril's *Catechetical Lectures* has been published in many languages and editions. However, the great reverence which the ancient Church showed for the Christian Mysteries—carefully preserving them from the gaze of those who were merely curious or who, being outside the Church and uncommitted to Christianity, might easily misunderstand or distrust them—is still kept by Orthodox Christians today who are serious about their faith. Even today we are not to "cast our pearls before swine"—to speak much of the Mysteries of the Orthodox Faith to those who are merely curious about them but do not seek to join themselves to the Church.

instructed us that we should turn to the east in prayer? Which of the saints left us in written form the words of invocation during the transformation of the bread of the Eucharist and the Chalice of blessing? For we are not satisfied with the words which are mentioned in the Epistles or the Gospels, but both before them and after them we pronounce others also as having great authority for the Mystery, having received them from the unwritten teaching. By what Scripture, likewise, do we bless the water of Baptism and the oil of anointing and, indeed, the one being baptized himself? Is this not the silent and secret tradition? And what more? What written word has taught us this anointing with oil itself?[15] Where is the triple immersion and all the rest that has to do with Baptism, the renunciation of Satan and his angels to be found? What Scripture are these taken from? Is it not from this unpublished and unspoken teaching which our Fathers have preserved in a silence inaccessible to curiosity and scrutiny, because they were thoroughly instructed to preserve in silence the sanctity of the Mysteries? For what propriety would there be to proclaim in writing a teaching concerning that which it is not allowed for the unbaptized even to behold?" (*On the Holy Spirit*, chap. 27).

From these words of St. Basil the Great we may conclude: first, that the Sacred Tradition of the teaching of faith is that which may be traced back to the earliest period of the Church, and, second, that it was carefully preserved and unanimously acknowledged among the Fathers and teachers of the Church during the epoch of the great Fathers and the beginning of the Ecumenical Councils.

Although St. Basil has given here a series of examples of the "oral" tradition, he himself in this very text has taken a step towards the "recording" of this oral word. During the era of the freedom and triumph of the Church in the 4th century, almost all of the tradition in general received a written form and is now preserved in the literature of the Church, which comprises a supplement to the Holy Scripture.

We find this sacred ancient Tradition

---

[15] That is, the anointing of those being baptized; the anointing of the Sacrament of Unction, on the other hand, is clearly indicated in Scripture (James 5:14).

a) in the most ancient record of the Church, the Canons of the Holy Apostles;[16]

b) in the Symbols of Faith of the ancient local churches;

c) in the ancient Liturgies, in the rite of Baptism, and in other ancient prayers;

d) in the ancient Acts of the Christian martyrs. The Acts of the martyrs did not enter into use by the faithful until they had been examined and approved by the local bishops; and they were read at the public gatherings of Christians under the supervision of the leaders of the churches. In them we see the confession of the Most Holy Trinity, the Divinity of the Lord Jesus Christ, examples of the invocation of the saints, of belief in the conscious life of those who had reposed in Christ, and much else;

e) in the ancient records of the history of the Church, especially in the book of Eusebius Pamphili, Bishop of Caesarea,[17] where there are gathered many ancient traditions of rite and dogma—in particular, there is given the canon of the sacred books of the Old and New Testaments;

f) in the works of the ancient Fathers and teachers of the Church;

g) and, finally, in the very spirit of the Church's life, in the preservation of faithfulness to all her foundations which come from the Holy Apostles.

The Apostolic Tradition which has been preserved and guarded by the Church, by the very fact that it has been kept by the Church, becomes the Tradition of the Church herself, it "belongs" to her, it testifies to her; and, in parallel to Sacred Scripture, it is called by her "*Sacred* Tradition."

The witness of Sacred Tradition is indispensable for our certainty that all the books of Sacred *Scripture* have been handed down to us from Apostolic times and are of Apostolic origin.

---

[16] See p. 34, note 9 above.

[17] English translation: Eusebius, *The History of the Church from Christ to Constantine*, G. A. Williamson, trans. (Baltimore: Penguin Books, 1965).

Sacred Tradition is necessary for the correct understanding of separate passages of Sacred Scripture, and for refuting heretical reinterpretations of it, and, in general, so as to avoid superficial, one-sided, and sometimes even prejudiced and false interpretations of it.

Finally, Sacred Tradition is also necessary because some truths of the faith are expressed in a completely definite form in Scripture, while others are not entirely clear and precise and therefore demand confirmation by the Sacred Apostolic Tradition.

The Apostle commands, *Therefore, brethren, stand fast, and hold the traditions which ye have been taught, whether by word, or our epistle* (II Thes. 2:15).

Besides all this, Sacred Tradition is valuable because from it we see how the whole order of Church organization, the canons, the Divine services and rites are rooted in and founded upon the way of life of the ancient Church. Thus, the preservation of "Tradition" expresses the *succession* of the very essence of the Church.

The Catholic Consciousness of the Church

The Orthodox Church of Christ is the Body of Christ, a spiritual *organism* whose Head is Christ. It has a single spirit, a single common faith, a single and common catholic *consciousness*, guided by the Holy Spirit; and its reasonings are based on the concrete, definite foundations of Sacred Scripture and Sacred Apostolic Tradition. This catholic consciousness is always with the Church, but, in a more definite fashion, this consciousness is expressed in the Ecumenical Councils of the Church. From profound Christian antiquity, local councils of separate Orthodox Churches gathered twice a year, in accordance with the 37th Canon of the Holy Apostles.[18] Likewise, often in the history of the Church there were councils of regional bishops representing a wider area than individual Churches and, finally, councils of bishops of the

---

[18] The 37th Apostolic Canon begins: "Let there be a meeting of the bishops twice a year, and let them examine amongst themselves the decrees concerning religion and settle the ecclesiastical controversies which may have occurred..." (*Seven Ecumenical Councils*, NPNF, p. 596).

whole Orthodox Church of both East and West. Such *Ecumenical* Councils the Church recognizes as seven in number. The Ecumenical Councils formulated precisely and confirmed a number of the fundamental truths of the Orthodox Christian Faith, defending the ancient teaching of the Church against the distortions of heretics. The Ecumenical Councils likewise formulated numerous laws and rules governing public and private Christian church life, which are called the Church canons, and required the universal and uniform observance of them. Finally, the Ecumenical Councils confirmed the dogmatic decrees of a number of *local* councils, and also the dogmatic statements composed by certain Fathers of the Church—for example, the confession of faith of St. Gregory the Wonderworker, Bishop of Neo-Caesarea,[19] the canons of St. Basil the Great,[20] and so forth.

When in the history of the Church it happened that councils of bishops permitted heretical views to be expressed in their decrees, the catholic consciousness of the Church was disturbed and was not pacified until authentic Christian truth was restored and confirmed by means of another council.[21] One must remember that the councils of the Church made their dogmatic decrees (*a*) after a careful, thorough and complete examination of all those places in Sacred Scripture which touch on a given question, (*b*) thus testifying that the Ecumenical Church has understood the cited passages of Sacred Scripture in precisely this way. In this way the decrees of the councils concerning faith express *the harmony of Sacred Scripture and the catholic Tradition of the Church.* For this reason *these decrees became themselves, in their turn, an authentic, inviolable, authoritative, Ecumenical and Sacred Tradition of*

---

[19] For the text of St. Gregory's "Canonical Epistle," see *The Seven Ecumenical Councils*, NPNF, p. 602.

[20] The text of St. Basil's canons may be found in *The Seven Ecumenical Councils*, NPNF, pp. 604–11.

[21] True councils—those which express Orthodox truth—are accepted by the Church's catholic consciousness; false councils—those which teach heresy or reject some aspect of the Church's Tradition—are rejected by the same catholic consciousness. The Orthodox Church is the Church not of "councils" as such, but only of the *true* councils, inspired by the Holy Spirit, which conform to the Church's catholic consciousness.

the Church, founded upon the facts of Sacred Scripture and Apostolic Tradition.

Of course, many truths of the faith are so immediately clear from Sacred Scripture that they were not subjected to heretical reinterpretations; therefore, concerning them there are no specific decrees of councils. Other truths, however, were confirmed by councils.

Among all the dogmatic decrees of councils, the Ecumenical Councils themselves acknowledge as primary and fundamental the Nicaeo-Constantinopolitan Symbol of Faith,[22] and they forbade any change whatsoever in it, not only in its ideas, but also in its words, either by addition or subtraction (decree of the Third Ecumenical Council, repeated by the Fourth, Fifth, Sixth, and Seventh Councils).

The decrees regarding faith which were made by a number of local councils, and also certain expositions of the faith by the Holy Fathers of the Church, are acknowledged as a guide for the whole Church and are numbered in the Second Canon of the Sixth Ecumenical Council (in Trullo).[23]

Dogmas and Canons

In ecclesiastical terminology *dogmas* are the truths of Christian teaching, the truths of faith, and *canons* are the prescriptions relating to Church order, Church government, the obligations of the Church hierarchy and clergy and of every Christian, which flow from the moral foundations of the evangelical and Apostolic teaching. *Canon* is a Greek word which literally means "a straight rod, a measure of precise direction."

---

[22] This is the "Creed" ("I believe in One God...") which is sung at every Divine Liturgy of the Orthodox Church and read at several other places in the daily Divine services.

[23] The "Quinisext" Council in Trullo (692) was actually held eleven years after the Sixth Ecumenical Council, but its decrees are accepted in the Orthodox Church as a continuation of those of the Sixth Council. The text of this Canon may be read in *The Seven Ecumenical Councils*, NPNF, p. 361, and the canons of the local councils and Holy Fathers which were approved in this Canon are printed elsewhere in the same volume (pp. 409–519, 589–615).

The Works of the Holy Fathers and Teachers of the Church as a Guide in Questions of Faith

For guidance in questions of faith, for the correct understanding of Sacred Scripture, and in order to distinguish the authentic Tradition of the Church from false teachings, we appeal to the works of the Holy Fathers of the Church, acknowledging that the *unanimous agreement* of all of the Fathers and teachers of the Church in teaching of the faith is an undoubted sign of truth. The Holy Fathers stood for the truth, fearing neither threats nor persecutions nor death itself. The Patristic explanations of the truths of the faith (1) gave precision to the expression of the truths of Christian teaching and created a unity of dogmatic language; (2) added testimonies of these truths from Sacred Scripture and Sacred Tradition, and also brought forth for them arguments based on reason. In theology, attention is also given to certain private opinions[24] of the Holy Fathers or teachers of the Church on questions which have not been precisely defined and accepted by the whole Church.[25] However, these opinions are not to be confused with dogmas, in the precise meaning of the word. There are some private opinions of certain Fathers and teachers which are not recognized as being in agreement with the general catholic faith of the Church, and are not accepted as a guide to faith.[26]

---

[24] In Greek, *theologoumena*.

[25] The Orthodox Christian is free to accept those *theologoumena* of the Holy Fathers that can be harmonized with the consensus of Patristic teaching. Most *theologoumena* fall in this category. One must reject only those *theologoumena* that clearly contradict the Patristic consensus—and especially those that have been condemned by a Church Council (as in the example given in the note below).—3RD ED.

[26] As an example of such [mistaken] "private opinions," one may take the mistaken opinion of St. Gregory of Nyssa that hell is not everlasting and that all—including the demons—are to be saved in the end. This opinion was rejected decisively at the Fifth Ecumenical Council as contradicting the Church's "catholic consciousness," but St. Gregory himself is still accepted as a saint and a Holy Father in the Orthodox Church and his other teachings are not questioned. On the Orthodox attitude towards such mistaken "private opinions" of the Fathers (and specifically,

The Truths of Faith in the Divine Services

The catholic consciousness of the Church, where it concerns the teaching of faith, is also expressed in the Orthodox Divine services which have been handed down to us by the Ecumenical Church. By entering deeply into the content of the Divine service books we make ourselves firmer in the dogmatic teaching of the Orthodox Church.[27]

The content of the Orthodox Divine services is the culminating expression of the teaching of the Holy Apostles and Fathers of the Church, both in the spheres of dogma and of morals. This is splendidly expressed in the hymn (the kontakion) which is sung on the day of the commemoration of the Holy Fathers of the Ecumenical Councils: "The preaching of the Apostles and the dogmas of the Fathers have imprinted upon the Church a single faith which, bearing the garment of truth woven of the theology from above, rightly dispenseth and glorifieth the great mystery of piety."

2. EXPOSITIONS OF CHRISTIAN TEACHING

The Symbolical Books

The interpretations of the *Symbol of Faith*, or the "Symbolic Guides" (from the Greek *symballo,* meaning "to unite"; *symbolon,* a uniting or conditional sign) of the Orthodox faith, in the common meaning of this term, are those expositions of Christian faith which are given in the *Book of Canons of the Holy Apostles, the Holy Local and Ecumenical Councils, and the Holy Fathers.* The theology of the Russian

---

concerning the teaching on this subject of such Fathers as St. Photius the Great and St. Mark of Ephesus), see the article "The Place of Blessed Augustine in the Orthodox Church" in *The Orthodox Word,* nos. 79 and 80 (1978). [Printed also as a separate book, Platina, Calif.: St. Herman Brotherhood, 1983; revised edition, 1996.]

[27] It should also be noted that the composers and compilers of the Divine services were often great theologians in their own right. For example, the *Octoechos,* or book of daily services in the Eight Tones, is essentially the work of St. John Damascene, the 8th-century Holy Father who summed up the Orthodox theology of the great Patristic age.

Church also makes use, as symbolical books, of those two expositions of the faith which in more recent times were evoked by the need to present the Orthodox Christian teaching against the teaching of the unorthodox confessions of the second millennium. These books include *The Confession of the Orthodox Faith* compiled by the Patriarch of Jerusalem, Dositheus, which was read and approved at the Council of Jerusalem in 1672[28] and, fifty years later, in answer to the inquiry received from the Anglican Church, was sent to that church in the name of all the Eastern Patriarchs and is therefore more widely known under the name of "The Encyclical of the Eastern Patriarchs on the Orthodox Faith."[29] Also included in this category is *The Orthodox Confession* of Peter Mogila, Metropolitan of Kiev,[30] which was examined and corrected at two local councils, that of Kiev in 1640 and Jassy in 1643, and then approved by four Ecumenical Patriarchs and the Russian Patriarchs Joachim and Adrian. *The Longer Catechism of the Orthodox, Catholic, Eastern Church* of Metropolitan Philaret of Moscow[31] enjoys a similar importance in the Russian Church, particularly the part which contains an exposition of the Symbol of Faith. This Catechism was "examined and approved by the Holy Synod and published for instruction in schools and for the use of all Orthodox Christians."[32]

Dogmatic Systems

The attempt at a comprehensive exposition of the whole Christian teaching we call a "system of dogmatic theology." A complete dog-

---

[28] Also known as the Council of Bethlehem.—3RD ED.

[29] This "Encyclical," comprised of Patriarch Dositheus's *Confession* of the 17th century, is not to be confused with the "Encyclical (or Reply) of the Eastern Patriarchs to Pope Pius IX" of 1848.—3RD ED.

[30] Metropolitan Peter Mogila of Kiev (1597–1646) was canonized as a saint in 1996 by the Ukrainian Orthodox Church (Moscow Patriarchate). Commemorated December 31.—3RD ED.

[31] Metrolopitan Philaret of Moscow (1782–1867) was canonized as a saint in 1994 by the Russian Orthodox Church (Moscow Patriarchate). Commemorated November 19.—3RD ED.

[32] This was in 1830.—3RD ED.

matic system, very valuable for Orthodox theology, was compiled in the 8th century by St. John Damascene under the title *Exact Exposition of the Orthodox Faith*. In this work, one may say, St. Damascene summed up the whole of the theological thought of the Eastern Fathers and teachers of the Church up to the 8th century.

Among Russian theologians, the most complete works of dogmatic theology were written in the 19th century by Metropolitan Macarius of Moscow (*Orthodox Dogmatic Theology*, two volumes), by Philaret, Archbishop of Chernigov (*Orthodox Dogmatic Theology*, in two parts), by Bishop Sylvester, rector of the Kiev Theological Academy (*Essay in Orthodox Dogmatic Theology, with an Historical Exposition of the Dogmas*, five volumes), by Archpriest N. Malinovsky (*Orthodox Dogmatic Theology*, four volumes, and *A Sketch of Orthodox Dogmatic Theology* in two parts), and by Archpriest P. Svietlov (*The Christian Teaching of Faith: An Apologetic Exposition*).[33]

3. DOGMATIC THEOLOGY

The dogmatic labor of the Church has always been directed towards the confirmation in the consciousness of the faithful of the truths of the faith which have been confessed by the Church from the beginning. This labor consists of indicating which way of thinking is the one that follows the Ecumenical Tradition. The Church's labor of

---

[33] These 19th-century Russian "systems" of theology have been out of fashion among Orthodox academic theologians in recent years, and some have criticized them for the supposed "Western influences" which they show. This criticism, while to a certain extent justified, has for the most part been one-sided and unfair, and has led some to a blind trust in *today's* Orthodox theologians as being untainted by "Western influence." The truth of the matter is that the division of theology into "categories," its "systematization" (which the present book itself follows) is a rather modern device borrowed from the West, but solely as an external organization of the subject-matter of theology. Fr. Michael himself has elsewhere defended these systems of theology for their usefulness in teaching theology in the schools against accusations of "scholasticism" which are totally unfair. In intent, these systems are only a 19th-century attempt to do what St. John Damascene did in the 8th century, and no one can deny that the basic *content* of these works is Orthodox.

instructing in the faith has been, in battling against heresies: (*a*) to find a precise form for the expression of the truths of the faith as handed down from antiquity, and (*b*) to confirm the correctness of the Church's teaching, founding it on Sacred Scripture and Sacred Tradition. In the teaching of the faith, it is the thinking of the Holy Apostles that was and remains the standard of the fullness and wholeness of the Christian worldview. A Christian of the 20th century cannot develop more completely or go deeper into the truths of the faith than the Apostles. Therefore, any attempt that is made—whether by individuals or in the name of dogmatic theology itself—to reveal new Christian truths, or new aspects of the dogmas handed down to us, or a new understanding of them, is completely out of place. The aim of dogmatic theology as a branch of learning is to set forth, with firm foundation and proof, the Orthodox Christian teaching which has been handed down.

Certain complete works of dogmatic theology set forth the thinking of the Fathers of the Church in an historical sequence. Thus, for example, the above-mentioned *Essay in Orthodox Dogmatic Theology* by Bishop Sylvester is arranged in this way. One must understand that such a method of exposition in Orthodox theology does not have the aim of investigating the "gradual development of Christian teaching"; its aim is a different one: it is to show that the complete setting forth, in historical sequence, of the ideas of the Holy Fathers of the Church on every subject confirms most clearly that the Holy Fathers in all ages thought the same about the truths of the faith. But, since some of them viewed the subject from one side, and others from another side, and since some of them brought forth arguments of one kind, and others of another kind, therefore the historical sequence of the teaching of the Fathers gives a complete view of the dogmas of the faith and the fullness of the proofs of their truth.

This does not mean that the theological exposition of dogmas must take an unalterable form. Each epoch puts forth its own views, ways of understanding, questions, heresies and protests against Christian truth, or else repeats ancient ones which had been forgotten. Theology naturally takes into consideration the inquiries of each age, answers them, and sets forth the dogmatic truths accordingly. In this sense, one may speak about the development of dogmatic theology *as a branch of learning*. But there are no sufficient grounds for speaking about the development of the Christian teaching of faith itself.

Dogmatics and Faith

Dogmatic theology is for the believing Christian. In itself it does not inspire faith, but presupposes that faith already exists in the heart. *I believed, wherefore I spake*, says a righteous man of the Old Testament (Ps. 115:1). And the Lord Jesus Christ revealed the mysteries of the Kingdom of God to His disciples *after* they had believed in Him: *Lord to whom shall we go? Thou hast the words of eternal life. And we believe and are sure that Thou art that Christ, the Son of the living God* (John 6:68–69). Faith, and more precisely *faith in the Son of God Who has come into the world*, is the cornerstone of Sacred Scripture; it is the cornerstone of one's personal salvation; and it is the cornerstone of theology. *But these are written, that ye might believe that Jesus is the Christ, the Son of God; and that believing ye might have life through His name* (John 20:31), writes the Apostle John at the end of his Gospel, and he repeats the same thought many times in his epistles; and these words of his express the chief idea of all of the writings of the Holy Apostles: *I believe*. All Christian theologizing must begin with this confession. Under this condition theologizing is not an abstract mental exercise, not an intellectual dialectics, but a dwelling of one's thought in Divine truths, a directing of the mind and heart towards God, and a recognition of God's love. For an unbeliever theologizing is without effect, because Christ Himself, for unbelievers, is *a stone of stumbling and a rock of offense* (I Peter 2:7–8; see Matt. 21:44).

Theology and Science; Theology and Philosophy

The difference between theology and the natural sciences, which are founded upon observation or experiment, is made clear by the fact that dogmatic theology is founded upon living and holy faith. Here the starting point is faith, and there, experience. However, the manners and methods of study are one and the same in both spheres; the study of facts, and deductions drawn from them. Only, with natural science the deductions are derived from facts collected through the observation of nature, the study of the life of peoples, and human creativity; while in theology the deductions come from the study of Sacred Scripture and Sacred Tradition. The natural sciences are empirical and technical, while our study is theological.

This clarifies the difference also between theology and philosophy. Philosophy is erected upon purely rational foundations and upon the deductions of the experimental sciences, to the extent that the latter are capable of being used for the higher questions of life; while theology is founded upon Divine Revelation. They must not be confused; theology is not philosophy even when it plunges our thinking into profound or elevated subjects of Christian faith which are difficult to understand.

Theology does not deny either the experimental sciences or philosophy. St. Gregory the Theologian considered it the merit of St. Basil the Great that he mastered dialectic to perfection, with the help of which he overthrew the philosophical constructs of the enemies of Christianity. In general, St. Gregory did not sympathize with those who expressed a lack of respect for outward learning. However, in his renowned homilies on the Holy Trinity, after setting forth the profoundly contemplative teaching of Tri-unity, he thus remarks of himself: "Thus, as briefly as possible I have set forth for you our love of wisdom, which is dogmatical and not dialectical, in the manner of the fishermen and not of Aristotle, spiritually and not cleverly woven, according to the rules of the Church and not of the marketplace" (Homily 22).

The course of dogmatic theology is divided into two basic parts: into the teaching (1) about God *in Himself* and (2) about God in His *manifestation* of Himself as Creator, Providence, Saviour of the world, and Perfecter of the destiny of the world.

The appearance of the Holy Trinity to the Patriarch Abraham in the form
of three Visitors (Gen. 18:1–3). *Icon by St. Andrew Rublev, ca. 1411.
Tretyakov Gallery, Moscow.*

Part I

GOD IN HIMSELF

Chapter 1

Our Knowledge of God

THE DOGMA OF FAITH

THE first word of our Christian Symbol of Faith is "I believe." All of our Christian confession is based upon faith. God is the first object of Christian *belief*. Thus, our Christian acknowledgment of the existence of God is founded not upon rational grounds, not on proofs taken from reason or received from the experience of our outward senses, but upon an inward, higher conviction which has a moral foundation.

In the Christian understanding, to believe in God signifies not only to *acknowledge* God with the mind, but also to *strive* towards Him with the heart.

We believe that which is inaccessible to outward experience, to scientific investigation, to being received by our outward organs of sense. St. Gregory the Theologian distinguishes between religious belief—"I believe in someone, in something"—and a simple personal belief—"I believe someone, I believe something." He writes: "It is not one and the same thing 'to believe in something' and 'to believe something.' We believe *in* the Divinity, but we simply believe any ordinary thing" ("On the Holy Spirit," part 3, p. 88 in the Russian edition of his *Works*; p. 319 in the NPNF English text).

Belief or Faith as an Attribute of the Soul

Christian faith is a mystical revelation in the human soul. It is broader, more powerful, closer to reality than *thought*. It is more complex than separate *feelings*. It contains within itself the feelings of love, fear, veneration, reverence, and humility. Likewise, it cannot be called a manifestation of the *will*, for although it moves mountains, the Christian renounces his own will when he believes, and entirely gives himself over to the will of God: "May Thy will be done in me, a sinner." The path to faith lies in the heart; it is inseparable from pure, sacrificial love, *working through love* (Gal. 5:6).

Of course, Christianity is bound up also with knowledge of the mind; it gives a worldview. But if it remained only a worldview, its power to move would vanish. Without faith it would not be the living bond between heaven and earth. Christian belief is something much greater than the "persuasive hypothesis" which is the kind of belief usually encountered in life.

The Power of Faith

The Church of Christ is founded upon faith as upon a rock which does not shake beneath it. By faith the saints conquered kingdoms, performed righteous deeds, closed the mouths of lions, quenched the power of fire, escaped the sharp sword, were strengthened in infirmity (Heb. 11:33–38). Being inspired by faith, Christians went to torture and death with joy. Faith is a rock, but a rock that is impalpable, free of heaviness and weight, that draws one upward and not downward.

He that believeth on Me, as the Scripture hath said, out of his belly shall flow rivers of living water, said the Lord (John 7:38); and the preaching of the Apostles, a preaching in the power of the word, in the power of the Spirit, in the power of signs and wonders, was a living testimony of the truth of the words of the Lord. Such is the mystery of living Christian faith.

The Source of Faith

If ye have faith, and doubt not … if ye shall say unto this mountain, Be thou removed, and be thou cast into the sea; it shall be done (Matt. 21:21). The history of the Church of Christ is filled with the miracles of the saints of all ages. However, miracles are not performed by faith in general, but by Christian faith. Faith is a reality not by the power of imagination and not by self-hypnosis, but by the fact that it binds one with the source of all life and power—with God. In the expression of the Hieromartyr Irenaeus, Bishop of Lyons, faith is a vessel by which water is scooped up; but one must be next to this water and must put the vessel into it: this water is the Grace of God. "Faith is the key to the treasure-house of God," writes St. John of Kronstadt (*My Life in Christ*, vol. 1, p. 242 in the Russian edition).

Faith is strengthened and its truth is confirmed by the benefits of its spiritual fruits which are known by experience. Therefore the Apostle instructs us, saying, *Examine yourselves, whether ye be in the faith; prove your own selves. Know ye not your own selves, how that Jesus Christ is in you, except ye be reprobates?* (II Cor. 13:5).

Yet, it is difficult to give a definition of what faith is. When the Apostle says, *Now faith is the substance of things hoped for, the evidence of things not seen* (Heb. 11:1), without touching here on the nature of faith, he indicates only what its gaze is directed towards: towards that which is awaited, towards the invisible; and thus he indicates precisely that faith is the penetration of the soul into the future ("the substance of things hoped for"), or into the invisible ("the evidence of things not seen"). This testifies to the mystical character of Christian faith.

THE NATURE OF
OUR KNOWLEDGE OF GOD

God in His Essence is incomprehensible.[1] God dwells *in the light which no man can approach unto; Whom no man hath seen, nor can see,* instructs the Apostle Paul (I Tim. 6:16).

In his *Catechetical Lectures* St. Cyril of Jerusalem instructs us: "We explain not what God is, but candidly confess that we have not exact knowledge concerning Him. For in what concerns God, to confess our

---

[1] The Holy Fathers make a distinction between God's Essence or Nature, which is inaccessible, unknowable, and incommunicable; and His Energy, which is inseparable from His Essence, and in which He goes forth from Himself, manifests, communicates, and gives Himself. (See Vladimir Lossky, *The Mystical Theology of the Eastern Church*, pp. 70, 86–87.)—3RD ED.

ignorance is the best knowledge" (Sixth Catechetical Lecture, NPNF, p. 33).

This is why there is no dogmatic value to be found in the various types of vast and all-encompassing conceptions and rational searchings on the subject of the inward life in God, and likewise in concepts fabricated by analogy with the life of the human soul. Concerning the "fellow inquirers" of his time, St. Gregory of Nyssa, the brother of St. Basil the Great, writes: "Men, having left off *delighting themselves in the Lord* (Ps. 36:4) and rejoicing in the peace of the Church, undertake refined researches regarding some kind of essences, and measure magnitudes, measuring the Son in comparison with the Father, and granting a greater measure to the Father. Who will say to them, 'That which is not subject to number cannot be measured; what is invisible cannot be valued; that which is fleshless cannot be weighed; that which is infinite cannot be compared; that which is incomparable cannot be understood as greater or less, because we know something as "greater" by comparing it with other things, but with something which has no end, the idea of "greater" is unthinkable.' *Great is our Lord, and great is His strength, and of His understanding there is no measure* (Ps. 146:5). What does this mean? Number what has been said, and you will understand the mystery."

The same hierarch further writes: "If someone is making a journey in the middle of the day, when the sun with its hot rays scorches the head and by its heat dries up everything liquid in the body, and under one's feet is the hard earth which is difficult for walking and waterless; and then such a man encounters a spring with splendid, transparent, pleasing and refreshing streams pouring out abundantly—will he sit down by the water and begin to reason about its nature, seeking out from whence it comes, how, from what, and all such things which idle speakers are wont to judge about, for example: is it a certain moisture which exists in the depths of the earth that comes to the surface under pressure and becomes water, or is it canals going through long desert places that discharge water as soon as they find an opening for themselves? Will he not rather, saying farewell to all rational deliberations, bend down his head to the stream and press his lips to it, quench his thirst, refresh his tongue, satisfy his desire, and give thanks to the One Who gave this Grace? Therefore, let you also imitate this thirsting one" (St. Gregory of Nyssa, "Homily on His Ordination," from his works in Russian, vol. 4).

Nevertheless, to a certain extent we *do* have a knowledge of God, a knowledge to the extent that He Himself has revealed it to men. One must distinguish between the *comprehension* of God, which in essence is impossible, and the *knowledge* of Him, even though incomplete, of which the Apostle Paul says, *For now we see through a glass, darkly*; and *I know in part* (I Cor. 13:12). The degree of this knowledge depends upon the ability of man himself to know.[2]

From whence do we derive knowledge of God?

a) It is revealed to men from the knowledge of nature, the knowledge of oneself, and the knowledge of all of God's creation in general. *For the invisible things of Him from the creation of the world are clearly seen, being understood by the things that are made, even His eternal power and Godhead* (Rom. 1:20); that is, what is invisible in Him, His eternal power and Godhead, is made visible from the creation of the world through observing the created things. Therefore, those men are without excuse who, having known God, did not glorify Him as God and did not give thanks, but became vain in their reasoning (Rom. 1:21). "The world is the kingdom of the Divine thought" (St. John of Kronstadt).

b) God has manifested Himself yet more in supernatural revelation and through the Incarnation of the Son of God. *God, who at sundry times and in divers manners spake in time past unto the fathers by the prophets, hath in these last days spoken unto us by His Son* (Heb. 1:1–2). *No man hath seen God at any time; the only begotton Son, Who is in the bosom of the Father, He hath declared Him* (John 1:18).

Thus did the Saviour Himself teach concerning the knowledge of God. Having said, *All things are delivered unto Me of My Father; and no*

---

[2] This distinction between what one might call the "absolute" unknowability of God and the "relative" knowability of Him is set forth by St. John Damascene in the *Exact Exposition of the Orthodox Faith* 1.1.

man knoweth the Son, but the Father; neither knoweth any man the Father, save the Son, the Saviour added, *and he to whomsoever the Son will reveal Him* (Matt. 11:27). And the Apostle John the Theologian writes in his epistle: *And we know that the Son of God is come, and hath given us an understanding, that we may know the true God* (I John 5:20).

Divine Revelation is given to us in the whole of Sacred Scripture and in Sacred Tradition, the preservation, instruction, and true interpretation of which are the duty and concern of the Holy Church of Christ.

But even within the boundaries which are given us in the light of Divine Revelation, we must follow the guidance of those who have purified their minds by an elevated Christian life and made their minds capable of contemplating exalted truths; that is, we must follow the guidance of the Fathers of the Church, and at the same time watch morally over ourselves. Of this St. Gregory the Theologian instructs us: "If you wish to be a theologian and worthy of the Divine, keep the laws; by means of the Divine laws go towards the high aim; for activity is the ascent to vision."[3] That is, strive and attain moral perfection, for only this path will give the possibility of ascending to the heights from whence Divine Truths are contemplated (Homily 20 of St. Gregory the Theologian).

The Saviour Himself has uttered: *Blessed are the pure in heart: for they shall see God* (Matt. 5:8).

The powerlessness of our mind to comprehend God is expressed by the Church also in the Divine services: "At a loss for words to express the meaning of Thine incomprehensible Thrice-radiant Godhead, we praise Thee, O Lord." That is, having no power to understand the mystical names of Thy Three-rayed Divinity, with our hearts we glorify Thee, O Lord (from the Canon of the Sunday Midnight Office, Tone 7, Canticle 4).

In antiquity certain of the heretics introduced the idea that God is

---

[3] "Activity" here is a technical term often encountered in Orthodox ascetic texts; it refers to the *means* (keeping the commandments, ascetic discipline, etc.) which lead one to the *end* of spiritual life ("vision" or "contemplation" of God).

entirely comprehensible, accessible to the understanding. They built their affirmations upon the idea that God is a simple essence, making from this the false conclusion that, being a simple essence, He has no inward content or qualities. Therefore, it was sufficient, they said, to name the names of God—for example *Theos* (God: "He Who Sees"), or Jehovah[4] ("He Who Is")—or to indicate His single characteristic, His "unoriginateness," in order to say everything that can be said about God. (Some of the Gnostics reasoned in this way—for example, Valentinus in the 2nd century, and Eunomius and the Anomoeans in the 4th century, thought this way.) The Holy Fathers replied to this heresy with a fervent protest, seeing in it an overthrowing of the essence of religion. Answering the heretics, they clarified and proved, both from the Scripture and by means of reason: (1) that the simplicity of God's Essence is united to the fullness of His attributes, the fullness of the content of the Divine Life, and (2) that the very names of God in the Divine Scripture—Jehovah, Elohim, Adonai, and others—do not express the very Essence of God, but primarily show the relation of God to the world and to man.

Other heretics in antiquity, for example the Marcionites, fell into the opposite extreme, affirming that God is completely unknown and inaccessible to our understanding. For this reason the Fathers of the Church showed that there is a degree of the knowledge of God which is possible, useful, and needful for us. St. Cyril of Jerusalem, in his *Catechetical Lectures*, teaches: "If someone says that the Essence of God is incomprehensible, then why do we speak about Him?[5] But is it really true that because I cannot drink the whole river I will not take water from it in moderation for my benefit? Is it really true that because my eyes are not in a condition to take in the whole sun, I am therefore un-

---

[4] *Jehovah* (*Yehowah*) is the New Latin transliteration of *Yahweh,* which in turn is a transliteration of the Hebrew tetragrammaton *YHWH.*—3RD ED.

[5] As we have seen (p. 55), the Divine Essence is of itself unknowable. However, we can know God through His Energies. St. Gregory Palamas writes: "To say that the Divine Essence is communicable not in itself but through its Energy, is to remain within the bounds of right devotion." (See Lossky, *Mystical Theology,* pp. 86–87.)—3RD ED.

able to behold as much as is needful for me? If, when going into some great garden, I cannot eat all the fruits, would you wish that I go away from it completely hungry?" (*Catechetical Lectures* 6.5).

It is well known how Blessed Augustine, when he was walking along the seashore thinking about God, saw a boy sitting at the seaside scooping water from the sea with a seashell and pouring it into a pit in the sand. This scene inspired him to think of the disproportion between our shallow minds and the greatness of God. It is just as impossible for our mind to hold a conception of God in all His greatness, as it is impossible to scoop up the sea with a seashell.

The Essence of God

"If you wish to speak or hear about God," St. Basil the Great theologizes, "renounce your own body, renounce your bodily senses, abandon the earth, abandon the sea, make the air to be beneath you; pass over the seasons of the year, their orderly arrangement, the adornments of the earth; stand above the ether, traverse the stars, their splendor, grandeur, the profit which they provide for the whole world, their good order, brightness, arrangement, movement, and the bond or distance between them. Having passed through all of this in your mind, go about heaven and, standing above it, with your thought alone, observe the beauties which are there: the armies of angels which are above the heavens, the chiefs of the archangels, the glory of the Dominions, the presiding of the Thrones, the Powers, Principalities, Authorities. Having gone past all this and left below the whole of creation in your thoughts, raising your mind beyond the boundaries of it, present to your mind the Essence of God, unmoving, unchanging, unalterable, dispassionate, simple, incomplex, indivisible, unapproachable light, unutterable power, infinite magnitude, resplendent glory, most desired goodness, immeasurable beauty that powerfully strikes the wounded soul, but cannot worthily be depicted in words."

Such exaltation of spirit is demanded in order for one to speak of God! But even under this condition the thoughts of man are capable only of dwelling on the attributes of the Divinity, not upon the very *Essence* of the Divinity.

There are in Sacred Scripture words concerning God which "touch on" or "come close" to the idea of His very Essence. These are expressions that are composed grammatically in such a way that, in their form, they answer not only the question "what kind?"—that is, what are the attributes of God—but they seem also to answer the question "who"—that is, "Who is God?" Such expressions are:

I Am He Who Is (in Hebrew, Jehovah) (Ex. 3:14).

I am Alpha and Omega, the beginning and the ending, saith the Lord, which is, and which was, and which is to come, the Almighty (Rev. 1:8).

The Lord is the True God (Jer. 10:10).

God is Spirit—the words of the Saviour to the Samaritan woman (John 4:24).

The Lord is that Spirit (II Cor. 3:17).

God is light, and in Him is no darkness at all (I John 1:5).

God is love (I John 4:8, 16).

Our God is a consuming fire (Heb. 12:29).

However, these expressions also must not be understood as indications of the very Essence of God. Only as concerns the name "He Who Is" did the Fathers of the Church say that it "in some fashion" (the expression of St. Gregory the Theologian) or "as it seems" (St. John Damascene) is a naming of the Essence. Although more rarely, this same significance has been given to the names "good" and "God" in the Greek language—*Theos*, meaning "He Who Sees." As distinct from everything "existing" and created, the Fathers of the Church applied to the existence of God the term "He Who is above all being," as in the kontakion, "The Virgin now giveth birth to Him Who is above all being." The Old Testament "Jehovah," "He Who Is," which was revealed by God to the Prophet Moses, has just such a profound meaning.[6]

Thus, one may speak only of the *attributes* of God, but not of the very Essence of God. The Fathers express themselves only indirectly

---

[6] That is to say: When we say that God is "He Who Is," we mean that He "is" in a superlative sense and not in the way that all of His creation "is"; and this is the same as saying that He is the One "Who is above all being" (kontakion of the Nativity of Christ).

61

concerning the Nature of the Divinity, saying that the Essence of God is "one, simple, incomplex." But this simplicity is not something without distinguishing characteristics or content; it contains within itself the fullness of the qualities of existence. "God is a sea of being, immeasurable and limitless" (St. Gregory the Theologian); "God is the fullness of all qualities and perfections in their highest and infinite form" (St. Basil the Great); "God is simple and incomplex; He is entirely feeling, entirely spirit, entirely thought, entirely mind, entirely source of all good things" (St. Irenaeus of Lyons).

The Attributes of God

Speaking of the attributes of God, the Holy Fathers indicate that their multiplicity, considering the simplicity of the Essence, is a result of our own inability to find a mystical and single means of viewing the Divinity. In God, one attribute is an aspect of another. God is righteous: this implies that He is also blessed and good and Spirit. The multiple simplicity in God is like the light of the sun, which reveals itself in the various colors which are received by bodies on the earth, for example, by plants.

In the enumeration of the attributes of God in the writings of the Holy Fathers and in the texts of the Divine services, there is a preponderance of expressions which are grammatically in a negative form, that is, with the prefixes "a-" or "un-". One must, however, keep in view that this negative form indicates a "negation of limits," as for example: "not unknowing" actually signifies "knowing." Thus, the negative form is really an *affirmation* of attributes which are without limit. We may find a model of such expressions in the *Exact Exposition of the Orthodox Faith* by St. John Damascene: "God is unoriginate, unending, eternal, constant, uncreated, unchanging, unalterable, simple, incomplex, bodiless, invisible, intangible, indescribable, without bounds, inaccessible to the mind, uncontainable, incomprehensible, good, righteous, the Creator of all creatures, the Almighty Pantocrator, He who looketh down upon all, whose Providence is over everything, Who has dominion over all, the Judge."

Our thoughts about God in general speak: (1) either about His distinction from the created world (for example, God is unoriginate, while the world has an origin; He is endless, while the world has an end; He is eternal, while the world exists in time); or (2) about the activities of God in the world and the relation of the Creator to His creations (Creator, Providence, Merciful, Righteous Judge).

In indicating the attributes of God, we do not thereby give a "definition" of the concept of God. Such a definition is essentially impossible, because every definition is an indication of "finiteness"[7] and signifies limitedness, incompleteness. But in God there are no limits, and therefore there cannot be a definition of the concept of the Divinity: "For a concept is itself a form of limitation" (St. Gregory the Theologian, Homily 28, his Second Theological Oration).

Our very reason demands the acknowledgment in God of a whole series of essential attributes. Reason tells us that God has a rational, free, and *personal* existence. If in the imperfect world we see free and rational *personal* beings, we cannot fail to recognize a free and rational personal existence in God Himself, Who is the Source, Cause, and Creator of all life.

Reason tells us that God is a *most perfect* Being. Every lack and imperfection are incompatible with the concept of "God."

Reason tells us that the most perfect Being can be only singular: God is *One*. There cannot be two perfect beings, since one would limit the other.

Reason tells us that God is a *self-existing* Being, since nothing can be the cause or condition of the existence of God.

What Does the Sacred Scripture Testify concerning the Attributes of God?

The attributes of God, taken directly from the word of God, are set forth in Metropolitan Philaret's *Longer Catechism of the Orthodox,*

---

[7] In Russian, Fr. Michael is indicating here the derivation of the word *opredeleniye* ("definition") from *predel* ("limit" or "boundary"). In English the same thing is true: "definition" derives from the Latin *finis*, "limit."

Catholic, Eastern Church.[8] Here we read: "Question: What idea of the Essence and essential attributes of God may be derived from Divine Revelation? Answer: That God is a Spirit, eternal, all-good, omniscient, righteous, almighty, omnipresent, unchangeable, all-sufficing to Himself, all-blessed." Let us stop to think about these attributes set forth in the catechism.

GOD IS SPIRIT. God is a Spirit (John 4:24) (the words of the Saviour in the conversation with the Samaritan woman). *The Lord is a Spirit, and where the Spirit of the Lord is, there is liberty* (II Cor. 3:17). God is foreign to every kind of bodily nature or materiality. At the same time the spirituality of God is higher, more perfect, than the spirituality that belongs to the created spiritual beings and the soul of man, which manifest in themselves only an "image" of the spiritual nature of God. God is a Spirit Who is most high, most pure, most perfect. It is true that in Sacred Scripture we find very many places where something bodily is symbolically ascribed to God. However, concerning the spiritual nature of God the Scripture speaks beginning with the very first words of the book of Genesis, and to the Prophet Moses God revealed Himself as *He Who Is,* as the pure, spiritual, most high Existence. Therefore, by bodily symbols the Scripture teaches us to understand the spiritual attributes and actions of God.

Let us quote here the words of St. Gregory the Theologian. He says: "According to the Scriptures God sleeps, He awakens, He grows angry, He walks, and He has the Cherubim as His throne. But when did He ever have infirmity? And have you ever heard that God is a body? Here there is presented something which does not exist in reality. For, in accordance with our own understanding we have given names to the things of God which are taken from ourselves. When God, for reasons known to Him alone, ceases His care and, as it were, takes no more concern for us, this means that He is 'sleeping'—because our sleep is a similar lack of activity and care. When, on the contrary, He suddenly begins to do good, this means He 'awakens.' He

---

[8] English translation (reprinted from the 1901 translation): *The Catechism of the Orthodox Church* (Willits, Calif.: Eastern Orthodox Books, 1971), p. 19.

chastises, and for this we have made it out that He is 'angry'—because chastisement among us is with anger. He acts sometimes here, sometimes there—and so, in our way of thinking, He walks, because walking is a going from one place to another. He reposes and as it were dwells in the holy powers—and we have called this a 'sitting,' and a 'sitting on a throne,' which is likewise characteristic of us, for the Divinity does not repose in any place as well as in the saints. A swift movement we call 'flying.' If there is a beholding, we speak of a 'face'; if there is a giving and a receiving, we speak of a 'hand.' Likewise, every other power and every other action of God are depicted among us by something taken from bodily things" (Homily 31, Fifth Theological Oration, "On the Holy Spirit," chap. 22; NPNF, pp. 324–25).

In connection with the accounts of the actions of God in the second and third chapters of the book of Genesis, Chrysostom instructs us: "Let us not pass over without attention, beloved, what is said by the Divine Scripture, and let us not look only at the words; but let us think that such simple words are used for the sake of our infirmity, and that everything is done in a most fitting way for our salvation. After all, tell me, if we wish to accept the words in a literal sense and do not understand what is communicated in a way befitting God, would not much then turn out to be strange? Let us look at the very beginning of the present reading. It says: *And they heard the voice of God walking in Paradise in the cool of the day,* and they were afraid (Gen. 3:8). What do you say: God walks? Do you then ascribe feet to Him? And are we not to understand by this anything higher? No, God does not walk—let us not think thus! How, in actual fact, could He Who is everywhere and fills all things, Whose throne is heaven and the earth the footstool of His feet—how could He walk in Paradise? What rational person would say this? But what then does it mean: *They heard the voice of God walking in Paradise in the cool of the day?* He wished to arouse in them such a feeling (of God's closeness) that it might make them upset—which in fact is what happened. They felt this and strove to conceal themselves from God Who was approaching them. Sin had occurred, and a transgression, and shame fell upon them. The unhypocritical judge, that is the *conscience,* having been aroused, called out with a loud voice, reproached them, and showed and, as it were, exhibited before their eyes the weight of the transgression. The Master created man in the beginning and placed in him the conscience as a never-silent accuser which cannot be seduced or deceived."

In connection with the image of the creation of woman, Chrysostom teaches: "It is said, *And He took one of his ribs* (Gen. 2:21). Do not understand these words in a human way, but understand that the crude utterances used are adapted to human weakness. After all, if Scripture had not used these words, how could we understand such unutterable mysteries? Let us not look only at the words, but let us receive everything in a fitting manner, as referring to God. This expression 'took' and all similar expressions are used for the sake of our weakness." In a similar way Chrysostom expresses himself regarding the words: *God formed man of the dust of the earth and breathed into him* (Gen. 2:7) (*Works of St. John Chrysostom*, vol. 4 [in Russian]).[9]

St. John Damascene devotes to this theme one chapter in his *Exact Exposition of the Orthodox Faith*. This chapter is called "On the things that are affirmed of God as if He had a body," and here he writes: "Since we find that in the Divine Scripture very much is said symbolically about God as if He had a body, we must know that it is impossi-

---

[9] It should not be thought that Fr. Michael is here stating that St. Chrysostom was *in general* opposed to "literal interpretations" of Scripture; when the literal sense was required, St. Chrysostom was quite "literal" in his interpretation. His point, and Fr. Michael's, is that all interpretations of Scripture should be as "befitting God"—and this sometimes requires a "literal" interpretation, and sometimes a metaphorical. In this same commentary on the book of Genesis, for example, St. Chrysostom writes: "When you hear that *God planted Paradise in Eden in the East,* understand the word 'planted' befittingly of God: that is, that He commanded; but concerning the words that follow, believe precisely that Paradise was created and in that very place where the Scripture has assigned it" (*Homilies on Genesis* 13.3). He also forbade an allegorical interpretation of the "rivers" and "waters" of Paradise, insisting that "the rivers are actually rivers and the waters are precisely waters" (13.4). Thus, when St. Chrysostom states that the word "take" in Genesis must be understood in a God-befitting way (i.e., it must not be understood literally, because God has no "hands"), he does not mean to deny that Eve was actually created from one of Adam's ribs, even though precisely *how* this was done remains a mystery to us (*Homilies on Genesis* 15.2–3).

ble for us who are men clothed in this crude flesh to think or speak about the Divine and lofty and immaterial actions of the Godhead, unless we use likenesses and images and symbols that correspond to our nature." And further, explaining the expressions concerning the eyes, ears, and hands of God, and other similar expressions, he concludes, "And to say it simply, everything that is affirmed of God as if He had a body contains a certain hidden meaning" (*Exact Exposition of the Orthodox Faith* 1.11; FC, pp. 191–93).

We today have become quite accustomed to the idea of God as pure Spirit. However, the philosophy of Pantheism ("God is all"), which is very widespread in our times, seeks to contradict this truth. Therefore, even now in the Rite of Orthodoxy sung on the Sunday of Orthodoxy, the first Sunday of Lent, we hear: "To those who say that God is not Spirit but flesh—Anathema."[10]

ETERNAL. The existence of God is outside time, for time is only a form of limited being, changeable being. For God there is neither past nor future; there is only the present. *In the beginning, O Lord, Thou didst lay the foundation of the earth, and the heavens are the works of Thy hands. They shall perish, but Thou abidest; and all like a garment shall grow old, and as a vesture shalt Thou fold them, and they shall be changed; but Thou art the same and Thy years shall not fail* (Ps. 101:26–28).

Certain Holy Fathers indicate a difference between the concepts of "eternity" and "immortality." "*Eternity* is ever-existent life, and this concept is applied usually to the one unoriginate Nature, in which everything is always one and the same. The concept of *immortality*, on the other hand, can be ascribed to one who has been brought into being and does not die, as, for example, an angel or a soul. *Eternal* in its precise meaning belongs to the Divine Essence, which is why it is applied usually only to the Worshipful and Reigning Trinity" (St. Isidore

---

[10] The Rite of Orthodoxy is celebrated after the Liturgy on the first Sunday of Lent in cathedral churches wherever a bishop presides. At this service anathemas are proclaimed against the heretics of ancient and modern times who have tried to overturn the dogmatic foundations of Orthodoxy. In many Orthodox jurisdictions today, however, under the influence of "ecumenical" ideas, this service has been abolished and replaced by a "pan-Orthodox" or "ecumenical" service.

of Pelusium). In this regard even more expressive is the phrase "the pre-eternal God."[11]

ALL-GOOD. Compassionate and merciful is the Lord, longsuffering and plenteous in mercy (Ps. 102:8). *God is love* (I John 4:16). The Goodness of God extends not to some limited region in the world, which is characteristic of love in limited beings, but to the whole world and all the beings that exist in it. He is lovingly concerned over the life and needs of each creature, no matter how small and, it might seem to us, insignificant. St. Gregory the Theologian writes: "If someone were to ask us what it is that we honor, and what we worship, we have a ready reply: we honor love" (Homily 23).

God gives to His creatures as many good things as each of them can receive according to its nature and condition, and as much as corresponds with the general harmony of the world. But it is to man that God reveals a particular goodness. "God is like a mother bird who, having seen her baby fall out of the nest, flies down herself to raise it up, and when she sees it in danger of being devoured by a serpent, with a pitiful cry she flies around it and all the other baby birds, not capable of being indifferent to the loss of a single one of them" (Clement of Alexandria, *Exhortation to the Greeks,* chap. 10). "God loves us more than a father or a mother or a friend, or anyone else can love, and even more than we can love ourselves, because He is concerned more for our salvation than even for His own glory. A testimony of this is the fact that He sent into the world for suffering and death (in human flesh) His only begotten Son, solely in order to reveal to us the path of salvation and eternal life" (St. Chrysostom, Commentary on Psalm 113). If man often does not understand the whole power of God's Goodness, this occurs because man concentrates his thoughts and desires too much on his earthly well-being. But God's Providence unites the giving to us of temporal, earthly goods together with the call to acquire for oneself, for one's soul, eternal good things.

OMNISCIENT. All things are naked and opened unto the eyes of Him (Heb. 4:13). *My being while it was still unformed Thine eyes did see* (Ps.

---

[11] As in the kontakion for the Nativity of Christ.

138:16). The knowledge of God is vision and immediate understanding of everything, both that which exists and that which is possible, the present, the past, and the future. Foreknowledge of the future is, strictly speaking, a spiritual vision, because for God the future is as the present. The foreknowledge of God does not violate the free will of creatures, just as the freedom of our neighbor is not violated by the fact that we see what he does. The foreknowledge of God regarding evil in the world and the acts of free beings is as it were crowned by the foreknowledge of the salvation of the world, when *God will be all in all* (I Cor. 15:28).

Another aspect of the omniscience of God is manifested in the *wisdom* of God. *Great is our Lord, and great is His strength, and of His understanding there is no measure* (Ps. 146:5). The Holy Fathers and teachers of the Church, following the word of God, have always indicated with great reverence the greatness of God's wisdom in the ordering of the visible world, dedicating to this subject whole works, as for example the Homilies on the Six Days (*Hexaemeron*), that is, the history of the creation of the world, written by such Fathers as Sts. Basil the Great, John Chrysostom, and Gregory of Nyssa. "One blade of grass or one speck of dust is enough to occupy your entire mind, in beholding the art with which it has been made" (Basil the Great). All the more have the Fathers reflected on God's wisdom in the economy of our salvation, in the Incarnation of the Son of God. The Sacred Scripture of the Old Testament concentrates its attention primarily on the wisdom of God in the orderly arrangement of the world: *In wisdom hast Thou made them all* (Ps. 103:26). In the New Testament, on the other hand, attention is concentrated on the economy of our salvation, in connection with which the Apostle Paul cries out: *O the depth of the riches both of the wisdom and knowledge of God* (Rom. 11:33). For it is by the wisdom of God that the whole existence of the world is directed to a single aim—to perfection and transfiguration for the glory of God.

ALL-RIGHTEOUS. Righteousness is understood in the word of God and in its general usage as having two meanings: (*a*) holiness, and (*b*) justice.

a) Holiness consists not only in the absence of evil or sin: holiness is the presence of higher spiritual values, joined to purity from sin.

Holiness is like the light, and the holiness of God is like the purest light. God is the "one alone holy" by nature. He is the Source of holiness for angels and men. Men can attain to holiness only in God, "not by nature, but by participation, by struggle and prayer" (St. Cyril of Jerusalem). The Scripture testifies that the angels who surround the throne of God ceaselessly declare the holiness of God, crying out to each other, *Holy, holy, holy, is the Lord of hosts, the whole earth is full of His glory* (Is. 6:3). As depicted in Scripture, the light of holiness fills everything that comes from God or serves God: *His holy name* (Ps. 32:21; 102:1; 104:3; 105:46); *His holy word* (Ps. 104:41); *the law is holy* (Rom. 7:12); *His holy arm* (Ps. 97:2); *O God, in the holy place is Thy way* (Ps. 76:13); *His holy throne* (Ps. 46:8); *holy is the footstool of His feet* (Ps. 98:5); *righteous is the Lord in all His ways, and holy in all His works* (Ps. 144:17); *holy is the Lord our God* (Ps. 98:9).

b) The *justice* of God is the other aspect of God's all-*righteousness; He will judge the peoples in uprightness* (Ps. 9:8). The Lord *will render to every man according to his deeds, for there is no respect of persons with God* (Rom. 2:6, 11).

How can one harmonize the Divine Love with God's justice, which judges strictly for sins and punishes the guilty? On this question many Fathers have spoken. They liken the anger of God to the anger of a father, who, with the aim of bringing a disobedient son to his senses, resorts to a father's means of punishing, at the same time himself grieving, simultaneously being sad at the senselessness of his son and sympathizing with him in the pain he is causing him. This is why God's justice is always mercy also, and His mercy is justice, according to the words: *Mercy and truth are met together, justice and peace have kissed each other* (Ps. 84:10).

The *holiness* and *justice* of God are closely bound to each other. God calls everyone to eternal life in Him, in His Kingdom, and this means in His Holiness. But into the Kingdom of God nothing unclean can enter. The Lord cleanses us by His chastisements, as by Providential acts which forewarn and correct for the sake of His *love* towards His creation. For we must undergo the judgment of justice, a judgment which for us is terrible: how can we enter into the kingdom of holiness and light, and how would we feel there, being unclean, dark, and not having in ourselves any seeds of holiness, not having in ourselves any kind of positive spiritual or moral value?

ALMIGHTY (omnipotent). He spake, and they came into being; He commanded, and they were created—thus the Psalmist expressed God's almightiness (Ps. 32:9). God is the Creator of the world. It is He who cares for the world in His Providence. He is the Pantocrator. He is the one *Who alone doeth wonders* (Ps. 71:19). But if God tolerates evil and evil people in the world, this is not because He cannot annihilate evil, but because he has given freedom to spiritual beings and directs them so that they might freely, of their own free will, reject evil and turn to good.

With regard to casuistical questions concerning what God "cannot" do, one must answer that the omnipotence of God is extended to everything which is pleasing to His thought, to His goodness, to His will.

OMNIPRESENT. Whither shall l go from Thy Spirit? And from Thy presence whither shall I flee? If I go up into heaven, Thou art there; if I go down into hades, Thou are present there. If I take up my wings toward the dawn, and make mine abode in the uttermost parts of the sea, even there shall Thy hand guide me, and Thy right hand shall hold me (Ps. 138:6–9).

God is not subject to any limitation in space, but He fills everything. Filling everything, God, as a simple Being, is present in every place, not as it were in some part of Him, or by merely sending down some power from Himself, but in all His Being; and He is not confused with that in which He is present. "The Divinity penetrates everything without being mingled with anything, but nothing can penetrate Him" (St. John Damascene). "That God is present everywhere we know, but how, we do not understand, because we can understand only a sensuous presence, and it is not given to us to understand fully the Nature of God" (St. John Chrysostom).[12]

---

[12] St. Gregory Palamas teaches that both God's Essence and His Energies, being inseparable from each other, are present everywhere in creation. (See the *Philokalia*, vol. 4, p. 390.)—3RD ED.

UNCHANGEABLE. In *the Father of lights* there is *no variableness, neither shadow of turning* (James 1:17). God is perfection, and every change is a sign of imperfection and therefore is unthinkable in the most perfect Being, in God. Concerning God one cannot say that any kind of process is being performed in Him, whether of growth, change of appearance, evolution, progress, or anything of the like.

But unchangeability in God is not some kind of immovability; it is not a being closed up within Himself. Even while He is unchanging, His Being is life, filled with power and activity. God in Himself is life, and life is His Being.

The unchangeability of God is not violated by the begetting of the Son and the procession of the Spirit, for to God the Father there belongs fatherliness, and to His Son sonship, and to the Holy Spirit, procession which is "eternal, unending, and unceasing" (St. John Damascene). The words, filled with mystery, "the begetting of the Son" and "the procession of the Spirit," do not express any kind of change in the Divine life or any kind of process; for our limited minds, "begetting" and "procession" are simply placed in opposition to the idea of "creation" and speak of the single *Essence* of the Persons or Hypostases in God. The creation is something outward in relation to the one who creates, whereas the "sonship" of God is an inward unity, a unity of the Nature of the Father and the Son; such also is the "procession" from the Essence of God, the procession of the Spirit from the Father Who causes it.

The unchangeability of God is not violated by the Incarnation and becoming man of the Word, the Son of God. Only creatures in their limitedness lose what they had or acquire what they did not have; but the Divinity of the Son of God remained after the Incarnation the same as it was before the Incarnation. It received in its Hypostasis, in the oneness of the Divine Hypostasis, human nature from the Virgin Mary, but it did not form from this any new, mixed nature, but preserved Its Divine Nature unchanged.

The unchangeability of God is not contradicted, likewise, by the creation of the world. The world is an existence which is outward with relation to the Nature of God, and therefore it does not change either the Essence or the attributes of God. The origin of the world is only *a manifestation* of the power and thought of God. The power and thought of God are eternal and are eternally active, but our creaturely mind cannot understand the concept of this activity in the eternity of God. The world is not co-eternal with God; it is created. But the creation of the world is the realization of the eternal thought of God (Blessed Augustine). The world is not like God in its essence, and therefore it has to be changeable and is not without a beginning; but these attributes of the world do not contradict the fact that its Creator is unchangeable and without beginning (St. John Damascene).

SELF-SUFFICING TO HIMSELF AND ALL-BLESSED. These two expressions are close to one another in meaning.

Self-sufficing must not be understood in the sense of "satisfied with oneself." Rather, it signifies the fullness of possession, complete blessedness, the fullness of all good things. Thus, in the prayers before Communion we read: "I know that I am not worthy or sufficient that Thou shouldest come under the roof of the house of my soul" (Second Prayer). And again, "I am not worthy or sufficient to behold and see the heights of heaven" (Prayer of Symeon the Translator). "Sufficient" signifies here "spiritually adequate," "spiritually wealthy." In God is the *sufficiency* of all good things. *O the depth of the riches both of the wisdom and knowledge of God!* exclaims the Apostle Paul, *for of Him, and through Him, and to Him, are all things* (Rom. 11:33, 36). God has no need for anything, since *He giveth to all life, and breath, and all things* (Acts 17:25). Thus God is Himself the *source* of all life and of every good thing; from Him all creatures derive their sufficiency.

All-Blessed. In his epistles, the Apostle Paul twice calls God "blessed": *According to the glorious Gospel of the blessed God* (I Tim. 1:11); *which in His times He shall show, who is the blessed and only Potentate, the King of kings and Lord of lords* (I Tim. 6:15). The word "all-blessed" must be understood not in the sense that God, having everything within Himself, would be indifferent to the sufferings of the world created by Him; but in this sense: that from Him and in Him, His creatures derive their blessedness. God does not "suffer," but He is "merciful." Christ "suffereth as mortal" (Canon of Pascha)—not in

His Divinity, but in His humanity. God is the *source* of blessedness. In Him is the fullness of joy, sweetness, rejoicing for those who love Him, as it says in the Psalm: *Thou wilt fill me with gladness with Thy countenance; delights are in Thy right hand forever* (Ps. 15:11).

The blessedness of God has its reflection in the unceasing praise, glorification, and thanksgiving which fill the universe, which come from the higher powers—the Cherubim and Seraphim who surround the throne of God and are flaming with fragrant love for God. These praises are offered up from the whole angelic world and from every creature in God's world: "The sun sings Thy praises; the moon glorifies Thee; the stars supplicate before Thee; the light obeys Thee; the deeps are afraid at Thy presence; the fountains are Thy servants" (Prayer of the Great Blessing of Water, Menaion, Jan. 5; *Festal Menaion*, p. 356).

The Unity of God

"Therefore, we believe in one God: one principle, without beginning, uncreated, unbegotten, indestructible and immortal, eternal, unlimited, uncircumscribed, unbounded, infinite in power, simple, uncompounded, incorporeal, unchanging, dispassionate, constant, unchangeable, invisible, source of goodness and justice, light intellectual and inaccessible; power which is not subject to any measure, but which is measured only by His own will, for He can do all things whatsoever He pleases ...; one Essence, one Godhead, one power, one will, one operation, one principality, one authority, one dominion, one kingdom, known in three perfect Hypostases, and known and worshipped with one worship" (St. John Damascene, *Exact Exposition of the Orthodox Faith* 1.8; FC, p. 177).

The truth of the *oneness* of God is so evident at the present time to human awareness that it needs no proofs from the word of God or simply from reason. It was a little different in the early Christian Church, when this truth had to be set forth against the idea of dualism—the acknowledgment of two gods, good and evil—and against the polytheism of the pagans which was then popular.

I believe in one God. These are the first words of the Symbol of Faith (the Creed). God possesses all the fullness of most perfect being. The idea of fullness, perfection, infinity, all-embracingness in God does not allow us to think of Him other than as One, that is, as singular and having one Essence in Himself. This demand of our awareness is expressed by one of the ancient Church writers in the words, "If God is not one, there is no God" (Tertullian). In other words, a divinity limited by another being loses his divine dignity.

The whole of the New Testament Sacred Scripture is filled with the teaching of the one God. *Our Father which art in heaven*, we pray in the words of the Lord's Prayer (Matt. 6:9). *There is none other God but one*, as the Apostle Paul expressed this fundamental truth of faith (I Cor. 8:4).

The Sacred Scripture of the Old Testament is entirely penetrated with monotheism. The history of the Old Testament is the history of the battle for faith in the one true God against pagan polytheism. The desire of some historians of religion to find traces of a supposed "original polytheism" in the Hebrew people in certain Biblical expressions—as, for example, the plural number in the name of God, "Elohim"—or to find a faith in a "national God" in such phrases as "the God of gods," "the God of Abraham, Isaac, and Jacob"—does not correspond to the authentic meaning of these expressions.

1. *Elohim.* For a simple Jew this is a form of reverence and respect (an example of this may be seen in the Russian and other European languages, where the second person plural, "you" as opposed to "thou," is used to express respect). For the Divinely inspired writer, the Prophet Moses, the plural number of the word without doubt contains, in addition, the profound mystical meaning of an insight into the Three Persons in God. No one can doubt that Moses was a pure monotheist and, knowing the spirit of the Hebrew language, he would not use a name that contradicted his faith in the one God.

2. *The God of gods* is an expression that sets faith in the *true* God against the worship of idols; those who worshipped them called their idols "gods," but for the Jews these were *false* gods. This expression is used freely in the New Testament by the Apostle Paul; after saying that

there is none other God but one, he adds: *for though there be that are called gods, whether in heaven or in earth (as there be gods many, and lords many), but to us there is but one God, the Father, of Whom are all things, and we in Him; and one Lord Jesus Christ, by Whom are all things, and we by Him* (I Cor. 8:4–6).

3. *The God of Abraham, Isaac and Jacob* is an expression that expresses only the chosenness of the Hebrew people as the "inheritor of the promises" given to Abraham, Isaac, and Jacob.

The Christian truth of the oneness of God is deepened by the truth of the *Tri-hypostatical unity.*

Chapter 2

The Dogma of the Holy Trinity

G OD is one in Essence and triple in Persons. The dogma of the Trinity is the second fundamental dogma of Christianity. A whole series of the Church's great dogmas are founded immediately upon it, beginning first of all with the dogma of our Redemption. Because of its special importance, the doctrine of the All-Holy Trinity constitutes the content of all the Symbols of Faith which have been and are now used in the Orthodox Church, as well as all the private confessions of faith written on various occasions by the shepherds of the Church.

Because the dogma of the All-Holy Trinity is the most important of all Christian dogmas, it is at the same time the most difficult for the limited human mind to grasp. This is why no battle in the history of the ancient Church was as intense as that over this dogma and the truths which are immediately bound up with it.

The dogma of the Holy Trinity includes in itself two fundamental truths:

A. God is one in Essence, but triple in Person. In other words, God is a Tri-unity, is Tri-hypostatical, is a Trinity One in Essence.

B. The Hypostases have personal or hypostatic attributes: God the Father is unbegotten; the Son is begotten from the Father; the Holy Spirit proceeds from the Father.

We worship the All-Holy Trinity with a single and inseparable worship. In the Church Fathers and the Divine services, the Trinity is often called a *Unity in Trinity*, a *Tri-hypostatical Unity*. In most cases, prayers addressed to one Person of the Holy Trinity end with a glorification or doxology to all three Persons (for example, in a prayer to the Lord Jesus Christ: "For most glorious art Thou, together with

Thine unoriginate Father, and the All-Holy Spirit, unto the ages. Amen").

The Church, addressing the All-Holy Trinity in prayer, invokes It in the singular, not the plural, number. For example, "For Thee" (and not "You") "all the heavenly powers praise, and to Thee (not "to You") we send up glory, to the Father, to the Son, and to the Holy Spirit, now and ever and unto the ages of ages. Amen."

Acknowledging the mystical nature of this dogma, the Church of Christ sees in it a great revelation which exalts the Christian faith incomparably above any confession of simple monotheism, such as may be found in non-Christian religions. The dogma of the Three Persons indicates the fullness of the mystical inward life in God, for *God is love,* and the love of God cannot merely be extended to the world created by Him: in the Holy Trinity this love is directed within the Divine Life also. The dogma of the Three Persons indicates even more clearly for us the closeness of God to the world: God *above* us, God *with* us, God *in* us and in all creation.

Above us is God the Father, the ever-flowing Source, as it is expressed in the Church's prayer, the Foundation of all being, the Father of mercies Who loves and cares for us, His creation—for we are His children by Grace.

With us is God the Son, begotten by Him, Who for the sake of Divine love has manifested Himself to men as Man so that we might know and see with our own eyes that God is with us most intimately, partaker of flesh and blood with us (Heb. 2:14) in the most perfect way.

In us and in all creation—by His Power and Grace—is the Holy Spirit, Who fills all things, is the Giver of Life, Life-Creator, Comforter, Treasury and Source of good things. Having an eternal and pre-eternal existence, the Three Divine Persons were *manifested* to the world with the coming and Incarnation of the Son of God, being "one Power, one Essence, one Godhead" (Stichera for Pentecost, Glory on "Lord, I have cried").

Because God in His very Essence is wholly consciousness and thought and self-awareness, each of these three eternal manifestations of Himself by the one God has self-awareness, and therefore each one is a *Person*. And these Persons are not simply forms or isolated manifestations or attributes or activities; rather, the Three Persons are contained in the very Unity of God's Essence. Thus, when in Christian doctrine we speak of the Tri-unity of God, we speak of the mystical inward life hidden in the depths of the Divinity, revealed to the world in time, in the New Testament, by the sending down of the Son of God from the Father into the world and by the activity of the wonderworking, life-giving, saving power of the Comforter, the Holy Spirit.

Indications of the Trinity of Persons in God in the Holy Scripture of the Old Testament

The truth of the Tri-unity of God is only expressed in a veiled way in the Old Testament, only half-revealed. The Old Testament testimonies of the Trinity are revealed and explained in the light of *Christian faith*, as the Apostle Paul wrote concerning the Jews: *But even unto this day, when Moses is read, the veil is upon their heart. Nevertheless, when it shall turn to the Lord, the veil shall be taken away.... It is taken away in Christ* (II Cor. 3:15–16, 14).

The chief passages in the Old Testament which testify to the Trinity of God are the following:

Genesis 1:1, and the following verses: the name of God ("Elohim") in the Hebrew text has the grammatical form of the plural number.

Genesis 1:26: *And God said, Let us make man in our image, after our likeness.* The plural number here indicates that God is not one Person.

Genesis 3:22: *And the Lord God said, Behold, Adam is become as one of us, to know good and evil.* (These are the words of God before the banishment of our ancestors from Paradise.)

Genesis 11:6–7: Prior to the confusion of tongues at the building of the tower of Babylon, the Lord said: *Let us go down, and there confound their language.*

Genesis 18:1–3, concerning Abraham: *And the Lord appeared unto him at the oak of Mamre.... And he* (Abraham) *lifted up his eyes and looked, and lo, three men stood by him … and he bowed himself toward the ground and said, My Lord, if now I have found favor in Thy sight, pass not away, I pray Thee, from Thy servant.* Blessed Augustine says of this: "Do you see that Abraham meets Three but bows down to One?… Having beheld Three, he understood the mystery of the Trinity, and having bowed down to One, he confessed One God in Three Persons."

In addition, the Fathers of the Church see an indirect reference to the Trinity in the following passages:

Numbers 6:24–26: The priestly blessing indicated by God through Moses is in a triple form: *The Lord bless thee.… The Lord make His face shine on thee.… The Lord lift up His countenance upon thee.*

Isaiah 6:3: The doxology of the Seraphim who stand about the throne of God is in a triple form: *Holy, holy, holy, is the Lord of hosts.*

Psalm 32:6: *By the Word of the Lord were the heavens established, and all the might of them by the Spirit of His mouth.*

Finally, one may indicate those passages in the Old Testament Revelation where the Son of God and the Holy Spirit are referred to separately. For example, concerning the Son:

Psalm 2:7: *Thou art My Son; this day have I begotten Thee.*

Psalm 109:3: *From the womb before the morning star have I begotten Thee.*

Concerning the Spirit:

Psalm 142:12: *Thy good Spirit shall lead me in the land of uprightness.*

Isaiah 48:16: *The Lord God, and His Spirit, hath sent me.*

*The Divinely Revealed Teaching
of the Holy Trinity in the New Testament*

The Trinity of Persons in God was revealed in the New Testament in the coming of the Son of God and in the sending down of the Holy Spirit. The sending to earth of God the Word and the Holy Spirit by the Father constitutes the content of all the New Testament writings. Of course, this manifestation to the world of the Triune God is given here not in a dogmatic formula, but in an account of the manifestations and deeds of the Persons of the Holy Trinity.

The manifestation of God in Trinity was accomplished at the Baptism of the Lord Jesus Christ, which is why this Baptism itself is called the "Theophany" or "manifestation of God." The Son of God, having become man, accepted baptism by water; the Father testified of Him; and the Holy Spirit confirmed the truth spoken by the voice of God by His manifestation in the form of a dove, as is expressed in the troparion of this feast: "When Thou, O Lord, wast baptized in the Jordan, the worship of the Trinity was made manifest. For the voice of the Father bore witness unto Thee, calling Thee the beloved Son; and the Spirit in the form of a dove confirmed His word as sure and steadfast. O Christ our God Who hast appeared and enlightened the world, glory to Thee."

In the New Testament Scriptures there are expressions concerning the Triune God; and these, in a most condensed but at the same time precise form, express the truth of the Trinity:

Matthew 28:19: *Go ye therefore, and teach all nations, baptizing them in the name of the Father, and of the Son, and of the Holy Spirit.* Of this, St. Ambrose of Milan notes: "The Lord said, 'In the name' and not 'in the names,' because God is One. There are not many names; therefore there are not two gods, and not three gods."

II Corinthians 13:14: *The Grace of the Lord Jesus Christ, and the love of God, and the communion of the Holy Spirit, be with you all. Amen.*

John 15:26: *But when the Comforter is come, Whom I will send unto you from the Father, even the Spirit of Truth, Who proceedeth from the Father, He shall testify of Me.*

I John 5:7: *For there are three that bear record in heaven, the Father, the Word, and the Holy Spirit: and these three are one.* (This verse is missing in the ancient Greek manuscripts that have been preserved, and is present only in Western, Latin manuscripts.)

In addition, St. Athanasius the Great interprets as a reference to the Trinity the following text of the Epistle to the Ephesians (4:6): *One God and Father of all, Who is above all* (God the Father), *and through all* (God the Son), *and in you all* (God the Holy Spirit). Indeed, the whole

Epistle of the Apostle Paul to the Ephesians—especially the first three dogmatical chapters—is a revelation of the truth of the "Trinitarian economy" of our salvation.

The Confession of the Dogma of the Holy Trinity in the Ancient Church

The truth of the Holy Trinity has been confessed by the Church of Christ in all of its fullness and completeness from the very beginning. For example, St. Irenaeus of Lyons, a disciple of St. Polycarp of Smyrna, who was himself instructed by the Apostle John the Theologian, speaks clearly of the universality of faith in the Holy Trinity: "Although the Church is dispersed throughout the whole inhabited world, to the ends of the earth, it has received faith in the one God the Father Almighty, ... and in one Lord Jesus Christ the Son of God, Who was incarnate for the sake of our salvation, and in the Holy Spirit Who has proclaimed the economy of our salvation through the prophets.... Having received such a preaching and such a faith, the Church, although it is dispersed throughout the entire world, as we have said, carefully preserves this faith as if dwelling in a single house. It believes this (everywhere) identically, as if it had a single soul and a single heart, and it preaches it with one voice, teaching and transmitting it as if with a single mouth. Although there are many dialects in the world, the power of Tradition is one and the same. None of the leaders of the churches will contradict this, nor will anyone, whether powerful in words or unskilled in words, weaken the Tradition" (*Against Heresies* 1.10).

Defending the catholic truth of the Holy Trinity against heretics, the Holy Fathers not only cited as proof the witness of Sacred Scripture, as well as rational philosophical grounds for the refutation of heretical opinions, but they also relied upon the testimony of the first Christians. They indicated: (1) the example of the martyrs and confessors who were not afraid to declare their faith in the Father, Son, and Holy Spirit before their torturers; and they cited (2) the writings of the Apostolic Fathers and, in general, the ancient Christian writers, and

(3) the expressions which are used in the Divine services. Thus, St. Basil the Great quotes the Small Doxology: "Glory to the Father through the Son in the Holy Spirit," and another: "To Him (Christ) with the Father and the Holy Spirit may there be honor and glory unto the ages of ages." And St. Basil says that this doxology was used in the churches from the very time that the Gospel was announced. He likewise points to the thanksgiving of lamplighting time, or the Vesper Hymn, calling it an "ancient" hymn handed down "from the Fathers," and he cites from it the words: "We praise the Father and the Son and the Holy Spirit of God" in order to show the faith of the ancient Christians in the equal honor of the Holy Spirit with the Father and the Son.

There are likewise many testimonies from the ancient Fathers and teachers of the Church concerning the fact that the Church from the first days of her existence has performed baptism in the name of the Father and the Son and the Holy Spirit, as three Divine Persons, and has accused the heretics who tried to perform baptism either in the name of the Father alone, considering the Son and the Holy Spirit to be lower powers, or in the name of the Father and the Son, and even of the Son alone, thus belittling the Holy Spirit (see the testimonies of Justin the Martyr, Tertullian, Irenaeus, Cyprian, Athanasius, Hilary, Basil the Great, and others).

The Church, however, has experienced great disturbances and undergone a great battle in the defense of the dogma of the Holy Trinity. The battle was chiefly fought on two points: first on the affirmation of the truth of the oneness of Essence and equality of honor of the *Son of God* with God the Father; and then on the affirmation of the oneness of honor of the *Holy Spirit* with God the Father and God the Son.

In the ancient period, the dogmatic aim of the Church was to find such precise words for this dogma as could best protect the dogma of the Holy Trinity against the reinterpretations of heretics. Desiring to bring the mystery of the All-Holy Trinity a little closer to our earthly concepts, to bring what is beyond understanding a little closer to that which is understandable, the Fathers of the Church used comparisons from nature. Among these comparisons are: (*a*) the sun, its rays, and light; (*b*) the root, trunk, and fruit of a tree; (*c*) a spring of water and the fountain and river that issue from it; (*d*) three candles burning simultaneously which give a single inseparable light; (*e*) fire, and the light and warmth which come from it; (*f*) mind, will, and memory; (*g*) consciousness, knowledge, and desire; and the like. But this is what St. Gregory the Theologian says regarding these attempts at comparison: "I have very carefully considered this matter in my own mind, and have looked at it in every point of view, in order to find some likeness of this mystery, but I have been unable to discover anything on earth with which to compare the Nature of the Godhead. For even if I did happen upon some tiny likeness, it escaped me for the most part, and left me down below with my example. I picture to myself a spring, a fountain, a river, as others have done before, to see if the first might be analogous to the Father, the second to the Son, and the third to the Holy Spirit. For in these there is no distinction in time, nor are they torn away from their connection with each other, though they seem to be parted by three personalities. But I was afraid in the first place that I should present a flow in the Godhead, incapable of standing still; and secondly, that by this figure a numerical unity would be introduced. For the spring and the fountain and the river are numerically one, though in different forms.

"Again, I thought of the sun and a ray and light. But here again there was a fear lest people should get an idea of composition in the Uncompounded Nature, such as there is in the sun and the things that are in the sun. And in the second place lest we should give Essence to the Father but deny Personality to the Others and make Them only powers of God, existing in Him and not Personal. For neither the ray nor the light is another sun, but they are only emanations from the sun, and qualities of its essence. And lest we should thus, as far as the illustration goes, attribute both Being and Not-being to God, which is even more monstrous…. In a word, there is nothing which presents a standing point to my mind in these illustrations from which to consider the Object which I am trying to represent to myself, unless one may indulgently accept one point of the image while rejecting the rest. Finally, then, it seems best to me to let the images and the shadows go, as being deceptive and very far short of the truth, and clinging myself to the more reverent conception, and resting upon few words, using the guidance of the Holy Spirit, keeping to the end as my genuine comrade and companion the enlightenment which I have received from Him, and passing through this world to persuade others also to the best of my power to worship Father, Son, and Holy Spirit, the one Godhead and Power" (St. Gregory the Theologian, Homily 31, "On the Holy Spirit," sections 31–33; NPNF, p. 328).

The Personal Attributes of the Divine Persons

The Personal or Hypostatical attributes of the All-Holy Trinity are designated thus: the Father is unbegotten; the Son is pre-eternally begotten; the Holy Spirit proceeds from the Father.

"Although we have been taught that there is a distinction between begetting and procession, what this distinction consists of, and what is the begetting of the Son and the procession of the Holy Spirit from the Father—this we do not know" (St. John Damascene).

No kind of logical calculation as to what begetting and procession mean is capable of revealing the inner mystery of the Divine life. Arbitrary conceptions can even lead to a distortion of the Christian teaching. The very expressions that the Son is "begotten of the Father" and that the Spirit "proceeds from the Father" are simply a precise transmission of the words of Sacred Scripture. Of the Son it is said that He is "the only begotten" (John 1:14; 3:16; and other places); likewise, *From the womb before the morning star have I begotten Thee* (Ps. 109:3); *The Lord said unto Me: Thou art My Son, this day have I begotten Thee* (Ps. 2:7; the words of this Psalm are also cited in the Epistle to the Hebrews, 1:5; 5:5). The dogma of the procession of the Holy Spirit rests upon the following direct and precise expression of the Saviour: *But when the Comforter is come, Whom I will send unto you from the Father, even the Spirit of Truth, Who proceedeth from the Father, He shall testify of Me* (John 15:26). On the foundation of the above-cited expressions, of the Son it is usually said, in the past tense, that He is "begotten," and of the Spirit in the present tense that He "proceeds." However, these various grammatical forms of tense do not indicate any relation to time at all. Both begetting and procession are "from all eternity," "outside of time." Concerning the begetting of the Son, theological terminology sometimes also uses the present tense form—"He is begotten from all eternity" of the Father. However, the Holy Fathers more usually use the expression of the Symbol of Faith: "begotten."[1]

The dogma of the begetting of the Son from the Father and the procession of the Holy Spirit from the Father shows the mystical inner relations of the Persons in God and the life of God within Himself. One must clearly distinguish these relations which are pre-eternal, from all eternity, and outside of time, from the manifestations of the Holy Trinity in the created world, from the activities and manifestations of God's *Providence* in the world as they have been expressed in such events as the creation of the world, the coming of the Son of God to earth, His Incarnation, and the sending down of the Holy Spirit. These providential manifestations and activities have been accomplished *in time*. In historical time the Son of God was born of the Virgin Mary by the descent upon her of the Holy Spirit: *The Holy Spirit shall come upon thee, and the power of the highest shall overshadow thee; therefore also that holy thing which shall be born of thee shall be called the Son of God* (Luke 1:35). In historical time the Holy Spirit descended upon Jesus at the time of His Baptism by John. In historical time the Holy Spirit was sent down by the Son from the Father, appearing in the form of fiery tongues. The Son came to earth through the Holy Spirit. The Spirit is sent down by the Son in accordance with the promise: *the Comforter ... Whom I will send unto you from the Father* (John 15:26).

Concerning the pre-eternal begetting of the Son and the procession of the Spirit one might ask: "When was this begetting and this procession?" St. Gregory the Theologian replies: "This was before *when* itself. You have heard about the begetting; do not be curious to know in what form this begetting was. You have heard that the Spirit

---

[1] The English translation does not preserve the distinction of tenses in the Russian and Greek verbs here; the single English word "begotten" is used to translate both the reflexive, passive form of the present tense and the past participle.

proceeds from the Father; do not be curious to know how He proceeds."

Although the meaning of the words "begetting" and "procession" are beyond us, this does not decrease the importance of these conceptions in the Christian teaching regarding God. They indicate the wholeness of Divinity of the Second and Third Persons. The existence of the Son and the Spirit rests inseparably in the very Essence of God the Father; hence we have the expressions regarding the Son: *From the womb … have I begotten Thee*—from the womb, that is, from the Essence. By means of the words "begotten" and "proceeds," the existence of the Son and the Spirit is set in opposition to any kind of creatureliness, to everything that was created and was called by the will of God out of nonexistence. An existence which comes from the *Essence of God* can only be Divine and eternal; therefore the word of God says of the Son Who came down to earth: *the only begotten Son, Who IS in the bosom of the Father* (John 1:18); and concerning the Holy Spirit: *Whom I will send … Who PROCEEDETH from the Father.* (Here the grammatical present tense signifies eternity.)

That which is begotten is always of the same essence as the one that begets. But that which is created and made is of another, lower essence, and is *external* with relation to the Creator.

The Name of the Second Person—The Word

Often in the Holy Fathers and in the Divine service texts, the Son of God is called the Word or Logos. This has its foundation in the first chapter of the Gospel of John the Theologian.

The concept or name "Word" we find in its exalted significance many times in the books of the Old Testament. Such are the expressions of the Psalter: *Forever, O Lord, Thy Word abideth in heaven* (Ps. 118:89); *He sent forth His Word and He healed them* (Ps. 106:20)—a verse which refers to the Exodus of the Hebrews from Egypt; *By the Word of the Lord were the heavens established* (Ps. 32:6). The author of the Wisdom of Solomon writes: *Thine all-powerful Word leaped from heaven, from the royal throne, into the midst of the land that was doomed, as a stern warrior carrying the sharp sword of Thine authentic command, and stood and filled all things with death, and touched heaven while standing on the earth* (Wis. 18:15–16).

With the help of this Divine name, the Holy Fathers make attempts to explain somewhat the mystery of the relationship of the Son to the Father. St. Dionysius of Alexandria (a disciple of Origen) explains this relationship in the following way: "Our thought utters from itself the word according to what the Prophet has said: *My heart hath poured forth a good word* (Ps. 44:1). Thought and word are separate one from the other, and each occupies its special and separate place: while thought remains and moves in the heart, the word is on the tongue and the lips. However, they are inseparable, and not for one moment are they deprived of each other. Thought does not exist without word, nor word without thought, having received its existence in thought. Thought is, as it were, a word hidden within, and word is thought which has come without. Thought is transformed into word, and word transmits thought to the hearers. In this way, thought, with the help of the word, is instilled in the souls of the listeners, entering them together with the word. Thought, coming from itself, is as it were the father of the word; and the word is, as it were, the son of the thought. Before the thought the word was impossible, and the word does not come from anywhere outside, but rather from the thought itself. Thus also, the Father, the greatest and all-embracing Thought, has a Son, the Word, His first Interpreter and Herald" (quoted in St. Athanasius, *De Sententia Dionisii*, no. 15).

This same likeness, the relationship of word to thought, is also used much by St. John of Kronstadt in his reflections on the Holy Trinity in *My Life in Christ*.

In the quoted citation from St. Dionysius of Alexandria, the quotation from the Psalter shows that the ideas of the Fathers of the Church were based upon the use of the term "Word" in the Sacred Scripture not only of the New Testament, but of the Old Testament as well. There is thus no reason to assert that the term "Logos" or "Word" was borrowed by Christianity from philosophy, as certain Western interpreters assert.

Of course, the Fathers of the Church, as well as the Apostle John the Theologian himself, were not unaware of the conception of the "Logos" as it was interpreted in Greek philosophy and in the Jewish philosopher, Philo of Alexandria (the concept of the Logos as a personal being intermediate between God and the world, or as an impersonal divine power); but they sharply *contrasted* this understanding of the Logos with the Christian understanding of the Word—the only begotten Son of God, one in Essence with the Father, and equal in Divinity to the Father and the Spirit.

On the Procession of the Holy Spirit

The ancient Orthodox teaching of the personal attributes of the Father, Son, and Holy Spirit was distorted in the Latin Church by the creation of a teaching of the procession, outside of time and from all eternity, of the Holy Spirit from the Father *and the Son*—the *Filioque*. The idea that the Holy Spirit proceeds from the Father and the Son originated in certain expressions of Blessed Augustine. It became established in the West as obligatory in the 9th century, and when Latin missionaries came to the Bulgarians in the middle of the 9th century, the *Filioque* was in their Symbol of Faith.[2]

As differences between the papacy and the Orthodox East became sharper, the Latin dogma became more and more strengthened in the West; finally it was acknowledged in the West as a universally obligatory dogma. Protestantism inherited this teaching from the Roman Church.

The Latin dogma of the *Filioque* is a substantial and important deviation from Orthodox truth. This dogma was subjected to a detailed examination and accusation, especially by Patriarchs Photius (9th cen-

---

[2] In the 9th century the *Filioque* was not yet obligatory in Rome. However, the Germans had already inserted it into their Creed, and, with the approval of Pope Nicholas I, they made it obligatory among the Bulgarians they were evangelizing. This was until 870, when the Bulgarian Church was assigned to the Patriarchate of Constantinople and the German missionaries were expelled from Bulgaria. (See Timothy [Bishop Kallistos] Ware, *The Orthodox Church*, pp. 54–56.)—3RD ED.

tury) and Michael Cerularius (11th century), and likewise by St. Mark of Ephesus, who took part in the Council of Florence (1439). Adam Zernikav (18th century), who converted from Roman Catholicism to Orthodoxy, cites about a thousand testimonies from the writings of the Holy Fathers of the Church in favor of the Orthodox teaching of the Holy Spirit in his work, *Concerning the Procession of the Holy Spirit.*

Out of "missionary" aims, the Roman Church has, in more recent times, disguised the difference (or rather, the importance of the difference) between the Orthodox teaching on the Holy Spirit and the Roman teaching. With this in mind, the popes have kept the ancient Orthodox text of the Symbol of Faith, without the words "and from the Son," for the Uniates and the "Eastern Rite." But this cannot be regarded as a kind of half-rejection by Rome of its own dogma. At best, it is only a disguise for the Roman view that the Orthodox East is backward in dogmatic development, that one must be condescending to this backwardness, and that the dogma expressed in the West in a developed form (*explicite*, in accordance with the Roman theory of the "development of dogmas") is concealed in the Orthodox dogma in a still undeveloped form (*implicite*). But in Latin dogmatic works which are intended for internal use, we encounter a definite treatment of the Orthodox dogma of the procession of the Holy Spirit as a "heresy." In the officially approved Latin dogmatic work of the doctor of theology, A. Sanda, we read: "Opponents (of the present Roman teaching) are the schismatic Greeks, who teach that the Holy Spirit proceeds from the Father alone. Already in the year 808 Greek monks protested against the introduction by the Latins of the word *Filioque* into the Creed.... Who the originator of this heresy was, is unknown." (Dr. A. Sanda, *Sinopsis Theologiae Dogmaticae Specialis*, vol. 1 [Herder edition, 1916], p. 100.)

However, the Latin dogma agrees neither with Sacred Scripture nor with the universal Sacred Tradition of the Church; and it does not even agree with the most ancient tradition of the Local Church of Rome.

In their defense, Roman theologians cite a series of passages from Sacred Scripture where the Holy Spirit is called "of Christ," where it is said that He is given by the Son of God; from this they conclude that He proceeds also from the Son. The most important of these passages cited by Roman theologians are: the words of the Saviour to His disciples concerning the Holy Spirit, the Comforter: *He shall take of Mine, and shall show it unto you* (John 16:15); the words of the Apostle Paul, *God hath sent forth the Spirit of His Son into your hearts* (Gal. 4:6); the words of the same Apostle, *Now if any man have not the Spirit of Christ, he is none of His* (Rom. 8:9); and from the Gospel of John, *He breathed on them, and saith unto them, Receive ye the Holy Spirit* (John 20:22).

In like fashion, the Roman theologians find in the works of the Holy Fathers of the Church passages where often there is mention of the sending of the Holy Spirit "through the Son" and sometimes even of a "proceeding through the Son."

However, no reasoning of any kind can obscure the perfectly precise words of the Saviour: *the Comforter ... Whom I will send unto you from the Father,* and immediately afterwards, *the Spirit of Truth, Who proceedeth from the Father* (John 15:26). The Holy Fathers of the Church could not possibly place in the words "through the Son" anything that is not contained in Sacred Scripture.

In the present case, Roman Catholic theologians are either confusing two dogmas—that is, the dogma of the personal existence of the Hypostases, and the dogma of the Oneness of Essence which is immediately bound up with it, although it is a separate dogma—or else they are confusing the inner relations of the Hypostases of the All-Holy Trinity with the providential actions and manifestations of the Father, the Son, and the Holy Spirit, which are directed towards the world and the human race. That the Holy Spirit is One in Essence with the Father and the Son, that therefore He is the Spirit of the Father and of the Son, is an indisputable Christian truth, for God is a Trinity One in Essence and Indivisible.

This idea is clearly expressed by Blessed Theodoret: "Concerning the Holy Spirit, it is said not that He *has existence* from the Son or through the Son, but rather that He proceeds from the Father and *has the same Nature* as the Son, is in fact the Spirit of the Son as being One in Essence with Him" (Bl. Theodoret, "On the Third Ecumenical Council").

In the Orthodox Divine services also, we often hear these words addressed to the Lord Jesus Christ: *By Thy Holy Spirit* enlighten us, instruct us, preserve us." The expression, "the Spirit of the Father and the Son," is likewise in itself quite Orthodox. But these expressions refer to the dogma of the Oneness of Essence, and it is absolutely essential to distinguish this from another dogma, the dogma of the begetting and the procession, in which, as the Holy Fathers express it, is shown the *Cause of the existence* of the Son and the Spirit. All of the Eastern Fathers acknowledge that the Father is *monos aitios*, the "*sole Cause*" of the Son and the Spirit. Therefore, when certain Church Fathers use the expression "through the Son," they are, precisely by means of this expression, preserving the dogma of the procession *from the Father* and the inviolability of the dogmatic formula, "proceedeth from the Father." The Fathers speak of the Son as "through" so as to defend the expression "from," which refers only to the Father.

To this, one should add that the expression, "through the Son," which is found in certain Holy Fathers, in the majority of cases refers definitely to the manifestations of the Holy Spirit *in the world*, that is, to the providential actions of the Holy Trinity, and not to the life of God in Himself. When the Eastern Church first noticed a distortion of the dogma of the Holy Spirit in the West and began to reproach the Western theologians for their innovations, St. Maximus the Confessor (in the 7th century), desiring to defend the Westerners, justified them precisely by saying that by the words "from the Son" they intended to indicate that the Holy Spirit is *given* to creatures through the Son, that He is *manifested*, that He is *sent*—but not that the Holy Spirit has His existence from Him. St. Maximus the Confessor himself held strictly to the teaching of the Eastern Church concerning the procession of the Holy Spirit from the Father and wrote a special treatise about this dogma.

The providential sending of the Spirit by the Son of God is spoken of in the words, *Whom I will send unto you from the Father.* Also, we pray: "O Lord, Who didst send down Thine All-Holy Spirit at the third hour upon Thine apostles, Him take not away from us, O Good One, but renew Him in us who pray to Thee" (troparion of the Third Hour on weekdays of Great Lent; also said silently by the priest before the Consecration at the Liturgy). Confusing the texts of Sacred Scripture which speak of the "procession" with the others which speak of the "sending" of the Holy Spirit, Roman theologians transferred the concept of providential relations to the very existence of the Godhead, to the relations there between the Persons of the Holy Trinity.

Apart from the *dogmatic* side, by introducing a new dogma the Roman Church violated the decree of the Third and subsequent Ecumenical Councils (4th to 7th centuries), which forbade the introduction of any kind of change into the Nicaean Symbol of Faith after the Second Ecumenical Council had given it its final form. Thus, the Roman Church also performed a serious *canonical* violation.

But when Roman theologians try to say that the whole difference between Roman Catholicism and Orthodoxy in the teaching on the Holy Spirit is that they teach the procession "also from the Son" while we teach of the procession "through the Son," in such an assertion there is hidden at the very least a misunderstanding (even though sometimes our Church writers also follow the Catholics and allow themselves to repeat this idea). The expression "through the Son" does not at all comprise a *dogma* of the Orthodox Church; it is only an *explanatory means* of certain Holy Fathers in their teaching on the Holy Trinity, whereas the very *meaning* of the teaching of the Orthodox Church in essence is different from that of Roman Catholicism.

The Oneness of Essence, the Equality of Divinity, and the Equality of Honor of the Persons of the Holy Trinity

The Three Hypostases of the Holy Trinity have one and the same Essence; each of the Hypostases has the fullness of Divinity unharmed and immeasurable; the Three Hypostases are equal in honor and worship.

As for the fullness of Divinity of the *First Person* of the Holy Trinity, there have been no heretics in the history of the Church of Christ who have denied or lessened it. However, we do encounter departures from the authentic Christian teaching regarding God the Father. Thus, in antiquity under the influence of the Gnostics, and more recently under the influence of the so-called philosophy of idealism in the first half of the 19th century (chiefly Schelling), there arose a teaching of God as the Absolute, God detached from everything limited and finite (the very word "absolute" means "detached") and therefore having no immediate contact with the world and requiring an intermediary. Thus, the concept of the Absolute was connected with the name of God the Father and the concept of the intermediary with the name of the Son of God. Such a conception is in total disharmony with the Christian understanding and with the teaching of the word of God. The word of God teaches us that God is near to the world, that *God is love*, and that God—God the Father—so loved the world that He gave His only begotten Son so that all who believe in Him might have eternal life. To God the Father, inseparably from the Son and the Spirit, belongs the creation of the world and a ceaseless Providence over the world. If in the word of God the Son is called an Intermediary, this is because the Son of God took upon Himself human nature, became the God-Man, and united in Himself Divinity with humanity, united the earthly with the heavenly. But this is not at all because the Son is, as it were, some indispensable binding principle between God the Father Who is infinitely remote from the world, and the finite, creaturely world.

In the history of the Church, the *chief* dogmatic work of the Holy Fathers was directed towards affirming the truth of the Oneness of Essence, the fullness of Divinity, and the equality of honor of the *Second* and *Third* Hypostases of the Holy Trinity.

The Oneness of Essence, the Equality of Divinity, and the Equality of Honor of God the Son with God the Father

In earliest Christian times, until the Church's faith in the Oneness of Essence and the equality of the Persons of the Holy Trinity had been precisely formulated in strictly defined terminology, it happened that

94

even those Church writers who were careful to be in agreement with the universal consciousness of the Church and had no intention to violate it with any personal views of their own, sometimes, together with clear Orthodox thoughts, used expressions concerning the Divinity of the Persons of the Holy Trinity which were not entirely precise and did not clearly affirm the equality of the Persons.

This can be explained, for the most part, by the fact that in one and the same term some shepherds of the Church placed one meaning and others, another meaning. The concept of "essence" was expressed in the Greek language by the word *ousia,* and this word was in general understood by everyone in the same way. Using the word *ousia,* the Holy Fathers referred it to the concept of "Person." But a lack of clarity was introduced by the use of another word, "Hypostasis." Some signified by this term the "Persons" of the Holy Trinity, and others the "Essence." This circumstance hindered mutual understanding. Finally, following the authoritative example of St. Basil the Great, it became accepted to understand by the word Hypostasis the Personal attributes in the Triune Divinity.

But apart from this, there were heretics in the ancient Christian period who consciously denied or lessened the Divinity of the Son of God. Heresies of this type were numerous and from time to time caused strong disturbances in the Church. Such, for example, were the following heretics:

1. In the Apostolic Age—the Ebionites (after the name of the heretic Ebion).[3] The Holy Fathers testify that the Holy Evangelist John the Theologian wrote his Gospel against them.

2. In the 3rd century, Paul of Samosata, who was accused by two councils of Antioch in the same century.

3. The most dangerous of all the heretics was Arius, the presbyter of Alexandria, in the 4th century. Arius taught that the Word, or Son of God, received the beginning of His existence in time, although before anything else; that He was created by God, although subse-

---

[3] It has also been suggested that their name comes from the Hebrew word *ebion,* meaning "poor." See Appendix II, p. 374 below.—3rd Ed.

quently God created everything through Him; that He is called the Son of God only because He is the most perfect of all the created spirits, and has a nature which, being different from the Father's, is not Divine.

This heretical teaching of Arius disturbed the whole Christian world, since it drew after it very many people. In 325 the First Ecumenical Council was called against this teaching, and at this Council 318 of the chief hierarchs of the Church unanimously expressed the ancient teaching of Orthodoxy and condemned the false teaching of Arius. The Council triumphantly pronounced anathema against those who say that there was a time when the Son of God did not exist, against those who affirm that He was created, or that He is of a different essence from God the Father. The Council composed a Symbol of Faith, which was confirmed and completed later at the Second Ecumenical Council. The unity and equality of honor of the Son of God with God the Father was expressed by this Council in the Symbol of Faith by these words: "of One Essence with the Father."

After the Council, the Arian heresy was divided into three branches and continued to exist for some decades. It was subjected to further refutation in its details at several local councils and in the works of the great Fathers of the Church of the 4th century and part of the 5th century (Sts. Athanasius the Great, Basil the Great, Gregory the Theologian, John Chrysostom, Gregory of Nyssa, Epiphanius, Ambrose of Milan, Cyril of Alexandria, and others). However, the spirit of this heresy even later found a place for itself in various false teachings both of the Middle Ages and of modern times.

In answering the opinions of the Arians, the Fathers of the Church did not overlook a single one of the passages in Holy Scripture which had been cited by the heretics in justification of their idea of the inequality of the Son with the Father. Concerning the expressions in Sacred Scripture which seem to speak of the inequality of the Son with the Father, one should bear in mind the following: (*a*) that the Lord Jesus Christ is not only God, but also became Man, and such expressions can be referred to His humanity; (*b*) that in addition, He, as our Redeemer, during the days of His earthly life was in a condition of voluntary belittlement: *He humbled Himself, and became obedient unto death* (Phil. 2:7–8). In keeping with these words of the Apostle, the Fathers of the Church express this condition by the words *ekkenosis, kenosis*, which mean a pouring out, a lessening, a belittlement. "Foreseeing Thy Divine self-emptying upon the Cross, Habakkuk cried out marvelling" (Canon for the Matins of Great Saturday). Even when the Lord speaks of His own Divinity, He, being sent by the Father and having come to fulfill upon the earth the will of the Father, places Himself in *obedience* to the Father, being One in Essence and equal in honor with Him as the Son, giving us an example of obedience. This relationship of submission refers not to the Essence (*ousia*) of the Divinity, but to the activity of the Persons in the world: the Father is He Who sends; the Son is He Who is sent. This is the obedience of love.

Such is the precise significance, for example, of the words of the Saviour in the Gospel of John: *My Father is greater than I* (John 14:28). One should note that these words are spoken to His disciples in His farewell conversation after the words which express the idea of the fullness of His Divinity and the Unity of the Son with the Father: *If a man love me, he will keep my words: and My Father will love him, and We will come unto him and make Our abode with him* (v. 23). In these words the Saviour joins the Father and Himself in the single word "We," and speaks equally in the name of His Father and in His own name; but, since He has been sent by the Father into the world (v. 24), He places Himself in a relationship of submission to the Father (v. 28).

A detailed examination of similar passages in Sacred Scripture (for example, Mark 13:32; Matt. 26:39; Matt. 27:46; John 20:17) is to be found in St. Athanasius the Great (in his sermons against the Arians), in St. Basil the Great (in his fourth book against Eunomius), in St. Gregory the Theologian, and in others who wrote against the Arians.

However, if there are such unclear expressions in the Sacred Scripture about Jesus Christ, there are many, one might even say innumerable, passages that testify of the Divinity of the Lord Jesus Christ. First of all, the Gospel as a whole testifies of Him. With regard to separate passages, we will indicate here only a few of the more important ones. Some of these passages say that the Son of God is true God; others state that He is equal to the Father; still others say that He is One in Essence with the Father.

It is essential to keep in mind that to call the Lord Jesus Christ God—*Theos*—in itself speaks of the fullness of Divinity in Him. Speaking of the Son, the Apostle Paul says that *in Him dwelleth all the fullness of the Godhead bodily* (Col. 2:9).

That the Son of God is true God is shown by the following:

a) He is directly called God in Sacred Scripture:

In the beginning was the Word, and the Word was with God, and the Word was God. The same was in the beginning with God. All things were made by Him; and without Him was not anything made that was made (John 1:1–3).

Great is the mystery of godliness: God was manifest in the flesh (I Tim. 3:16).

And we know that the Son of God is come and hath given us an understanding that we may know Him that is true; and we are in Him that is true, even in His Son Jesus Christ. This is the true God, and eternal life (I John 5:20).

… Of whom as concerning the flesh Christ came, Who is over all, God blessed for ever. Amen (Rom. 9:5).

My Lord and my God—the exclamation of the Apostle Thomas (John 20:28).

Take heed therefore unto yourselves, and to all the flock, over the which the Holy Spirit hath made you bishops, to feed the Church of God, which He hath purchased with His own blood (Acts 20:28).

We should live soberly, righteously, and godly in this present world; looking for that blessed hope, and the glorious appearing of the great God and our Saviour Jesus Christ (Titus 2:12–13). That the title of "great God" belongs here to Jesus Christ is made clear for us from the sentence construction in the Greek language (a common article for the words "God and Saviour"), as well as from the context of this chapter.

b) He is called the "only begotten":

And the Word was made flesh, and dwelt among us, and we beheld His glory, the glory as of the only begotten of the Father (John 1:14, 18).

For God so loved the world, that He gave His only begotten Son, that whosoever believeth in Him should not perish, but have everlasting life (John 3:16).

(*c*) He is equal in honor to the Father:

My Father worketh hitherto, and I work (John 5:17).

For what things soever He doeth, these also doeth the Son likewise (John 5:19).

For as the Father raiseth up the dead, and quickeneth them, even so the Son quickeneth whom He will (John 5:21).

For as the Father hath life in Himself, so hath He given to the Son to have life in Himself (John 5:26).

That all men should honor the Son, even as they honor the Father (John 5:23).

(*d*) He is One in Essence with the Father:

I and My Father are one (John 10:30)—in Greek, *en esmen*, one in essence.

I am in the Father, and the Father in Me (John 14:11; 10:38).

All Mine are Thine, and Thine are Mine (John 17:10).

(*e*) The word of God likewise speaks of the eternity of the Son of God:

I am Alpha and Omega, the beginning and the ending, saith the Lord, which is, and which was, and which is to come (Rev. 1:8).

And now, O Father, glorify Thou Me with Thine own self with the glory which I had with Thee before the world was (John 17:5).

(*f*) Of His omnipresence:

And no man hath ascended up to heaven, but He that came down from heaven, even the Son of Man Who is in heaven (John 3:13).

For where two or three are gathered together in My name, there am I in the midst of them (Matt. 18:20).

(*g*) Of the Son of God as the Creator of the world:

All things were made by Him; and without Him was not anything made that was made (John 1:3).

For by Him were all things created, that are in heaven, and that are in earth, visible and invisible, whether they be Thrones, or Dominions, or Principalities, or Powers: all things were created by Him, and for Him: and He is before all things, and by Him all things consist (Col. 1:16–17).

The word of God speaks similarly of the other Divine attributes of the Lord Jesus Christ.

As for Sacred Tradition, it contains entirely clear testimonies of the universal faith of Christians in the first centuries in the true Divinity of the Lord Jesus Christ. We see the universality of this faith in:

1) the Symbols of Faith which were used before the Council of Nicaea in every Local Church;

2) the Confessions of Faith which were composed at the councils or in the name of a council by the pastors of the Church prior to the 4th century;

3) the writings of the Apostolic Fathers and the teachers of the Church during the first centuries; and

4) the written testimonies of men who were outside of Christianity and related that the Christians worshipped "Christ as God" (for example, the letter of Pliny the Younger to the Emperor Trajan; the testimony of the writer Celsus, who was an enemy of Christians; and others).

The Oneness of Essence, the Equality of Divinity, and the Equality of Honor of the Holy Spirit with God the Father and God the Son

In the history of the ancient Church, whenever heretics tried to lessen the Divine dignity of the Son of God, this was usually accompanied by a lessening on their part of the dignity of the Holy Spirit.

In the 2nd century the heretic Valentinus falsely taught that the Holy Spirit was not distinct in His nature from the angels. The Arians thought the same thing. But the chief of the heretics who distorted the apostolic teaching concerning the Holy Spirit was Macedonius, who occupied the cathedra of Constantinople as archbishop in the 4th century and found followers for himself among former Arians and Semi-Arians. He called the Holy Spirit a creation of the Son, and a servant of the Father and the Son. Accusers of his heresy were Fathers of the Church like St. Basil the Great, St. Gregory the Theologian, St. Athanasius the Great, St. Gregory of Nyssa, St. Ambrose, St.

Amphilocius, Diodore of Tarsus, and others, who wrote works against the heretics. The false teaching of Macedonius was refuted first in a series of local councils and finally at the Second Ecumenical Council of Constantinople in 381. In preserving Orthodoxy, the Second Ecumenical Council completed the Nicaean Symbol of Faith with these words: "And in the Holy Spirit, the Lord, the Giver of Life, Who proceedeth from the Father, Who with the Father and the Son is equally worshipped and glorified, Who spake by the Prophets," as well as those articles of the Creed which follow this in the Nicaeo-Constantinopolitan Symbol of Faith.

From among the numerous testimonies in Holy Scripture which concern the Holy Spirit, it is especially important to have in mind those passages which (*a*) confirm the teaching of the Church that the Holy Spirit is not an impersonal Divine power, but a Person of the Holy Trinity, and (*b*) which affirm His Oneness in Essence and equal Divine dignity with the First and Second Persons of the Holy Trinity.

a) A testimony of the first kind—that the Holy Spirit is a Person—we have in the words of the Lord in His farewell conversation with His disciples, where He calls the Holy Spirit the "Comforter" *Whom I will send unto you from the Father, even the Spirit of Truth, Who proceedeth from the Father, He shall testify of Me* (John 15:26). *And when He is come, He will reprove the world of sin, and of righteousness, and of judgment: of sin, because they believe not on Me; of righteousness, because I go to My Father, and ye see Me no more; of judgment, because the prince of this world is judged* (John 16:8–11).

The Apostle Paul speaks clearly of the Spirit as a Person when, in examining the various gifts of the Holy Spirit—the gifts of wisdom, knowledge, faith, healings, miracles, the discerning of spirits, diverse tongues, and the interpretation of tongues—he concludes: *But all these worketh that one and the selfsame Spirit, dividing to every man severally as He will* (I Cor. 12:11).

b) The Apostle Peter speaks of the Spirit as God in the words addressed to Ananias, who had concealed the price of his property: *Why hath Satan filled thine heart to lie to the Holy Spirit?... Thou hast not lied unto men, but unto God* (Acts 5:3–4).

Concerning the equality of honor and the Oneness of Essence of the Spirit with the Father and the Son there is the testimony of such passages as:

… *Baptizing them in the name of the Father, and of the Son, and of the Holy Spirit* (Matt. 28:19).

The Grace of the Lord Jesus Christ, and the love of God (the Father), *and the communion of the Holy Spirit, be with you all. Amen* (II Cor. 13:14). Here all three Persons of the Holy Trinity are named as equal. And in the following words the Saviour Himself expressed the Divine dignity of the Holy Spirit: *And whosoever speaketh a word against the Son of Man, it shall be forgiven him: but whosoever speaketh against the Holy Spirit, it shall not be forgiven him, neither in this world, neither in the world to come* (Matt. 12:32).

Transition to the Second Part of Dogmatic Theology

When man's mind is directed towards the understanding of *the life of God in Himself*, his thought is lost in its own helplessness and can only acknowledge the immeasurable and unattainable *grandeur* of God, and the endless, unfathomable *difference* between creature and God—a difference so great that it is impossible to compare them.

But when the same mind of a believing man is turned to *the knowledge of God in the world*, to God's activities in the world, it sees everywhere and in everything the *power, mind, goodness, and mercy of God: The invisible things of Him from the creation of the world are clearly seen, being understood by the things that are made, even His eternal power and Godhead* (Rom. 1:20).

Further, *turning to his own soul*, looking deep within himself, concentrating in prayer, being in the Church of Christ, to the degree of his own spiritual growth a man becomes capable of understanding that which is inexpressible in words: *the closeness of God* to His creation, and especially His closeness to man.

Yet further, before the spiritual eyes of a believing Christian there stands an abyss: the limitless and bright, all-surpassing *love of God* for each one of us, as revealed in the sending down to the world and the death on the Cross of the Son of God for our *salvation*.

The final aim of Dogmatic Theology in its Second Part is the recognition of the wisdom and goodness of God, the closeness of God, the love of God; and from our side, a recognition of what is necessary for man to receive salvation and draw near to God.

This Second Part thus treats of God, the Creator and Providence, our Saviour and Sanctifier, and the Accomplisher of the destiny of the world.

The Saviour.
Icon by St. Andrew Rublev, second decade of the 15th century.
Tretyakov Gallery, Moscow.

Part II

GOD MANIFEST
IN THE WORLD

Chapter 3

God and the Creation

*I*N *the beginning God created the heaven and the earth* (Gen. 1:1). Moses' Divinely inspired account of the creation of the world, set forth on the first page of the Bible, stands in exalted grandeur, quite independent of the ancient mythological tales of the origin of the world, as well as from the various hypotheses, constantly replacing each other, concerning the beginning and development of the world order. It is extremely brief, but in this brevity is embraced the whole history of the creation of the world.[1]

The direct purpose of the God-seer Moses was—by means of an account of the creation—to instill in his people, and through them in the whole of mankind, the fundamental truths of God, of the world, and of man.[2]

A. *Of God.* The chief truth expressed in Genesis is of *God as the One Spiritual Essence independent of the world.* The first words of the

---

[1] St. John Chrysostom affirms that Moses was a prophet of things of the past: "All the other prophets spoke either of what was to occur after a long time or of what was about to happen then; but he, the blessed [Moses], who lived many generations after [the creation of the world], was vouchsafed by the guidance of the right hand of the Most High to utter what had been done by the Lord before his own birth. It is for this reason that he begins to speak thus: *In the beginning God created the heaven and the earth,* as if calling out to us all with a loud voice: It is not by the instruction of men that I say this; He Who called them [heaven and earth] out of non-being into being—it is He Who has roused my tongue to relate of them. And therefore I entreat you, let us pay heed to these words as if we heard not Moses but the very Lord of the universe Who speaks through the tongue of Moses, and let us take leave for good of our own opinions" (*Homilies on Genesis* 2.2; Russian ed., p. 9).—3RD ED.

[2] For a detailed Patristic commentary on the book of Genesis, see Fr. Seraphim Rose, *Genesis, Creation and Early Man* (Platina, Calif.: St. Herman of Alaska Brotherhood, 2000).—3RD ED.

book of Genesis, *In the beginning God created,* tell us that God is the sole extra-temporal, eternal, self-existing Being, the Source of all being, the Spirit above this world, since He existed also before the creation of the world. His Being is outside of space, not bound even to heaven, since heaven was created together with the earth. God is One. God is Personal, Intellectual Essence.

After presenting in order the stages of the creation of the world, the writer of Genesis concludes his account with the words, *And God saw everything that He had made, and, behold, it was very good* (Gen. 1:31).

B. *Of the world.* From the magnificent schema given by Moses of the origin of the world, there follow a series of direct conclusions about the world, namely:

1. *How the world arose:*
   a) the world does not exist eternally, but has appeared in time;
   b) it did not form itself, but is dependent on the will of God;
   c) it appeared not in a single instant, but was created in sequence;[3]
   d) it was created not out of necessity, but by the free desire of God;
   e) it was created by the Word of God, with the participation of the Life-giving Spirit.

2. *What the nature of the world is:*

---

[3] Concerning the Six Days of creation, St. John Chrysostom speaks thus in his *Homilies on Genesis:* "The blessed Moses, instructed by the Divine Spirit, teaches us with great precision [so that we might] know clearly both the sequence of created things and how each thing was created. You see, if God in His care for our salvation had not directed the tongue of the Biblical author in this way, it would have been sufficient to say that God made heaven and earth, the sea and living things, and not add the order of the days, nor what was created first and what later. But, lest he leave any grounds of excuse to those bent on folly, he explains in this way both the order of created things and the number of days, and he teaches us everything with great considerateness so that we may learn the whole truth and not turn our minds to the error of those uttering ideas from their own reasoning. But we are able to know the ineffable power of our Creator" (*Homilies on Genesis* 7.10; FC, pp. 96–97).—3RD ED.

a) the world in its essence is distinct from God. It is not
   (1) part of His Essence,
   (2) nor an emanation of Him,
   (3) nor His body;

b) it was created not out of any eternally existing material but was brought into being out of complete non-being;

c) everything that is on the earth was created from the elements of the earth, was "brought forth" by the water and the earth at the command of God, except for the soul of man, which bears in itself the image and likeness of God.

3. *What the consequences of the creation are:*

   a) God remains in His Nature distinct from the world, and the world from God;

   b) God did not suffer any loss and did not acquire any gain for Himself from the creation of the world;

   c) In the world there is nothing uncreated, apart from God Himself;

   d) Everything was created *very good*—which means that evil did not appear together with the creation of the world.

C. *Of man.* Man is the highest creation of God on earth. Recognizing this, man would belittle himself if he would not think, and be exalted in thought, about His Creator, glorifying Him, giving thanks to Him, striving to be worthy of His mercy.

But these things—glory, thanksgiving, prayer—are possible only on the foundations that are given in Moses' account of the creation of the world. Without the acknowledgment of a *Personal* God, we could not turn to Him: we would be like orphans, knowing neither father nor mother.

If we were to acknowledge that the world is co-eternal with God, in some way independent of God, in some way equal to God, or else born from God by emanation—this would be the same as saying that the world itself is like God in dignity, and man, as the most developed manifestation of nature in the world, might be able to consider himself as a divinity who has no accountability before a Higher Principle. Such a concept would lead to the same negative and grievous moral consequences, to the moral fall of men, as does simple atheism.

But the world had a beginning. The world was created in time. There is a Higher, Eternal, Most-wise, Almighty, Good Power over us, towards Whom the spirit of a believing man joyfully strives and to Whom he clings, crying with love: *How magnified are Thy works, O Lord! In wisdom hast Thou made them all; the earth is filled with Thy creation.... Let the glory of the Lord be unto the ages* (Ps. 103:26, 33).

The Manner of the World's Creation

The world was created out of nothing. It is better to say: it was brought into being from non-being, as the Fathers usually express themselves, since if we say "out of," we are evidently already thinking of material—but "nothing" is not a "material." However, it is conditionally acceptable and entirely allowable to use this expression for the sake of its simplicity and brevity.

That creation is a bringing into being from complete non-being is shown in many passages in the word of God:

God made them out of things that did not exist (II Maccabees 7:28); *things which are seen were not made of things which do appear* (Heb. 11:3);

God ... calleth those things which be not as though they were (Rom. 4:17).

Time itself received its beginning at the creation of the world: until then there was only eternity. The Sacred Scripture also says that *by Him* (His Son) *He made the ages* (Heb. 1:2). The word "ages" here has the significance of "time."

God created the world by His *thought,* by His will, by His word or command. *For He spake, and they came to be; He commanded, and they were created* (Ps. 148:5). "Spake" signifies a command. By the "word" of God, the Fathers of the Church note, we must understand here not any kind of articulate sound or word like ours; no, this creative word signifies only the command or the expression of the almighty will of God, which brought the universe into existence out of nothingness.

St. Damascene writes: "Now, because the good and transcendentally good God was not content to contemplate Himself, but by a superabundance of goodness saw fit that there should be some things to benefit by and participate in His goodness, He brings all things from nothingness into being and creates them, both visible and invisible, and also man, who is made up of both. By thinking He creates, and, with the Word fulfilling and the Spirit perfecting, the thought becomes deed" (*Exact Exposition* 2.2; FC, p. 205).

Thus, although the world was created in time, God had the thought of its creation from eternity (Augustine, *Against Heresies*). However, we avoid the expression "He created out of His thought," so as not to give occasion to think that He created out of His own Essence.[4] If the word of God does not give us the right to speak of the "pre-eternal being" of the whole world, so also, on the same foundation one must recognize as unacceptable the idea or the "pre-eternal existence of mankind," which has been trying to penetrate into our theology through one of the contemporary philosophical-theological currents.

The Holy Church, being guided by the indications of Sacred Scripture, confesses *the participation of all the Persons of the Holy Trinity* in the creation. In the Symbol of Faith we read: "I believe in one God, the Father Almighty, Maker of heaven and earth, and of all things visible and invisible; and in one Lord Jesus Christ, the Son of God … *through Whom all things were made.*… And in the Holy Spirit, the Lord, *the Giver of life.*" St. Irenaeus of Lyons writes: "The Son and the Holy Spirit are, as it were, the hands of the Father"

---

[4] The Holy Fathers teach that the act of creating pertains to God's Energies, while the pre-eternal begetting of the Son and procession of the Holy Spirit pertain to God's Essence. As St. Gregory Palamas points out, "If the act of creating is not distinct from that of begetting and of procession, then created things will in no way differ from Him Who is begotten and Him Who proceeds…. For this reason St. Cyril [of Alexandria], affirming the distinction between God's Essence and Energy, says, 'The act of generation pertains to the Divine Nature, whereas the act of creating pertains to His Divine Energy.' Then he clearly underscores what he has affirmed by saying, 'Nature and Energy are not identical'" (St. Gregory Palamas, *Philokalia*, vol. 4, p. 392, quoting St. Cyril of Alexandria, *Treasuries* 18).—3RD ED.

(*Against Heresies* 5.6). The same idea is found in St. John of Kronstadt (*My Life in Christ*).

The Motive for the Creation

Concerning the motive for the creation in the mind of God, the *Orthodox Confession* and the *Longer Catechism*[5] express it thus: The world was created by God "so that other beings, glorifying Him, might be *participants of His goodness.*" The idea of the mercy and goodness of God, as expressed in the creation of the world, is to be found in many Psalms, for example, Psalms 102 and 103 ("Bless the Lord, O my soul"), which call on one to glorify the Lord and give thanks for one's existence and for all of God's Providence. The same thoughts are expressed by the Fathers of the Church. Thus, Blessed Theodoret writes: "The Lord God has no need of anyone to praise Him; but by His goodness alone He granted existence to angels, archangels, and the whole creation." And further: "God has need of nothing; but He, being an abyss of goodness, deigned to give existence to things which did not exist." And St. John Damascene says (as we have just seen): "The good and transcendentally good God was not content to contemplate Himself, but by a superabundance of goodness saw fit that there should be some things to benefit by and participate in His goodness."[6]

The Perfection of the Creation

The word of God and the Fathers of the Church teach that everything created by God was *good*, and they indicate the good order of the world as created by the Good one. The irrational creation, not having in itself any moral freedom, is morally neither good nor evil. The

---

[5] See p. 45 above.

[6] In Orthodox doctrine, this participation ultimately means deification (*theosis*), which is man's union with God and participation in God's life through the Divine, Uncreated Energies. Man was created to be the link between the visible creation and God through his own deification. This teaching will be brought out further in later sections of the present book.—3RD ED.

rational and free creation becomes evil when it inclines away from God, that is, following its sinful attraction, and not because it was created thus. *And God saw that it was good* (Gen. 1:4, 10, 12, 18, 21, 25). *And, behold, it was very good* (Gen. 1:31).

God created the world perfect. However, Revelation does not say that the present world was perfect to such an extent that it had no need of, or would be incapable of, further perfecting, whether in the days of its creation or in its later and present condition. The earthly world in its highest representatives—mankind—was foreordained to a new and higher form of life. Divine Revelation teaches that the present condition of the world will be replaced at some time by a better and more perfect one, when there will be *new heavens and a new earth* (II Peter 3:13), and the creation itself *will be delivered from the bondage of corruption* (Rom. 8:21).[7]

To the question: How did the life of God proceed before the creation of the world? Blessed Augustine replies: "My best answer is: I do not know." St. Gregory the Theologian reflects: "He contemplated the beloved radiance of His own goodness": "Inasmuch as one cannot ascribe to God inactivity and imperfection, what then occupied the Divine thought before the Almighty, reigning in the absence of time, created the universe and adorned it with forms? It contemplated the beloved radiance of His own goodness, the equal and equally perfect splendor of the Triply shining Divinity known only to the Divinity and to whomever God reveals it. The world-creating Mind likewise beheld, in His great conceptions, the world's forms devised by Him, which, even though they were brought forth subsequently, were present for God even then. With God, everything is before His eyes: that which will be, that which was, and that which is now" (St. Gregory the Theologian, Homily 4, "On the World").

To the question: How was God's omnipotence expressed before there was a world? St. Methodius of Patara notes: "God Omnipotent is outside every dependence upon the things created by Him."

---

[7] See p. 151, note 1; pp. 344–46; and pp. 345–46, note 7 below.—3RD ED.

THE CREATION, NATURE, AND PURPOSE
OF THE ANGELIC WORLD

The first and highest place in the whole ladder of created being is occupied by the pure and fleshless spirits. They are beings not only comparatively higher and more perfect,[8] but they also have a very important influence on the life of men, even though they are invisible to us.

What has been revealed to us about them? How and when did they come into being? What nature was given them? And are they all of an equal stature? What is their purpose, and the form of their existence?

Angels in Sacred Scripture

The name "angel" means "messenger." This word defines chiefly their service to the human race. And mankind knew about their existence from its first days in Paradise. We see a reflection of this fact in other ancient religions also, not only in the Jewish.

After the banishment from Paradise of mankind which had fallen into sin, a *Cherubim* was placed with a flaming sword, turned to guard the entrance to Paradise (Gen. 3:24). Abraham, when sending his servant to Nahor, encouraged him with the conviction that the Lord would send His *angel* with him and order well his way (Gen. 24:7). Ja-

---

[8] St. Gregory Palamas writes: "Every noetic being, since it is likewise created in the image of God, is our fellow servant, even if certain noetic beings [the angels] are more honorable than us in that they possess no body and so more closely resemble the utterly bodiless and Uncreated Nature. Or, rather, those noetic beings who have kept their rank and who maintain the purpose for which they were created deserve our homage and are far superior to us, even though they are our fellow-servants" (*Philokalia*, vol. 4, p. 357). Elsewhere the same Saint writes: "Even though we still bear God's image to a greater degree than the angels, yet as regards the likeness of God we fall far short of them. This is especially true if we compare our present state with that of the good angels.... The perfection of the Divine likeness is accomplished by means of the Divine illumination that issues from God" (ibid., p. 376). On why man bears God's image to a greater degree than the angels, see p. 138, note 19 below.—3RD ED.

cob saw angels, both during sleep (in the vision of the mystical ladder, on the way to Mesopotamia; Gen. 28:12), and while awake (on the way home to Esau, when he saw a "host" of the angels of God; Gen. 32:1–2). In the Psalter, angels are often spoken of: *Praise Him, all ye His angels* (Ps. 148:2); *He shall give His angels charge over thee, to keep thee in all thy ways* (Ps. 90:11). Similarly, we read about them in the book of Job and in the Prophets. The Prophet Isaiah saw *Seraphim* surrounding the Throne of God (chap. 6); the Prophet Ezekiel saw *Cherubim* in the vision of the House of God (chap. 10).

The New Testament Revelation contains much information and many mentions of angels. An angel informed Zachariah of the conception of the Forerunner; an angel informed the Most Holy Virgin Mary of the birth of the Saviour, and appeared in sleep to Joseph; a numerous multitude of angels sang the glory of the Nativity of Christ; an angel announced the good tidings of the birth of the Saviour to the shepherds; an angel prevented the Magi from returning to Herod; angels served Jesus Christ after His temptation in the wilderness; an angel appeared to strengthen Him in the Garden of Gethsemane; angels informed the Myrrhbearing Women about His Resurrection; and the Apostles were told by them of His Second Coming, at the time of His Ascension into heaven. Angels freed the bonds of Peter and other Apostles (Acts 5:19), and those of Peter alone (Acts 12:7–15); an angel appeared to Cornelius and gave him instruction to call the Apostle Peter to instruct him in the word of God (Acts 10:3–7); an angel informed the Apostle Paul that he must appear before Caesar (Acts 27:23–24). A vision of angels is the foundation of the revelations given to St. John the Theologian in the Apocalypse.

The Creation of Angels

In the Symbol of Faith we read, "I believe in one God ... Maker of heaven and earth, and of all things visible and *invisible*." The invisible, angelic world was created by God, and created before the visible world. *When the stars were made, all My angels praised Me with a loud voice,* said the Lord to Job (Job 38:7, Septuagint). The Apostle Paul writes: *By Him were all things created that are in heaven, and that are in earth, visible and invisible, whether they be thrones, or dominions, or principalities, or powers* (Col. 1:16). The Fathers of the Church understand the word "heaven" in the first words of the book of Genesis (*In the beginning God created the heaven and the earth*) as being not the physical heaven, which was formed later, but the invisible heaven, or the dwelling place of the powers on high, and they expressed the idea that God created the angels long before He created the visible world (Sts. Ambrose, Jerome, Gregory the Great [the Dialogist], Anastasius of Sinai), and that at the creation of the visible world the angels already stood before the Face of the Creator and served Him. St. Gregory the Theologian reflects on this: "Since for the goodness of God it was not sufficient to be occupied only with the contemplation of Himself, but it was needful that good should extend further and further, so that the number of those who have received Grace might be as many as possible (because this is characteristic of the highest Goodness)—therefore, God devised first of all the angelic heavenly powers: and the thought became deed, which was fulfilled by the Word, and perfected by the Spirit.... And inasmuch as the first creatures were pleasing to Him, He devised another world, material and visible, the orderly composition of heaven and earth, and that which is between them." St. John Damascene also follows the thought of St. Gregory the Theologian (*Exact Exposition* 2.3).

The Nature of Angels

By their nature, angels are active spirits which have intelligence, will, and knowledge. They serve God, fulfill His providential will, and glorify Him. They are fleshless spirits and, in so far as they belong to the invisible world, they cannot be seen by our bodily eyes. The angels, instructs St. John Damascene, "do not appear exactly as they are to the just and to them that God wills them to appear to. On the contrary, they appear under such a different form as can be seen by those who behold them" (*Exact Exposition* 2.3; FC, p. 206). In the account of the book of Tobit, the angel who accompanied Tobit and his son told them of himself: *All these days I merely appeared to you and did not eat or drink, but you were seeing a vision* (Tobit 12:19).

"Now," as St. John Damascene expresses it, "compared with us, the angel is said to be incorporeal and immaterial, although in comparison with God, Who alone is incomparable, everything proves to be gross and material—for only the Divinity is truly immaterial and incorporeal" (*Exact Exposition* 2.3; FC, p. 205).

The Degree of Angelic Perfection

The angels are most perfect spirits. They surpass man by their spiritual powers; however, they also, as created beings, bear in themselves the seal of limitation. Being fleshless, they are less dependent than men on space and place, and, so-to-speak, pass through vast spaces with extreme rapidity, appearing wherever it is required for them to act. However, one cannot say that they exist entirely independent of space and place, nor that they are everywhere present. The Sacred Scripture depicts angels sometimes descending from heaven to the earth, sometimes ascending from earth to heaven, and thus one must suppose that they cannot be both on earth and in heaven at the same time.[9]

Immortality is an attribute of angels, as is clearly testified by the Scriptures, which teach that they cannot die (Luke 20:36). However, their immortality is not a Divine immortality, that is, something self-existing and unconditional; rather, it depends, just as does the immortality of human souls, entirely upon the will and mercy of God.[10]

As fleshless spirits, the angels are capable of inward *self-development* to the highest degree. Their minds are more elevated than the human mind; according to the explanation of the Apostle Peter, in their might

---

[9] The Holy Fathers teach this quite explicitly. Thus, St. Basil the Great writes: "We believe that each (of the heavenly powers) is in a definite place. For the angel who stood before Cornelius was not at the same time with Philip (Acts 10:3; 8:26); and the angel who spoke with Zachariah near the altar of incense (Luke 1:11) did not at the same time occupy his own place in heaven" ("On the Holy Spirit," chap. 23; Russian ed. of Soikin, St. Petersburg, 1911, vol. 1, p. 622). Likewise, St. John Damascene teaches: "The angels are circumscribed, because when they are in heaven they are not on earth, and when they are sent to earth by God they do not remain in heaven" (*Exact Exposition* 2.3; FC, p. 206).

[10] See p. 134, note 16 below.—3RD ED.

117

and power they surpass all earthly governments and authorities (II Peter 2:10–11). The nature of an angel is higher than the nature of a man, as the Psalmist says when, with the aim of exalting man, he remarks that man is *a little lower than the angels* (Ps. 8:5).

However, the exalted attributes of angels have their limits. Scripture indicates that they do not know the depths of the Essence of God, which is known to the Spirit of God only (*the things of God knoweth no man, but the Spirit of God,* I Cor. 2:11). They do not know the future, which is also known to God alone: *But of that day and hour knoweth no man, no, not the angels which are in heaven* (Mark 13:32). Likewise, they do not understand completely the mystery of the Redemption, although they wish to penetrate it (*which things the angels desire to look into;* I Peter 1:12). And they do not even know all human thoughts (III Kings 8:39). Finally, they cannot of themselves, without the will of God, perform miracles: *Blessed is the Lord, the God of Israel, Who alone doeth wonders* (Ps. 71:19).

The Number and Ranks of Angels

Sacred Scripture presents the angelic world as extraordinarily large. When the Prophet Daniel saw the Ancient of Days in a vision, it was revealed to his gaze that *thousand thousands ministered unto Him, and ten thousand times ten thousand stood before Him* (Daniel 7:10). *A multitude of the heavenly host* praised the coming to earth of the Son of God (Luke 2:13).

"Reckon," says St. Cyril of Jerusalem, "how many are the Roman nation; reckon how many the barbarian tribes now living, and how many have died within the last hundred years; reckon how many nations have been buried during the last thousand years; reckon all from Adam to this day. Great indeed is the multitude, but yet it is little, for the angels are many more. They are the *ninety and nine* sheep, but mankind is the single *one* (Matt. 18:12). For according to the extent of universal space, must we reckon the number of its inhabitants. The whole earth is but as a point in the midst of the one heaven, and yet contains so great a multitude; what a multitude must the heaven which encircles it contain? And must not the heaven of heavens contain unimaginable numbers? And it is written, *thousand thousands ministered unto Him, and ten thousand times ten thousand stood before Him* (Dan. 7:10); not that the multitude is only so great, but because the Prophet could not express more than these" (St. Cyril of Jerusalem, *Catechetical Lectures* 15.24; NPNF, pp. 111–12).

With such a multitude of angels it is natural to suppose that in the world of angels, just as in the material world, there are various degrees of perfection; and therefore various stages, or *hierarchical degrees*, of the heavenly powers. Thus, the word of God calls some of them "angels" and others "archangels" (I Thes. 4:16; Jude, v. 9).

The Orthodox Church—guided by the views of the ancient writers of the Church and the Church Fathers, and in particular by the work *The Heavenly Hierarchy,* which bears the name of St. Dionysius the Areopagite—divides the angelic world into nine choirs or ranks, and these nine into three hierarchies, with three ranks in each. In the first hierarchy are those who are closest to God: the Thrones, Cherubim, and Seraphim. In the second, middle hierarchy, are the Authorities, Dominions, and Powers. In the third, closer to us, are the Angels, Archangels, and Principalities (*The Orthodox Confession*).

We find this enumeration of the nine choirs of angels in the Apostolic Constitutions,[11] in Sts. Ignatius the God-bearer, Gregory the Theologian, and Chrysostom; later, in Sts. Gregory the Dialogist, John Damascene, and others. Here are the words of St. Gregory the Dialogist on this subject: "We accept nine ranks of angels, because from the testimony of the word of God we know about Angels, Archangels, Powers, Authorities, Principalities, Dominions, Thrones, Cherubim, and Sera-

---

[11] The "Apostolic Constitutions" are a 4th- and 5th-century collection of texts on Christian doctrine, worship, and discipline which give much information on the life of the early Church (though not necessarily of the time of the Apostles). While given respect as an ancient Christian text, this collection, owing to some un-Orthodox additions made to it at different times, has not had the authority in the Church which is enjoyed by other early texts. It should be distinguished from the "Apostolic Canons," which were accepted by the Quinisext Council (692) as authoritative for the Church; but this same Council rejected the Apostolic Constitutions as a whole because of the "adulterous matter" which had been added to them (Canon 2; *Seven Ecumenical Councils,* NPNF, p. 361).

phim. Thus, concerning the existence of Angels and Archangels, almost every page of Sacred Scripture testifies; of the Cherubim and Seraphim, as is well known, the prophetic books speak often; the Apostle Paul enumerates four other ranks in his Epistle to the Ephesians, saying that God (the Father) placed His Son *far above all Principality, and Authority, and Power, and Dominion* (Eph. 1:21). And in his Epistle to the Colossians he writes: *By Him were all things created, that are in heaven, and that are in earth, visible and invisible, whether Thrones, or Dominions, or Principalities, or Powers* (Col. 1:16). And so, when we join Thrones to these four of which he speaks to the Ephesians, that is, Principalities, Authorities, Powers and Dominions, we have five separate ranks; and when we join to them the Angels, Archangels, Cherubim and Seraphim, it is clear that there are nine ranks of angels."

Indeed, turning to the books of Sacred Scripture, we find the names of the nine ranks which have been listed above, and more than nine are not mentioned. Thus, the name "Cherubim" we read in the book of Genesis (chap. 3), in Psalms 79 and 98, and in Ezekiel, (chaps. 1 and 10); "Seraphim" we find in Isaiah (chap. 6); "Powers" we find in the Epistle to the Ephesians (chap. 1), and in Romans (chap. 8); "Thrones," "Principalities," "Dominions," and "Authorities" all in Colossians (chap. 1) and Ephesians (chaps. 1 and 3); "Archangels" are in I Thessalonians (chap. 4) and Jude (v. 9); "Angels" are in I Peter (chap. 3), Romans (chap. 8), and other books. On this foundation the number of the ranks of angels is usually limited in the teaching of the Church to nine.

Certain Fathers of the Church express their private pious opinion that the division of the angels into nine ranks includes only those names and ranks which have been revealed in the word of God, but does not include many other names and ranks which have not been revealed to us in this present life but will become known only in the future life. This idea is developed by St. Chrysostom, Blessed Theodoret, and Blessed Theophylactus. "There are," says Chrysostom, "in truth, other powers whose very names we do not know.... Angels, Archangels, Thrones, Dominions, Principalities, and Authorities are not the only inhabitants of the heavens; there are also innumerable other kinds, and unimaginably many classes which no words are capable of depicting. And how is it evident that there are powers beyond those mentioned above, and powers whose very names we do not know? The Apostle Paul, having spoken of the one, mentions the other also when he testifies of Christ: *and set Him at His own right hand in the heavenly places, far above every Principality, and Power, and Might, and Dominion, and every name that is named, not only in this world, but also in that which is to come* (Eph. 1:20–21). Do you see that there are some names which will be known then, but that are now unknown? Therefore he also said, *every name that is named, not only in this world, but also in that which is to come.*" This opinion is taken by the Church as a private one.

In general, the ancient shepherds considered the doctrine of the celestial hierarchy a mystical one. "How many ranks of heavenly beings there are," reflects St. Dionysius in the *Heavenly Hierarchy,* "of what sort they are, and in what way the mysteries of their sacred order are performed is known precisely only to God, Who is the Cause of their hierarchy. Likewise, they themselves know their own powers, light, and order beyond this world. But we can speak of this only to the degree that God has revealed this to us through the heavenly powers themselves, as ones who know themselves" (*Heavenly Hierarchy,* chap. 6). Similarly, Blessed Augustine reflects: "That there are Thrones, Dominions, Principalities, and Authorities in the heavenly mansions, I believe unwaveringly, and that they are distinct one from the other, I hold without doubt; but of what sort they are, and in precisely what way they are distinguished among themselves, I do not know."

In Sacred Scripture, some of the higher angels are given their own names. There are two such names in the canonical books: "Michael" (which means "Who is like God?"; Dan. 10:13; 12:1; Jude, v. 9; Apoc. 12:7–8) and "Gabriel" ("Man of God"; Dan. 8:16, 9:21; Luke 1:19, 26). Three angels are mentioned by name in the non-canonical books: "Raphael" ("The Help of God"; Tobit 3:17, 12:12–15); "Uriel" ("Fire of God"; III Esdras 4:1, 5:20); "Salathiel," ("Prayer to God"; III Esdras 5:16). Apart from this, pious tradition ascribes names to two other angels: "Jegudiel" ("Praise of God") and "Barachiel" ("Blessing of God");

these names are not to be found in the Scriptures. Moreover, in the third book of Esdras there is mention of yet another, "Jeremiel" ("the Height of God"; III Esdras 4:36); but judging from the context of this passage, this name is the same as "Uriel."

Thus, names have been given to *seven* of the higher angels, corresponding to the words of the Apostle John the Theologian in the Apocalypse: *Grace be unto you, and peace from Him Who is, and Who was, and Who is to come; and from the seven spirits who are before His throne* (Apoc. 1:4).

The Ministry of the Angels

What, finally, is the purpose of the beings of the spiritual world? It is evident that they were ordained by God to be the most perfect reflections of His grandeur and glory, with inseparable participation in His blessedness. If it has been said concerning the visible heavens that *the heavens declare the glory of God*, then all the more is this the aim of the spiritual heavens. This is why St. Gregory the Theologian calls them "reflections of the perfect Light," or secondary lights.

The angels in the ranks which are close to the human race are presented in Sacred Scripture as heralds of God's will, guides of men, and servants of their salvation. The Apostle Paul writes, *Are they not all ministering spirits, sent forth to minister for them who shall be heirs of salvation?* (Heb. 1:14).

Not only do angels hymn the glory of God, but they also serve Him in the works of His Providence for the material and sensible world. Of this service the Holy Fathers frequently speak: "Some of them stand before the great God; others, by their cooperation, uphold the whole world" (St. Gregory the Theologian, "Mystical Hymns," Homily 6). The angels "are appointed for the governance of the elements and the heavens, the world and everything that is in it" (Athenagoras). "Different individuals of them embrace different parts of the world, or are appointed over different districts of the universe, as He knoweth Who ordered and distributed it all; combining all things in one, solely with a view to the consent of the Creator of all things" (St. Gregory the Theologian, Homily 28; NPNF, p. 300).

In some Church writers there is to be found the opinion that special angels are placed over separate aspects of the kingdom of nature—the inorganic, the organic, and the animal (Origen, Blessed Augustine). The latter opinion has its source in the Apocalypse, where mention is made of angels who, in accordance with God's will, are in charge of certain earthly elements. The Seer of mysteries (St. John) writes, in the 16th chapter, verse 5, of the Apocalypse: *And I heard the angel of the waters say;* in Apocalypse 7:1 he says: *I saw four angels standing on the four corners of the earth, holding the four winds of the earth, that the wind should not blow on the earth, nor on the sea, nor on any tree;* and in Apocalypse 14:18: *And another angel came out from the altar, who had power over fire; and he cried out.* In the vision of the Prophet Daniel there are angels to whom God has entrusted the care of the fate of the peoples and kingdoms which exist upon the earth (Daniel chaps. 10, 11, and 12).

The Orthodox Church believes that every man has his own guardian angel, if he has not put him away from himself by an impious life. The Lord Jesus Christ has said: *Take heed that ye despise not one of these little ones, for I say unto you, that their angels do always behold the face of My Father which is in heaven* (Matt. 18:10).

MAN, THE CROWN OF CREATION

In the ladder of the earthly creation, man is placed on the highest rung, and in relationship to all earthly beings he occupies the reigning position. Being earthly, according to his gifts he approaches the heavenly beings, for he is *a little lower than the angels* (Ps. 8:5). And the Prophet Moses depicts man's origin in this way: After all the creatures of the earth had been created, *God said, Let Us make man in Our image, after Our likeness; and let him have dominion over the fish of the sea and over the fowl of the air ... and over all the earth.... So God created man in His own image, in the image of God created He him* (Gen. 1:26–27).

1. In itself, the *counsel* of God, which is not indicated at the creation of the other creatures of the earth, clearly speaks of the fact that

man was to be a special creation, distinct from the others, the highest, most perfect on earth, having also a higher purpose in the world.

2. The concept of man's high purpose and his special significance is emphasized yet more in the fact that the counsel of God ordained that man be created *in the image and likeness of God,* and that in fact he was created in God's image. Every image necessarily presupposes a similarity with its archetype; consequently, the presence of God's image in man testifies to a reflection of the very attributes of God in man's spiritual nature.

3. Finally, certain details of man's creation which are given in the second chapter of Genesis emphasize once more a special preeminence of human nature. To be precise, it is said there: *And God formed man of the dust of the earth, and breathed into his nostrils the breath of life; and man became a living soul* (Gen. 2:7). Two actions, or two aspects of action, are distinguished here, and they may be understood as simultaneous: the formation of the body, and the giving of life to it. St. John Damascene notes: "The body and the soul were formed at the same time—not one before and the other afterwards, as the ravings of Origen would have it" (*Exact Exposition* 2.12; FC, p. 235). According to the description of the book of Genesis, God created the body of man from already existing earthly elements; and He created it in a very special fashion: not by His command or word alone, as was done in the creation of the other creatures, but by His own direct action. This shows that man, even in his bodily organization, is a being surpassing all other creatures from the very beginning of his existence. Further, it is said that God breathed into his face the breath of life and the man became a living soul. As one who has received the breath of life, in this figurative expression, from the mouth of God Himself, man is thus a living, organic union of the earthly and the heavenly, the material and the spiritual.

4. From this follows the exalted view of the significance of the human *body* as is set forth generally in the Sacred Scripture. The body must serve as the companion, organ, and even fellow laborer of the soul. It depends on the soul itself whether to lower itself to such an extent that it becomes the slave of the body, or, being guided by an en-

lightened spirit, to make the body its obedient executor and fellow laborer. Depending upon the soul, the body can be a vessel of sinful impurity and foulness, or it can become a temple of God, participating with the soul in the glorification of God. This is taught in Sacred Scripture (Rom. 13:14; Gal. 3:3; I Cor. 9:27; Gal. 5:24; Jude, vv. 7–9; I Cor. 3:16–17; I Cor. 6:20). Even with the death of the body, the bond of the soul with the body is not cut off forever. The time will come when the bodies of men will arise in a renewed form and will again be united forever with their souls, in order to receive a part in eternal blessedness or torment, corresponding to the good or evil deeds performed by men with the participation of the body in the course of earthly life (II Cor. 5:10).

An even more exalted view is instilled in us by the word of God regarding the nature of *the soul*. At the creation of the soul, God took nothing of it from the earth, but imparted it to man solely by His creative inbreathing. This clearly shows that, in the conception of the word of God, the human soul is an essence completely separate from the body and from everything material and composed of elements, having a nature not earthly, but above the world, heavenly. The high preeminence of man's soul compared to everything earthly was expressed by the Lord Jesus Christ in the words: *What is a man profited, if he shall gain the whole world, and lose his own soul? Or what shall a man give in exchange for his soul?* (Matt. 16:26). The Lord instructed His disciples: *Fear not them which kill the body, but are not able to kill the soul* (Matt. 10:28).

Concerning the exalted dignity of the soul, St. Gregory the Theologian expresses himself thus: "The soul is the breath of God, and while being heavenly, it endures being mixed with what is of the dust. It is a light enclosed in a cave, but still it is divine and inextinguishable…. The Word spoke, and having taken a part of the newly created earth, with His immortal hands formed my image and imparted to it His life; because He sent into it the spirit, which is a ray of the invisible Divinity" (Homily 7, "On the Soul").

Nevertheless, one cannot make such exalted figurative expressions of the Holy Fathers into a foundation for teaching that the soul is "divine" in the full sense of the word, and that, consequently, it had an eternal existence of its own before its incarnation in earthly man, in Adam. (This view is found in those contemporary theological-philosophical currents which follow V. S. Soloviev.) The very statement that the soul is of heavenly origin does not mean that the soul is Divine in essence.[12] "He breathed the breath of life" (Gen. 2:7) is an anthropomorphic expression, and there is no basis for understanding it as meaning that he gave something of His Divine Essence. After all, man's breathing is not an "outbreathing" of the elements of human nature itself, or even of its physical essence. Likewise, from the Biblical expression one cannot draw the conclusion that the soul proceeded from the Essence of God or is an element of the Divinity. Chrysostom writes: "Certain senseless ones, being drawn away by their own conceptions, without thinking of anything in a God-befitting manner, and without paying any attention to the adaptation of the expressions (of Scripture), dare to say that the soul has proceeded from the Essence of God. Oh, frenzy! Oh, folly! How many paths of perdition has the devil opened up for those who wish to serve him! In order to understand this, behold the opposite ways in which these people go: some, seizing on the phrase, 'He breathed,' say that souls proceed from the Essence of God; others, on the contrary, affirm that souls are converted into the essence of the lowest irrational creatures. What can be worse than such folly?" (*Homilies on Genesis* 13.2).

---

[12] Vladimir Lossky further elucidates the meaning of the above passage of St. Gregory the Theologian: "The 'breath of God' points to a mode of creation, by virtue of which the human spirit is intimately connected with Grace, and is produced by it in the same way as a movement of air is produced by the breath, contains the breath and is inseparable from it. It is a participation in the Divine Energy proper to the soul, which is meant by [St. Gregory's] phrase 'part of the Deity'" (*The Mystical Theology of the Eastern Church,* p. 118).

In Orthodox theology, the word "Grace" is often employed to denote the Uncreated Energy, Power, or Operation of God. As noted above (p. 55, note 1), the Holy Fathers make a distinction between God's Essence and His Energies. God is wholly present in His Energies. Therefore, when man was created in Grace, he had God Himself dwelling within him and participated in God's life through the Divine Energies.—3RD ED.

That St. Gregory the Theologian spoke of the divinity of the soul not in the strict sense of the word is evident from another homily of his: "The Nature of God and the nature of man are not identical; or, to speak more generally, the Nature of the Divine and the nature of the earthly are not identical. In the Divine Nature, both existence itself and everything in It which has existence are unchangeable and immortal; for, in that which is constant, everything is constant. But what is true of our nature? It flows, is corrupted, and undergoes change after change" (Homily 19, "On Julian").

We have already spoken in the section on the attributes of God (on God as Spirit) of the question as to how one should understand anthropomorphic expressions about God. Here let us only cite the argument of Blessed Theodoret: "When we hear in the account of Moses that God took *dust* from the earth and formed man, and we seek out the meaning of this utterance, we discover in it the special good disposition of God towards the human race. For the great Prophet notes, in his description of the creation, that God created all the other creatures by His word, while man He created with His own hands. But just as we understand by 'word' not a commandment, but the will alone, so also, in the formation of the body, (we should understand) not the action of hands, but the greatest attentiveness to this work. For in the same way that now, by His will, the fruit is generated in a mother's womb, and nature follows the laws which He gave to it from the very beginning—so also then, by His will the human body was formed from the earth, and dust became flesh." In another passage Blessed Theodoret expresses himself in a general way: "We do not say that the Divinity has hands ... but we affirm that every one of these expressions indicates a greater care on God's part for man than for the other creatures" (quoted in the *Orthodox Dogmatic Theology* of Metr. Macarius, vol. 1, p. 430–31).

The Soul as an Independent Substance
Distinct from the Body

The ancient Fathers and teachers of the Church, strictly following the Sacred Scripture in the teaching on the independence of the soul and its value in itself, explained and revealed the distinctness of the soul from the body in order to refute the materialistic opinion that the soul is only an expression of the harmony of the members of the body, or is a result of the body's physical activity, and that it does not have its own particular spiritual substance or nature. Appealing to simple observation, the Church Fathers show:

a) That it is characteristic of the soul to *govern* the strivings of the body, and characteristic of the body to accept this governance (Athenagoras and others).

b) That the body is, as it were, a tool or instrument of an artist, while the soul is the *artist* (Sts. Irenaeus, Gregory of Nyssa, Cyril of Jerusalem, and others).

c) That the soul is not unconditionally subject to the impulses of the body; it is even capable *of entering into warfare* with the strivings of the body as with something foreign and hostile to it, and is able to gain a victory over them, thus showing that it is not the same thing as the body but is an invisible essence, is of a different nature, surpassing every bodily nature (Origen).

d) That it is *intangible and ungraspable,* and is neither blood, nor air, nor fire, but a self-moving principle (Lactantius).

e) That the soul is a power which brings all the members of the organism into full *harmony* and full *unity* (Sts. Athanasius the Great, Basil the Great).

f) That the soul possesses *reason, self-awareness,* and *free will* (Origen and others).

g) That man, while he is in the body on earth, mentally thinks of that which is *heavenly* and beholds it; being mortal in his body, he reasons about immortality and often, out of love for virtue, he draws upon himself suffering and death; having a body which is temporal, with his mind he contemplates the eternal and *strives towards it,* disdaining that which is under his feet: the body itself would never have imagined such things (St. Athanasius the Great).

h) Speaking of the very nature of the soul, the Fathers and teachers of the Church point to the *simplicity* and *immateriality* of the soul, as opposed to the complexity and material crudeness of the body;

they indicate its invisibility and complete absence of form, and in general the fact that it is not subject to any of the measurements (space, weight, etc.) to which the body is subject (Origen and others).

With regard to the fact that the conditions of the body are reflected in the activities of the soul, and that these conditions can weaken and even corrupt the soul—for example, during illness, old age, or drunkenness—the Fathers of the Church often compare the body to an instrument used in steering. The different degrees of the soul's manifestation in the body testify only to the instability of the instrument—the body. Those conditions of the body which are unfavorable for the manifestation of the soul may be compared to a sudden storm at sea which hinders the pilot from manifesting his art but does not prove that he is absent. As another example, one might take an untuned harp, from which even the most skilled musicians cannot bring forth harmonious sounds (Lactantius). So also, poor horses give no opportunity for a horseman to demonstrate his skill (Blessed Theodoret).

Certain ancient Fathers (Sts. Ambrose, Gregory the Dialogist, John Damascene), while acknowledging the spirituality of the soul as distinct from the body, at the same time also ascribe a certain comparative bodiliness or materiality to the soul. By this supposed attribute of the soul they had in mind to distinguish the spirituality of the human soul, as also the spirituality of angels, from the most pure spirituality of God, in comparison with which everything must seem material and crude.[13]

The Origin of the Souls of Individual Men

How the soul of each individual man originates is not fully revealed in the word of God; it is "a mystery known to God alone" (St. Cyril of Alexandria), and the Church does not give us a strictly defined teaching on this subject. She decisively rejected only Origen's view, which had been inherited from the philosophy of Plato, concerning the preexistence of souls, according to which souls come to earth from

---

[13] On the "materiality" of angels in comparison with God, see p. 117 above.—3RD ED.

a higher world. This teaching of Origen and the Origenists was condemned by the Fifth Ecumenical Council.

However, this conciliar decree did not establish whether the soul is created from the souls of a man's parents and only in this general sense constitutes a new creation of God, or whether each soul is created immediately and separately by God, being joined at a definite moment to the body which is being or has been formed. In the view of certain Fathers of the Church (Clement of Alexandria, John Chrysostom, Ephraim the Syrian, Theodoret), each soul is created separately by God, and some of them refer its union with the body to the fortieth day after the body's formation. (Roman Catholic theology is decisively inclined toward the view that each soul is separately created; this view has been set forth dogmatically in several papal bulls, and Pope Alexander VII linked with this view the dogma of the Immaculate Conception of the Most Holy Virgin Mary.)

In the view of other teachers and Fathers of the Church (Tertullian, Gregory the Theologian, Gregory of Nyssa, Macarius the Great, Anastasius of Sinai),[14] both soul and body receive their beginning simultaneously and mature together; the soul proceeds from the souls of the parents just as the body proceeds from the bodies of the parents. In this way "creation" is understood here in a broad sense as the participation of the creative power of God which is present and essential everywhere, for every kind of life. The foundation of this view is the fact that in the person of our forefather Adam, God created the human race—*He hath made of one blood all nations of men* (Acts 17:26). From this it follows that in Adam the soul and body of every man was given in potentiality. But God's decree is brought into reality in such a way that God holds all things in His hand: *He giveth to all life, and breath, and all things* (Acts 17:25). God, having created, *continues to create.*

St. Gregory the Theologian says: "Just as the body, which was originally formed in us of dust, became subsequently the current of human bodies as has not been cut off from the first-formed root, in one man

---

[14] Also, St. Maximus the Confessor. See *The Cosmic Mystery of Jesus Christ,* pp. 72–74.—3RD ED.

including others—so also the soul, being inbreathed by God, from that time comes together into the formed composition of man, being born anew, and from the original seed (St. Gregory evidently means here a spiritual seed) being imparted to many and always preserving a constant form in mortal members.... Just as the breath in a musical pipe produces sounds depending upon the width of the pipe, so also the soul, appearing powerless in an infirm body, becomes manifest as the body is strengthened and reveals then all its intelligence" (Homily 7, "On the Soul"). St. Gregory of Nyssa has the same view.

In his diary, St. John of Kronstadt has this observation: "What are human souls? They are all one and the same soul, one and the same breathing of God, which God breathed into Adam, which from Adam until now is disseminated to the whole human race. Therefore all men are the same as one man, or one tree of humanity. From this there follows the most natural commandment, founded upon the unity of our nature: *Thou shalt love the Lord thy God* (thy Prototype, thy Father) *with all thy heart, and with all thy soul, and with all thy strength, and with all thy mind; and thy neighbor* (for who is closer to me than a man who is like me and of the same blood with me?) *as thyself* (Luke 10:27). There is a natural need to fulfill these commandments" (*My Life in Christ*).

The Immortality of the Soul

Faith in the immortality of the soul is inseparable from religion in general and, all the more, comprises one of the fundamental objects of the Christian faith.

Nor is this idea foreign to the *Old Testament*. It is expressed in the words of Ecclesiastes: *Then shall the dust return to the earth as it was, and the spirit shall return to God Who gave it* (Eccl. 12:7). The whole account in the third chapter of Genesis—from the words of God's warning: *Of the tree of the knowledge of good and evil thou shalt not eat of it: for in the day that thou eatest thereof thou shalt surely die* (Gen. 2:17)—is the answer to the question of the appearance of death in the world, and thus it is in itself an expression of the idea of immortality. The idea that man was foreordained to immortality, that immortality is possible, is contained in the words of Eve: *Of the fruit of the tree which is in the midst of Paradise, God hath said, ye shall not eat of it, neither shall ye touch it, lest ye die* (Gen. 3:3). The same thought is expressed by the Psalmist in the words of the Lord: *I said: Ye are gods, and all of you the sons of the Most High. But like men ye die, and like one of the rulers do ye fall* (Ps. 81:6–7).

One must emphasize the fact that the idea of immortality is present without any doubt in the Old Testament, because there exists an opinion that denies that the Jews had faith in the immortality of the soul. In the accounts of Moses there are indications of faith in the immortality of the soul. Concerning Enoch, Moses remarks that *he was not; for God took him*—that is, he went to God without undergoing death (Gen. 5:24). From the Biblical expressions concerning the deaths of Abraham (Gen. 25:8), Aaron and Moses (Deut. 32:50), *and he was gathered to his people,* it is illogical to understand that this means they were placed in the same grave or place, or even in the same land with their people, since each of these Old Testament righteous ones died not in the land of his ancestors but in the new territory of their resettlement (Abraham) or their wandering (Aaron and Moses). Patriarch Jacob, having received news that his son had been torn to pieces by beasts, says: *I will go down into hades unto my son, mourning* (Gen. 37:35, Septuagint). "Hades" here clearly means not the tomb, but the place where the soul dwells. This condition of the soul after death was expressed in the Old Testament as a descent into the underworld, that is, as a joyless condition in a region where even the praise of the Lord is not heard; this is expressed in a number of passages in the book of Job and in the Psalms.

But already in the Old Testament, and especially as the coming of the Saviour approaches, there is heard a hope that the souls of righteous men will escape this joyless condition. For example, in the Wisdom of Solomon we find: *The souls of the righteous are in the hand of God, and no torment will ever touch them.... The righteous live for ever, and their reward is with the Lord* (3:1; 5:15). The hope of the future deliverance from hades of the souls of the righteous is more clearly and distinctly expressed in the words of the Psalmist: *My flesh shall dwell in hope, for thou wilt not abandon my soul in hades, nor wilt thou suffer Thy Holy One to see corruption* (Ps. 15:9–10; see also Ps. 48:16).

The Lord Jesus Christ often pointed to the immortality of the soul as the foundation of pious life, and He accused the Sadducees, who denied immortality. In His farewell conversation with His disciples the Lord told them that He was going to prepare a place for them so that they might be where He Himself would be (John 14:2–3). And to the thief He said: *Verily I say unto thee, today shalt thou be with Me in Paradise* (Luke 23:43).

In the New Testament, generally speaking, the truth of the immortality of the soul is the object of a more *complete* revelation, making up one of the fundamental parts of Christian faith itself. This truth inspires a Christian, filling his soul with the joyful hope of eternal life in the Kingdom of the Son of God. St. Paul writes: *For to me ... to die is gain ... having a desire to depart, and to be with Christ* (Phil. 1:21, 23). *For we know that, if our earthly house of this tabernacle were dissolved, we have a building of God, a house not made with hands, eternal in the heavens. For in this we groan, earnestly desiring to be clothed upon with our house which is from heaven* (II Cor. 5:1–2).

It goes without saying that the Holy Fathers and teachers of the Church have unanimously preached the immortality of the soul,[15]

---

[15] For example, St. Athanasius the Great writes: "That the soul is immortal is a further point of the Church's teaching which you must know.... For if when coupled with the body it lived a life outside the body, much more shall its life continue after the death of the body, and live without ceasing by reason of God Who made it thus by His own Word, our Lord Jesus Christ" (*Against the Heathen* 33; NPNF, pp. 21–22).

St. Gregory Palamas writes: "The soul of each man is also the life of the body that it animates, and possesses a quickening activity in relation to something else, namely, to the body that it quickens. Yet the soul has life not only as an activity but also as its essence, since it is self-existent; for it possesses a spiritual and a noetic life that is evidently different from the body's and from what is actuated by the body. Hence when the body dissolves the human soul does not perish with it; and not only does it not perish but it continues to exist immortally, since it is not manifest only in relation to something else, but possesses its own life as its essence" (*Philokalia,* vol. 4, p. 359).—3RD ED.

with this distinction only, that some acknowledge the soul as being immortal by nature, while others—the majority—say that it is immortal by the Grace of God. "God wishes that the soul might live" (St. Justin Martyr); "the soul is immortal by the Grace of God Who makes it immortal" (St. Cyril of Jerusalem and others). The Holy Fathers by this emphasize the difference between the immortality of man and the immortality of God, Who is immortal by the very *Essence* of His nature and therefore *Who only hath immortality,* according to the Scripture (I Tim. 6:16).[16]

Observation shows that faith in the immortality of the soul has always been inwardly inseparable from faith in God, to such an extent that the degree of the former is determined by the degree of the latter. The more lively is one's faith in God, the more firm and undoubting is one's faith in the immortality of the soul. And, on the contrary, the weaker and more lifeless is one's belief in God, the greater the wavering and doubt one brings to the truth of the immortality of the soul. One who completely loses or stifles faith in God within oneself usually ceases to believe in the immortality of the soul or the future life at all. And this is surely understandable. A man receives the power of faith from the very Source of life, and if he cuts off his tie with this Source, he loses this stream of living power, and then no rational proofs or persuasions will be able to pour the power of faith into him.

One might also make the opposite conclusion. In those confessions and worldviews—even though they might be Christian—where the power of faith in the active existence of the soul beyond the grave has grown dim, where there is no prayerful remembrance of the dead, Christian faith itself is in a condition of decline. One who believes in God and acknowledges God's love cannot allow the thought that one's Heavenly Father might wish to completely cut off one's life and deprive one of the bond with Himself, just as a child who loves his

---

[16] St. John Damascene points out that "Angels are immortal, not by nature, but by Grace; for, naturally, everything that has a beginning has an end" (*Exact Exposition* 2.3; FC, p. 206). What he says of angels can likewise be applied to human souls, since they too have a definite beginning.—3RD ED.

mother and is loved by her in turn does not believe that she would not wish him to have life.

One may rightly say that in the Orthodox Eastern Church the acknowledgment of the immortality of the soul occupies a fitting central place in the system of teaching and in the life of the Church. The spirit of the Church typicon, the content of the Divine services and separate prayers, all support and animate in the faithful this awareness, this belief in a life beyond the grave for the souls of our close ones who have died, as well as a belief in our own personal immortality. This belief sheds a bright ray on the whole life's work of an Orthodox Christian.

Soul and Spirit

The spiritual principle in man which is opposed to the body is designated in Sacred Scripture by two terms which are almost equal in significance: "spirit" and "soul." The use of the word "spirit" in place of "soul," or both terms used in exactly the same meaning, is encountered especially in the Apostle Paul. This is made evident, for example, by placing the following texts side by side: *Glorify God in your body and in your spirit, which are God's* (I Cor. 6:20); *Let us cleanse ourselves from all filthiness of the flesh and spirit* (II Cor. 7:1); and, *We are not of them who draw back unto perdition, but of them that believe to the saving of the soul* (Heb. 10:39).

In addition, there are two passages in the writings of this Apostle where soul and spirit are mentioned side by side, and this gives occasion to ask the question: Is the Apostle not indicating that, besides the soul, there is also a "spirit" that is an essential part of human nature? Likewise, in the writings of certain Holy Fathers, particularly in the ascetic writings, a distinction is made between soul and spirit. The first passage in the Apostle Paul is in the Epistle to the Hebrews: *The word of God is quick, and powerful and sharper than any two-edged sword, piercing even to the dividing asunder of soul and spirit, and of the joints and marrow, and is a discerner of the thoughts and intents of the heart* (Heb. 4:12). Another passage from the same Apostle is in the Epistle to the Thessalonians: *Your whole spirit and soul and body be preserved blameless unto the coming of our Lord Jesus Christ* (I Thes. 5:23). It is not

135

difficult, however, to see that in the first passage the spirit is to be understood not as a substance that is separate and independent from the soul, but only as the inward and most hidden side of the soul. Here the relation of soul and spirit is made parallel to the relationship between the members of the body and the brain; and just as the brain is the inward part of the same bodily nature—or is a content as compared to its container—so also the spirit is evidently considered by the Apostle as the hidden part of the soul of a man.[17]

In the second passage, by "spirit" is evidently meant that special higher harmony of the hidden part of the soul which is formed through the Grace of the Holy Spirit in a Christian—the "spirit" of which the Apostle says elsewhere: *quench not the spirit* (I Thes. 5:19), and *fervent in spirit* (Rom. 12:11). Thus, the Apostle is not thinking here of all men in general, but only of Christians or believers. In this sense the Apostle contrasts the "spiritual" man with the "natural" or fleshly man (I Cor. 2:14–15). The spiritual man possesses a soul, but being reborn, he cultivates in himself the seeds of Grace; he grows and brings forth fruits of the spirit. However, by carelessness towards his spiritual life he may descend to the level of the fleshly or natural man (*Are ye so foolish? Having begun in the spirit, are ye now made perfect by the flesh?* [Gal. 3:3]). Therefore, there are no grounds for supposing that the thinking of the Apostle Paul is not in agreement with the teaching that the nature of man consists of two parts.

This same idea of the spirit as the higher, Grace-given form of the life of the human soul is evidently what was meant by those Christian teachers and Fathers of the Church in the first centuries who distinguished in man a spirit as well as a soul. This distinction is found in St. Justin Martyr, Tatian, St. Irenaeus, Tertullian, Clement of Alexandria, St. Gregory of Nyssa, St. Ephraim the Syrian, and likewise in later writers and ascetics. However, a significant majority of the Fathers and

---

[17] In this sense, "spirit" corresponds to the Greek word *nous*, which is the highest part of the human soul, and the faculty by which man knows God and enters into communion with Him. In the words of St. John Damascene, "The soul does not have the *nous* as something distinct from itself, but as its purest part, for as the eye is to the body, so is the *nous* to the soul" (*Exact Exposition* 2.12; FC, p. 236).—3RD ED.

teachers of the Church directly acknowledge that man's nature has two parts: body and soul (Sts. Cyril of Jerusalem, Basil the Great, Gregory the Theologian, John Chrysostom, John Damascene, Blessed Augustine). Blessed Theodoret writes: "According to the teaching of Apollinarius (the heretic) there are three composite parts in a man: the body, the animal soul, and the rational soul, which he calls the mind. But the Divine Scripture acknowledges only one soul, not two, and this is clearly indicated by the history of the creation of the first man. God, having formed the body from the dust and breathed a soul into it, showed in this wise that there are two natures in man, and not three."[18]

The Image of God in Man

The sacred writer of the account of man's creation relates: *And God said: Let us make man in Our image, after Our likeness.... So God created man in His own image, in the image of God created He him; male and female created He them* (Gen. 1:26–27).

In what does the image of God in us consist? The Church's teaching tells us only that in general man was created "in the image," but precisely what part of our nature manifests this image is not indicated. The Fathers and teachers of the Church have answered this question in various ways: some see it (the image) in reason, others in free will, still others in immortality. If one brings together their ideas, one obtains a complete conception of what the image of God in man is, according to the teaching of the Holy Fathers.

First of all, the image of God may be seen only in the soul, not in the body. According to His Nature, God is most pure Spirit, not clothed in any kind of body and not a partaker of any kind of

---

[18] The Patristic consensus on this subject is that man is composed of body and soul, and the spirit (*nous*) is the highest and purest part of the soul. The spirit (*nous*) of man is created, and must never be confused with the Holy Spirit, Who is Uncreated. At Baptism, however, the Uncreated Grace of God, which man lost at the fall, is once again united with the *nous*. Thus, St. Diadochus of Photike writes: "The Grace of God dwells in the very depths of the soul—that is to say, in the *nous*" (*Philokalia*, vol. 1, p. 280).—3RD ED.

materiality. Therefore the image of God can refer only to the immaterial soul—many Fathers of the Church have considered it necessary to give this warning.[19]

Man bears the image of God in the higher qualities of the soul, especially in the soul's immortality, in its freedom of will, in its reason, and in its capability for pure love without thought of gain.

a) The eternal God gave immortality of soul to man, even though the soul is immortal not by nature but only by the goodness of God.

b) God is completely free in His actions, and He gave to man free will and the ability to act freely within certain boundaries.

c) God is most wise, and He has given man a reason which is capable of being not limited only to earthly, animal needs and to the visible side of things, but is capable of penetrating to their depths, of recognizing and explaining their inward meaning. Man's reason is able to rise to the level of that which is invisible and to strive in thought towards the very Source of all that exists—God. Man's reason makes his will conscious and authentically free, because it can choose that which

---

[19] Some of the Holy Fathers—St. Justin Martyr (*On the Resurrection,* chap. 7), St. Irenaeus of Lyons (*Against Heresies* 5.6), and St. Epiphanius of Cyprus (*The Medicine Chest* 70.3)—state that the "image of God" refers to the whole man. However, the vast majority of Holy Fathers teach that the "image of God" refers to man's soul, or, more particularly, to the highest faculty of the soul: the *nous.* Many of them categorically deny that the "image" refers to the body. Thus, for example, Nicetas Stithatos writes: "Only in ignorance would one claim that man is created in the image of God with respect to the organic structure of his body. He is in the image by virtue of the spiritual nature of his *nous"* (*Philokalia,* vol. 4, pp. 139–40). St. Gregory Palamas likewise writes: "To know that we have been created in God's image prevents us from deifying even the noetic world. 'Image' here refers not to the body but to the nature of the *nous"* (*Philokalia,* vol. 4, p. 357). St. John Damascene and St. Gregory Palamas make a further distinction in this teaching, which may point to a deeper unity between those who say the "image" refers to the whole man and those who say it refers to the soul. According to Sts. John and Gregory, while the "image of God" refers to the soul, human beings are more in the image of God than are angels, because the human soul governs and gives life to (animates) the body (St. John Damascene, *On the Two Wills in Christ* 16.5–10, 30.9–11; St. Gregory Palamas, *Philokalia,* vol. 4, pp. 362–64).—3RD ED.

corresponds to man's highest dignity rather than that to which his lower nature inclines him.

d) God created man in His goodness, and He has never left him nor ever will leave him without His love. Man, having received his soul from the breathing of God, strives towards his first Principle, God, as towards something akin to himself, seeking and thirsting for union with Him. This is specifically shown in the straight and upright posture of his body, and his gaze, which turns up towards heaven. Thus, this striving towards and love for God expresses the image of God in man.

In summary, one may say that all of the good and noble qualities and capabilities of the soul are an expression of the image of God in man.

Is there a distinction between the "image" and the "likeness" of God? The majority of the Holy Fathers and teachers of the Church reply that there is. They see the image of God in the very *nature* of the soul, and the likeness in the moral *perfecting* of man in virtue and sanctity, in the acquirement of the gifts of the Holy Spirit. Consequently, we receive the image of God from God together with existence, but the likeness we must acquire ourselves, having received the possibility of doing this from God.[20]

To become "in the likeness" depends upon our will; it is acquired in accordance with our own activity. Therefore, concerning the "counsel" of God it is said: *Let us make man in Our image, after Our likeness* (Gen. 1:26), but with regard to the very act of creation it is said: *God created man in His own image* (Gen. 1:27). About this St. Gregory of Nyssa reasons: By God's "counsel," we were given the potential to be "in His likeness."

---

[20] St. John Damascene: "From the earth God formed man's body and by His own inbreathing gave him a rational and understanding soul, which last we say is the Divine image—for the 'according to His image' means the *nous* and free will, while the 'according to His likeness' means such likeness in virtue as is possible" (*Exact Exposition* 2.12; FC, p. 236).—3RD ED.

The Purpose of Man

Having raised man above all the earthly world, having given him reason and freedom, having adorned him with His own image, the Creator thus indicated to man his especially high purpose. God and the spiritual world lie before man's spiritual gaze; before his bodily gaze lies the material world.

a) The first purpose of man is the glory of God. Man is called to remain faithful to his bond with God, to strive towards Him with his soul, to acknowledge Him as his Creator, to glorify Him, to rejoice in union with Him, to live in Him. *He filled them with knowledge and understanding,* says the most wise son of Sirach with regard to the gifts God has given to man; *He set His eye upon their hearts to show them the majesty of His works. And they will praise His holy name, to proclaim the grandeur of His works* (Sirach 17:6–10). For if all of creation is called, according to its ability, to glorify the Creator (as is stated, for example, in Psalm 148), then of course man, as the very crown of creation, is all the more intended to be the conscious, rational, constant, and most perfect instrument of the glory of God on earth.

b) For this purpose, man should be worthy of his Prototype. In other words, he is called to perfect himself, to guard his likeness to God, to restore and strengthen it; he is called to develop and perfect his moral powers by means of good deeds. This requires that a man take care for his own good, and his true good lies in blessedness in God. Therefore one must say that *blessedness* in God is the aim of man's existence.[21]

c) Man's immediate physical gaze is directed to the world.

---

[21] Ultimately, this means union with God or deification (*theosis*) through participation in the Uncreated Energies. Archimandrite George of Grigoriou Monastery, Mount Athos, observes concerning this: "Man must not only better himself, become more moral, more just, more chaste, more careful. Of course, all this must happen, but it is not the most important purpose, the final purpose, for which our Creator and Maker created man. What is that purpose? Deification—to unite man with God, not externally or sentimentally, but truly" (*Deification as the Purpose of Man's Life,* p. 13).—3rd Ed.

Man has been placed as the crown of earthly creation and the king of nature, as is shown in the first chapter of the book of Genesis. In what way should this be manifested? Metropolitan Macarius speaks of it thus in his *Orthodox Dogmatic Theology:* "As the image of God, the son and inheritor in the house of the Heavenly Father, man has been placed as a kind of intermediary between the Creator and the earthly creation: in particular he has been foreordained to be a *prophet* for it, proclaiming the will of God in the world in word and deed; he is to be its *chief priest,* in order to offer a sacrifice of praise and thanksgiving to God on behalf of all those born of earth, thus bringing down upon earth the blessings of heaven; he is to be head and *king,* so that by concentrating the aims of all existing visible creatures in himself, he might through himself unite all things with God,[22] and thus keep the whole chain of earthly creatures in a harmonious bond and order."

Thus was the first man created, capable of fulfilling his purpose and of doing so freely, voluntarily, joyfully, according to the attraction of his soul, and not by compulsion.

The idea of man's royal position on earth causes the Psalmist to praise the Creator ecstatically: *O Lord, our Lord, how wonderful is Thy name in all the earth! For Thy magnificence is lifted high above the heavens.... For I will behold the heavens, the works of Thy fingers, the moon and the stars, which Thou hast founded. What is man, that Thou art mindful of him? Or the son of man, that Thou visitest him? Thou hast made him a little lower than the angels, with glory and honor hast Thou crowned him, and Thou hast set him over the works of Thy hands.... O Lord, our Lord, how wonderful is Thy name in all the earth!* (Ps. 8:1, 3–5, 8).

---

[22] This Patristic teaching finds its fullest expression in the writings of St. Maximus the Confessor. Vladimir Lossky writes: "It was the Divinely appointed function of the first man, according to St. Maximus, to unite in himself the whole of created being; and at the same time to reach his perfect union with God and thus grant the state of deification to the whole creation.... Since this task which was given to man was not fulfilled by Adam, it is in the work of Christ, the second Adam, that we can see what it was meant to be" (*Mystical Theology,* pp. 109–10).—3RD ED.

From the Majesty of the Creation
to the Incomparable Majesty of the Creator

The Apostle instructs: *The invisible things of Him from the creation of the world are clearly seen ... even His eternal power and Godhead* (Rom. 1:20). That is, the invisible things of God are seen through beholding the creation. In all epochs of human history, the best minds, reflecting deeply on the world, have paused with astonishment before the majesty, harmony, beauty, and rationality of the order of the world, and have been raised up from this to reverent thoughts of the goodness, majesty, and wisdom of the Creator. St. Basil the Great, in his homilies on the Six Days (*Hexaemeron*), examines the first words of the book of Genesis—*In the beginning God created the heaven and the earth*—and then calls on his hearers: "Let us glorify the superb Artist Who created the world most wisely and skillfully; and from the beauty of that which is visible, let us understand Him Who surpasses all in beauty: from the majesty of these sensible and limited bodies let us make a conclusion regarding Him Who is endless, Who surpasses every majesty, and in the multitude of His power surpasses every understanding." And then, going to the second homily, as it were pausing in hopelessness at penetrating further into the depths of creation, he utters these words: "If the entrance to the holy is such, and the entryway of the temple is so praiseworthy and majestic ... then what is to be said of the Holy of Holies? And who is worthy to enter into the Holy Place? Who will stretch forth his gaze to that which is hidden?"

Chapter 4

The Providence of God

God's General Providence over the World

MY Father worketh hitherto, and I work (John 5:17). In these words of the Lord Jesus Christ is contained the truth of God's constant care and providing for the world. Although God *rested on the seventh day from all His works* (Gen. 2:2–3), He did not abandon the world. God *giveth to all life, and breath, and all things.... In Him we live, and move, and have our being* (Acts 17:25, 28). The power of God keeps the world in existence and participates in all the activities of the created powers. The constancy of the so-called "laws of nature" is an activity of the living will of God; by themselves these "laws" would be powerless and ineffective.

The Providence of God embraces everything in the world. God provides not only for the great and the immense, but also for the small and apparently insignificant; not only over the heaven and the earth, angels and men, but also over the smallest creatures, birds, grasses, flowers, trees. The whole of Sacred Scripture is filled with the thought of God's unwearying providential activity.

By God's good will the universe stands, and the whole immense space of the world. God fills the heavens and the earth (Jer. 23:24); *when Thou turnest away Thy face, everything is troubled* (Ps. 103:30).

By God's Providence the world of vegetation lives on the earth. God *covereth heaven with clouds, Who prepareth rain for the earth, Who maketh grass to grow on the mountains, and green herb for the service of man* (Ps. 146:8–9). Nor does He leave without His care the lilies of the field, adorning them and other flowers with a beauty which astonishes us (Matt. 6:29).

The Providence of God extends to the whole of the animal kingdom: *The eyes of all look to Thee with hope, and Thou givest them their food in due season. Thou openest Thy hand and fillest every living thing with Thy blessing* (Ps. 144:16–17). God cares even for the smallest bird: *One of them shall not fall on the ground without your Father* (Matt. 10:29).

But it is man who is the chief object of God's Fatherly Providence on earth. God knows the thoughts of each man (Ps. 138:2), his feelings (Ps. 7:9), even his sighs (Ps. 37:9). He provides what is needful even before He is asked (Matt. 6:32) and bends His ear to the supplication of those who ask (Ps. 85:1), fulfilling what is asked if only the request comes from a sincere and living faith (Matt. 17:20) and is for the good of the one who asks and helps one's search for the Kingdom of God (Matt. 6:33). God directs the steps of the man who does not know his own way (Prov. 20:24). He makes poor and enriches, He brings down and raises up, He causes wounds and Himself binds them up, He strikes and heals (Job 5:18). Loving the righteous, He spares sinners also: *Not unto the end will He be angered, neither unto eternity will He be wroth* (Ps. 102:8). He is long-suffering, in order by means of His goodness to lead sinners to repentance (Rom. 2:4). This all-embracing, ceaseless activity of God in the world is expressed in the Symbol of Faith when we call God "Almighty."

As for the seeming injustices of life, when we see virtuous men suffer while the impious are prosperous, Chrysostom exhorts us in the following words: "If the Kingdom of Heaven is open to us and a reward is shown to us in the future life, then it is not worth investigating why the righteous endure sorrows here while the evil live in comfort. If a reward is waiting there for everyone, according to their just deserts, why should we be disturbed by present events, whether they are fortunate or unfortunate? By these misfortunes God exercises those who are submissive to Him as manful warriors; and the weaker, negligent ones, and those unable to bear anything difficult, He exhorts ahead of time to perform good deeds" ("To Stagirius the Ascetic," Homily 1.8, in *Works of St. John Chrysostom* in Russian, vol. 1, part 1, p. 184). And in fact, we ourselves often see that the best teachers and upbringers are the experiences and misfortunes which men undergo.

In essence, God's Providence over the world is a ceaseless and inseparable activity, even though our limited minds receive this activity of God in the varied and changing world under different forms and appearances. The activity of God's Providence is not, so to speak, an interference in the course of the life given to the world at its creation; it is not a series of private intrusions of God's will into the life of the world. The life of the world is constantly in God's right hand: "The world could not stand for an instant if God were to remove His Providence from it" (Bl. Augustine). "The almighty and most holy Word of the Father, being in the midst of all things and manifesting everywhere His powers, illuminating all things visible and invisible, embraces and contains everything in Himself, so that nothing is without participation in His power; He gives life to and preserves everything everywhere, every creature separately and all creatures together" (St. Athanasius the Great, *Against the Heathen,* chap. 42).

In this regard one must note yet another aspect which causes man to pause in reverent astonishment. This is the fact that, while the Creator contains everything in His right hand, from the very day of creation He gave to all organic beings, and even to the vegetable kingdom, a *freedom* of growth and development, the use of their own powers and of the surrounding environment, each in its own measure and according to its nature and organization. Even greater freedom did the Creator give to man, His rational and morally responsible creation—the highest creation on earth. With this variety of strivings—natural, instinctive, and in the rational world also morally free—God's Providence comes together in such a way that all of them are held in themselves and are directed in accordance with the general providential plan. All of the imperfections, sufferings, and diseases, which proceed from the collision of these separate strivings in the world, are corrected and healed by God's goodness; this goodness calms hostility and directs the life of the whole world towards the good goal which has been established for it from above. And, further, to the rational creatures of God, this goodness opens up the way to the ceaseless glorification of God.

No matter how much humanity violates its purpose in the world, no matter how much it falls, no matter how much the masses of mankind, led by their evil leaders, are inclined to renounce the commandments of God and God Himself, as we see at the present time—the history of the world will still culminate in the attainment of the goal established for it by God's Providence: the triumph of God's righteousness, following which there will be the *Kingdom of Glory,* when *God will be all in all* (I Cor. 15:28).

Beholding the majesty, wisdom, and goodness of God in the world, the Apostle Paul cries out: *O the depth of the riches both of the wisdom and knowledge of God! ... For who hath known the mind of the Lord? Or who hath been His counsellor? Or who hath first given to Him, and it shall be recompensed unto him again? For of Him, and through Him, and to Him are all things: to Whom be glory for ever. Amen* (Rom. 11:33–36).

God's Providence over Man before the Fall

Having created man, the Creator did not leave the first-created ones without His Providence. The Grace of God dwelt constantly in our first ancestors and, in the expression of the Holy Fathers, served as a kind of heavenly clothing for them.[1] They had a perfect feeling of closeness to God. God Himself was their first Instructor and Teacher, and He vouchsafed His immediate revelations to them. Appearing to them, He conversed with them and revealed His will to them.[2]

---

[1] St. John Damascene: "He [Adam] had the indwelling God as a dwelling place and wore Him as a glorious garment. He was wrapped about with His Grace, and, like some one of the angels, he rejoiced in the enjoyment of that one most sweet fruit which is the contemplation of God, and by this he was nourished" (*Exact Exposition* 2.11; FC, p. 232).—3RD ED.

[2] Adam and Eve were not deified at the time of their creation, but were created *for* deification. Deification, as we have seen, refers to union with God through participation in His Uncreated Energies, but it does not mean the appropriation of God's Essence. St. John Damascene writes: "God made man a living being to be governed here according to this present life, and then to be removed elsewhere, that is, to the world to come, and so to complete the mystery by becoming deified through reversion to God—this, however, not by being transformed into the Divine Essence, but by participation in the Divine illumination" (*Exact Exposition* 2.12; FC, p. 235).—3RD ED.

Chapters two and three of the book of Genesis depict for us the life of the first people.

God placed Adam and Eve in Paradise, the Garden of Eden, the "Paradise of delight," where there grew every tree that was pleasant to the sight and good for food, commanding them to dress and keep it. The Garden of Eden was such a splendid place that the first people must have been involuntarily aroused to a feeling of joy and their minds raised to the most perfect Artist of the world. Labor itself must have facilitated the development both of their physical and spiritual powers.

As the writer of Genesis informs us, God brought all living creatures to man so that he might name them. It is clear that on the one hand this gave man the opportunity to become acquainted with the wealth and variety of the animal kingdom, and, on the other, facilitated the development of his mental capabilities, giving him a more complete knowledge of himself by comparison with the world which lay before his eyes, and an awareness of his royal superiority over all the other creatures of earth.

Understandably, the original condition of the first people was one of spiritual childhood and simplicity joined to moral purity. But this condition contained the opportunity for a speedy and harmonious development and growth of all man's powers, directed towards a moral likeness to God and the most intimate union with Him.

Man's mind was pure, bright, and sound. But at the same time it was a mind limited and untested by the experience of life, as was revealed at the time of the fall into sin. Man's mind had yet to develop and be perfected.

Morally, the first-created man was pure and innocent. The words, *They were both naked, the man and his wife, and were not ashamed* (Gen. 2:25), are interpreted by St. John Damascene as "the pinnacle of dispassion." However, one should not understand this purity of the first people as meaning that from the very beginning they already possessed all virtues and were not in need of perfection. No, Adam and Eve, although they came from the hands of the Creator pure and innocent, had yet to be confirmed in the good and grow spiritually, with the help of God, by means of their own actions. "Man," as St. Irenaeus expresses it, "having received existence, was to grow and mature, then become strong. In reaching full maturity he would be glorified and, being glorified, he would be vouchsafed to see God."

Man came from the hands of the Creator faultless also in *body*. His body, so remarkable in its organization, without any doubt received no inward or outward defects from the Creator. It possessed faculties which were fresh and uncorrupted. It had in itself not the least disorder and was able to be free of diseases and sufferings. Indeed, diseases and sufferings are presented in the book of Genesis as the consequences of our first ancestors' fall and as chastisements for sin.

Additionally, the book of Genesis gives a mystical indication of the Tree of Life, the tasting of which was accessible to the first ancestors before the fall into sin and preserved them from physical death. Death was not a necessity for man: "God created man neither completely mortal nor immortal, but capable of both the one and the other" (St. Theophilus of Antioch; see in Bishop Sylvester, *An Essay in Orthodox Dogmatic Theology,* vol. 3, p. 379).

But no matter how perfect the natural powers of man were, as a limited creature he required even then constant strengthening from the Source of all life, from God, just as do all created beings. Appropriate means for man's strengthening on the path of good were needed. Such an elementary means was the *commandment not to taste* of the tree of the knowledge of good and evil. This was a commandment of *obedience.* Free obedience is the path to moral advancement. Where there is voluntary obedience there is (*a*) the cutting off of the way to self-esteem; (*b*) respect and trust for that which is above us; (*c*) continence. Obedience acts beneficially upon the mind, humbling its pride; upon the feelings, limiting self-love; and upon the will, directing the freedom of man towards the good. The Grace of God cooperates and strengthens one on this path. This was the path which lay before the first people, our first ancestors.

"God made man sinless and endowed with freedom of will. By being sinless I do not mean being incapable of sinning, for only the Divinity is incapable of sinning, but having the tendency to sin not in his nature but, rather, in his power of choice—that is to say, having the power to persevere and progress in good with the help of Divine Grace, as well as having the power to turn from virtue and fall into vice" (St. John Damascene, *Exact Exposition* 2.12; FC, p. 235).

In general, it is difficult if not impossible for contemporary man to imagine man's true condition in Paradise, a condition that joined together moral purity, clarity of mind, the perfection of first-created nature, and nearness to God, with a general spiritual childlikeness. But in any case it must be noticed that the traditions of all peoples speak of precisely such a condition, which the poets call the "golden age" of mankind (the traditions of the Chinese, the Indians, the Persians, the Greeks, and others). The great minds of pagan antiquity expressed the certainty that the ancients were more pure and moral than later men (Socrates); and that the most ancient religious traditions and conceptions were more perfect than the later pagan conceptions, because the first men were nearer to God and knew Him as their Creator and Father (Plato and Cicero).

Chapter 5

Concerning Evil and Sin

1. Evil and Sin in the World

EVIL and misfortune. "Evil," in our ordinary usage of words, is the name of two kinds of manifestations. We often understand by this word anything in general which evokes misfortune and causes suffering. But in a more precise, direct sense, evil is a name for negative manifestations of the moral order which proceed from the evil direction of the will and a violation of God's laws.

It is clear that misfortunes in the physical world—for example, earthquakes, storms, floods, landslides, and the rest—are in themselves neither good nor evil. In the general world system they are what shadows are to bright colors in the art of painters, what crude sounds are to soft sounds in music, and so forth. This is the way in which Holy Fathers such as Blessed Augustine and St. Gregory the Theologian treat these manifestations. One cannot deny that such manifestations of the elements are often the cause of misfortunes and sufferings for sensible creatures and for man; but one can only bow down in reverence before the all-wise order of the world, where the endlessly various and mutually opposed strivings on the part of blind elemental powers and organic creatures, which collide with each other at every moment, are in mutual agreement and are brought into harmony, becoming a source of constant renewal in the world.

Suffering and sin. To a certain extent, the unpleasant, shadowy sides of our human life make us value and sense more highly the joyful sides of life. But the word of God itself tells us that difficult sufferings, sorrows, and afflictions cannot be acknowledged as manifestations completely in accordance with law and therefore normal; rather, they are a deviation from the norm. The sufferings of the human race began with the appearance of moral evil and are the consequences of sin, which entered into our life at that time. Of this the first pages of the Bible testify: *I will greatly multiply thy sorrow and thy sighing; in pain thou shalt bring forth children* (the words addressed to Eve after the fall into sin); *Cursed is the ground for thy sake; in sorrow shalt thou eat of it all the days of thy life* (the words spoken to Adam; Gen. 3:16–17). Sufferings are given to man as a means of chastisement, enlightenment, and correction. According to St. Basil the Great, sufferings and death itself "cut off the growth of sin." Numerous examples of the awareness of the tie between suffering and sin as a result of its cause are given to us in the word of God: *Lay hold of chastisement, lest at any time the Lord be angry* (Ps. 2:12); *it is good for me that Thou hast humbled me, that I might learn Thy statutes* (Ps. 118:71). Careful observation itself shows that the causes of diseases and sufferings, in the overwhelming majority of cases, are men themselves, who have created artificial and abnormal conditions for their existence, introducing a cruel mutual warfare while chasing after their own egotistic physical well-being; and sometimes these things are the direct result of a certain demonic attitude—pride, revenge, and malice.

As the word of God instructs us, the consequences of moral evil spread from people to the animal world and to the whole of creation: *For we know that the whole creation groaneth and travaileth in pain together until now,* the Apostle Paul writes, and he further explains: *For the creation was made subject to vanity, not willingly, but by reason of him who hath subjected it in hope: because the creation itself also shall be delivered from the bondage of corruption into the glorious liberty of the children of God* (Rom. 8:22, 20–21).[1]

---

[1] It is the consensus of the Holy Fathers that the entire creation was brought into *the bondage of corruption* through man's sin (see p. 344 below). Commenting on Romans 8:20, St. John Chrysostom writes: "What means, *For the creation was made subject to vanity?* It became corruptible. Why, and by what cause? By your fault, O man. Because you received a body mortal and subject to sufferings, so the earth also

The essence of moral evil. The Holy Fathers indicate that evil is not some kind of essence which has any actual independent existence, like the elements and powers of the world which were created by God.[2] Evil is only a deviation of living beings from that original condition in which the Creator placed them, into a condition which is opposed to this. Therefore, it is not God Who is the cause of moral evil; rather, it proceeds from creatures themselves, for they have deviated from the agreement of their will with the will of God. The essence of evil consists in the violation of God's will, the commandments of God, and the moral law which is written in the human conscience. This violation is called *sin.*

The origin of evil. But from whence did moral evil arise? God created the world pure, perfect, free from evil. Evil entered the world as a consequence of the fall, which occurred, according to the word of God, originally in the world of fleshless spirits, and then in the human race, and was reflected in the whole of living nature.

---

was subject to a curse, and brought forth thorns and thistles." Later in the same section, St. John writes: "Just as the creation became corruptible when your body became corruptible, so also when your body will be incorrupt [i.e., after the General Resurrection], the creation also will follow after it and become corresponding to it" (*Homilies on Romans,* Homily 14.5; *Works,* in Russian, vol. 9, p. 665; NPNF, pp. 444–45).

St. Symeon the New Theologian states specifically that the entire earth, and not just Paradise, was created incorrupt: "God did not, as some people think, just give Paradise to our ancestors at the beginning, nor did He make only Paradise incorruptible. No!... The whole world had been brought into being by God as one thing, as a kind of paradise, at once incorruptible yet material and perceptible" (*On the Mystical Life,* vol. 1, p. 21).—3RD ED.

[2] St. Diadochus of Photiki: "Evil does not exist by nature, nor is any man naturally evil, for God made nothing that was not good. When in the desire of his heart someone conceives and gives form to what in reality has no existence, then what he desires begins to exist. We should therefore turn our attention away from the inclination to evil and concentrate it on the remembrance of God; for good, which exists by nature, is more powerful than our inclination to evil. The one has existence while the other does not, except when we give it existence through our actions" (*Philokalia,* vol. 1, p. 253).—3RD ED.

2. The Fall in the Angelic World:
The World of Dark and Evil Spirits

According to the testimony of the word of God, the origin of sin comes from the devil: *He that committeth sin is of the devil; for the devil sinneth from the beginning* (I John 3:8). The word "devil" means "slanderer." Bringing together the evidence of Sacred Scripture, we see that the devil is one of the rational spirits or angels who deviated into the path of evil. Possessing, like all rational creatures, the freedom which was given him for becoming perfect in the good, he "abode not in the truth" and fell away from God.[3] The Saviour said of him: *He was a murderer from the beginning, and abode not in the truth, because there is no truth in him. When he speaketh a lie, he speaketh of his own: for he is a liar and the father of it* (John 8:44). He drew the other angels after himself into the fall. In the epistles of the Apostle Jude and the Apostle Peter, we read of the angels *which kept not their first estate, but left their own habitation* (Jude, v. 6; compare with II Peter 2:4).

What was the cause of the fall in the angelic world? From this same Divine Revelation we can conclude that the reason was *pride: the beginning of sin is pride,* says the son of Sirach (Sir. 10:13). The Apostle Paul, warning the Apostle Timothy against making bishops of those who are newly converted, adds: *Lest being lifted up with pride he fall into the condemnation of the devil* (I Tim. 3:6).

The evil spirits are mentioned in only a few passages in the Old Testament Revelation. These places are the following: We read of the "serpent," the tempter of the first people, in the third chapter of the book of Genesis. The activities of "Satan" in the life of the righteous

---

[3] St. John Damascene: "Every rational being is free. The angelic nature, then, insofar as it is rational and intelligent, is free; while, insofar as it is created, it is changeable and has the power to persevere and progress in good or to turn to evil.

"Although man, by reason of the infirmity of his body, is capable of repentance, the angel, because of his incorporeality, is not" (*Exact Exposition* 2.3; FC, p. 206).—3RD ED.

Job are related in the first chapter of the book of Job. In First Kings it is said concerning Saul that *an evil spirit troubled him* after *the Spirit of the Lord departed from him* (I Kings 16:14—I Sam. in KJV). In First Paralipomenon (Chronicles), chapter 21, we read that when the thought came to King David to make a census of the people, it was because *Satan stood up against Israel, and provoked David to number Israel.* In the book of the Prophet Zachariah it is said concerning his vision of the chief priest, Joshua, that Joshua was resisted by "the devil" ("Satan" in KJV; Zach. 3:1). In the book of the Wisdom of Solomon it is said that *through the devil's envy death entered the world* (Wis. 2:24). Likewise, in Deuteronomy 32:17 it is said: *They sacrificed unto devils, not to God;* and in Psalm 105:35: *And they sacrificed ... unto demons.*

An incomparably more complete representation of the activity of Satan and his angels is contained in the New Testament Revelation. From it we know that Satan and the evil spirits are constantly attracting people to evil. Satan dared to tempt the Lord Jesus Christ Himself in the desert. The evil spirits rush into the souls and even into the bodies of men; of this there is the testimony of many events in the Gospel and of the teachings of the Saviour. Concerning the habitation of evil spirits in men, we know from the numerous healings by the Saviour of the demon-possessed. Evil spirits spy, as it were, on the carelessness of man so as to attract him to evil: *When the unclean spirit is gone out of a man, he walketh through dry places seeking rest, and findeth none. Then he saith, I will return into my house from whence I came out; and when he is come, he findeth it empty, swept, and garnished. Then goeth he, and taketh with himself seven other spirits more wicked than himself and they enter in and dwell there: and the last state of that man is worse than the first* (Matt. 12:43–45). With regard to the healing of the bent woman, the Saviour said to the ruler of the synagogue: *And ought not this woman, being a daughter of Abraham, whom Satan hath bound, lo, these eighteen years, be loosed from this bond on the sabbath day?* (Luke 13:16).

Likewise, the Sacred Scripture calls evil spirits "unclean spirits," "spirits of evil," "devils," "demons," "angels of the devil," "angels of

Satan." Their chief, the devil, is also called the "tempter," "Satan," "Beelzebub," "Belial," the "prince of devils," and other names like "Lucifer" (the morning star).

Taking the form of a serpent, the devil was the tempter and the cause of the fall into sin of the first people, as is related in the third chapter of the book of Genesis. In the Apocalypse he is called *the great dragon, that old serpent* (Apoc. 12:9).

The devil and his angels are deprived of remaining in the heavenly dwellings of light. *I beheld Satan as lightning fall from heaven,* said the Lord to His disciples (Luke 10:18). Being cast down from the world above, the devil and his servants act in the world under the heaven, among men on earth, and they have taken into their possession, as it were, hell and the underworld. The Apostle calls them *principalities, powers, the rulers of the darkness of this world* (Eph. 6:12). The devil is *the prince of the power of the air* (Eph. 2:2), and his servants, the fallen angels, are *the spirits of wickedness under the heaven* (Eph. 6:12).

3. Man's Fall into Sin

Why was man's fall into sin possible? The Creator imparted to man three great gifts at his creation: freedom, reason, and love. These gifts are indispensable for the spiritual growth and blessedness of man. But where there is freedom there is the possibility of wavering in one's choice; thus, temptation is possible. The temptation for *reason* is to grow proud in mind; instead of acknowledging the wisdom and goodness of God, to seek the knowledge of good and evil outside of God; to desire oneself to be a "god." The temptation for the feeling of *love* is: in place of love for God and one's neighbor, to love oneself and everything that satisfies the lower desires and gives temporary enjoyment. This possibility of temptation and fall stood before mankind, and the first man did not stand firm against it.

Let us make note here of St. John of Kronstadt's reflection on this subject. He writes: "Why did God allow the fall of man, his beloved creation and the crown of all the earthly creatures? To this question one must reply thus: If man is not to be allowed to fall, then he cannot be created in the image and likeness of God, he cannot be granted free will, which is an inseparable feature of the image of God; but he would have to be subject to the law of necessity, like the soulless creation—the sky, the sun, stars, the circle of the earth, and all the elements—or like the irrational animals. But then there would have been no king over the creatures of the earth, no rational hymn-singer of God's goodness, wisdom, creative almightiness, and Providence. Then man would have had no way to show his faithfulness and devotion to the Creator, his self-sacrificing love. Then there would have been no exploits in battle, no merits, and no incorruptible crowns for victory; there would have been no eternal blessedness, which is the reward for faithfulness and devotion to God, and no eternal repose after the labors and struggles of our earthly pilgrimage."

The history of the fall into sin. The writer of Genesis does not tell us whether our first ancestors lived for a long time in the blessed life of Paradise. Speaking of their fall, he indicates that they did not come to the temptation of themselves, but were led to it by the *tempter.*

Now the serpent was more subtil than any of the beasts of the earth which the Lord God had made. And he said unto the woman: Yea, hath God said, Ye shall not eat of every tree of Paradise? And the woman said unto the serpent, We may eat of the fruit of the trees of Paradise: but of the fruit of the tree which is in the midst of Paradise, God hath said, Ye shall not eat of it, neither shall ye touch it, lest ye die. And the serpent said unto the woman: Ye shall not surely die. For God doth know that in the day ye eat thereof, then your eyes shall be opened, and ye shall be as gods, knowing good and evil. And when the woman saw that the tree was good for food, and that it was pleasant to the eyes, and a tree to be desired to make one wise, she took of the fruit thereof, and did eat, and gave also to her husband with her, and he did eat (Gen. 3:1–6).

The Christian Church has always understood the serpent, the tempter, to be the devil, who took the form of a serpent as corresponding best to his sneaky, cunning, and poisonous character. The clear words of our Lord Himself about the devil confirm this interpretation:

He was a murderer from the beginning (John 8:44). In the Apocalypse of John the Theologian he is called *the great dragon, that old serpent* (Apoc. 12:9). In the book of the Wisdom of Solomon it says: *Through the devil's envy death entered the world* (Wis. 2:24).

What was the sin in the eating of the fruit? The transgression of our first ancestors was this: Having been tempted by the serpent, they violated the direct commandment of God not to eat of the forbidden tree. The fulfillment of this commandment would have shown *obedience* to God and *trust* in His words, as well as *humility* and *continence*—a summing up of the simple and natural virtues. The eating of the forbidden fruit immediately drew after itself the whole sum of lamentable moral and physical consequences.

The moral consequences of the fall. The eating of the fruit was only the beginning of moral deviation, the first push; but it was so poisonous and ruinous that it was already impossible to return to the previous sanctity and righteousness; on the contrary, there was revealed an inclination to travel farther on the path of apostasy from God. This is seen in the fact that they immediately noticed their nakedness and, hearing the voice of God in Paradise, they hid from Him and, justifying themselves, only increased their guilt. In Adam's replies to God, we see from the beginning his desire to flee from God's sight and an attempt to hide his guilt; we see the untruth in his saying that he had hidden from God only because he was naked; and then the attempt at self-justification and the desire to transfer his guilt to another, his wife. Blessed Augustine says: "Here was pride, because man desired to be more under his own authority than under God's; and a mockery of what is holy, because he did not believe God; and murder, because he subjected himself to death; and spiritual adultery, because the immaculateness of the human soul was defiled through the persuasion of the serpent; and theft, because they made use of the forbidden tree; and the love of acquisition, because he desired more than was necessary to satisfy himself."

Thus, with the first transgression of the commandment, the principle of sin immediately entered into man—"the law of sin" (*nomos tis amartias*). It struck the very nature of man and quickly

157

began to root itself in him and develop.[4] Of this sinful principle which entered human nature, the Apostle Paul wrote: *For I know that in me (that is, in my flesh) dwelleth no good thing: for to will is present with me; but how to perform that which is good I find not.... For I delight in the law of God after the inward man: but I see another law in my members, warring against the law of my mind, and bringing me into captivity to the law of sin which is in my members* (Rom. 7:18, 22–23). The sinful inclinations in man have taken the reigning position; man has become *the servant of sin* (Rom. 6:17). Both the mind and the feelings have become darkened in him, and therefore his moral freedom often does not incline towards the good, but towards evil. *Lust* and *pride* have appeared in the depths of man's impulses to activity in life. Of this we read in I John 2:15–16: *Love not the world, neither the things that are in the world.... For all that is in the world, the lust of the flesh, and the lust of the eyes, and the pride of life, is not of the Father, but is of the world.* The *lust of the flesh* is a weakening of the authority of the spirit over the body, a subjection of it to the lower, fleshly desires; the *lust of the eyes* means the false idols and attachments, greed and hunger for the world, envy; and *pride* is self-esteem, egoism, self-exaltation, a despising of others who are weaker, love of self, and vainglory.

Contemporary psychological observations also lead investigators to the conclusion that lust and pride (the thirst for being better than others) are the chief levers of the strivings of contemporary fallen mankind, even when they are deeply hidden in the soul and are not completely conscious.

---

[4] With the entrance of sin, man lost the Grace in which he had been created. Because his nature had become corrupted by sin, Grace was now foreign to it. St. John Damascene writes: "And so, man succumbed to the assault of the demon, the author of evil; he failed to keep the Creator's commandment and was stripped of Grace and deprived of that familiarity which he had enjoyed with God" (*Exact Exposition* 3.1, p. 267). Likewise, St. Symeon the New Theologian writes: "When with his whole soul he (Adam) believed the serpent and not God, then Divine Grace which had rested on him stepped away from him, so that he became the enemy of God by reason of the unbelief which he had shown to His words" (*First-Created Man*, pp. 43–44).—3RD ED.

The physical consequences of the fall. The physical consequences of the fall are diseases, hard labor, and death. These were the natural result of the moral fall, the falling away from communion with God, man's departure from God.[5] Man became subject to the *corrupt elements of the world,* in which dissolution and death are active. Nourishment from the Source of Life and from the constant renewal of all of one's powers became weak in men. Our Lord Jesus Christ indicated the dependence of illnesses on sin when he healed the paralytic, saying to him: *Behold, thou art made whole; sin no more, lest a worse thing come unto thee* (John 5:14).

With sin, *death* entered into the human race. Man was created immortal in his soul, and he could have remained immortal also in body if he had not fallen away from God. The Wisdom of Solomon says: *God did not make death* (Wis. 1:13). Man's body, as was well expressed by Blessed Augustine, does not possess "the impossibility of dying," but it did possess "the possibility of not dying," which it has now lost. The writer of Genesis informs us that this "possibility of not dying" was maintained in Paradise by eating the fruit of the *Tree of Life,* of which our first ancestors were deprived after they were banished from Paradise. *As by one man sin entered into the world, and death by sin; and so death passed upon all men, for that all have sinned* (Rom. 5:12). The

---

[5] When man lost the Grace of God, he experienced spiritual death, and this spiritual death made him subject to physical death. Thus, St. Gregory Palamas writes: "It was indeed Adam's soul that died by becoming through his transgression separated from God; for bodily he continued to live after that time, even for 930 years. The death, however, that befell the soul because of the transgression not only crippled the soul and made man accursed; it also rendered the body itself subject to fatigue, suffering, and corruptibility, and finally handed it over to death" (*Philokalia,* vol. 4, p. 296).

Elsewhere St. Gregory Palamas expounds further on what is meant by the death of the soul: "Physical death is when the soul leaves the body and is separated from it. The death of the soul is when God leaves the soul and is separated from it, although in another way, the soul remains immortal. Once separated from God it becomes more ugly and useless than a dead body, but unlike such a body it does not disintegrate after death since it is not composite" (*Homilies,* vol. 1, p. 184).—3RD ED.

Apostle calls death the "wages," that is, the payment or reward for sin: *The wages of sin is death* (Rom. 6:23).[6]

Misfortunes and death as chastisements of God. Physical misfortunes are not only a consequence of sin; at the same time they are chastisements from God, as was revealed in the words of God to our first parents when they were banished from Paradise. It is clear that these chastisements are given as a means of preventing man from a further and final fall.

Concerning the meaning of labors and diseases in fallen man, St. Cyril of Alexandria says that man, "having received as his lot an exhausting fast and sorrows, was given over to illnesses, sufferings, and the other bitter things of life as to a kind of bridle. Because he did not sensibly restrain himself in that life which was free of labors and sorrows, he was given over to misfortunes so that by sufferings he might heal in himself the disease which came upon him in the midst of blessedness" ("On the Incarnation of the Lord").

Of death, this same Holy Father says: "By death the Giver of the Law stopped the spread of sin, and in the very chastisement revealed His love for mankind. Inasmuch as He, in giving the commandment, joined death to the transgression of it, and inasmuch as the criminal thus fell under this chastisement, so He arranged that the chastisement itself might serve for salvation. For death dissolves this animal nature of ours and thus, on the one hand, stops the activity of evil, and on the other delivers a man from illnesses, frees him from labors, puts an end to his sorrows and cares, and stops his bodily sufferings. With such a love for mankind has the Judge mixed the chastisement" (the same Homily).

The loss of the Kingdom of God as the most severe consequence of the fall. However, the final and most important consequence of sin was

---

[6] St. John Damascene: "He [man] was clothed with the roughness of his wretched life—for that is what the fig leaves signify—and put on death, that is to say, the mortality and the grossness of the flesh—for this is what the garment of skins signifies; he was excluded from Paradise by the just judgment of God; and was condemned to death and made subject to corruption" (*Exact Exposition* 3.1, p. 267).—3RD ED.

not illness and physical death, but the loss of Paradise. This loss of Paradise is the same thing as the loss of the Kingdom of God. In Adam all mankind was deprived of the future blessedness which stood before it, the blessedness which Adam and Eve had partially tasted in Paradise.[7] In place of the prospect of life eternal, mankind beheld death, and behind it hell, darkness, rejection by God. Therefore, the sacred books of the Old Testament are filled with dark thoughts concerning existence beyond the grave: *For in death there is none that is mindful of Thee, and in hades who will confess Thee?* (Ps. 6:5). This is not a denial of immortality, but a reflection of the hopeless darkness beyond the grave. Such awareness and sorrow were eased only by the hope of future deliverance through the coming of the Saviour: *I know that my Redeemer liveth, and that He shall stand at the latter day upon the earth: And though my skin hath been destroyed, yet in my flesh shall I see God* (Job 19:25–26). *Therefore did my heart rejoice and my tongue was glad; moreover, my flesh shall dwell in hope. For Thou wilt not abandon my soul in hades, nor wilt Thou suffer Thy Holy One to see corruption* (Ps. 15:9–10).

God's mercy to fallen man. After man's fall into sin, God did not reject man the sinner. He took away from him neither His image,[8] which distinguished him from the animal world, nor the freedom of his will, nor his reason, by which man was capable of understanding spiritual principles, nor his other capabilities. God acted towards him as does a

---

[7] In other words, the way to deification was barred to man. See pp. 167–68, note 14 below.—3RD ED.

[8] St. Gregory Palamas writes that the human soul "possesses the image of God inalienably, even if it does not recognize its own dignity, or think and live in a manner worthy of the Creator's image within it. After our forefather's transgression in Paradise through the tree, we suffered the death of our soul—which is the separation of the soul from God—prior to our bodily death; yet although we cast away our divine likeness, we did not lose our divine image. Thus when the soul renounces its attachment to inferior things and cleaves through love to God and submits itself to Him through acts and modes of virtue, it is illuminated and made beautiful by God and is raised to a higher level, obeying His counsels and exhortations; and by these means it regains the truly eternal life" (*Philokalia*, vol. 4, p. 363).—3RD ED.

physician and educator: He covered his nakedness with clothing, moderated his self-esteem and pride, his fleshly desires and passions, by means of healing measures—labor and diseases—giving to them an educational significance. We ourselves can see the educational effect of labor, and the cleansing effect of disease on the soul. God subjected man to physical death so as not to hand him over to final spiritual death—that is, so that the sinful principle in him might not develop to the extreme, so that he might not become like Satan.

However, this natural bridle of suffering and death does not uproot the very source of evil. It only restrains the development of evil. It was most necessary for mankind to have a supernatural power and help which might perform an inward reversal within him and give to man the possibility to turn away from a gradually deepening descent and towards victory over sin and a gradual ascent to God. God's Providence foresaw the future fall of man's free will which had not become strong. Foreseeing the fall, He prearranged an arising. Adam's fall into sin was not an absolute perdition for mankind. The power which was to give rebirth, according to God's pre-eternal determination, was the descent to earth of the Son of God.

4. Original Sin

By *original sin* is meant the sin of Adam, which was transmitted to his descendants and weighs upon them.[9] The doctrine of original sin has great significance in the Christian worldview, because upon it rests a whole series of other dogmas.

The word of God teaches us that through Adam "all have sinned": *By one man sin entered into the world, and death by sin; and so death*

---

[9] The expression "original sin" has become traditional in Latin theology since the time of Blessed Augustine (see p. 169, note 15 below). Contemporary Orthodox writers generally prefer the expression "ancestral sin" (*progoniki amartia, to propartorikon amartia*), which is common among the Greek Fathers. When such writers do speak of "original sin," they are usually careful to distinguish the Eastern Orthodox conception from the Latin conception, as Fr. Michael proceeds to do here.—3RD ED.

passed upon all men, for that all have sinned (Rom. 5:12). *For who will be clean of defilement? No one, if he have lived even a single day upon earth* (Job 14:4–5, Septuagint). *For behold, I was conceived in iniquities, and in sins did my mother bear me* (Ps. 50:5); "the seed of corruption is in me" (Evening Prayers).

The common faith of the ancient Christian Church in the existence of original sin may be seen in the Church's ancient custom of baptizing infants. The Local Council of Carthage in 252, composed of 66 bishops under the presidency of St. Cyprian, decreed the following against heretics: "Not to forbid (the Baptism) of an infant who, scarcely born, has sinned in nothing apart from that which proceeds from the flesh of Adam. He has received *the contagion of the ancient death* through his very birth,[10] and he comes, therefore, the more easily

---

[10] The Eastern Orthodox Holy Fathers often affirm that all of Adam's descendants inherit his sin, in accordance with the words of St. Paul: *By one man's disobedience, many were made sinners* (Rom. 5:19). However, in saying this they do not mean that the *guilt* of Adam's sin was imputed to his descendants; rather, it was the *consequences* of that sin that were transmitted. These consequences, as we have seen, include suffering, death, and physical corruption; a corruption of human nature; and a consequent loss of the indwelling Grace of God. As Fr. Michael explains (see pp. 157–58, 169), the corruption of human nature entails an *inclination* or *tendency* toward sin.

St. Cyril of Alexandria well expresses the Orthodox teaching on the transmission of ancestral sin: "What has Adam's guilt to do with us? Why are we held responsible for his sin when we were not even born when he committed it? Did not God say: *The parents will not die for the children, nor the children for the parents, but the soul which has sinned, it shall die* (Deut. 24:16)? We have become sinners because of Adam's disobedience in the following manner…. After he fell into sin and surrendered to corruption, impure lusts [or pleasures] invaded the nature of his flesh, and at the same time the evil law of our members was born. For our nature contracted the disease of sin because of the disobedience of one man, that is, Adam, and thus many became sinners. This was not because they sinned along with Adam, because they did not then exist, but because they had the same nature as Adam, which fell under the law of sin. Thus, just as human nature acquired the weakness of corruption in Adam because of disobedience, and evil desires [or passions] invaded it, so the same nature was later set free by Christ, Who was obedient to God the Father and did not commit sin" (Commentary on Romans 5:18, *Patrologiae Cursus Completus, Series Graeca*, vol. 74, pp. 788–89).—3RD ED.

to the reception of the remission of sins in that it is not his own but the sins of another that are remitted."[11]

This is the way in which the "Encyclical of the Eastern Patriarchs" defines the result of the fall into sin: "Fallen through the transgression, man became like the irrational creatures. That is, he became darkened and was deprived of perfection and dispassion. But he was not deprived of the nature and power which he had received from the All-Good God. For had he been so deprived, he would have become irrational, and thus not a man. But he preserved that nature with which he had been created, and the free, living and active natural power, so that, according to nature, he might choose and do the good, and flee and turn away from evil" ("Encyclical of the Eastern Patriarchs," par. 14).

In the history of the ancient Christian Church, Pelagius and his followers denied the inheritance of sin (the heresy of Pelagianism). Pelagius affirmed that every man only repeats the sin of Adam, performing anew his own personal fall into sin, and following the example of Adam because of his own weak will. However, his nature remains the same as when it was created, innocent and pure, the same as that of the first-created Adam. Moreover, disease and death are characteristic of this nature from the creation, and are not the consequences of original sin.

Blessed Augustine stepped out against Pelagius with great power and proof. He cited (a) testimonies from Divine Revelation concerning original sin, (b) the teaching of the ancient shepherds of the Church, (c) the ancient custom of baptizing infants, and (d) the sufferings and misfortunes of men, including infants, which are a consequence of the universal and inherited sinfulness of men. However, Augustine did not escape the opposite extreme, setting forth the idea that in fallen man any independent freedom to do good has been completely annihilated, unless Grace comes to his aid.

---

[11] The same thing is stated in Canon 110 of the "African Code," approved by 217 bishops at Carthage in 419 and ratified by the Council in Trullo (692) and the Seventh Ecumenical Council (787). Canon 110 ends: "On account of this rule of faith even infants, who could have committed as yet no sin themselves, therefore are truly baptized for the remission of sins, in order that what in them is the result of generation may be cleansed by regeneration" (*Seven Ecumenical Councils,* NPNF, p. 497).

Out of this dispute in the West there subsequently were formed two tendencies, one of which was followed by Roman Catholicism, and the other by Protestantism. Roman Catholic theologians consider that the consequence of the fall was the removal from men of a *supernatural gift* of God's grace, after which man remained in his "natural" condition, his nature not harmed but only brought into disorder because the flesh, the bodily side, has come to dominate over the spiritual side; original sin in this view consists in the fact that the *guilt* before God of Adam and Eve has passed to all men.[12]

The other tendency in the West sees in original sin the complete perversion of human nature and its corruption to its very depths, to its very foundations (the view accepted by Luther and Calvin). As for the newer sects of Protestantism, reacting in their turn against the extremes of Luther, they have gone as far as the complete denial of original, inherited sin.

Among the shepherds of the Eastern Church there have been no doubts concerning either the teaching of the inherited ancestral sin in

---

[12] Roman Catholic teaching on inherited guilt is based on the works of Blessed Augustine, who wrote: "Even of believing husbands and wives are born guilty persons ... on account of original sin" ("Treatise against Two Letters of the Pelagians, chap. 11); "The fault of our nature remains in our offspring so deeply impressed as to make it [our offspring] guilty" ("On Original Sin," chap. 44); "Inasmuch as infants are not held bound by any sins of their own actual life, it is the guilt of original sin which is healed in them by the grace of Him Who saves them by the laver of regeneration [i.e., in Baptism]" ("On the Baptism of Infants," chap. 24); "Until, then, this remission of sins takes place in the offspring, they have within them the law of sin in such manner, that it is really imputed to them as sin; in other words, with that law there is attaching to them its sentence of guilt, which holds them debtors to eternal condemnation" ("On Marriage and Concupiscence," chap. 37). This concept of inherited guilt was affirmed at the fifth session of the Council of Trent (1546), which, in defining the Roman teaching on original sin, referred to "the guilt of original sin." In the 17th and 18th centuries, some Roman Catholic theologians continued to develop Blessed Augustine's teaching on inherited guilt. However, it was in Protestantism rather than Roman Catholicism that the doctrine of inherited guilt (also known as the doctrine of "imputed sin") was given its most extreme formulations.—3RD ED.

general, or the consequences of this sin for fallen human nature in particular.

Orthodox theology does not accept the extreme points of Blessed Augustine's teaching; but equally foreign to it is the (later) Roman Catholic point of view, which has a very legalistic, formal character. The foundation of the Roman Catholic teaching lies in (*a*) an understanding of the sin of Adam as an *infinitely great offense* against God; (*b*) after this offense there followed the *wrath* of God; (*c*) the wrath of God was expressed in the *removal of the supernatural gifts* of God's grace;[13] and (*d*) the removal of grace drew after itself the submission

---

[13] According to the *Catholic Encyclopedia,* "Original sin is the privation of sanctifying grace" (1911 edition, vol. 11, p. 314). As noted above (p. 158, note 4), the Orthodox Holy Fathers also teach that man lost the Grace of God at the time He fell. However, the Orthodox teaching on this subject is different from the Roman Catholic teaching in two ways.

First of all, in Roman Catholic teaching grace is a *created* phenomenon: "It is not a substance that exists by itself, or apart from the soul; therefore it is a physical accident inhering in the soul.... Sanctifying grace may be philosophically termed a 'permanent, supernatural quality of the soul'" (*Catholic Encyclopedia,* 1911 edition, vol. 6, p. 705). According to Orthodox theology, on the other hand, Grace is the *Uncreated* Energy of God Himself, which at the time of man's creation was intimately connected with his soul. Man *participated* in the Divine life through the Divine Energy, and this participation was proper to the original nature of man.

Vladimir Lossky comments on the difference between the Roman Catholic doctrine of supernatural (created) grace and the Orthodox doctrine of Divine (Uncreated) Grace: "For Eastern [Orthodox] tradition the created supernatural has no existence. That which Western theology calls by the name *supernatural* signifies for the East *Uncreated*—the Divine Energies ineffably distinct from the Essence of God. The difference consists in the fact that the Western conception of grace implies the idea of causality, grace being represented as an effect of the Divine Cause, exactly as in the act of creation; while for Eastern theology there is a natural procession, the Energies shining forth eternally from the Divine Essence. It is in the creation alone that God acts as cause, in producing a new subject called to participate in the Divine fullness; preserving it, saving it, *granting* Grace to it, and guiding it towards its final goal. In the Energies *He is,* He exists, He eternally manifests Himself" (*Mystical Theology,* pp. 88–89).

Secondly, in Roman Catholic teaching original sin consists only in the privation of sanctifying grace (also called "original justice"), while the nature of man remained the same after the fall as it had been before the fall. In this view, the nature of man

of the spiritual principle to the *fleshly principle,* and a falling deeper into sin and death. From this comes a particular view of the redemption performed by the Son of God. In order to restore the order which had been violated, it was necessary first of all to give satisfaction for the offense given to God, and by this means to *remove the guilt* of mankind and the punishment that weighs upon him.

The consequences of ancestral sin are accepted by Orthodox theology differently.

After his first fall, man *himself* departed in soul from God and became unreceptive to the Grace of God which was opened to him; he ceased to listen to the Divine voice addressed to him, and this led to the further deepening of sin in him.

However, God has never deprived mankind of His mercy, help, Grace, and especially His chosen people; and from this people there came forth great righteous men such as Moses, Elijah, Elisha, and the later prophets. The Apostle Paul, in the eleventh chapter of the Epistle to the Hebrews, lists a whole choir of Old Testament righteous ones, saying that they are those *of whom the world was not worthy* (Heb. 11:38). All of them were perfected not without a gift from above, not without the Grace of God.[14] The book of Acts cites the words of the first martyr, Stephen, where he says of David that he

---

has not become corrupted; rather, the privation of grace *in itself* constitutes "a stain, a moral deformity" (*Catholic Encyclopedia,* vol. 11, p. 314). According to Orthodox theology, on the other hand, man's nature was corrupted at the fall, and this corruption caused man to lose the indwelling of Grace and deprived him of participation in God. As Vladimir Lossky notes, "The deprivation of Grace is not the cause, but rather the consequence of the decadence of our nature" (*Mystical Theology,* p. 132).—3RD ED.

[14] Between the time of man's fall and his redemption by Christ, Grace could act on man temporarily from the outside, but could not dwell within him, united with his soul, as it was before the fall. Vladimir Lossky writes: "From the fall until the day of Pentecost, the Divine Energy, deifying and Uncreated Grace, was foreign to our human nature, acting on it only from the outside.... The prophets and righteous men of the Old Testament were the instruments of Grace. Grace acted by them, but did not become their own, their personal strength. Deification, union with God by Grace, had become impossible" (*Mystical Theology,* p. 133). That is why, in II Corinthians, St. Paul says the glory (Grace beheld as Uncreated Light)

found favor (Grace) *before God, and desired to find a tabernacle of the God of Jacob* (Acts 7:46)—that is, to build a Temple for Him. The greatest of the prophets, St. John the Forerunner, was *filled with the Holy Spirit even from his mother's womb* (Luke 1:15). But the Old Testament righteous ones could not escape the general lot of fallen mankind after death, remaining in the darkness of hell, until the founding of the Heavenly Church—that is, until the Resurrection and Ascension of Christ. The Lord Jesus Christ destroyed the gates of hell and opened the way into the Kingdom of Heaven.

One must not see the essence of sin—including original sin—only in the dominance of the fleshly over the spiritual, as Roman Catholic theology teaches. Many sinful inclinations, even very serious ones, have to do with qualities of a *spiritual* order: such, for example, is pride, which, according to the words of the Apostle, is the source, together with lust, of the general sinfulness of the world (I John

---

that shone temporarily from Moses' face is exceeded and surpassed by the glory that is given to Christians, whose souls can be united with Grace forever: *If the ministry of death, engraved in letters on stone, was accompanied by such glory that the sons of Israel could not bear to gaze at the face of Moses because of the glory, transitory though it was, that shone from it, then how much greater must the glory be that accompanies the ministry of the Spirit?... Indeed, what once seemed full of glory now seems to have no glory at all, because it is outshone by a glory that is so much greater. If what was transitory came with glory, what endures will be far more glorious* (II Cor. 3:7–11). Commenting on this passage of Scripture, St. Macarius the Great writes: "St. Paul says 'transitory' because it was Moses' mortal body that shone with the glory of light.... A little later he affirms that the everlasting and immortal glory of the Spirit shines even now with immortal and indestructible power in the immortal inner being of the saints: *With unveiled face we all*—all, that is to say, who through perfect faith are born in the Spirit—*reflect as in a mirror the glory of the Lord, and are transfigured into the same image from glory to glory, through the Lord Who is the Spirit* (II Cor. 3:18). The words with *unveiled face* indicate the [unveiled] soul; St. Paul adds that when one turns back to the Lord the veil is taken off, and that the Lord is the Spirit. By this he clearly shows that from the time of Adam's transgression a veil of darkness has encroached upon mankind and has covered the soul. But we believe that through the illumination of the Spirit this veil is now removed from truly faithful and saintly souls. It was for this reason that Christ came; and to those who truly believe in Him God has given the Grace to attain to this measure of holiness" (*Philokalia*, vol. 3, pp. 347–48).—3RD ED.

2:15–16). Sin is also present in evil spirits who have no flesh at all. In Sacred Scripture the word "flesh" signifies a condition of not being reborn, a condition opposed to being reborn in Christ: *That which is born of the flesh is flesh, and that which is born of the Spirit is spirit* (John 3:6). Of course, this is not to deny that a whole series of passions and sinful inclinations originate in bodily nature, which Sacred Scripture also shows (Romans, chap. 7).

Thus, original sin is understood by Orthodox theology as a sinful inclination which has entered into mankind and become its spiritual disease.[15]

---

[15] Perhaps no doctrine of the Orthodox Church has caused such heated discussions and misunderstandings in our day as has this doctrine of original or ancestral sin. The misunderstandings usually occur either from the desire to define the doctrine too precisely, or from overreactions to this over-definition. The expressions of the early Fathers in general (apart from Blessed Augustine in the West) do not go into the "how" of this matter, but simply state: "When Adam had transgressed, his sin reached unto all men" (St. Athanasius the Great, *Four Discourses Against the Arians* 1.51; NPNF, p. 336).

Some Orthodox Christians have mistakenly defended the Augustinian notion of "original guilt"—that is, that all men have inherited the guilt of Adam's sin—and others, going to the opposite extreme, have denied altogether the inheritance of sinfulness from Adam. Fr. Michael rightly points out, in his balanced presentation, that from Adam we have indeed inherited our tendency towards sin, together with the death and corruption that are now part of our sinful nature; but we have not inherited the guilt of Adam's personal sin.

The term "original sin" itself comes from Blessed Augustine's treatise *De Peccato Originale* [On Original Sin], and a few people imagine that merely to use this term implies acceptance of Augustine's exaggerations of this doctrine. This, of course, need not be the case. [See p. 162, note 9 above.]

[The Latin exaggeration of the doctrine may be seen to have derived, at least in part, from a Latin mistranslation of Romans 5:12.] The King James Version rightly translates Romans 5:12: "And so death passed upon all men, *for that all have sinned.*" The Latin translation of the latter clause, *"in whom* all have sinned," overstates the doctrine and might be interpreted to imply that all men are *guilty* of Adam's sin.

Chapter 6

God and the Salvation of Mankind

THE ECONOMY OF OUR SALVATION

*B*LESSED *be the God and Father of our Lord Jesus Christ, Who hath blessed us with all spiritual blessings in heavenly places in Christ: According as He hath chosen us in Him before the foundation of the world, that we should be holy and without blame before Him in love: Having predestined us unto the adoption of children by Jesus Christ to Himself, according to the good pleasure of His will, to the praise of the glory of His Grace, wherein He hath made us accepted in the Beloved: In Whom we have redemption through His blood, the forgiveness of sins, according to the riches of His Grace, wherein He hath abounded toward us in all wisdom and prudence, having made known unto us the mystery of His will, according to His good pleasure, which He hath purposed in Himself: That in the dispensation of the fullness of times He might gather together in one all things in Christ, both which are in heaven, and which are on earth* (Eph. 1:3–10).

For God so loved the world, that He gave His only begotten Son, that whosoever believeth in Him should not perish, but have everlasting life (John 3:16; the conversation with Nicodemus).

But God, Who is rich in mercy, for His great love wherewith He loved us, even when we were dead in sins, hath quickened us together with Christ (Eph. 2:4–5).

Herein is love, not that we loved God but that He loved us, and sent His Son to be the propitiation for our sins…. We love Him, because He first loved us (I John 4:10, 19).

God, in foreknowledge of the fall of man, foreordained the salva-

170

tion of men, even *before the foundation of the world* (Eph. 1:4). The word of God calls the Saviour the Lamb of God *foreordained before the foundation of the world* (I Peter 1:20).

THE PREPARATION OF THE HUMAN RACE TO RECEIVE THE SAVIOUR

But when the fullness of the time was come, God sent forth His Son, made of a woman, made under the law, to redeem them that were under the law, that we might receive the adoption of sons (Gal. 4:4–5).

In what consists this "fullness of time" which was ordained for the work of redemption? In the verses which precede the quoted words of the Apostle Paul in the Epistle to the Galatians, the Apostle speaks of the time before the coming of the Saviour as being *when we were children* (Gal. 4:3). Thus, he calls the period of the Old Testament "childhood," the time of upbringing, the guidance of children under the law of Moses; while the coming of the Saviour is the end of "childhood."

We can understand the significance of this preparatory period if we are guided by the parable of the *Prodigal Son*. The father sorrowed over the departure from his house of his beloved son. However, not violating the dignity and freedom of his son, he waited until the son, having experienced the bitterness of evil and recalled the goodness of life in his father's house, himself became homesick for the father's house and opened his soul for the father's love. Thus it was with the human race also. *My soul thirsteth after Thee like a waterless land* (Ps. 142:6) could have been said by the best part of mankind; it had become a "thirsty land," having tasted to the dregs the bitterness of estrangement from God.

The Lord did not abandon men, did not turn utterly away, but from the moment of the fall into sin led them toward the future salvation.

1. Having cut off the criminality of the original mankind by means of the Flood, the Lord chose first from the descendants of Noah, who had been saved from the Flood, a single race for the preservation of piety and faith in the one true God, and likewise of faith in

the coming Saviour. This was the race of Abraham, Isaac and Jacob, and then the whole Hebrew people. In His care for His chosen people, God led them out of slavery, preserved them in the desert, settled them in a land flowing with milk and honey; He made covenants—the covenant of circumcision and the covenant of the law of Sinai; He sent them judges and prophets, warned them, chastised them, and again had mercy, leading them out of the Babylonian captivity; and finally, from their midst He prepared a chosen one, who became the Mother of the Son of God.

The chosenness of the Hebrew people was confirmed by the Lord Jesus Christ when He said to the Samaritan woman that *salvation is of the Jews* (John 4:22). The writings of the Apostles testify abundantly to the same thing: the speeches of the first martyr Stephen and the Apostle Peter in the book of Acts, the Epistles of the Apostle Paul to the Romans and Galatians, and other places in Sacred Scripture.

2. Further, preparation for the reception of the Saviour consisted of (*a*) the comforting promises of God, and (*b*) the prophecies of the prophets concerning His coming.

a) *The promises of God* began in Paradise. The words of the Lord to the serpent concerning "the Seed of the woman" possess a mystical significance: *And I will put enmity between thee and the woman, and between thy seed and her seed; it shall bruise thy head, and thou shalt bruise his heel* (Gen. 3:15). The promise given here concerning the Seed of the woman became even clearer for the chosen ones of faith with the increase of prophecies about the Saviour Who Himself would endure suffering from the violence of the devil (Ps. 21), and strike him down: *And the great dragon was cast out, that old serpent, called the devil, and Satan, which deceiveth the whole world; he was cast out into the earth, and his angels were cast out with him* (Apoc. 12:9).

Further, there was the promise to Abraham: *And in thy seed shall all the nations of the earth be blessed* (Gen. 22:18)—a promise repeated to Isaac and Jacob (Gen. 26:4; 28:14). Its authentic significance was also gradually revealed to the Jews, during the period of their captivities and other misfortunes, as the promise of a Saviour of the world.

b) *Prophecies:* the blessing of Judah. The Patriarch Jacob, in blessing one of his sons just before his death, uttered an even more definite prophecy concerning the Saviour: *A ruler shall not fail from Judah, nor a prince from his loins, until there come the thing stored up for him* (in the Hebrew: *until there come a reconciler*); *and he is the expectation of nations* (Gen. 49:10, Septuagint). In other words, the authority of the tribe of Judah shall not cease until the Reconciler, the hope of the nations, comes; and consequently, the termination of the authority of the tribe of Judah will be a clear sign of the coming of the Saviour. The ancient Jewish teachers saw in the "Reconciler" the awaited Messiah, to whom they applied this name (in Hebrew *Shiloh*, the Reconciler).

Another prophecy consists of the words of Moses to his people: *Thy Lord thy God will raise up unto thee a prophet from the midst of thee, of thy brethren, like unto me; unto him ye shall hearken* (Deut. 18:15). After Moses there were many great prophets among the Hebrews, but to none of them were the words of Moses referred. And the same book of Deuteronomy testifies of the time close to Moses: *And there arose not a prophet since in Israel like unto Moses* (Deut. 34:10). The Lord Jesus Christ Himself referred the words of Moses to Himself: *For had ye believed Moses, ye would have believed Me: for he wrote of Me* (John 5:46).

Then came numerous prophecies in the form of prefigurations in the Psalms, of which the most expressive is Psalm 21, which the ancient rabbis recognized as a hymn of the Messiah. It includes a depiction of the severe and tormenting sufferings which the Saviour bore upon the Cross: *O God, my God, attend to me; why hast Thou forsaken me?... All that look upon me have laughed me to scorn; they have spoken with their lips and have wagged their heads: He hoped in the Lord; let Him deliver him.... I have been poured out like water, and scattered are all my bones.... They have parted my garments amongst themselves, and for my vesture have they cast lots....* Near the end of the Psalm are these words which concern the triumph of the Church: *In the great church will I confess Thee.... The poor shall eat and be filled.... Their hearts shall live for ever and ever.*

A number of other Psalms also contain such prophecies or prefigurations. Some of these proclaim the sufferings of the Saviour

(Psalms 39, 68, 108, 40, 15, 8), while others proclaim His glory (Psalms 2, 109, 44, 67, 117, 96, 94).

Finally, closer to the end of the Old Testament period, numerous prophecies appear in the books of the so-called major and minor prophets, and these ever more clearly reveal the imminent coming of the Son of God. They speak of the Forerunner of the Lord, of the time, place, and conditions of the Saviour's birth, of His spiritual-bodily image (His meekness, humility, and other features), of the events preceding the betrayal of the Lord, of His sufferings and Resurrection, of the descent of the Holy Spirit, of the character of the New Testament, and of other aspects of the Lord's coming.

Among these prophecies a special place belongs to the fifty-third chapter of the Prophet Isaiah, which gives an image of the Saviour's sufferings on the Cross. Here is how Isaiah prefigures the redeeming sufferings of the Messiah, Christ: *Who hath believed our report? and to Whom is the arm of the Lord revealed? For He shall grow up before Him as a tender plant, and as a root out of a dry ground: He hath no form nor comeliness; and when we shall see Him, there is no beauty that we should desire Him. He is despised and rejected of men; a man of sorrows, and acquainted with grief: and we hid as it were our faces from Him; He was despised, and we esteemed Him not. Surely He hath borne our griefs, and carried our sorrows: yet we did esteem Him stricken, smitten of God, and afflicted. But He was wounded for our transgressions, He was bruised for our iniquities: the chastisement of our peace was upon Him; and with His stripes we are healed. All we like sheep have gone astray; we have turned every one to his own way; and the Lord hath laid on Him the iniquity of us all. He was oppressed, and He was afflicted, yet He opened not His mouth: He is brought as a lamb to the slaughter, and as a sheep before her shearers is dumb, so He openeth not His mouth. He was taken from prison and from judgment: and who shall declare His generation? for He was cut off out of the land of the living: for the transgression of my people was He stricken.... And He was numbered with the transgressors; and He bare the sin of many, and made intercession for the transgressors* (Is. 53:1–8, 12, KJV; the Septuagint text is only slightly different).

In the Prophet Daniel we read the revelation given to him by the

Archangel Gabriel concerning the seventy weeks (490 years)—the period of time from the decree for the restoration of Jerusalem before Christ, until His death and the cessation of the Old Testament, that is, the cessation of sacrifices in the Temple of Jerusalem (Dan. 9:24–27).

These promises and prophecies, first of all, gave support to the chosen people, especially during the difficult periods of its life; they gave support to its firmness, faith, and hope. Secondly, they prepared the people so that they would be able to recognize by these prophecies that the time of the promise was near, and that they might recognize the Saviour Himself in the form given Him by the prophets.

Thanks to these prophecies, as the time of the Saviour's coming neared, the expectation of Him was intense and vigilant among pious Jews. We see this in the Gospels. This is revealed in the expectation of Symeon the God-receiver, to whom it was declared that he would not see death until he had beheld Christ the Lord (Luke 2:26). It is revealed in the reply of the Samaritan woman to the Saviour: *I know that Messiah cometh, which is called Christ: when He is come, He will tell us all things* (John 4:25). It is revealed in the questions of the Jews who came to John the Baptist, "Art thou the Christ?" (John 1:20–25); in the words addressed by Andrew, the first-called Apostle, after his first meeting with Christ, to his brother Simon: *We have found the Messiah* (John 1:41), and likewise in the similar words of Philip to Nathaniel in the evangelist's account of their calling to the apostleship (John 1:44–45). Another testimony to it is the people's attitude at the time of the Lord's entrance into Jerusalem.

3. To what has been said above must be added the fact that it was not only the Jews who were being prepared for the reception of the Saviour, but also the whole world, although to a lesser degree.

Even in the pagan world there were preserved—even though in a distorted form—traditions concerning the origin and originally blessed condition of mankind (the Golden Age), concerning the fall of our first ancestors in Paradise, concerning the Flood as a consequence of man's corruption, and—most important of all—the tradition of a coming Redeemer of the human race and the expectation of His coming, as may be seen in the works of Plato, Plutarch, Virgil, Ovid,

Strabo, and likewise in the history of the religions of the ancient world (for example, the prediction of the sibyls,[1] of which we read in Cicero and Virgil).

The pagans found themselves in contact with the chosen people by means of mutual visits, sea voyages, wars, the captivities of the Jews (especially the Assyrian and Babylonian captivities), and trade, and thanks to the dispersion of the Jews into the various countries of the three parts of the old world towards the end of the Old Testament period. Under these conditions, the light of faith in the One God and hope in a Redeemer could be spread to other peoples also.

Over two centuries prior to Christ's Nativity, a translation of the sacred books of the Hebrews had been made into Greek, and many pagan scholars, writers, and educated people in general made use of it; there are various testimonies of this, particularly among the ancient Christian writers.

From the Sacred Scripture we know that apart from the chosen people there were other people also who had preserved faith in the One God, and were on the way to the acceptance of piety. We learn of this in the account of Melchisedek in the book of Genesis (Gen. 14:18); in the history of Job; in the account of the father-in-law of Moses, Jethro of Midian (Exodus, chap. 18); in the account of Balaam, who prophecied concerning the Messiah (*I shall see Him, but not now; I shall behold Him, but not nigh*—Num. 24:17); and in the repentance of the Ninevites after the preaching of Jonah. The readiness of many of the best people in the pagan world for the reception of the good news of the Saviour is also attested to by the fact that by the preaching of the Apostles the Church of Christ was quickly planted in every country of the pagan world, and that Christ Himself sometimes encountered in the pagans such faith as He did not find in the Jews themselves.

But when the fullness of the time was come (Gal. 4:4), or, in other words:

---

[1] The sibyls were pagan seeresses whose oracles and predictions were highly regarded in pagan Rome. These oracles referred for the most part to the destiny of peoples, kingdoms, and rulers, and some of them hinted at the coming of Christ.

—when the human race, following after Adam, had tasted in full measure, spiritually speaking, of the tree of the knowledge of good and evil, and had come to know in experience the sweetness of doing good and the bitterness of evil-doing;

—when for the most part mankind had reached an extreme degree of impiety and corruption;

—when the best, although smallest, part of humanity had an especially great thirst, longing, and desire to see the promised Redeemer, Reconciler, Saviour, Messiah;

—when, finally, by God's will, the political conditions were ready because the whole of the civilized part of humanity had been united under the authority of Rome—something which strongly favored the spreading of faith and the Church of Christ;

—then *the promised and expected Son of God came to earth.*

THE INCARNATION OF THE SON OF GOD

In the beginning was the Word, and the Word was with God, and the Word was God. The same was in the beginning with God. All things were made by Him; and without Him was not anything made that was made.... And the Word was made flesh, and dwelt among us ... (John 1:1–3, 14).

Thus does the Evangelist John announce the glad tidings and theologize in the first lines of his Gospel. The Orthodox Church places this account at the head of all the Gospel readings, offering it to us at the Divine Liturgy on the day of holy Pascha, and beginning the yearly cycle of readings from the Gospel with this one.

Great is the mystery of godliness: God was manifest in the flesh (I Tim. 3:16).

The unutterable, unknowable, invisible, unattainable God, the Second Person of the Holy Trinity, became man in the form of the God-Man, the Lord Jesus Christ, and dwelt among men on earth.

The preaching of the God-Manhood of the incarnate Son of God constitutes the content of the words of the Saviour Himself, the content of the whole message of good tidings announced by the Apostles,

177

the essence of the four Gospels and all of the Apostolic writings, the foundation of Christianity, and the foundation of the teaching of the Church.

The Lord Jesus Christ: True God

The good tidings of the Gospel are the good tidings of the incarnate *Son of God* Who became man, having come down from heaven to earth.

Faith in Jesus Christ—that He is the Son of God—is the firm foundation or *rock* of the Church, according to the Lord's own words: *Upon this rock I will build My Church* (Matt. 16:18).

With these good tidings the Apostle Mark begins his account: *The beginning of the Gospel of Jesus Christ, the Son of God* (Mark 1:1).

With this same truth of faith the Evangelist John concludes the main text of his Gospel: *But these are written, that ye might believe that Jesus is the Christ, the Son of God; and that believing ye might have life through His name* (John 20:31; the last verse of the next to the last chapter)—that is, the preaching of the Divinity of Jesus Christ was the aim of the whole Gospel.

That holy thing which shall be born of thee shall be called the Son of God (Luke 1:35)—the Archangel Gabriel addressed the Virgin Mary.

At the Baptism of the Saviour these words were heard: *This is My beloved Son;* the same thing was repeated at the Lord's Transfiguration (Matt. 3:17, 17:5).

Simon confessed, *Thou art the Christ, the Son of the living God* (Matt. 16:16), and this confession served for the promise that the Church of Christ would be built upon the rock of this confession.

The Lord Jesus Christ Himself testified that He is the Son of God the Father: *All things are delivered unto Me of My Father: and no man knoweth the Son, but the Father; neither knoweth any man the Father, save the Son, and he to whomsoever the Son will reveal Him* (Matt. 11:27). Here Christ speaks of Himself as the only Son of the only God the Father.

In order that the words, "the Son of God," might not be understood in a metaphorical or conditional sense, the Sacred Scripture joins to them the expression, "only begotten"—that is, the Only One begotten of the Father: *And the Word was made flesh and dwelt among us (and we beheld His glory, the glory as of the only begotten of the Father), full of grace and truth* (John 1:14; see also John 1:18).

For God so loved the world, that He gave His only begotten Son, that whosoever believeth in Him should not perish, but have everlasting life (John 3:16).

Likewise, the Sacred Scripture uses the word "true," calling Christ the True Son of the True God: *And we know that the Son of God is come, and hath given us an understanding, that we may know Him that is true; and we are in Him that is true, even in His Son Jesus Christ. This is the true God, and eternal life* (I John 5:20).

Similarly, the word "His own" is used in connection with the Son of God: *He Who spared not His own* (in the Greek, *idion*) *Son, but delivered Him up for us all, how shall He not with Him also freely give us all things?* (Rom. 8:32).

The only begotten Son of God is True God even while in human flesh: *Whose* (that is, the Israelites) *are the fathers, and of whom as concerning the flesh Christ came, Who is over all, God blessed for ever. Amen* (Rom. 9:5).

Thus, all the fullness of Divinity remains in the human form of Christ: *For in Him dwelleth all the fullness of the Godhead bodily* (Col. 2:9).

The First Ecumenical Council of Nicaea was convoked for the confirmation of this truth in the clear awareness of all Christians, as the foundation of the Christian faith, and for this purpose it composed the Symbol of Faith (the Creed) of the Ecumenical Church.

The Human Nature of the Lord Jesus Christ

Being perfect God, Christ the Saviour is at the same time also perfect Man.

As Man, Christ was born when for Mary, His mother, *the days were accomplished that she should be delivered* (Luke 2:6). He gradually *grew,*

179

and waxed strong in spirit (Luke 2:40). As Mary's son, He *was subject unto* her and her spouse (Luke 2:51). As Man, He was baptized of John in the Jordan; He went about the cities and villages with the preaching of salvation; not once before His Resurrection did he encounter a need to prove His humanity to anyone. He experienced hunger and thirst, the need for rest and sleep, and He suffered painful feelings and physical sufferings.

Living the physical life natural to a man, the Lord also lived the life of the soul as a man. He strengthened His spiritual powers with fasting and prayer. He experienced human feelings: joy, anger, sorrow. He expressed them outwardly: *He was troubled in spirit* (John 13:21), showed dissatisfaction, shed tears—for example, at the death of Lazarus. The Gospels reveal to us a powerful spiritual battle in the garden of Gethsemane on the night before He was taken under guard: *My soul is exceeding sorrowful, even unto death* (Matt. 26:38)—thus did the Lord describe the state of His soul to His disciples.

The rational, conscious human will of Jesus Christ unfailingly placed all human strivings in submission to the Divine will in Himself. A strikingly evident image of this is given in the Passion of the Lord, which began in the garden of Gethsemane: *O My Father, if it be possible, let this cup pass from Me: nevertheless, not as I will, but as Thou wilt* (Matt. 26:39). *Not my will, but Thine, be done* (Luke 22:42).

Concerning the truth of the Saviour's fully human nature, the Holy Fathers of the Church speak thus:

St. Cyril of Alexandria: "If the nature which He received had not had a human mind, then the one who entered into battle with the devil was God Himself; and it was therefore God who gained the victory. But if God was victorious, then I, who did not participate in this victory at all, do not receive any benefit from it. Therefore I cannot rejoice over it, for I would then be boasting of someone else's trophies."

St. Cyril of Jerusalem: "If the becoming man was a phantom, then salvation is a dream." Other Holy Fathers expressed themselves similarly.

The Church's Battle with Errors concerning the Divinity and Humanity of Jesus Christ

The Church has always strictly guarded the correct teaching of the two natures of the Lord Jesus Christ, seeing in this an indispensable condition of faith, without which salvation is impossible.

The errors with regard to this teaching have been various, but they may be reduced to two groups: In one, we see the denial or lessening of the Divinity of Jesus Christ; in the other we see a denial or lessening of His humanity.

A. As was already mentioned in the chapter on the Second Person of the Holy Trinity, the spirit of the Jewish disbelief in the Divinity of Christ, the denial of His Divinity, was reflected in the Apostolic age in the heresy of Ebion, from whom these heretics received the name of Ebionites. A similiar teaching was spread in the 3rd century by Paul of Samosata, who was denounced by two councils of Antioch. Slightly different was the false teaching of Arius and the various Arian currents in the 4th century. They thought that Christ was not a simple man, but the Son of God, created rather than begotten, and the most perfect of all the created spirits. The heresy of Arius was condemned at the First Ecumenical Council in 325, and Arianism was refuted in detail by the most renowned Fathers of the Church during the course of the 4th and 5th centuries.

In the 5th century there arose the heresy of Theodore of Mopsuestia, which was supported by Nestorius, Archbishop of Constantinople. Those who held this heresy acknowledged the Lord Jesus Christ to be only the "bearer" of the Divine principle, and therefore they ascribed to the Most Holy Virgin the title of *Christotokos* but not Theotokos—"Birthgiver of Christ," but not "Birthgiver of God." According to Nestorius, Jesus Christ united within Himself two natures and two different persons, Divine and human, which touched each other but were separate; and after His birth He was Man, but not God. St. Cyril of Alexandria stepped forward as the chief accuser of

Nestorius. Nestorianism was accused and condemned by the Third Ecumenical Council (431).

B. The other group erred in denying or lessening the humanity of Jesus Christ. The first heretics of this sort were the Docetists, who acknowledged the flesh and matter to be an evil principle with which God could not be joined; therefore, they considered that Christ's flesh was only pretended or "seeming" (Greek: *dokeo*, "to seem").

At the time of the Ecumenical Councils, Apollinarius, Bishop of Laodicea, taught incorrectly concerning the humanity of the Saviour. Although he acknowledged the reality of the Incarnation of the Son of God in Jesus Christ, he affirmed that His humanity was incomplete: affirming the tripartite composition of human nature, he taught that Christ had a human soul and body, but that His spirit (or "mind") was not human but Divine, and that this comprised the Saviour's Divine Nature, which abandoned Him at the moment of His sufferings on the Cross.

Refuting these opinions, the Holy Fathers explained that it is the free human spirit that comprises the basic essence of man. It is this which, possessing freedom, was subjected to the fall and, being defeated, was in need of salvation. Therefore the Saviour, in order to restore fallen man, Himself possessed this essential part of human nature; or, to speak more precisely, He possessed not only the lower but also the higher side of the human soul.[2]

In the 5th century there was another heresy which lessened the humanity of Christ: that of the *Monophysites*. It arose among the monks of Alexandria and was the opposite of and a reaction against Nestorianism, which had lessened the Saviour's Divine Nature. The Monophysites considered that in Jesus Christ the principle of the flesh had been swallowed up by the spiritual principle, the human by the Divine, and therefore they acknowledged in Christ only *one* nature. Monophysitism, also called the heresy of Eutyches, was rejected at the Fourth Ecumenical Council, that of Chalcedon (451).

---

[2] Here again, the higher side of the soul refers to the *nous*.—3RD ED.

A corollary of the rejected heresy of the Monophysites was the teaching of the Monothelites (from the Greek *thelima,* "desire" or "will"), who set forth the idea that in Christ there is only one *will.* Starting from a fear that acknowledging a human will in Christ would permit the idea of two persons in Him, the Monothelites acknowledged only one, Divine will in Christ. But, as the Fathers of the Church have explained, such a teaching abolished the whole labor for the salvation of mankind by Christ, since this consisted of the free subjection of the human will to the Divine will: *Not My will, but Thine, be done,* the Lord prayed. This error was rejected by the Sixth Ecumenical Council (681).

Both of these kinds of error, which were overcome in the history of the ancient Church, continue to find refuge for themselves partly in a hidden form but in part openly in the Protestantism of the last centuries. Protestantism, therefore, to a large extent refuses to recognize the dogmatic decrees of the Ecumenical Councils.

The Manner of the Union of the Two Natures in the Person of the Lord Jesus Christ

At three Ecumenical Councils—the Third (of Ephesus, against Nestorius), the Fourth (of Chalcedon, against Eutyches), and the Sixth (the third one of Constantinople, against the Monothelites)—the Church revealed the dogma of the one Hypostasis of the Lord Jesus Christ in two natures, Divine and human; and with two wills, the Divine will and the human will, the latter being entirely in subjection to the former.

The Third Ecumenical Council, that of Ephesus in 431, approved the exposition of faith of St. Cyril of Alexandria concerning the fact that "the Divinity and humanity composed a single Hypostasis of the Lord Jesus Christ by means of the unutterable and inexplicable union of these distinct natures in one."

The Fourth Ecumenical Council, that of Chalcedon in 451, putting an end to Monophysitism, precisely formulated the manner of the union of the two natures in the one Person of the Lord Jesus

Christ, acknowledging the very essence of this union to be mystical and inexplicable. The definition of the Council of Chalcedon reads as follows:

"Following the Holy Fathers we teach with one voice that the Son and our Lord Jesus Christ is to be confessed as one and the same (Person), that He is perfect in Godhead and perfect in manhood, very God and very man, of a reasonable soul and (human) body, one in Essence with the Father as touching His Godhead, and one in essence with us as touching His manhood; made in all things like unto us, as touching sin only excepted; begotten of His Father before the world according to His Godhead, but in the last days for us men and for our salvation born of the Virgin Mary the Theotokos, according to His manhood. This one and the same Jesus Christ, the only begotten Son, must be confessed to be in two natures, unconfusedly, immutably, indivisibly, inseparably ... not separated or divided into two persons, but one and the same Son and only begotten God the Word, our Lord Jesus Christ, as the prophets of old time have spoken concerning Him, and as the Lord Jesus Christ hath taught us, and as the Creed of the Fathers hath delivered to us" (*Seven Ecumenical Councils*, NPNF, pp. 264–65).

ꙗ The manner of this union of the natures is expressed in the Chalcedonian definition in the words: "Unconfusedly and immutably." The Divine and human natures in Christ do not mingle and are not converted one into the other.

"Indivisibly, inseparably." Both natures are forever united, not forming two persons which are only morally united, as Nestorius taught. They are inseparable from the moment of conception (that is, the man was not formed first, and then God was united to him; but God the Word, descending into the womb of Mary the Virgin, formed a living human flesh for Himself). These natures were also inseparable at the time of the Saviour's sufferings on the Cross, at the moment of death, at the Resurrection and after the Ascension, and unto the ages of ages. In His deified flesh the Lord Jesus Christ will also come at His Second Coming.

Finally, the Sixth Ecumenical Council, in the year 681 (the third Council of Constantinople), decreed that there be confessed two wills in Christ and two operations: "Two natural wills not contrary the one to the other ... but His human will follows and that not as resisting and reluctant, but rather as subject to His Divine and omnipotent will" (from the "Definition of Faith" of the Sixth Ecumenical Council, *Seven Ecumenical Councils*, NPNF, p. 345).

The human nature—or, in the terminology of the Holy Fathers, the "flesh of the Lord"—united with the Godhead, was enriched by Divine powers without losing anything of its own attributes, and became a participant of the Divine dignity but not of the Divine Nature. The flesh, being deified, was not destroyed, "but continued in its own state and nature," as the Sixth Ecumenical Council expressed it (*loc. cit.*).[3]

Corresponding to this, the *human will* in Christ was not changed

---

[3] St. John Damascene: "The word *destruction* (*phthora*) has two meanings. Thus, it means human sufferings such as hunger, thirst, weariness, piercing with nails, death—that is, separation of the soul from the body—and the like. In this sense, we say that the Lord's body was destructible, because He endured all these things freely. Destruction, however, also means the complete dissolution of the body and its reduction to the elements of which it was composed. By many this is more generally called *corruption* (*diaphthora*). This the Lord's body did not experience, as the Prophet David says: *For Thou wilt not abandon my soul in hades, nor wilt Thou suffer Thy Holy One to see corruption* (Ps. 15:10).

"Therefore, it is impious to say with the insane Julian and Gaianus [Julian of Halicarnassus and Gaianus of Alexandria, originators of the Aphthartodocetist heresy] that before the Resurrection the Lord's body was indestructible in the first sense. For, if it was thus incorruptible, then it was not consubstantial with us, and the things such as hunger, the thirst, the nails, the piercing of the side, and death which the Gospel says happened did not really happen, but only seemed to. But, if they only seemed to happen, then the mystery of the Incarnation is a hoax and a stage trick; it was in appearance and not in truth that He was made man and in appearance and not in truth that we have been saved. But far be it, and let those who say this have no part in salvation. We, however, have gained and shall obtain the true salvation. Moreover, in the second sense of the word destruction, we confess that the Lord's body was indestructible, that is to say, incorruptible, even as it has been handed down to us by the inspired Fathers. Nevertheless, we do say that after the Saviour's Resurrection the body of the Lord is indestructible in the first sense, too. And through His body the Lord has granted the resurrection and consequent incorruptibility to our body, also, Himself becoming the firstfruits of the resurrection and incorruptibility and impassibility" (*Exact Exposition* 3.28; FC, pp. 333–34).—3RD ED.

into the Divine will and was not destroyed, but remained whole and operative. The Lord completely subjected it to the Divine will, which in Him is one with the will of the Father: *I came down from heaven, not to do Mine own will, but the will of Him that sent Me* (John 6:38).

In his *Exact Exposition of the Orthodox Faith*, St. John Damascene speaks thus of the union of the two natures in the person of the Lord Jesus Christ:

"Just as we confess that the Incarnation was brought about without transformation or change, so also do we hold that the deification of the flesh was brought about. For the Word neither overstepped the bounds of His own Divinity nor the Divine prerogatives belonging to it just because He was made flesh, and when the flesh was made Divine it certainly did not change its own nature or its natural properties. For, even after the union, the natures remained unmingled and their properties unimpaired. Moreover, by reason of its most unalloyed union with the Word, that is to say, the hypostatic union, the Lord's flesh was enriched with the Divine operations but in no way suffered any impairment of its natural properties. For not by its own operation does the flesh do Divine works, but by the Word united to it, and through it the Word shows His own operation. Thus, the steel which has been heated burns, not because it has a naturally acquired power of burning, but because it has acquired it from its union with the fire" (*Exact Exposition* 3.17; FC, pp. 316–17). The union of the two natures in Christ is defined by St. John Damascene as "mutually immanent" (*Exact Exposition* 3.7; FC, p. 284).

Concerning the manner of the union of the two natures in Christ, one must of course have in mind that the Councils and Church Fathers had only one aim: to defend the faith from the errors of heretics. They did not strive to reveal entirely the very essence of this union, that is, the mystical transfiguration of human nature in Christ, concerning which we confess that in His human flesh Christ sits at the right hand of God the Father, that in this flesh He will come with glory to judge the world and His Kingdom will have no end, and that believers receive communion of His life-giving Flesh and Blood in all times throughout the whole world.

The Sinlessness of the Human Nature of Jesus Christ

The Fifth Ecumenical Council condemned the false teaching of Theodore of Mopsuestia, which stated that the Lord Jesus Christ was not deprived of inward temptations and the battle with passions. If the word of God says that the Son of God came *in the likeness of sinful flesh* (Rom. 8:3), it is thereby expressing the idea that this flesh was true human flesh, but not sinful flesh; rather, it was completely pure of every sin and corruption, both of the ancestral sin and of voluntary sin.[4] In His earthly life the Lord was free of any sinful desire, of every inward temptation; for the human nature in Him does not exist separately, but is united hypostatically to the Divinity.

The Unity of the Hypostasis of Christ

With the union in Christ the God-Man of two natures, there remains in Him one Person, one Personality, one Hypostasis. This is important to know because in general oneness of consciousness and

---

[4] When the Son of God became incarnate, He voluntarily assumed the passibility and mortality that were the consequences of Adam's sin (see p. 185, note 3 above), while remaining Himself wholly sinless. As St. Maximus the Confessor asserts, this "sin" transmitted from Adam (i.e., suffering and death) is itself innocent and blameless (*Ad Thalassium* 42, in St. Maximus, *The Cosmic Mystery of Jesus Christ*, p. 119). Thus, St. Paul could say of Christ: *He* (God) *hath made Him Who knew no sin to be sin for us* (II Cor. 5:21).

Christ did *not* assume the corruption of human nature and inclination toward sin that all other people have inherited from Adam. In this sense, Christ remained free of ancestral sin. While being *passible* (that is, subject to suffering), He was completely free of sinful passions and of the disease of sin.

St. Gregory Palamas writes concerning the sinlessness of Christ: "Having conceived, she [the Holy Virgin] gave birth, and it was as if the Victor over the devil, being both man and God, had drawn to Himself the root of the human race but not its sin (cf. Heb. 4:15). For He was the only one neither shapen in iniquity nor conceived in sin (cf. Ps. 50:5), that is to say, in the fleshly pleasure, passion, and unclean thoughts that belong to our nature defiled by transgression. The point of this was that the nature He assumed should be wholly pure and unsullied, so that He Himself would not need to be purified, but would in His wisdom accept everything for our sake" (*Homilies*, vol. 1, p. 182).—3RD ED.

self-awareness is dependent on oneness of personality. In the confession of faith of the Council of Chalcedon we read: "Not separated or divided into two persons, but one and the same Son and only begotten God the Word...." The Divine Hypostasis is inseparable in a single Hypostasis of the Word. This truth is expressed in the first chapter of the Gospel of John: *In the beginning was the Word, and the Word was with God, and the Word was God;* and further: *And the Word was made flesh, and dwelt among us* (John 1:1, 14). On this foundation, in some passages of Sacred Scripture human attributes are indicated as belonging to Christ *as God,* and Divine attributes are indicated as belonging to the same Christ *as man.* Thus, for example, in I Corinthians 2:8 it is said: *Had they known it, they would not have crucified the Lord of glory.* Here the Lord of glory—God—is called crucified (for the "King of Glory" is God, as we read in Psalm 23:10: *Who is this King of Glory? The Lord of hosts, He is the King of Glory*). The truth of the unity of the Hypostasis of Christ as a Divine Hypostasis is explained by St. John Damascene in the *Exact Exposition of the Orthodox Faith* (3.7–8).

The One Worship of Christ

To the Lord Jesus Christ as to one person, as the God-Man, it is fitting to give a single inseparable worship, both according to Divinity and according to humanity, precisely because both natures are inseparably united in Him. The decree of the Fathers of the Fifth Ecumenical Council (the Ninth Canon against Heretics) reads: "If anyone shall take the expression, Christ ought to be worshipped in His two natures, in the sense that he wishes to introduce thus two adorations, the one in special relation to God the Word and the other as pertaining to the Man ... and does not venerate, by one adoration, God the Word made man, together with His flesh, as the Holy Church has taught from the beginning: let him be anathema" (*Seven Ecumenical Councils*, NPNF, p. 314).

A Word on the Latin Cult of the "Heart of Jesus"

In connection with this decree of the Council it may be seen how out of harmony with the spirit and practice of the Church is the cult of the "Sacred Heart of Jesus" which has been introduced into the Roman Catholic Church. Although the above-cited decree of the Fifth Ecumenical Council touches only on the separate worship of the Divinity and the humanity of the Saviour, it still indirectly tells us that in general the veneration and worship of Christ should be directed to Him as a whole and not to parts of His Being; it must be one. Even if by "heart" we should understand the Saviour's love itself, still neither in the Old Testament nor in the New was there ever a custom to worship separately the love of God, or His wisdom, or His creative or providential power, or His sanctity. All the more must one say this concerning the parts of His bodily nature. There is something unnatural in the separation of the heart from the general bodily nature of the Lord for the purpose of prayer, contrition, and worship before Him. Even in the ordinary relationships of life, no matter how much a man might be attached to another—for example, a mother to a child—he would never refer his attachment to the heart of the beloved person, but will refer it to the given person as a whole.

DOGMAS CONCERNING THE MOST HOLY MOTHER OF GOD

Two dogmas concerning the Mother of God are bound up, in closest fashion, with the dogma of God the Word's becoming man. They are (*a*) her Ever-virginity, and (*b*) her name of Theotokos. They proceed immediately from the dogma of the unity of the Hypostasis of the Lord from the moment of His Incarnation—the Divine Hypostasis.

A. The Ever-Virginity of the Mother of God

The birth of the Lord Jesus Christ from a *Virgin* is testified to directly and deliberately by two Evangelists, Matthew and Luke. This dogma was entered into the Symbol of Faith of the First Ecumenical Council, where we read: *Who for the sake of us men and for our salvation came down from heaven and was incarnate by the Holy Spirit and the Virgin Mary and became man.* The *Ever-virginity* of the Mother of God is testified by her own words, handed down in the Gospel, where she expressed awareness of the immeasurable majesty and height of her chosenness: *My soul doth magnify the Lord.... For, behold, from henceforth all generations shall call me blessed.... For He that is mighty hath done to me great things; and holy is His name* (Luke 1:46–49).

The Most Holy Virgin preserved in her memory and in her heart both the announcement of the Archangel Gabriel and the inspired words of righteous Elizabeth when she was visited by Mary: *And whence is this to me, that the Mother of my Lord should come to me?* (Luke 1:43); both the prophecy of the righteous Symeon on meeting the Infant Jesus in the Temple, and the prophecy of the righteous Anna on the same day (Luke 2:25–38). In connection with the account of the shepherds of Bethlehem concerning the words of the angels to them, and of the singing of the angels, the Evangelist adds: *But Mary kept all these things, and pondered them in her heart* (Luke 2:19). The same Evangelist, having told of the conversation of the Most Holy Mother with the twelve-year-old Jesus after their visit to Jerusalem on the Feast of Pascha, ends his account with the words: *But His mother kept all these sayings in her heart* (Luke 2:51). The Evangelists speak also of the understanding of the majesty of her service in the world by the righteous Joseph, her espoused husband, whose actions were many times guided by an angel.

When the heretics and simple blasphemers refuse to acknowledge the Ever-virginity of the Mother of God on the grounds that the Evangelists mention the "brothers and sisters of Jesus,"[5] they are refuted by the following facts from the Gospel:

(*a*) In the Gospels there are named four "brothers" (James, Joses,

---

[5] Another verse of Scripture that some have used to argue against the Ever-virginity of the Mother of God is Matthew 1:25: *And* (Joseph) *knew her not until she had brought forth her firstborn son.* As the Orthodox Holy Fathers have pointed out, however, the word "until" does not signify that Mary remained a virgin only until a certain time. In the Sacred Scripture, the word "until" (*eos*) and words similar to it often signify eternity. For example, when Christ says, *Lo, I am with you always, even until* (*eos*) *the end of the world* (Matt. 28:20), we are obviously not to believe that Christ will cease to be with His disciples after the end of the world. See St. John Maximovitch, *The Orthodox Veneration of Mary the Birthgiver of God*, pp. 31–32, where other examples from Scripture are given.—3RD ED.

Simon and Jude), and there are also mentioned the "sisters" of Jesus—no fewer than three, as is evident in the words: *and His sisters, are they not ALL with us?* (Matt. 13:56).

On the other hand, (*b*) in the account of the journey to Jerusalem of the twelve-year-old boy Jesus, where there is mention of the *kinsfolk and acquaintances* (Luke 2:44) in the midst of whom they were seeking Jesus, and where it is likewise mentioned that Mary and Joseph every year journeyed from faraway Galilee to Jerusalem, no reason is given to think that there were present other younger children with Mary: it was thus that the first twelve years of the Lord's earthly life proceeded.

c) When, about twenty years after the above-mentioned journey, Mary stood at the Cross of the Lord, she was *alone,* and she was entrusted by her Divine Son to His disciple John; and *from that hour that disciple took her unto his own home* (John 19:27). Evidently, as the ancient Christians also understood it, the Evangelists speak either of "half" brothers and sisters or of cousins.[6]

B. The Most Holy Virgin Mary Is Theotokos

With the dogma of the Son of God's becoming man is closely bound up the naming of the Most Holy Virgin Mary as *Theotokos* (Birth-giver of God). By this name the Church confirms its faith that God the Word became Man truly and not merely in appearance; a faith that, in the Person of the Lord Jesus Christ, God was joined to Man from the very instant of His conception in the womb of the Virgin Mary, and that He, being perfect Man, is also perfect God.

At the same time the name of Theotokos is the highest name that exalts or glorifies the Virgin Mary.

---

[6] The generally accepted Orthodox tradition is that the "brothers" and "sisters" of the Lord are the children of Joseph by an earlier marriage. See Archbishop John Maximovitch, *The Orthodox Veneraton of the Mother of God* (Platina, Calif.: St. Herman Brotherhood, 1978), p. 24. [Revised edition: *The Orthodox Veneration of Mary the Birthgiver of God,* 1994, pp. 32–33.]

The name "Theotokos" has a direct foundation in Sacred Scripture. The Apostle Paul writes:

a) When the fullness of the time was come, God sent forth His Son, made of a woman (Gal. 4:4). Here is expressed the truth that a woman gave birth to the Son of God.

b) God was manifest in the flesh (I Tim. 3:16): the flesh was woven for God the Word by the Most Holy Virgin Mary.

At the meeting of the Virgin Mary, after the Annunciation, with the righteous Elizabeth, *Elizabeth was filled with the Holy Spirit, and she spake out with a loud voice, and said: Blessed art thou among women, and blessed is the fruit of thy womb. And whence is this to me, that the Mother of my Lord should come to me?... And blessed is she that believed: for there shall be a performance of those things which were told her from the Lord* (Luke 1:41–45). Thus Elizabeth, being filled with the Holy Spirit, calls Mary the Mother of the Lord, the God of Heaven; it is precisely the God of Heaven that she is here calling "Lord," as is clear from her further words: "She that believed ... those things which were told her from the Lord"—the Lord God.

Concerning the birth of God *from a virgin* the Old Testament Scriptures speak:

The Prophet Ezekiel writes of his vision: *Then said the Lord unto me: This gate shall be shut, it shall not be opened, and no man shall enter in by it; because the Lord the God of Israel hath entered in by it, therefore it shall be shut* (Ezek. 44:2).

The Prophet Isaiah prophesies: *Behold, a virgin shall conceive, and bear a son, and shall call His name Immanuel, which is to say: God is with us.... For unto us a Child is born, unto us a Son is given: and the government shall be upon His shoulder; and His name shall be called Messenger of Great Counsel, Wonderful, Counselor, the Mighty God, Potentate, the Prince of Peace, Father of the age to come* (Is. 7:14, 9:6, Septuagint; Matt. 1:23).

In the first centuries of the Church of Christ, the truth of God the Word's becoming man and His birth of the Virgin Mary was the catholic faith. Therefore, the Apostolic Fathers expressed themselves thus: "Our God Jesus Christ was in the womb of Mary"; "God took flesh of the Virgin Mary" (St. Ignatius the God-bearer, St. Irenaeus). Exactly the same expressions were used by Sts. Dionysius and Alexander of Alexandria (3rd and 4th centuries). The Fathers of the 4th century, Sts. Athanasius, Ephraim the Syrian, Cyril of Jerusalem, and Gregory of Nyssa, called the Most Holy Virgin the Theotokos.

In the 5th century, because of the heresy of Nestorius, the Church triumphantly confessed the Most Holy Virgin Mary to be Mother of God at the Third Ecumenical Council, accepting and confirming the following words of St. Cyril of Alexandria: "If anyone will not confess that Immanuel is very God, and that therefore the Holy Virgin is Theotokos, inasmuch as in the flesh she bore the Word of God made flesh: let him be anathema" (*Seven Ecumenical Councils*, NPNF, p. 206).

Blessed Theodoret also, who previously had been on friendly terms with Nestorius, when later condemning his stubbornness in heresy wrote: "The first stage in these new teachings of Nestorius was the opinion that the Holy Virgin, from whom God the Word took flesh and was born in the flesh, should not be acknowledged as Theotokos but only as Christotokos; whereas the ancient and most ancient proclaimers of the true Faith, in accordance with the Apostolic Tradition, had taught that the Mother of the Lord should be named and confessed to be Theotokos."

The Proclamation by the Roman Church of the Dogma of the Immaculate Conception and the Dogma of the Bodily Assumption of the Mother of God

The dogma of the Immaculate Conception was proclaimed by a Bull of Pope Pius IX in 1854. The definition of this dogma says that the Most Holy Virgin Mary at the moment of her conception was cleansed of ancestral sin. In essence this is a direct deduction from the Roman teaching on original sin. According to the Roman teaching, the burden of the sin of our first ancestors consists in the removal from mankind of a supernatural gift of grace. But here there arose a theological question: if mankind had been deprived of the gifts of grace, then how is one to understand the words of the Archangel addressed to Mary: "Rejoice, thou that art *full of Grace*, the Lord is with thee. *Blessed* art thou among women.... Thou hast found Grace with God" (Luke 1:28, 30)? One could only conclude that the Most Holy Virgin Mary had been removed from the general law of the "deprivation of grace" and of the guilt of the sin of Adam. And since her life was holy from her birth, consequently she received, in the form of an exception, a supernatural *gift*, a grace of sanctity, even before her birth, that is, at her conception. Such a deduction was made by the Latin theologians. They called this removal a "privilege" of the Mother of God. One must note that the acknowledgment of this dogma was preceded in the West by a long period of theological dispute, which lasted from the 12th century, when this teaching appeared, until the 17th century, when it was spread by Jesuits in the Roman Catholic world.[7]

In 1950, the so-called Jubilee Year, the Roman Pope Pius XII triumphantly proclaimed a second dogma, the dogma of the Assumption of the Mother of God with her body into heaven. Dogmatically this teaching was deduced in Roman theology from the Roman dogma of the Immaculate Conception and is a further logical deduction from the Roman teaching on original sin. If the Mother of God was removed from the general law of original sin, this means that she was given from her very conception supernatural gifts: righteousness and immortality, such as our first ancestors had before their fall into sin, and she should not have been subject to the law of bodily death. Therefore, if the Mother of God died, then, in the view of the Roman theologians, she accepted death voluntarily so as to emulate her Son; but death had no dominion over her.

The declaration of both dogmas corresponds to the Roman theory of the "development of dogmas." The Orthodox Church does not accept the Latin system of arguments concerning original sin. In

---

[7] Further on the Immaculate Conception, see Archbishop John Maximovitch, *The Orthodox Veneration of the Mother of God*, pp. 35–47. [Revised edition, 1994, pp. 47–61.]

particular, the Orthodox Church, confessing the perfect personal immaculateness and perfect sanctity of the Mother of God, whom the Lord Jesus Christ by His birth from her made to be more honorable than the Cherubim and more glorious beyond compare than the Seraphim—has not seen and does not see any grounds for the establishment of the dogma of the Immaculate Conception in the sense of the Roman Catholic interpretation, although it does venerate the conception of the Mother of God, as it does also the conception of the Holy Prophet and Forerunner John.

On the one hand, we see that God did not deprive mankind, even after its fall, of His Grace-giving gifts, as for example, the words of the 50th Psalm indicate: *Take not Thy Holy Spirit from me.... With Thy governing Spirit establish me;* or the words of Psalm 70: *On Thee have I been made fast from the womb; from my mother's womb Thou art my Protector.*[8]

On the other hand, in accordance with the teaching of Sacred Scripture, in Adam all mankind tasted the forbidden fruit. Only the God-Man Christ begins with Himself the new mankind, freed by Him from the sin of Adam. Therefore, He is called the *Firstborn among many brethren* (Rom. 8:29), that is: the First in the new human race; He is the "new Adam." The Most Holy Virgin was born as subject to the sin of Adam together with all mankind, and with him she shared the need for redemption ("Encyclical of the Eastern Patriarchs," par. 6).[9] The pure and immaculate life of the Virgin Mary up to the Annunciation by the Archangel, her freedom from personal sins, was the fruit of the union of her spiritual labor upon herself and the abun-

---

[8] For a description of how Grace acted on man between the time of the fall and the coming of Christ, see pp. 167–68, note 14 above.—3RD ED.

[9] In other words, the Virgin Mary was born with the *inclination* toward sin which, as we have seen (pp. 157–58; p. 163, note 10; p. 169; p. 169, note 15), was a consequence of the fall of man. St. John (Maximovitch) of Shanghai and San Francisco writes: "None of the ancient Holy Fathers say that God in miraculous fashion purified the Virgin Mary while yet in the womb; and many directly indicate that the Virgin Mary, just as all men, endured a battle with sinfulness, but was victorious over temptations and was saved by her Divine Son" (*The Orthodox Veneration of Mary the Birthgiver of God,* p. 51).—3RD ED.

dance of Grace that was poured out upon her. "Thou hast found Grace with God," the Archangel said to her in his greeting: "thou hast found," that is, attained, acquired, earned. The Most Holy Virgin Mary was prepared by the best part of mankind as a worthy vessel for the descent of God the Word to earth. The coming down of the Holy Spirit ("the Holy Spirit shall come upon thee") totally sanctified the womb of the Virgin Mary for the reception of God the Word.

One must acknowledge that the very principle of a preliminary "privilege" is somehow not in harmony with Christian concepts, for *there is no respect of persons with God* (Rom. 2:11).

As for the tradition concerning the assumption of the body of the Mother of God: the belief in the assumption of her body after its burial does exist in the Orthodox Church. It is expressed in the content of the service for the feast of the Dormition of the Mother of God, and also in the *Confession* of the Jerusalem Council of the Eastern Patriarchs in 1672. St. John Damascene in his second homily on the Dormition relates that once the Empress Pulcheria (5th century), who had built a church in Constantinople, asked the Patriarch of Jerusalem, Juvenal, a participant in the Council of Chalcedon, for relics of the Most Holy Virgin Mary to place in the church. Juvenal replied that, in accordance with ancient tradition, the body of the Mother of God had been taken to heaven, and he joined to this reply the well-known account of how the Apostles had been assembled in miraculous fashion for the burial of the Mother of God, how after the arrival of the Apostle Thomas her grave had been opened and her body was not there, and how it had been revealed to the Apostles that her body had ascended to heaven.[10] Written church testimonies on this subject date in general to a relatively late period (not earlier than the 6th century), and the Orthodox Church, with all its respect for them, does not ascribe to them the significance of a dogmatic source. The Church, accepting the tradition of the ascension of the body of the Mother of God, has not regarded and does not regard this pious tradition as one of the fundamental truths or dogmas of the Christian faith.

---

[10] See *On the Dormition of Mary: Early Patristic Homilies*, pp. 224–26.—3RD ED.

The Cult of the "Immaculate Heart" of the Most Holy Virgin in the Roman Church

In a way similar to the veneration of the "Sacred Heart" of Jesus, there has been established by the Roman Church the cult of the "Immaculate Heart of the Most Holy Virgin," which has received a universal dissemination. In essence one can say of it the same thing that was said above about the veneration of the heart of Jesus.

THE DOGMA OF REDEMPTION

The Lamb of God Who Taketh Away the Sin of the World (John 1:29)

The dogma of salvation in Christ is the central dogma of Christianity, the heart of our Christian faith. The Lord Jesus Christ is the Redeemer and Saviour of the human race. All the preceding history of mankind up to the Incarnation of the Son of God, in the clear image given both in the Old Testament and the New Testament Scriptures, is a *preparation* for the coming of the Saviour. All the following history of mankind, after the Resurrection and Ascension of the Lord, is the *actualization* of the salvation which had been accomplished: the reception and assimilation of it by the faithful. The *culmination* of the great work of salvation is bound up with the end of the world. The Cross and the Resurrection of Christ stand at the very center of human history.

Neither descriptions nor enumerations can take in the majesty, breadth, power, and significance of the earthly ministry of Christ; there is no measuring-stick for the all-surpassing wealth of God's love, manifest in His mercy for the fallen and for sinners in miracles, in healings, and finally, in His innocent sacrificial death, with prayer for His crucifiers. Christ took upon Himself the sins of the entire world; He received in Himself the guilt of all men. He is the Lamb slaughtered for the world. Are we capable of embracing in our thoughts and expressing in our usual, everyday conceptions and words all the economy of our salvation? We have no words for heavenly mysteries.

"We the faithful, speaking on things that pertain to God, touch upon an ineffable mystery, the Crucifixion that mind cannot comprehend, and the Resurrection that is beyond description: for today death and hell are despoiled, while mankind is clothed in incorruption" (Sedalion after the second kathisma, Sunday Matins, Tone 3).

However, as we see from the writings of the Apostles, the very truth of salvation, the truth of this mystery, was for the Apostles themselves entirely clear in its undoubtedness and all-embracingness. Upon it they base all their instruction, by means of it they explain events in the life of mankind, they place it as the foundation of the life of the Church and the future fate of the whole world. They constantly proclaim the good news of salvation in the most varied expressions, without detailed explanations, as a self-evident truth. They write: "Christ saved us"; "you are redeemed from the curse of the law"; "Christ has justified us"; "you are bought at a dear price"; Christ "has covered our sins"; He is a "propitiation for our sins"; by Him we have been "reconciled with God"; He is "the sole Chief Priest"; "He has torn up the handwriting against us and nailed it to the Cross"; He "was made a curse for us"; we have peace with God "by the death of His Son"; we have been "sanctified by His blood"; we have been "resurrected together with Christ." In such expressions, chosen here at random, the Apostles have contained a truth which in its very essence surpasses human understanding, but which is clear for them in its meaning and in its consequences. In a simple and accessible way this truth has penetrated from their lips into the hearts of the faithful so that they all might know what is *the economy of the mystery, which from the beginning of the world hath been hid in God, Who created all things by Jesus Christ* (Eph. 3:9). Let us, therefore, examine the teaching of the Apostles.

In the preaching of the Apostles, especially worthy of attention is the fact that they precisely teach us to distinguish between the truth of the salvation of mankind as a whole, which has already been accomplished, and another truth—the necessity for a personal reception and assimilation of the gift of salvation on the part of each of the faithful, and the fact that this latter salvation depends upon each one himself.

Ye are saved through faith, and that not of yourselves: it is the gift of God, writes the Apostle Paul (Eph. 2:8); but he also teaches, *Work out your own salvation with fear and trembling* (Phil. 2:12).

Man's salvation consists in the acquirement of eternal life in God, in the Kingdom of Heaven. *But nothing unclean can enter the Kingdom of God* (cf. Eph. 5:5; Apoc. 21:27). God is Light, and there is no darkness in Him, and those who enter the Kingdom of God must themselves be sons of the Light. Therefore, entrance into it necessarily requires purity of soul, a garment of *holiness, without which no man shall see the Lord* (Heb. 12:14).[11]

The Son of God came into the world in order (*a*) *to open the path* to mankind in its entirety for the personal salvation of each of us; and in order by this means (*b*) to direct the hearts of men to the search, to the thirst for the Kingdom of God, and *to give help, to give power on this path of salvation for the acquirement of personal spiritual purity and sanctity.* The first of these has been accomplished by Christ entirely. The second depends upon ourselves, although it is accomplished by the *activity of the Grace of Christ* in the Holy Spirit.

THE GENERAL ECONOMY OF SALVATION

A. The Condition of the World before the Coming of the Saviour

In the prophetic books of the Old Testament, and in particular in the psalms of David, the chosen Hebrew people, as the representative

---

[11] The Orthodox Church takes a *maximalist* approach to salvation, seeing it as a *process* which ends in deification (*theosis*). As Harry Boosalis (St. Tikhon's Seminary, South Canaan, Pa.) explains: "For the Orthodox Church, salvation is more than the pardon of sins and transgressions. It is more than being justified or acquitted for offenses committed against God. According to Orthodox teaching, salvation certainly includes forgiveness and justification, but is by no means limited to them. For the Fathers of the Church salvation is the acquisition of the Grace of the Holy Spirit. To be saved is to be sanctified and to participate in the life of God—indeed to *become partakers of the Divine Nature* (II Peter 1:4)" (*Orthodox Spiritual Life according to St. Silouan the Athonite*, p. 19).—3rd Ed.

of all mankind, is presented as "the planting of God," as the vineyard of God (see Isaiah 5:7, 61:3). The image of a garden, having the same meaning, is given also in the Gospel. A vineyard or garden must bear fruits. Preserving and guarding His planting, the Lord expects fruits from it. But what should be done with a fruit garden when it bears no fruits, and, what is more, is infected with a disease? Should it be looked after if it does not justify its purpose?

The axe is laid unto the root of the trees; therefore, every tree which bringeth not forth good fruit is hewn down, and cast into the fire (Matt. 3:10). Thus did St. John the Forerunner warn and accuse the people before the coming of the Lord.

The Lord speaks of the same thing, and gives to His disciples the parable of the fig tree. *A certain man had a fig tree planted in his vineyard; and he came and sought fruit thereon, and found none. Then said he unto the dresser of his vineyard, Behold, these three years I come seeking fruit on this fig tree, and find none; cut it down; why cumbereth it the ground? And he answering said unto him, Lord, let it alone this year also, till I shall dig about it, and dung it. And if it bear fruit, well; and if not, then after that thou shalt cut it down* (Luke 13:6–9).

Like this fig tree, the human race was fruitless. Once already it had been exterminated by the flood. Now it would have been doomed—it would have doomed itself—to the loss of eternal life, to the general loss of the Kingdom of God, because it had lost all value as not having fulfilled its purpose and as drowning in evil.

Hath not the potter power over the clay?... What if God, willing to show His wrath, and to make His power known, endured with much long-suffering the vessels of wrath fitted unto destruction: and that He might make known the riches of His glory on the vessels of mercy, which He had afore prepared unto glory ...? (Rom. 9:21–23).

Mankind, in the person of its best representatives, acknowledged its unfulfilled debt, the heavy debt of numerous preceding generations and of its own age. It was a debtor unable to pay. This feeling of guilt in its purest form was present in the Jewish people. Mankind tried to erase its sins by means of sacrifices, which expressed the giving over to God of the best part of what was in man's possession, in the possession of his family, as a gift to God. But these sacrifices were not capable of *regenerating* men.[12]

Let us quote here the words of the holy righteous Fr. John of Kronstadt, from his sermon on the feast of the Exaltation of the Cross of the Lord: "Let us enter into the meaning of the mystery of the Cross.... The world, that is, the human race, would have been given over to eternal death, to eternal torments, according to the unchanging, most strict justice of God, if the Son of God had not become, out of His limitless goodness, a voluntary Intermediary and Redeemer of mankind, which was criminal, defiled and corrupted by sin. For, by the deception of the serpent, the murderer of men, it was cast down into a frightful abyss of lawlessness and perdition.... However, so that men might be capable of this reconciliation and redemption from above, it was necessary for the Son of God to descend into the world, to take upon Himself a human soul and body, and become the God-Man, in order that in His own Person, in His human nature, He might fulfill all the righteousness of God which had been brazenly violated by all manner of human unrighteousness; in order that He might fulfill the whole law of God, even to the least iota, and become the greatest of righteous men for the whole of unrighteous mankind, and teach mankind righteousness with repentance for all its unrighteousness and show forth the fruits of repentance. This He fulfilled, not being guilty of a single sin, and was the only perfect man, in hypostatical union with the Divinity" (Sermon on the Feast of the Exaltation: "The Meaning of the Mystery of the Cross").

---

[12] St. Gregory Palamas writes: "Before Christ we all shared the same ancestral curse and condemnation poured out on all of us from our single Forefather, as if it had sprung from the root of the human race and was the common lot of our nature. Each person's individual action attracted either reproof or praise from God, but no one could do anything about the shared curse and condemnation, or the evil inheritance that had been passed down to him and through him would pass to his descendants." As we have seen, this inheritance entailed a corrupted human nature, bringing about the death of both the soul and the body. "But Christ came," says St. Gregory, "setting human nature free and changing the common curse into a shared blessing" (*Homilies,* vol. 1, p. 52).—3RD ED.

B. The General Salvation of the World in Christ

How was the general justification of human existence accomplished, and in what did it consist?[13] It was accomplished by the *Incarnation of God*, together with all the further events in the life of the Lord Jesus Christ.[14] The light of Sanctity shone forth upon the earth. In the person of the Immaculate, Most Pure Virgin Mary, the Mother of God, all mankind was sanctified. By the steps of the Saviour, by His Baptism in the Jordan, by His life on earth, the very nature of the earth was sanctified. The Gospel teaching and the deeds of mercy of Jesus Christ kindled love and faith in the hearts of the disciples of Christ, to

---

[13] What Fr. Michael here calls "general salvation" and "general justification" might also be called the *objective* dimension of salvation. This is the *free gift* that *came upon all men unto justification of life* (Rom. 5:18). Christ has saved our *nature:* through His Incarnation, death and Resurrection, physical death will not hold us, and all mankind has been made subject to future resurrection. Further, Christ has opened to human nature the *possibility* of being deified and united to God eternally in the Kingdom of Heaven.

Together with this, there is the *subjective* dimension of salvation, or what Fr. Michael calls "personal salvation." Each of us must come to Christ and receive salvation from Him personally, freely, and willingly, so that we may be united with Christ and one day be resurrected unto life rather than unto damnation (cf. John 5:29). (See p. 340, note 4 below.)—3RD ED.

[14] Our redemption by Jesus Christ began with His Incarnation. In assuming human nature, Christ deified it. By uniting the separated natures—Divine and human—in one Person, He overcame the barrier of nature that separated man from God. This was in order for Christ's true followers to be deified: not by nature and Sonship, as Christ was, but by Grace and adoption.

But with Christ's Incarnation, other barriers between man and God still remained. Because of his spiritual corruption, man was an impure vessel. Because of the barrier of sin, man could not receive and keep the Grace of God within himself. So Christ, having overcome the barrier of nature at His Incarnation, now had to break down the barrier of sin. He would do this through His death. As St. Nicholas Cabasilas says, Christ broke down the three barriers that separated man from God: the barrier of nature by His Incarnation, the barrier of sin by His death, and the barrier of death by His Resurrection (St. Nicholas Cabasilas, *The Life in Christ,* pp. 105–106).—3RD ED.

such an extent that they "left everything" and followed after Him. And, above all this, in His voluntary death on the Cross, there is a manifestation, "surpassing the understanding," of the heights of the love of Christ,[15] concerning which the Apostle Paul reasons thus:

The love of God is shed abroad in our hearts by the Holy Spirit which is given unto us. For when we were yet without strength, in due time Christ died for the ungodly. For scarcely for a righteous man will one die; yet peradventure for a good man some would even dare to die. But God

---

[15] Christ's Incarnation, death and Resurrection, which He accomplished for the salvation of mankind, expressed God's truth, righteouness and justice on the one hand, and His mercy and love on the other. St. Gregory Palamas says the following concerning Divine justice: "The pre-eternal, uncircumscribed and almighty Word and omnipotent Son of God could clearly have saved man from mortality and servitude to the devil without Himself becoming man.... But the Incarnation of the Word of God was the method of deliverance most in keeping with our nature and weakness, and most appropriate for Him Who carried it out, for this method had justice on its side, and God does not act without justice. As the Psalmist and Prophet says, *God is righteous and loveth righteousness* (Ps. 10:7), *and there is no unrighteousness in him* (91:15)" (*Homilies*, vol. 1, p. 179). (See also p. 215, note 25 below.)

St. Isaac the Syrian writes concerning how God's plan of salvation also manifested His love: "God the Lord surrendered His own Son to death on the Cross for the fervent love of creation. *For God so loved the world that He gave His only begotten Son* to death for our sake (cf. John 3:16). This was not, however, because He could not have redeemed us in another way, but so that His surpassing love, manifested hereby, might be a teacher unto us. And by the death of His only begotten Son He made us near to Himself. Yea, if He had had anything more precious, He would have given it to us, so that by it our race might be His own" (*Ascetical Homilies*, pp. 345–46).

St. Cyril of Jerusalem describes how both God's truth and His love were manifested in His work of redemption. Having recounted Christ's crucifixion, St. Cyril says: "These things the Saviour endured, and *made peace through the blood of His Cross*, for *things in earth, and things in heaven* (Col. 1:20). For we were enemies of God through sin (cf. Romans 5:10), and God had appointed the sinner to die. There must needs therefore have happened one of two things: either that God, in His truth, should destroy all men, or that in His loving-kindness He should cancel the sentence. But behold the wisdom of God; He preserved both the truth of His sentence, and the exercise of His loving-kindness. Christ took our sins *in His own body on the tree, that we* by His death *might die to sin, and live unto righteousness* (I Peter 2:24)" (*Catechetical Lectures* 23.33; NPNF, p. 91).—3RD ED.

commendeth His love towards us, in that, while we were yet sinners, Christ died for us (Rom. 5:5–8). And the Apostle concludes his thought with this: By this means was accomplished the fact that *when we were enemies, we were reconciled to God by the death of His Son* (Rom. 5:10); *by the righteousness of one the free gift came upon all men unto justification of life* (Rom. 5:18).[16]

1. This general economy of the salvation of the world is presented in the Sacred Scripture of the New Testament in various words similar in significance, as for example: justification, reconciliation, redemption, propitiation, forgiveness, deliverance.

---

[16] See also Hebrews 2:9: *That He* (Christ) *by the Grace of God should taste death for every man.*

St. Athanasius the Great explains how Christ died in place of us in order to free us from the law of sin and death: "Taking a body like our own, because all our bodies were liable to corruption and death, He [Christ] surrendered His body to death in place of all, and offered it to the Father. This He did out of sheer love for us, so that in His death all might die, and the law of death thereby be abolished....

"The Word perceived that corruption could not be got rid of otherwise than through death; yet He Himself, as the Word, being immortal and the Father's Son, was such as could not die. For this reason, therefore, He assumed a body capable of death, in order that it, through belonging to the Word Who is above all, and, itself remaining incorruptible through His indwelling, might thereafter put an end to corruption for all others as well, by the Grace of the Resurrection. It was by surrendering to death the body which He had taken, as an offering and sacrifice free from every stain, that he forthwith abolished death for His human brethren by the offering of an equivalent" (*On the Incarnation,* pp. 34–35).

In the same work St. Athanasius says that, since death "was the penalty for the Transgression" (p. 34) and "was a debt owing which must needs be paid," Christ "surrendered His own temple to death in place of all, to settle man's account with death and free him from the primal transgression" (p. 49).

Through His death and Resurrection, Christ freed man from both spiritual and bodily death. As will be remembered, at his fall man died spiritually, and this spiritual death made him subject to physical death. St. Gregory Palamas writes that "Of necessity bodily death followed upon this spiritual death, so the evil one caused our double death by his [Adam's] single death.... The good Lord healed this twofold death of ours through His single bodily death, and through the one Resurrection of His body He gave us a twofold resurrection. By means of His bodily death He destroyed him who had the power over our souls and bodies in death, and rescued us from his tyranny over both" (*Homilies,* vol. 1, pp. 196–97).—3RD ED.

Here are some texts relating to this general economy:

John 1:29: *Behold the Lamb of God, Who taketh away the sin of the world.*

I John 2:2: *And He is the propitiation for our sins, and not for ours only, but also for the sins of the whole world.*

II Cor. 5:15: *He (Christ) died for all, that they who live should not henceforth live unto themselves, but unto Him Who died for them, and rose again.*

I Tim. 2:5–6: *For there is one God, and one mediator between God and men, the man Christ Jesus; Who gave Himself a ransom for all.*[17]

I Tim. 4:10: *Trust in the living God, Who is the Saviour of all men, especially of those that believe.*

2. In addition to the broad significance of the salvation of the world here indicated, the death of Christ and His subsequent descent into hades (I Peter 3:19–20, 4:6; Eph. 4:8–10) signify in a narrower sense the deliverance from hades of the souls of the reposed first ancestors, prophets, and righteous ones of the pre-Christian world; and thus they express the special significance of the Cross of the Lord for the Old Testament world, a significance which comes from the death of Christ accomplished upon it: *for the redemption of the transgressions that were under the first testament* (Heb. 9:15).[18] In accordance with this, our Orthodox hymns for Sunday also sing of the mystical truth of the victory over hades and the deliverance of souls from it: "Today Adam dances for joy and Eve rejoices, and with them the prophets and Patriarchs unceasingly sing of the Divine triumph of Thy power" (Sunday kontakion, Tone 3).

3. The deliverance from hades testifies also to the *lifting of the curses* which were placed in the Old Testament: (*a*) the curses in the third chapter of the book of Genesis, which were joined to the depriva-

---

[17] Cf. the words of Christ Himself in Matt. 20:28: *The Son of Man came ... to give His life* (as) *a ransom for many.*—3RD ED.

[18] The entire verse reads: *He (Christ) is the mediator of the new testament, that by means of death, for the redemption of the transgressions that were under the first testament, they which are called might receive the promise of eternal inheritance.*—3RD ED.

tion of life in Paradise of Adam and Eve and their descendants;[19] and then (*b*) the curses placed by Moses, in the book of Deuteronomy (chap. 28), for the stubborn non-fulfillment of the laws given through him.

C. The Personal Rebirth and New Life in Christ

The transition from the idea of the general economy of God to the call for the personal salvation of men is clearly expressed in the following words of Apostle Paul: *God was in Christ, reconciling the world unto Himself, not imputing their trespasses unto them: and hath committed unto us the word of reconciliation.... We pray you in Christ's stead, be ye reconciled to God* (II Cor. 5:19–20).

The personal salvation of man is expressed in Sacred Scripture usually in the same terminology, in the same words, as is the salvation of the world in the broad sense of the word ("justification," "redemption," "reconciliation"), as we see in the text we have cited above. Only the words are applied here in a narrower significance. Here the Apostles already have in mind men who have come to believe in Christ and have received Holy Baptism. The common phrases used to express both kinds of salvation may be seen in the following examples:

Titus 3:5–7: He (Christ) *according to His mercy saved us, by the washing of regeneration* (in Baptism), *and renewing of the Holy Spirit ... that being justified by His Grace, we might be made heirs according to the hope of eternal life.*

Eph. 4:30: *Grieve not the Holy Spirit of God, whereby ye are sealed unto the day of redemption* (that is to say, the day of Baptism and the receiving of the seal of the Holy Spirit).

---

[19] St. Symeon the New Theologian writes concerning this: "Since Adam had fallen under the curse, and through him all people also who proceed from him, therefore the sentence of God concerning this could in no way be annihilated; and therefore Christ was for us a curse (cf. Gal. 3:13), through being hung upon the tree of the Cross, so as to offer Himself as a sacrifice to His Father, as has been said, and to annihilate the sentence of God by the superabundant worth of the sacrifice. For what is greater and higher than God?" (*First-Created Man*, p. 47).—3RD ED.

But the chief place among all such expressions with relation to Christians is the conception of "resurrection in Christ." The mystery of Baptism is a personal resurrection in Christ: *Ye are risen with Him* (Col. 2:12).

The Apostle Peter writes in his First Catholic Epistle: *Baptism doth also now save us ... by the Resurrection of Jesus Christ* (I Peter 3:21). The very preaching of the Apostles is, in its essence, the preaching of the Resurrection of Christ.

Baptism by water is called in the Apostolic Scriptures likewise a *new birth, adoption, sanctification. But ye are washed, ye are sanctified, ye are justified in the name of the Lord Jesus* (I Cor. 6:11). *As many of you as have been baptized into Christ have put on Christ* (Gal. 3:27).[20]

From this it is clear that in the mystery of redemption *the Cross and*

---

[20] St. Symeon the New Theologian explains how, through the sacrifice of Christ, man can be cleansed of sin and delivered from spiritual death, receiving within himself the Grace of God as Adam had it before the fall: "One Person of the Holy Trinity, namely the Son and Word of God, having become incarnate, offered Himself in the flesh as a sacrifice to the Divinity of the Father, and of the Son Himself, and of the Holy Spirit, in order that the first transgression of Adam might be benevolently forgiven for the sake of this great and fearful work, that is, for the sake of this sacrifice of Christ, and in order that by its power there might be performed another new birth and re-creation of man in Holy Baptism, in which we also are cleansed by water mingled with the Holy Spirit. From that time people are baptized in water, are immersed in it and taken out from it three times, in the image of the three-day burial of the Lord, and after they die in it to this whole evil world, in the third bringing out from it they are already alive, as if resurrected from the dead, that is, their souls are brought to life and again receive the Grace of the Holy Spirit as Adam had it before the transgression. Then they are anointed with Holy Myrrh, and by means of it are anointed with Jesus Christ, and are fragrant in a way above nature. Having become in this way worthy of being associates of God, they taste His Flesh and drink His Blood, and by means of the sanctified bread and wine become of one Body and Blood with God Who was incarnate and offered Himself as a sacrifice. After this it is no longer possible that sin should reign and tyrannize over them, for they are gods by Grace....

"Thus God, Who is incomparably higher than the visible and invisible creation, accepted human nature, which is higher than the whole visible creation, and offered it as a sacrifice to His God and Father.... Honoring the sacrifice, the Father could not leave it in the hands of death. Therefore, He annihilated His sentence and resurrected from the dead first of all and at the beginning Him Who had given Himself as

Resurrection of the Lord are inseparable. In the consciousness of the Church this truth is expressed in full measure in the Paschal hymns, which confess the power of the Resurrection of Christ not only for the personal salvation of the Christian, but also in the final, complete justification of the world: "Passover of incorruption, salvation of the world" (Exapostilarion of Pascha). *By the Cross* has been accomplished the cleansing of the sins of the world, the reconciliation with God; *by the Resurrection* new life has been brought into the world.

The Word "Redemption" in the Usage of the Apostles

The totality of the consequences of the Cross and Resurrection are usually expressed by the Apostles, and therefore in theological terminology also, by the single concept of "redemption," which literally signifies a "ransom," an offering of payment.[21] This conception is sufficiently vivid and lively that it has been accessible to the under-

---

a sacrifice for the redemption and as a replacement for men who are of the same race as Himself; and afterwards, in the last day of the end of this world, He will resurrect also all men. Moreover, the souls of those who believe in Jesus Christ, the Son of God, in this great and fearful sacrifice, God resurrects in the present life; and a sign of this resurrection is the Grace of the Holy Spirit which He gives to the soul of every Christian, as if giving a new soul" (*First-Created Man*, pp. 46–48).—3RD ED.

[21] St. John Damascene explains how Christ offered Himself as a ransom for us when He died on the Cross: "Since our Lord Jesus Christ was without sin (*for He committed no sin, He Who took away the sin of the world, nor was there any deceit found in his mouth* [cf. Isaiah 53:9, John 1:29]), He was not subject to death, since death came into the world through sin [cf. Rom. 5:12]. He dies, therefore, because He took on Himself death on our behalf, and He makes Himself an offering to the Father for our sakes. For we had sinned against Him, and it was meet that He should receive a ransom for us, and that we should thus be delivered from the condemnation. God forbid that the blood of the Lord should have been offered to the tyrant [i.e., the devil]. Wherefore death approaches, and swallowing up the body as a bait is transfixed on the hook of Divinity, and after tasting of a sinless and life-giving body, perishes, and brings up again all whom of old he had swallowed up. For just as darkness disappears on the introduction of light, so is death repulsed before the assault of life, and brings life to all, but death to the destroyer" (*Exact Exposition* 3.27; NPNF, p. 72).

Likewise, St. Gregory Palamas writes: "The Lord patiently endured for our sake a death He was not obliged to undergo, to redeem us, who were obliged to suffer

standing of people even of the lowest rank of society. But this vividness in itself has inspired attempts to ask further questions which do not relate to the essence of salvation. Therefore, St. Gregory the Theologian puts off these further questions and establishes the essence of the present expression in the following reflection:

"To whom was that Blood offered that was shed for us, and why was it shed? I mean the precious and glorious Blood of our God and High Priest and Sacrifice. We were detained in bondage by the evil one, sold under sin, and received pleasure in exchange for wickedness. Now, since a ransom belongs only to him who holds in bondage, I ask to whom was this offered and for what cause? If to the evil one, fie upon the outrage! The robber receives ransom, not only from God, but a ransom which consists of God Himself, and has such an illustrious payment for his tyranny, a payment for whose sake it would have been right for him to have left us alone altogether. But if to the Father, I ask, first, how? For it was not by Him that we were being oppressed: and next, on what principle did the Blood of His only begotten Son delight the Father, Who would not receive even Issac when he was being offered by his father, but changed the sacrifice, putting a ram in the place of the human victim? Is it not evident that the Father accepts the sacrifice not because He demanded it or because He felt any need for it, but

---

death, from servitude to the devil and death, by which I mean death both of the soul and of the body, temporary and eternal. Since He gave His Blood, which was sinless and therefore guiltless, as a ransom for us who were liable to punishment because of our sins, He redeemed us from our guilt. He forgave our sins, tore up the record of them on the Cross and delivered us from the devil's tyranny (cf. Col. 2:14–15). The devil was caught by the bait. It was as if he opened his mouth and hastened to pour out for himself our ransom, the Master's Blood, which was not only guiltless but full of Divine power. Then instead of being enriched by it he was strongly bound and made an example in the Cross of Christ" (*Homilies,* vol. 1, pp. 200–201).

St. John Chrysostom further highlights this teaching: "It is as if, at a session of a court of justice, the devil should be addressed as follows: 'Granted that you destroyed all men because you found them guilty of sin; but why did you destroy Christ? Is it not very evident that you did so unjustly? Well then, through Him the whole world will be vindicated" (*Commentary on the Gospel of St. John,* Homily 67; FC, p. 232).—3RD ED.

on account of the economy: because humanity must be sanctified by the Humanity of God, that He might deliver us Himself, and overcome the tyrant, and draw us to Himself by the mediation of His Son, Who also arranged this to the honor of the Father, Whom it is manifest that He obeys in all things?" (St. Gregory the Theologian, Second Oration on Pascha, chap. 22).[22]

In this theological reflection of St. Gregory the Theologian, the idea which appears in the First Catholic Epistle of the Apostle Peter is given complete expression: *Ye were not redeemed with ... vain conversation received by tradition from your fathers, but with the precious blood of Christ, as of a lamb without blemish and without spot, Who verily was foreordained before the foundation of the world* (I Peter 1:18–20).

For a theological definition of the concept of "redemption," a philological examination of the Greek words which correspond to this concept has great importance.

In the Greek text of the New Testament Scriptures, this concept is expressed by two words, and each of them has a significant shade of meaning. The first of them *lytro-o,* means "to buy off," "to ransom." In

---

[22] Here St. Gregory the Theologian, while fully accepting the teaching of Christ's death as being a sacrifice, rejects a theory that had been invented to explain it; i.e., that the sacrifice was offered by Christ as a ransom to the devil. Such a theory existed in his time, having been developed by Origen and St. Gregory of Nyssa. The Holy Fathers after St. Gregory the Theologian also rejected this theory; as, for example, St. John Damascene (see pp. 208–9, note 21 above). They often spoke of the sacrifice as being offered to God the Father, and sometimes they spoke of it as being offered to the Holy Trinity, since the Father, Son and Holy Spirit are One God (see, for example, the quotes of St. Symeon the New Theologian above: p. 206, note 19; pp. 207–8, note 20). (At two Local Councils held in Constantinople in 1156–1157, it was affirmed that the sacrifice was offered to the Holy Trinity.)

St. Gregory the Theologian considered it fitting to see the sacrifice as having been offered to and accepted by God the Father—not, however, in the sense that the Father "demanded it or felt any need for it," but rather for the sake of the economy, that is, because this was in accordance with the Divine plan for the salvation of mankind.

In the same vein, St. John Chrysostom writes concerning Christ's sufferings on the Cross: "If He suffered this, then He suffered it not for His own sake, and not for the sake of His Father, but rather that through the Cross mankind might be saved" (*Works,* in Russian, vol. 2, p. 890).—3RD ED.

those times the world knew three forms of ransoming people, namely (according to Greek dictionaries), (1) ransoming from captivity; (2) ransoming from prison, for example for debts; and (3) ransoming from slavery. In the Christian meaning, the Apostles use this term to express the moment in the accomplishment of our salvation that is joined to the Cross of Christ, that is, the deliverance from the sinful world, from the power of the devil, the liberation from the curses, the liberation of the righteous from the bonds of hades. These are the same three forms of "ransoming": ransoming from the captivity of sin, ransoming from hades, ransoming from slavery to the devil.

The second verb, *agorazo,* signifies "to buy for oneself," "to buy at the marketplace" (*agora* means "marketplace"). The image utilized in this term refers only to believers, to Christians. Here it has an especially rich significance. This verb is encountered three times in the writings of the Apostles, namely:

I Cor. 6:19–20: *What? Know ye not that your body is the temple of the Holy Spirit Who is in you, Whom ye have from God, and ye are not your own? For ye are bought with a price.*

I Cor. 7:23: *Ye are bought with a price; be not ye the servants of men.*

Apoc. 5:9, the hymn in heaven to the Lamb: *Thou wast slain, and hast redeemed us to God by Thy blood.*

In all three places this verb signifies that Christ has acquired us for Himself so that we might belong to Him entirely, as bought slaves belong to their Master. It remains for us to reflect upon the depth of this image, which was placed in the word by the Apostles themselves.

On the one hand, the name "slaves" of Christ signifies a complete, unconditional giving over of oneself in obedience to Him Who has redeemed us all. Such precisely did the Apostles feel themselves to be. It is sufficient to read the first verses of a number of the Epistles of the Apostles. In the first words they call themselves the slaves (or servants)[23] of Christ: *Simon Peter, a servant and an apostle of Jesus Christ* (II Peter); *Jude, the servant of Jesus Christ, and brother of James* (Jude); *Paul, a servant of Jesus Christ, called to be an apostle* (Romans); *Paul and*

---

[23] In Greek, *douloi.*—3rd Ed.

Timothy, the servants of Jesus Christ (Philippians). Such a self-awareness should be present, according to the teaching of the Apostles, in all believers. The Holy Church in precisely the same way at all times has called and does call the members of the Church, in the language of the Divine services, "slaves (servants) of God."

But there is another side. The Saviour addresses His disciples in His farewell conversation with them: *Ye are My friends, if ye do whatsoever I command you* (John 15:14); and in the same place He calls them "My children" (John 13:33); *as the Father hath loved Me, so have I loved you* (John 15:9). And the Apostles teach: *Ye have received the spirit of adoption* (Rom. 8:15); *we are the children of God; and if children, then heirs; heirs of God, and joint-heirs with Christ* (Rom. 8:16–17). And the Holy Apostle John, he who lay upon the breast of Christ, cries out in inspiration: *Beloved, now we are the sons of God, and it doth not yet appear what we shall be; but we know that, when He shall appear, we shall be like Him; for we shall see Him as He is* (I John 3:2).

He Who sanctifies and they who are sanctified are all of the One (God); therefore Christ calls those who have been sanctified His brothers (Heb. 2:11). Most important, He is the *captain of* (our) *salvation* (Heb. 2:10); He is the High Priest of the New Testament. *Wherefore in all things it behooved Him to be made like unto His brethren, that He might become a merciful and faithful High Priest in things pertaining to God, to make reconciliation for the sins of the people. For in that He Himself hath suffered, being tempted, He is able to succor them that are tempted* (Heb. 2:17–18). Of Him we ask forgiveness of our sins; for the Heavenly Father does not judge anyone, but has given judgment over entirely to the Son, that all might worship the Son as they worship the Father. The Son Himself proclaimed before His Ascension: *All power is given unto Me in heaven and in earth* (Matt. 28:18). This is why almost all our prayers—whether for ourselves, for our fathers and brethren, for the living and the dead—we offer to the Son of God. We are in the house of God, we are the house of Christ. Therefore for us it is easy, joyful, and saving to have communion with all the heavenly members of this house: with the Most Holy Theotokos, with the Apostles, the

Prophets, the Martyrs, the Hierarchs, and the monastic Saints—a single Church of heaven and earth! It is for this that we have been bought by Christ.

So great are the consequences of the Sacrifice of Christ which was offered on the Cross and signed by the Resurrection of Christ! This is the meaning of the new song before the Lamb at His throne, which was given in the Apocalypse to the Apostle John the Theologian: *Thou wast slain, and has redeemed us to God by Thy blood* (Apoc. 5:9). We have been purchased *for God*.

Therefore, let not the sorrowful spiritual condition of the world which we observe confuse us. We know that the salvation of the children of the Church, the slaves of the Christ, is being accomplished. And the salvation of the world, in the broad, eschatological meaning of the word, has already been accomplished. But, as the Apostle Paul instructs us, *We are saved by hope; but hope that is seen is not hope: for what a man seeth, why doth he yet hope for? But if we hope for that we see not, then do we with patience wait for it* (Rom. 8:24–25). The spiritual forces in the world may be hidden, but they are not extinguished. The heavenly-earthly body of the Church of Christ grows and draws the world near to the mystical day of the triumphant and glorious open manifestation of the Son of Man, the Son of God, when, after the great and righteous General Judgment, the renewal and transfiguration of the world will be revealed, and He Who sits on the throne will say, *Behold, I make all things new* (Apoc. 21:5). And there will be a new heaven and a new earth. Amen.

A Note on the Roman Catholic Teaching

The interpretation of the truth of the Redemption was greatly complicated thanks to the direction which was given to it in the Western theology of the Middle Ages. The figurative expressions of the Apostles were accepted in medieval Roman Catholic theology in their literal and overly narrow sense, and the work of redemption was interpreted as a "satisfaction"—more precisely, a satisfaction for offending God, and even more precisely, "the satisfaction of God (God in the

Holy Trinity) for the offense caused to Him by the sin of Adam." It is easy to see that the foundation of such a view is the special Latin teaching on original sin: that man in the transgression of Adam "infinitely offended" God and evoked God's wrath; therefore, it was required that God be offered complete satisfaction in order that the guilt might be removed and God might be appeased; this was done by the Saviour when He accepted death on the Cross: the Saviour offered an infinitely complete satisfaction.[24]

This one-sided interpretation of Redemption became the reigning one in Latin theology and it has remained so up to the present time. In Protestantism it evoked the opposite reaction, which led in the later sects to the almost complete denial of the dogma of Redemption and to the acknowledgment of no more than a moral or instructive significance for Christ's life and His death on the Cross.

The term "satisfaction" has been used in Russian Orthodox theology, but in a changed form: "the satisfaction of God's righteousness." The expression "to satisfy the righteousness of God," one must acknowledge, is not entirely foreign to the New Testament, as may be seen from the words of the Saviour Himself: *Thus it becometh us to ful-*

---

[24] Thomas Aquinas set forth the Roman Catholic teaching as follows: "The passion of Christ is the cause of our reconciliation with God ... through its being a sacrifice most acceptable to God, for this is properly the effect of a sacrifice, that through it God is appeased, as even man is ready to forgive an injury done to him by accepting a gift which is offered to him.... And so in the same way, what Christ suffered was so great a good that, on account of that good found in human nature, God has been appeased over all the offenses of mankind" (*Summa Theologica* 3, Question 49, article 4).

The same teaching is found in the *Catholic Encyclopedia:* "Redemption has reference to both God and man. On God's part, it is the acceptation of satisfactory amends whereby the Divine honor is repaired and the Divine wrath appeased.... The judicial axiom *'honor est in honorante, injuria in injuriato'* (honor is measured by the dignity of him who gives it, offence by the dignity of him who receives it) shows that mortal sin bears in a way an infinite malice and that nothing short of a person possessing infinite worth is capable of making full amends for it.... 'For an adequate satisfaction,' says St. Thomas [Aquinas], 'it is necessary that the act of him who satisfies should possess an infinite value and proceed from one who is both God and Man'" (1911 edition, vol. 12, p. 678).—3RD ED.

fill all righteousness (Matt. 3:15).[25] An expression which is close in meaning to the present term, but which is more complete and is authentically Biblical, and gives a basis for the Orthodox understanding of the work of Redemption, is the word "propitiation," which we read in the First Epistle of John: *Herein is love, not that we loved God, but that He loved us, and sent His Son to be the propitiation for our sins* (I John 4:10). ("Propitiation" is a direct translation of the Greek word *ilasmos*. The same use of the word is to be found in I John 2:2, and in St. Paul's Epistle to the Hebrews, 2:17, where it is translated as "reconciliation" in the King James Version).

---

[25] St. Gregory Palamas sets forth the Orthodox understanding of how the Lord's manner of redeeming mankind was according to His righteousness and justice: "Man was justly abandoned by God in the beginning as he had first abandoned God. He had voluntarily approached the originator of evil, obeyed him when he treacherously advised the opposite of what God had commanded, and was justly given over to him. In this way, through the evil one's envy and the good Lord's just consent, death came into the world. Because of the devil's overwhelming evil, death became twofold, for he brought about not just physical but also eternal death.

"As we had been justly handed over to the devil's service and subjection to death, it was clearly necessary that the human race's return to freedom and life should be accomplished by God in a just way. Not only had man been surrendered to the envious devil by Divine righteousness, but the devil had rejected righteousness and become wrongly enamored by authority, arbitrary power and, above all, tyranny. He took up arms against justice and used his might against mankind. It pleased God that the devil be overcome first by the justice against which he continuously fought, then afterwards by power, through the Resurrection and future Judgment....

"The devil achieved his victory and man's fall unjustly and treacherously, but the Redeemer accomplished the final defeat of the originator of evil and the renewal of His creation with righteousness and wisdom. Earlier God left undone what it was in His power to do, so that He might first do what was fitting. In this way, justice was manifested more clearly, having been favored by Him Whose might is unconquerable. Men had to be taught to demonstrate righteousness in their actions now in the time of this mortal life, so that they might be strengthened to hold it fast when eternity comes" (*Homilies*, vol. 1. pp. 179–81).—3RD ED.

THE TRIPLE MINISTRY OF THE LORD

The systems of dogmatic theology, following the ancient custom, in order to gain a fuller illumination of the whole work of salvation accomplished by the Lord Jesus Christ, view it most often from three aspects, namely as (*a*) the High-Priestly ministry of the Lord, (*b*) His Prophetic ministry, and (*c*) His Royal ministry. These three aspects are called the triple ministry of the Lord.

The common feature of the three ministries, the Prophetic, the High-Priestly, and the Royal, is that in the Old Testament the calling to these three ministries was accompanied by anointing with oil, and those who worthily passed through these ministries were strengthened by the power of the Holy Spirit.

The very name "Christ" signifies "Anointed One." (The name "Jesus" signifies "Saviour.") The Lord Himself referred to Himself the words of the Prophet Isaiah when He read them in the Synagogue at Nazareth: *The Spirit of the Lord is upon Me, because He hath anointed Me to preach the Gospel to the poor; He hath sent Me to heal the broken-hearted, to preach deliverance to the captives, and recovering of sight to the blind, to set at liberty them that are bruised, to preach the acceptable year of the Lord* (Luke 4:18–19).

A. Christ the High Priest

The Lord Jesus Christ is not only the Lamb of God Who is offered as a sacrifice for the life of the world; He is at the same time also He Who offers, the Performer of the sacrifice, the High Priest. Christ is "He Who offereth and is offered; that accepteth and is distributed" (the secret prayer at the Cherubic Hymn in the Liturgy). He Himself is offered as a sacrifice, and He Himself also offers the sacrifice. He Himself both receives it and distributes it to those who come.

The Lord expressed His High-Priestly ministry on earth in its highest degree in the prayer to His Father which is called "the High-Priestly prayer," which was pronounced after the farewell conversation with His disciples in the night when He was taken by the soldiers: *For their sakes I sanctify Myself, that they also might be sanctified in the truth. Neither pray I for these alone, but for them also which shall believe on Me through their word* (John 17:19–20).[26] He expressed it likewise in the prayer in solitude in the garden of Gethsemane.

The Apostle Paul interprets the High-Priestly ministry of Christ in his Epistle to the Hebrews (chapters 5 to 10). He juxtaposes the High-Priestly ministry of Christ with the ministry of the Old Testament high priests and shows that the priesthood of Christ incomparably surpasses it:

There were many high priests according to the order of Aaron, since death did not allow there to be only one. But this One, according to the order of Melchisedek, as remaining eternally, has a priesthood that does not pass away (Heb. 7:23–24).

Those high priests had to offer sacrifice constantly; but Christ performed the sacrifice once, offering Himself as the sacrifice (Heb. 7:27).

Those high priests themselves were clothed with infirmity; but this High Priest is perfect forevermore (Heb. 7:28).

Those were priests of the earthly tabernacle made by hands; but this One is the sacred Performer of the eternal tabernacle not made with hands (Heb. 9:24).

Those high priests entered into the holy place with the blood of calves and goats; but this One with His own blood entered once into the holy place and obtained an eternal redemption (Heb. 9:12).

They were priests of the Old Testament; whereas this One is Priest of the New Testament (Heb. 8:6).

B. Christ the Evangelizer (The Prophetic Ministry of the Lord)

The evangelistic, or instructive, or prophetic ministry of the Lord Jesus Christ was expressed in the fact that He proclaimed to men, in all

---

[26] St. John Chrysostom explains these words of Christ: "What is the meaning of *I sanctify Myself?* [It means] 'I offer sacrifice to Thee.' Now, all sacrifices are called 'holy,' and things that are consecrated to God are called 'holy' in a special way.... Indeed, it is quite clear from the words that follow that in saying *I sanctify myself* He was indirectly referring to His immolation" (*Commentary on the Gospel of St. John,* Homily 82; FC, pp. 389–90).—3rd Ed.

the fullness and clarity accessible to them, the will of the heavenly Father, for the salvation of the world, and granted to them the new, more perfect law of faith and piety which serves for the purpose of the salvation of the whole human race. This ministry was performed immediately by the Lord Himself and through His disciples, who, in accordance with His commandment, proclaimed the good news to all peoples and handed it down to the Church in all times.

The Lord proclaimed the good news of (1) the teaching of faith, and (2) the teaching of life and piety.

The evangelical teaching of faith is the teaching:

a) concerning God, our All-Good Father, to Whom we are taught to appeal with the cry of a son: "Our Father." Concerning this revelation to men of the new, more perfect understanding of God, the Saviour speaks in the prayer before His sufferings: *I have manifested Thy name unto men,* and, *I have declared unto them Thy name* (John 17:6, 26);

b) concerning the coming of the *Word* into the world—the coming of the only begotten Son of God—for the salvation of men and their reunion with God;

c) concerning the Holy Spirit, our Comforter and Sanctifier;

d) concerning the nature and purpose of man; concerning sin, repentance, the means of salvation, sanctification and rebirth;

e) concerning the Kingdom of God and the New Testament Church;

f) concerning the final General Judgment and the final fate of the world and man.

The evangelical teaching of life and piety is the high commandment of love to God and neighbor, which is presented much more fully and elevatedly than in the Old Testament, and inspires one to the full devotion to God of a son. Many private commandments of this most perfect moral law are concentrated in the Sermon on the Mount. Such, for example, are the commandments of the forgiveness of offenses and love for one's enemies, of self-denial and humility, of true chastity (not only bodily but also spiritual), of mutual service according to the most exalted example of the Saviour Himself, and of the other things that are morally demanded of a Christian.

While the Old Testament law inspires one to fulfill the commandments chiefly for the sake of an earthly, temporal prosperity, the New Testament law inspires one to higher, eternal, spiritual goods.

The Old Testament law, however, was not abrogated by the Saviour, it was only elevated; it was given a more perfect interpretation; it was placed upon better foundations. With the coming of the New Testament, it was only the Jewish ritual law that was abrogated.

Concerning the relation of Christians to the Old Testament, the Blessed Theodoret reasons thus: "Just as mothers of just-born infants give nourishment by means of the breast, and then light food, and finally, when they become children or youths, give them solid food, so also the God of all things from time to time has given men a more perfect teaching. But, despite all this, we revere also the Old Testament as a mother's breast, only we do not take milk from there; for the perfect have no need of a mother's milk, although they should revere her because it was from her that they received their upbringing. So we also, although we do not any longer observe circumcision, the Sabbath, the offering of sacrifices, the sprinklings—nonetheless, we take from the Old Testament a different benefit: for it, in a perfect way, instructs us in piety, in faith in God, in love for neighbor, in continence, in justice, in courage, and above all it presents for imitation the examples of the ancient saints" (Blessed Theodoret, "Brief Exposition of Divine Dogmas").

The law of the Gospel is given for all times, unto the end of the age, and is not subject to being abrogated or changed.

The law of the Gospel is given for all men, and not for one people alone, as was the Old Testament law.

Therefore, the faith and teaching of the Gospel are called by the Fathers of the Church "Catholic," that is, embracing all men in all times.

C. Christ, the Head and King of the World
(The Royal Ministry of Christ)

The Son of God, the Creator and Master of heaven and earth, the Eternal King according to Divinity, is King also according to His

God-Manhood, both in His earthly ministry until His death on the Cross, and in His glorified condition after the Resurrection.

The Prophets prophesied of Him as a King, as we read in the Prophet Isaiah: *Unto us a Child is born, unto us a Son is given: and the government shall be upon His shoulder; and His name shall be called Messenger of Great Counsel, Wonderful, Counselor, the Mighty God, Potentate, the Prince of Peace, Father of the age to come.... Of the increase of His government and peace there shall be no end, upon the throne of David and upon His Kingdom* (Is. 9:6–7, Septuagint).

The Royal Ministry of the Lord before His Resurrection was expressed (*a*) in His miracles, in His authority over nature; (*b*) in His authority over the powers of hell, concerning which there is the testimony of His numerous exorcisms of demons and of the word of the Lord: *I beheld Satan as lightning fall from heaven* (Luke 10:18); and (*c*) in His authority over death, manifested in the resurrection of the son of the widow of Nain, the daughter of Jairus, and Lazarus of the four days.

The Lord Jesus Christ Himself speaks of Himself as a King before His Resurrection when He was being judged by Pilate: *My Kingdom is not of this world* (John 18:36–37).

When the Lord appeared in His glory to His disciples after the Resurrection, He said to them, *All power is given unto Me in heaven and in earth* (Matt. 28:18).

After His Ascension, the God-Man Christ is Head of heaven, earth, and the underworld.

In all its power, the royal might of the Lord Jesus Christ was revealed in His descent into hell and His victory over hell, His destruction of its bonds; further, in His Resurrection and victory over death; and finally, in the Ascension of Jesus Christ and the opening of the Kingdom of Heaven for all who believe in Him.

How is One to Understand "The Deification of Humanity in Christ"?

The human nature of the Lord Jesus Christ, through its union with the Divinity, participated in Divine qualities and was enriched by them, in other words, it was "deified." And not only was the human nature of the Lord Himself deified: through Him and in Him *our* humanity also is deified, for *He also Himself likewise took part in* our flesh and blood (Heb. 2:14), united Himself in the most intimate way with the human race, and consequently united it with the Divinity. Since the Lord Jesus Christ received flesh from the Ever-Virgin Mary, the Church books very frequently call her the fount of our deification: "Through her we have been deified." We are deified likewise through worthy reception of the Body and Blood of Christ.[27] However, one must understand the limits of the meaning of the term "deification,"

---

[27] Here Fr. Michael is speaking of the Orthodox doctrine of deification in the broad sense. As St. Symeon the New Theologian affirmed in the passage cited earlier (pp. 207–8, note 20), those who have received Baptism, Chrismation, and Communion are already in a sense "gods by Grace," because they have the Uncreated Energy of God dwelling within them. In his prepatory prayer for Holy Communion, St. Symeon says that all those who partake of the Holy Mysteries "with sincerity of heart are quickened and deified."

"Deification in the broad sense," writes Fr. Dumitru Staniloae, "begins at Baptism, and stretches out all along the whole of man's spiritual ascent; here his powers are also active, that is, during the purification from the passions, the winning of the virtues, and illumination" (*Orthodox Spirituality,* p. 363).

According to the experience of the Orthodox Church, deification may also be understood in a strict sense: that is, as God's full and perfect penetration of man, in which the operations and energies of human nature cease, having been replaced by the Divine Operations and Energies. Of such deification, St. Maximus the Confessor writes: "The soul becomes god and rests from all its mental and physical works by participation in Divine Grace; at the same time all the natural operations of the body rest with it. They are deified along with the soul in proportion to its participation in deification, to the extent that then only God will be visible, through the soul as well as through the body; the natural attributes are conquered by the over-abundance of glory" (*Selected Writings,* p. 167).

The ultimate state of man's deification will occur only after the General Resurrection, when the *whole man*—both body and soul—will dwell forever in a deified state, penetrated by Uncreated Light. The bodies of the saints will then be like the glorious body of Christ after His Resurrection. But even then, after the General Resurrection, the growth of the saints toward God will never end. "The progress will be endless," says St. Symeon, "for a cessation of this growing toward the end without ending would be nothing but a grasping at the ungraspable" (quoted in Archbishop Basil Krivocheine, *In the Light of Christ,* p. 386).—3RD ED.

since in the philosophic-religious literature of recent times, beginning with Vladimir Soloviev, there is a tendency towards an incorrect broadening of the meaning of the dogma of Chalcedon. The term "deification" does not mean the same thing as the term "God-Manhood," and one who is "deified" in Christ is not placed on the path to personal God-Manhood.[28] If the Church of Christ is called a Divine-Human organism, this is because the Head of the Church is Christ *God*, and the body of the Church is *humanity* reborn in Christ. In itself humanity in general, and likewise man individually, remains in that nature in which and for which it was created: for, in the person of Christ also, the human body and soul did not pass over into the Divine Nature, but were only united with it, united "without confusion or change." "For there never was, nor is, nor ever will be another Christ consisting

---

[28] The Orthodox teaching on deification, both in its broad and strict definitions, is radically different from Soloviev's idea of God-Manhood. According to Soloviev, man can unite the Divine Nature with his human nature, as Christ did (see Appendix I below). According to Orthodox theology, on the other hand, Christ was the only one to unite Divine Nature and human nature in one Person; the rest of mankind possesses only a human nature. But although we cannot become God by nature as Christ was and is, we can become "gods by Grace," being united with God and participating in Him through His Divine Energies.

Fr. Dumitru Staniloae explains: "God 'by Grace,' not by nature, means precisely that the nature of deified man remains unchanged, in the sense that it does not itself become the source of Divine Energies; it has them by Grace received as a gift. No matter how much the Divine Energies grow in it, it remains only a channel, a medium which reflects them—never will it assume the role of the source."

The deified Christian, Fr. Dumitru continues, "is as God, yes even god, but not God. He is a dependent god, or, to say it another way, a 'god by participation.' The consciousness of this dependence excludes the pantheistic identification of man with God.

"Deification is the passing of man from created things to the Uncreated, to the level of the Divine Energies. Man partakes of these, not of the Divine Essence. So it is understood how man assimilates more and more of the Divine Energies, without this assimilation ever ending, since he will never assimilate their Source itself, that is, the Divine Essence, and become God by Essence, or another Christ. In the measure in which man increases his capacity to become a subject of ever richer Divine Energies, these Energies from the Divine Essence are revealed to him in a greater proportion (*Orthodox Spirituality*, pp. 371, 373).—3RD ED.

of Divinity and humanity, Who remains in Divinity and humanity, the same being perfect God and perfect Man," as teaches St. John Damascene (*Exact Exposition* 3.3).

THE RESURRECTION OF CHRIST

THE SAVING FRUITS OF THE RESURRECTION OF CHRIST

The Resurrection of Christ is *the foundation and the crown of our Orthodox Christian faith.* The Resurrection of Christ is the first, most important, great truth, with the proclamation of which the Apostles began their preaching of the Gospel after the descent of the Holy Spirit. Just as by the death of Christ on the Cross our Redemption was accomplished, so by His Resurrection *eternal life was given to us.* Therefore, the Resurrection of Christ is the object of the Church's constant triumph, its unceasing rejoicing, which reaches its summit in the Feast of the Holy Christian Pascha—"Today all creation is glad and rejoices, for Christ has risen!" (Canon of Pascha, Canticle 9).

The saving fruits of the Resurrection of Christ are:

(*a*) the victory over hell and death; (*b*) the blessedness of the saints in heaven and the beginning of the existence of the Heavenly Church; and (*c*) the sending down of the Holy Spirit and the creation of the Church of Christ on earth.

A. The Victory over Hell and Death

Human existence after the loss of Paradise has two forms: (*a*) the earthly, bodily life; and (*b*) the life after death.

Earthly life ends with the death of the body. The soul preserves its existence after bodily death, but its condition after death, according to the word of God and the teaching of the Fathers of the Church, is diverse. Until the coming to earth of the Son of God, and until His Resurrection from the dead, the souls of the dead were in a condition of rejection, being far away from God, in darkness, in hell, in the underworld (the Hebrew "Sheol"; Gen. 37:35, Septuagint). To be in hell was like spiritual death, as is expressed in the words of the Old Testament Psalm: *In hades who will confess Thee?* (Ps. 6:5). In hell there were imprisoned also the souls of the Old Testament righteous ones. These righteous ones lived on earth with faith in the coming Saviour, as the Apostle Paul explains in the eleventh chapter of his Epistle to the Hebrews; and after death they languished in expectation of their redemption and deliverance. Thus it continued until the Resurrection of Christ, until the coming of the New Testament: *And these all, having obtained a good report through faith, received not the promise, God having provided some better thing for us, that they without us should not be made perfect* (Heb. 11:39–40). Our deliverance was also their deliverance.

Christ, after His death on the Cross, descended in His soul and in His Divinity into hell, at the same time that His body remained in the grave. He preached salvation to the captives of hell and brought up from there all the Old Testament righteous ones into the bright mansions of the Kingdom of Heaven. Concerning this raising up of the righteous ones from hell, we read in the Epistle of St. Peter: *For Christ also hath once suffered for sins, the just for the unjust, that He might bring us to God, being put to death in the flesh, but quickened by the Spirit; by which also He went and preached unto the spirits in prison* (I Peter 3:18–19). And in the same place we read further: *For this cause was the Gospel preached also to them that are dead, that they might be judged according to men in the flesh, but live according to God in the spirit* (I Peter 4:6). St. Paul speaks of the same thing: quoting the verse of the Psalm, *When He ascended up on high, He led captivity captive, and gave gifts unto men,* the Apostle continues: *Now that He ascended, what is it but that He also descended first into the lower parts of the earth? He that descended is the same also that ascended up far above all the heavens, that He might fill all things* (Eph. 4:8–10).

To use the words of St. John Chrysostom, "Hell was taken captive by the Lord Who descended into it. It was laid waste, it was mocked, it was put to death, it was overthrown, it was bound" (Homily on Pascha).

With the destruction of the bolts of hell—that is, the inescapability of hell—the power of death also was annihilated. First of all, death for righteous men became only a transition from the world below to the world above, to a better life, to life in the Light of the Kingdom of God; secondly, bodily death itself became only a temporary phenomenon, for by the Resurrection of Christ the way to the General Resurrection was opened to us. *Now is Christ risen from the dead, and become the firstfruits of them that slept* (I Cor. 15:20). The Resurrection of Christ is the pledge of our resurrection: *For as in Adam all die, even so in Christ shall all be made alive; but every man in his own order: Christ the firstfruits: afterward they that are Christ's at His coming* (I Cor. 15:22–23).[29] After this, death will be utterly annihilated. *The last enemy that shall be destroyed is death* (I Cor. 15:26).[30]

The troparion of Holy Pascha proclaims to us with special joy the victory over hell and death: "Christ is risen from the dead, trampling down death by death, and on those in the tombs bestowing life." Christ *ascended up far above all heavens, that He might fill all things* (Eph. 4:10).

B. The Blessedness of the Saints in Heaven, and the Beginning of the Existence of the Great Kingdom of Christ, the Heavenly Triumphant Church

Before His departure to the Father, the Lord Jesus Christ said to the Apostles: *In My Father's house are many mansions; if it were not so I would have told you. I go to prepare a place for you. And if I go and pre-*

---

[29] Speaking of Christ's Resurrection, St. John Damascene writes that "Through His [risen] body, the Lord has granted the resurrection and consequent incorruptibility to our body, also, Himself becoming the firstfruits of the resurrection and incorruptibility and impassibility" (*Exact Exposition* 3.28; FC, p. 334). For further discussion of how Christ's Resurrection makes all mankind subject to future resurrection, see chapter 10 below.—3rd Ed.

[30] It will be remembered that, according to the explanation of St. Nicholas Cabasilas (see p. 202, note 14 above), death was the last barrier separating man from God, and that Christ broke down this barrier through His Resurrection. St. Gregory Palamas writes: "By means of the one death and Resurrection of His Flesh, He healed our twofold death [i.e., spiritual and bodily] and freed us from our double captivity of soul and body" (*Homilies*, vol. 1, p. 196).—3rd Ed.

pare a place for you, I will come again, and receive you unto Myself; that where I am, there ye may be also (John 14:2–3). The Saviour prayed to the Father, *Father, I will that they also, whom Thou hast given Me, be with Me where I am; that they may behold My glory which Thou hast given Me* (John 17:24). And the Apostles express the desire to depart and to be with Christ (Phil. 1:23), knowing that they have *a house not made with hands, eternal in the heavens* (II Cor. 5:1).

A depiction of the life of the saints in heaven is given in the Apocalypse. St. John the Theologian saw around the throne of God in the heavens *four and twenty seats* and on them elders clothed in white garments and having crowns of gold on their heads (Apoc. 4:4). He saw under the heavenly altar *the souls of them that were slain for the Word of God, and for the testimony which they held* (Apoc. 6:9); and yet again he saw a *great multitude ... of all nations, and kindreds, and people,* standing before the Throne and before the Lamb and crying out: *Salvation to our God Who sitteth upon the Throne, and unto the Lamb* (Apoc. 7:9–10).

The bright mansions of the Heavenly Home are called in Sacred Scripture "the city of the living God," "Mount Zion," the "Heavenly Jerusalem," "the Church of the firstborn written in heaven."

And thus the great Kingdom of Christ has been opened in heaven. Into it have entered the souls of all the righteous and pious people of the Old Testament, those of whom the Apostle has said, *These all, having obtained a good report through faith, received not the promise* (until the coming to earth of the Son of God, and the general salvation), *that they without us should not be made perfect,* that is, attain the joy and blessedness of the Heavenly Church of Christ (Heb. 11:39–40). Into this Kingdom in the New Testament there entered the first ones who believed in Christ, the Apostles, first martyrs, confessors; and thus until the end of the world the Heavenly Home will be filled—the Jerusalem on high, the granary of God—until it shall come to its perfect fullness.

St. Symeon the New Theologian teaches the following: "It was fitting that there should be born all who have been foreknown by God, and that the world which is above this world, the Church of the firstborn, the heavenly Jerusalem, should be filled up; and then the fullness of the Body of Christ will be perfected, receiving in itself all those foreordained by God to be conformed to the image of His Son—these are the sons of the light and the day. Such are all those foreordained and forewritten, and included in the number of the saved, and those who are to be joined and united to the Body of Christ; and there will no longer be lacking in Him a single member. Thus is it in truth, as the Apostle Paul reveals when he says: *Till we all come in the unity of the faith ... unto a perfect man, unto the measure of the stature of the fullness of Christ* (Eph. 4:13). When they shall be gathered together and shall comprise the full Body of Christ, then also the higher world, the heavenly Jerusalem, which is the Church of the firstborn, will be filled up, and the body of the Queen of God, the Church, which is the Body of Christ God, will be revealed as entirely full and perfect" (Homily 45).

According to the teaching of Sacred Scripture, the blessedness of the souls of the righteous in heaven consists of (*a*) the repose or rest from labors; (*b*) nonparticipation in sorrows and sufferings (Apoc. 14:13, 7:16); (*c*) being together with and consequently being in the closest communion with the forefathers and other saints; (*d*) mutual communion between themselves and with thousands of angels; (*e*) standing before the Throne of the Lamb, glorifying Him and serving Him; (*f*) communion and reigning together with Christ; and (*g*) the joyous beholding face to face of God Almighty.

C. The Sending Down of the Holy Spirit and the Establishment of the Church of Christ on Earth

The Lord Jesus Christ, in His conversation with His disciples before His sufferings, promised them to send the Holy Spirit, the Comforter, Who would remain with them forever—the Spirit of Truth Who would instruct them in everything and remind them of all that He Himself had spoken to them, and would inform them of the future. Appearing after the Resurrection to His disciples, the Lord granted them the Grace-given power of the Holy Spirit with the words,

Receive ye the Holy Spirit: Whosesoever sins ye remit, they are remitted unto them; and whosesoever sins ye retain, they are retained (John 20:22–23). And ten days after His Ascension, the Lord, in accordance with His promise, sent down the Holy Spirit upon the disciples on the day of Pentecost in the form of fiery tongues.

The descent into the world by the Holy Spirit was expressed, first of all, in the extraordinary gifts of the Apostles in the form of signs, healings, prophecies, the gifts of tongues; and secondly, in all the Grace-given powers which lead the faithful of Christ to spiritual perfection and to salvation.

In the Holy Spirit, in His Divine power, is given us *all things that pertain unto life and godliness* (II Peter 1:3). *These Grace-given gifts are in the Holy Church which the Lord founded on earth.* They comprise the means of our sanctification and salvation.

An examination of these means of salvation is the subject of a new section of Dogmatic Theology—that concerning *the Church of Christ.*

Chapter 7

The Church of Christ

THE CONCEPT OF THE CHURCH OF CHRIST ON EARTH

IN the literal meaning of the word, the Church is the "assembly," in Greek, *ekklesia,* from *ekkaleo,* meaning "to gather." In this meaning it was used in the Old Testament also (the Hebrew *kahal*).

In the New Testament, this name has an incomparably deeper and more mystical meaning which is difficult to embrace in a short verbal formula. The character of the Church of Christ is best explained by the Biblical images to which the Church is likened.

The New Testament Church is the new planting of God, the garden of God, the vineyard of God. The Lord Jesus Christ, by His earthly life, His death on the Cross and His Resurrection, introduced into humanity new Grace-giving powers, a new life which is capable of great fruitfulness. These powers we have in the Holy Church which is His Body.

The Sacred Scripture is rich in expressive *images* of the Church. Here are the chief of them:

a) The image of the grapevine and its branches (John 15:1–8). *I am the true vine, and My Father is the Husbandman. Every branch in Me that beareth not fruit He taketh away; and every branch that beareth fruit, He purgeth it, that it may bring forth more fruit.... Abide in Me, and I in you. As the branch cannot bear fruit of itself, except it abide in the vine, no more can ye, except ye abide in Me. I am the Vine, ye are the branches. He that abideth in Me, and I in him, the same bringeth forth much fruit; for without Me ye can do nothing. If a man abide not in Me, he is cast forth as a branch, and is withered; and men gather them, and*

229

cast them into the fire, and they are burned.... Herein is My Father glorified, that ye bear much fruit; so shall ye be My disciples.

b) The image of the shepherd and the flock (John 10:1–16). *Verily, verily, I say unto you, he that entereth not by the door into the sheepfold, but climbeth up some other way, the same is a thief and a robber. But he that entereth in by the door is the shepherd of the sheep.... Verily, verily, I say unto you, I am the door of the sheep.... I am the door; by Me if any man enter in, he shall be saved, and shall go in and go out, and find pasture.... I am the good shepherd: the good shepherd giveth his life for the sheep.... I am the good shepherd, and know My sheep, and am known of mine ... and I lay down My life for the sheep. And other sheep I have, which are not of this fold: them also I must bring, and they shall hear My voice; and there shall be one fold, and one shepherd.*

c) The image of the head and the body (Eph. 1:22–23, and other places). The Father *hath put all things under His feet, and gave Him to be the head over all things to the Church, which is His Body, the fullness of Him that filleth all in all.*

d) The image of a building under construction (Eph. 2:19–22). *Now therefore ye are no more strangers and foreigners, but fellow citizens with the saints, and of the household of God; and are built upon the foundation of the Apostles and Prophets, Jesus Christ Himself being the chief cornerstone; in Whom all the building fitly framed together groweth unto a holy temple in the Lord; in Whom ye also are builded together for a habitation of God through the Spirit.*

e) The image of a house or family: *That thou mayest know how thou oughtest to behave thyself in the house of God, which is the Church of the living God, the pillar and ground of the Truth* (I Tim. 3:15). *Christ as a Son over His own house, Whose house are we* (Heb. 3:6).

To this same thing refer likewise other images from the Gospel: the fishing net, the field which has been sown, the vineyard of God.

In the Fathers of the Church one often finds a comparison of the Church in the world with a ship on the sea.

The Apostle Paul, comparing the life of the Church of Christ with a marriage, or with the relationship between man and wife, concludes his thoughts with these words: *This is a great mystery: but I speak con-*

cerning Christ and the Church (Eph. 5:32). The life of the Church in its essence is *mystical;* the course of its life cannot be entirely included in any "history." The Church is completely distinct from any kind whatever of organized society on earth.

The Beginning of the Church's Existence, Its Growth, and Its Purpose

The Church of Christ received its existence with the coming to earth of the Son of God, *when the fullness of the time was come* (Gal. 4:4), and with His bringing of salvation to the world.

The beginning of its existence in its complete form and significance, with the fullness of the gifts of the Holy Spirit, was the day of Pentecost, after the Ascension of the Lord. On this day, after the descent of the Holy Spirit upon the Apostles, in Jerusalem there were baptized about three thousand men. And, further, the Lord each day added those being saved to the Church. From this moment, the territory of the city of Jerusalem, then of Palestine, then of the whole Roman Empire, and even the lands beyond its boundaries, began to be covered with Christian communities or churches. The name "church" which belongs to every Christian community, even of a single house or family, indicates the unity of this part with the whole, with the body of the whole Church of Christ.

Being "the body of Christ," the Church *increaseth with the increase of God* (Col. 2:19). Comparing the Church with a building, the Apostle teaches that its building is not completed, but continues: *All the building fitly framed together groweth unto a holy temple in the Lord* (Eph. 2:21). This growth is not only in the sense of the visible, quantitative increase of the Church on earth; in even greater degree, this is a *spiritual growth,* the *perfection of the saints,* the filling up of the heavenly-earthly world through sanctity. Through the Church is accomplished *the dispensation of the fullness of times* foreordained by the Father, so that *He might gather together in one all things in Christ, both which are in heaven, and which are on earth* (Eph. 1:10).

In the sense of its earthly growth, the Church develops in the

231

spheres of Divine services and the canons; it is made richer by Patristic literature; it grows in the outward forms which are necessary for its earthly conditions of existence.

The Church is our spiritual Home. As with one's own home—and even more than that—a Christian's thoughts and actions are closely bound up with the Church. In it he must, as long as he lives on earth, work out his salvation, and make use of the Grace-given means of sanctification given him by it. It prepares its children for the heavenly homeland.

As to how, by the Grace of God, spiritual rebirth and spiritual growth occur in a man, in what sequence these usually occur, what hindrances must be overcome by him on the way of salvation, how he must combine his own indispensable labors with the Grace-given help of God—special branches of theological and spiritual learning are devoted to all these matters. These are called *moral theology* and *ascetic theology*.

Dogmatic Theology proper limits the subject of the Church to an examination of the Grace-given *conditions* and the mystical, Grace-given *means* furnished in the Church for the attainment of the aim of salvation in Christ.

THE HEAD OF THE CHURCH

The Saviour, in giving authority to the Apostles before His Ascension, told them very clearly that He Himself would not cease to be the invisible Shepherd and Pilot of the Church. *I am with you alway, even unto the end of the world* (every day constantly and inseparably; Matt. 28:20). The Saviour taught that He, as the Good Shepherd, had to bring in also those sheep who were not of this fold, so that there might be one flock and One Shepherd (John 10:16). *All power is given unto Me in heaven and in earth. Go ye, therefore, and teach all nations* (Matt. 28: 18–19). In all these words there is contained the idea that the highest Shepherd of the Church is Christ Himself. We must be aware of this so as not to forget the close bond and the inward unity of the Church on earth with the Heavenly Church.

The Lord Jesus Christ is also the *Founder* of the Church: *I will build My Church, and the gates of hell shall not prevail against it* (Matt. 16:18).

Christ is also the *Foundation* of the Church, its cornerstone: *Other foundation can no man lay than that is laid, which is Jesus Christ* (I Cor. 3:11).

He also is its *Head*. God the Father *gave Him to be the head over all things to the Church, which is His body, the fullness of Him that filleth all in all* (Eph. 1:22–23). *The Head is Christ, from Whom the whole body fitly joined together and compacted by that which every joint supplieth, according to the effectual working in the measure of every part, maketh increase of the body unto the edifying of itself in love* (Eph. 4:15–16). As all the members of our body comprise a full and living organism which depends upon its head, so also the Church is a spiritual organism in which there is no place where the powers of Christ do not act. It is "full of Christ" (Bishop Theophan the Recluse).[1]

Christ is the *Good Shepherd* of His flock, the Church. We have the *great Shepherd of the sheep,* according to the Apostle Paul (Heb. 13:20). The Lord Jesus Christ is the Chief of Shepherds. *Being examples to the flock,* the Apostle Peter entreats those who have been placed as shepherds in the Church, as their co-pastor (Greek: *syn-presbyteros*), *when the Chief Shepherd shall appear, ye shall receive a crown of glory that fadeth not away* (I Peter 5:1–4).

Christ Himself is the invisible Chief *Bishop* of the Church. The Hieromartyr Ignatius the God-bearer, an Apostolic Father, calls the Lord the "Invisible Bishop" (Greek: *episkopos aoratos*).

Christ is the eternal *High-Priest* of His Church, as the Apostle Paul explains in the Epistle to the Hebrews. The Old Testament Chief Priests *were many, because they were not suffered to continue by reason of death. But this one, because He continueth forever, hath an unchangeable priesthood. Wherefore He is able also to save them to the uttermost that*

---

[1] Bishop Theophan the Recluse was canonized by the Russian Orthodox Church (Moscow Patriarchate) in 1988. Commemorated January 10. See Appendix III, p. 398 below.—3RD ED.

come unto God by Him, seeing He ever liveth to make intercession for them (Heb. 7:23–25).

He is, according to the Apocalypse of St. John the Theologian, *He that is true, He that hath the key of David, He that openeth, and no man shutteth; and shutteth and no man openeth* (Apoc. 3:7).

The truth that Christ Himself is the Head of the Church has always in lively fashion run through, and continues to run through, the self-awareness of the Church. In our daily prayers also we read, "O Jesus, Good Shepherd of Thy sheep" (The Prayer of St. Antioch in the Prayers Before Sleep of the Orthodox Prayer Book).

Chrysostom teaches in his Homilies on the Epistle to the Ephesians as follows: "In Christ, in the flesh, God placed a single Head for everyone, for angels and men; that is, He gave one principle both to angels and men: to the one, Christ according to the flesh; and to the other, God the Word. Just as if someone should say about a house, that one part of it is rotten and the other part strong, and he should restore the house, that is, make it stronger, placing a stronger foundation under it; so also here, He has brought all under a single Head. Only then is union possible; only then will there be that perfect bond, when everything, having a certain indispensable bond with what is above, will be brought under a single Head" (*Works of St. John Chrysostom* in Russian, vol. 11, p. 14).

The Orthodox Church of Christ refuses to recognize yet another head of the Church in the form of a "Vicar of Christ on earth," a title given in the Roman Catholic Church to the Bishop of Rome. Such a title does not correspond either to the word of God or to the universal Church consciousness and tradition; it tears away the Church on earth from immediate unity with the heavenly Church. A vicar is assigned during the absence of the one replaced; but Christ is invisibly present in His Church always.

The rejection by the ancient Church of the view of the Bishop of Rome as the Head of the Church and Vicar of Christ upon earth is expressed in the writings of those who were active in the Ecumenical Councils.

The Second Ecumenical Council of bishops, after the completion of their activities, wrote an epistle to Pope Damasus and other bishops of the Roman Church, which ended thus: "When in this way the teaching of faith is in agreement, and Christian love is established in us, we will cease to speak the words which were condemned by the Apostle: *I am of Paul, I am of Apollos, I am of Cephas* (I Cor 1:12). And when we will all be manifest as of Christ, since Christ is not divided in us, then by God's mercy we will preserve the Body of Christ undivided, and will boldly stand before the throne of the Lord."

The leading personality of the Third Ecumenical Council, St. Cyril of Alexandria, in his "Epistle on the Holy Symbol," which is included in the Acts of this Council, writes: "The most holy Fathers ... who once gathered in Nicaea, composed the venerable Ecumenical Symbol (Creed). With them Christ Himself presided, for He said, *Where two or three are gathered together in My name, there am I in the midst of them* (Matt. 18:20). For how can there be any doubt that Christ presided at this Holy and Ecumenical Council? Because there a certain basis and a firm, unvanquishable foundation was laid, and even extended to the whole universe, that is, this holy and irreproachable confession. If it is thus, then can Christ be absent, when He is the Foundation, according to the words of the most wise Paul: *Other foundation can no man lay than that is laid, which is Jesus Christ* (I Cor. 3:11)?"

Blessed Theodoret, in a homily which was also placed in the Acts of the Third Ecumenical Council, addressing the heretics, the followers of Nestorius, says: "Christ is a stone of stumbling and a scandal for unbelievers, but does not put the believers to shame; a precious stone and a foundation, according to the word of Isaiah when he said that Christ is the stone which the builders rejected and which has become the cornerstone. Christ is the foundation of the Church. Christ is the stone which was taken out not with hands, and was changed into a great mountain and covered the universe, according to the prophecy of Daniel; it is for Him, with Him, and by the power of Him that we battle, and for Whose sake we are far removed from the reigning city, but are not excluded from the Kingdom of Heaven; for we have a city on high, Jerusalem, *whose builder and maker is God* (Heb. 11:10), as the Apostle Paul says."

Concerning the rock upon which the Lord promised the Apostle Peter to found His Church, St. Juvenal, Patriarch of Jerusalem, in his epistle to the clergy of Palestine after the Fourth Ecumenical Council of Chalcedon writes: "When the chief and first of the Apostles Peter said, *Thou art the Christ, the Son of the living God,* the Lord replied, *Blessed art thou, Simon Bar-Jonah: for flesh and blood hath not revealed it unto thee, but My Father Who is in heaven. And I say also unto thee, that thou art Peter, and upon this rock I will build My Church; and the gates of hell shall not prevail against it* (Matt. 16:17–18). On this confession the Church of God is made firm, and this faith, given to us by the Holy Apostles, the Church has kept and will keep to the end of the world."

The Close Bond between the Church of Christ on Earth and the Church of the Saints in Heaven

The Apostle instructs those who have come to believe in Christ and have been joined to the Church as follows: *Ye are come unto Mount Zion, and unto the city of the living God, the heavenly Jerusalem, and to an innumerable company of angels, to the general assembly and Church of the firstborn, which are written in heaven, and to God the Judge of all, and to the spirits of just men made perfect, and to Jesus, the Mediator of the new covenant* (Heb. 12:22–24). We are not separated from our dead brothers in the faith by the impassable abyss of death: they are close to us in God, *for all live unto Him* (Luke 20:38).

The Church hymns this relationship in the kontakion of the feast of the Ascension of the Lord: "Having accomplished for us Thy mission and united things on earth with things in heaven, Thou didst ascend into glory, O Christ our God, being nowhere separated from those who love Thee, but remaining ever present with us and calling: I am with you and no one is against you."

Of course, there is a distinction between the Church of Christ on earth and the Church of the saints in heaven: the members of the earthly Church are not yet members of the heavenly Church.

In this connection the "Encyclical of the Eastern Patriarchs" (17th century), in reply to the teaching of the Calvinists concerning the one invisible Church, thus formulates the Orthodox teaching about the Church: "We believe, as we have been instructed to believe, in what is called, and what in actual fact is, the Holy, Catholic, Apostolic Church, which embraces all those, whoever and wherever they might be, who believe in Christ, who being now on their earthly pilgrimage have not yet come to dwell in the heavenly homeland. But we do not in the least confuse the Church in pilgrimage with the Church that has reached the homeland, just because, as certain of the heretics think, one and the other both exist, and they both comprise as it were two flocks of the single Chief Shepherd, God, and are sanctified by the one Holy Spirit. Such a confusion of them is out of place and impossible, inasmuch as one is battling and is still on the way, while the other is already celebrating its victory and has reached the Fatherland and has received the reward, something which will follow also for the whole Ecumenical Church" ("Encyclical of the Eastern Patriarchs," par. 10).

And in actuality, the earth and the heavenly world are two separate forms of existence: there in heaven is bodilessness, here on earth are bodily life and physical death; there, those who have attained, here, those seeking to attain; here, faith, there, seeing the Lord face to face; here, hope, there, fulfillment.

Nonetheless, one cannot represent the existence of these two regions, the heavenly and the earthly, as completely separate. If we do not reach as far as the saints in heaven, the saints do reach as far as us. As one who has studied the whole of a science has command also over its elementary parts, just as a general who has entered into a country has command also over its borderlands; so those who have reached heaven have in their command what they have gone through, and *they do not cease to be participants in the life of the militant Church on earth.*

The Holy Apostles, departing from this world, put off the earthly body, but have not put off the Church body. They not only *were,* but they also *remain* the foundations of the Church. The Church is built *upon the foundation of the Apostles and Prophets, Jesus Christ Himself being the chief cornerstone* (Eph. 2:20). Being in heaven, they continue to be in communion with believers on earth.

Such an understanding was present in ancient Patristic thought, of both East and West. Here are the words of Chrysostom: "Again, the memorial of the martyrs, and again a feast day and a spiritual solemnity. They suffered, and we rejoice; they struggled, and we leap for joy; their crown is the glory of all, or rather, the glory of the whole Church. How can this be? you will say. The martyrs are our parts and members. But, *whether one member suffer, all the members suffer with it; or one member be honored, all the members rejoice with it* (I Cor. 12:26). The head is crowned, and the rest of the body rejoices. One becomes a victor in the Olympic games, and the whole people rejoices and receives him with great glory. If at the Olympic games those who do not in the least participate in the labors receive such satisfaction, all the more can this be with regard to the strugglers of piety. We are the feet, and the martyrs are the head; but *the head cannot say to the feet, I have no need of you* (I Cor. 12:21). The members are glorified, but the preeminence of glory does not estrange them from the bond with the other parts: for then especially are they glorious when they are not estranged from the bond with them." "If their Master is not ashamed to be our Head, then all the more are they not ashamed to be our members; for in them is expressed love, and love usually joins and binds things which are separate, despite their difference in dignity" (St. John Chrysostom, "Eulogy for the Holy Martyr Romanus").

"For the souls of the pious dead," says Blessed Augustine, "do not depart from the Church, which is the Kingdom of Christ. This is why, on the altar of the Lord, their memorial is performed in the offering of the Body of Christ.... Why should this be done if not because the faithful even after death remain members of it (the Church)?"

The ever-memorable Russian pastor St. John of Kronstadt, in his "Thoughts Concerning the Church," writes: "Acknowledge that all the saints are our elder brothers in the one House of the Heavenly Father, who have departed from earth to heaven, and they are always with us in God, and they constantly teach us and guide us to eternal life by means of the Church services, Mysteries, rites, instructions, and Church decrees, which they have composed—as for example, those concerning the fasts and feasts; so to speak, they serve together with us, they sing, they speak, they instruct, they help us in various temptations and sorrows. And call upon them as living with you under a single roof; glorify them, thank them, converse with them as with living people; and you will believe in the Church" (St. John of Kronstadt, "What Does It Mean to Believe In The Church? Thoughts concerning the Church and the Orthodox Divine Services").

The Church in its prayers to the apostles and hierarchs calls them its pillars, upon which even now the Church is established. "Thou art a pillar of the Church"; "ye are pillars of the Church"; "thou art a good shepherd and fervent teacher, O Hierarch"; "ye are the eyes of the Church of Christ"; "ye are the stars of the Church" (from various Church services). In harmony with the consciousness of the Church, the saints, going to heaven, comprise, as it were, the firmament of the Church. "Ye do ever illumine the precious firmament of the Church like magnificent stars, and ye shine upon the faithful, O divine Martyrs, warriors of Christ" (from the Common Service to Martyrs). "Like brightly shining stars ye have mentally shone forth upon the firmament of the Church, and ye do illumine the whole creation" (from the Service to Hieromartyrs).

There is a foundation for such appeals to the saints in the word of God itself. In the Apocalypse of St. John the Theologian we read: *Him that overcometh will I make a pillar in the temple of my God* (Apoc. 3:12). Thus the saints are pillars of the Church not only in the past, but in all times as well.

In this bond of the Church with the saints, and likewise in the Headship of the Church by the Lord Himself, may be seen one of the mystical sides of the Church. "By Thy Cross, O Christ, there is a single flock of angels and men; and in the one assembly heaven and earth rejoice, crying out, O Lord, glory to Thee" (Octoechos, Tone 1, Aposticha of Wednesday Matins).

THE ATTRIBUTES OF THE CHURCH

The ninth Article of the Symbol of Faith indicates the four basic signs of the Church: "We believe in One, Holy, Catholic and Apostolic Church." These attributes are called essential, that is, those without which the Church would not be the Church.

The Unity of the Church

In the Greek text the word "in One," is expressed as a numeral (*en mian*). Thus the Symbol of Faith confesses that the Church is one: (*a*) it is one as viewed from within itself, not divided; (*b*) it is one as viewed from without, that is, not having any other beside itself. Its unity consists not in the joining together of what is different in nature, but in inward agreement and unanimity. *There is one body and one Spirit, even as ye are called in one hope of your calling; one Lord, one faith, one baptism, one God and Father of all, Who is above all, and through all, and in you all* (Eph. 4:4–6).

Depicting the Church in parables, the Saviour spoke of one flock, of one sheepfold, of one grapevine, of one foundation-stone of the Church. He gave a single teaching, a single baptism, and a single communion. The unity of the faithful in Christ comprised the subject of His High-Priestly Prayer before His sufferings on the Cross; the Lord prayed *that they all may be one* (John 17:21).

The Church is one not only inwardly, but also outwardly. Outwardly its unity is manifested in the harmonious confession of faith, in the oneness of Divine services and Mysteries, in the oneness of the Grace-giving hierarchy, which comes in succession from the Apostles, in the oneness of canonical order.

The Church on earth has a visible side and an invisible side. The invisible side is: that its Head is Christ; that it is animated by the Holy Spirit; that in it is performed the inward mystical life in sanctity of the more perfect of its members.

However, the Church, by the nature of its members, is *visible,* since it is composed of men in the body; it has a visible hierarchy; it performs prayers and sacred actions visibly; it confesses openly, by means of words, the faith of Christ.

The Church does not lose its unity because side by side with the Church there exist Christian societies which do not belong to it. These societies are not in the Church, they are outside of it.

The unity of the Church is not violated because of temporary divisions of a nondogmatic nature. Differences between Churches arise frequently out of insufficient or incorrect information. Also, sometimes a temporary breaking of communion is caused by the personal errors of individual hierarchs who stand at the head of one or another local Church; or it is caused by their violation of the canons of the Church, or by the violation of the submission of one territorial ecclesiastical group to another in accordance with anciently established tradition. Moreover, life shows us the possibility of disturbances within a local Church, which hinder the normal communion of other Churches with the given local Church until the outward manifestation and triumph of the defenders of authentic Orthodox truth. Finally, the bond between Churches can sometimes be violated for a long time by political conditions, as has often happened in history.[2] In such cases,

---

[2] Two examples from recent Church history may serve to illustrate the character of these temporary divisions. In the early 19th century, when Greece proclaimed its independence from the Turkish Sultan, the parts of the Greek Church in Greece itself and in Turkey became outwardly divided. When the Patriarch of Constantinople, who was still under Turkish authority, was forced by the Sultan to excommunicate the "rebels" in Greece, the Orthodox in Greece refused to accept this act as having been performed under political coercion, but they did not cease to regard the Patriarch as a member of the same Orthodox Church as themselves, nor did they doubt that his non-political sacramental acts were Grace-giving. This division led to the formation today of two separate local Churches (in full communion with each other): those of Greece and Constantinople.

In the 20th-century Russian Orthodox Church, a church administration was formed in 1927 by Metropolitan Sergius (the Moscow Patriarchate) on the basis of submission to the dictation of the atheist rulers. Parts of the Church in Russia (the Catacomb or True Orthodox Church) and outside (the Russian Church Outside of Russia) refuse up to now to have communion with this administration because of its political domination by Communists; but the bishops of the Church Outside of Russia (about the Catacomb Church it is more difficult to make a general statement) do not deny the Grace of the Mysteries of the Moscow Patriarchate and still feel themselves to be one with its clergy and faithful who try not to collaborate with Communist aims. When Communism falls in Russia, these church bodies can once more be in communion or even be joined together, leaving to a future free council all judgments regarding the "Sergianist" period.

[Since Fr. Seraphim Rose wrote the above paragraph (in 1981), Communist totalitarianism has of course fallen in Russia. As a result, the Russian Orthodox Church

the division touches only outward relations, but does not touch or violate inward spiritual unity.

The truth of the One Church is defined by the Orthodoxy of its members, and not by their quantity at one or another moment. St. Gregory the Theologian wrote concerning the Orthodox Church of Constantinople before the Second Ecumenical Council as follows:

"This field was once small and poor.... This was not even a field at all. Perhaps it was not worth granaries or barns or scythes. Upon it there were no stacks or sheaves, but perhaps only small and unripe grass which grows *on the housetops,* with which *the reaper filleth not his hand,* which do not call upon themselves the blessing of those who pass by (Ps. 128:6–8). Such was our field, our harvest! Although it is great, fat, and abundant before Him Who sees what is hidden ... still, it is not known among the people, it is not united in one place, but is gathered little by little *as the summer fruits, as the grape gleanings of the vintage; there is no cluster to eat* (Micah 7:1). Such was our previous poverty and grief" (Farewell Sermon of St. Gregory the Theologian to the Fathers of the Second Ecumenical Council).

"And where are those," says St. Gregory in another Homily, "who reproach us for our poverty and are proud of their wealth? They consider great numbers of people to be a sign of the Church, and despise the small flock. They measure the Divinity (the Saint has in mind here the Arians, who taught that the Son of God was less than the Father) and they weigh people. They place a high value on grains of sand (that is, the masses) and belittle the luminaries. They gather into their treasure-house simple stones, and disdain pearls" (St. Gregory the Theologian, Homily 33, Against the Arians).

(Moscow Patriarchate) and the Russian Orthodox Church Outside of Russia are currently discussing the restoration of full eucharistic communion. Some members of the Catacomb Church—particularly those who never denied the Grace of the Mysteries of the Moscow Patriarchate—have already returned to the Patriarchate. Others, however, are entrenched in a sectarian mentality and have no intention of reuniting with the Church of Russia. In his time, Fr. Seraphim was aware of this problem of sectarianism in some Catacomb groups, and he wrote and spoke about it (see Hieromonk Damascene, *Father Seraphim Rose: His Life and Works,* p. 650).]

In the prayers of the Church are contained petitions for the ceasing of possible disagreements among the Churches: "Cause discords to cease in the Church; quickly destroy by the might of Thy Holy Spirit all uprisings of heresies" (Eucharistic Prayer at the Liturgy of St. Basil the Great). "We glorify Thee ... Thou one rule in Trinity, and beg for forgiveness of sins, peace for the world, and concord for the Church.... Grant peace and unity to Thy Church, O Thou Who lovest mankind" (Canon of the Sunday Midnight Office, Tone 8, Canticle 9).

The Sanctity of the Church

The Lord Jesus Christ performed the work of His earthly ministry and death on the Cross; Christ *loved the Church ... that He might present it to Himself a glorious Church, not having spot, or wrinkle, or any such thing; but that it should be holy and without blemish* (Eph. 5:25–27). The Church is holy through its *Head,* the Lord Jesus Christ. It is holy, further, through the presence in it of the *Holy Spirit* and His Grace-giving gifts, communicated in the Mysteries and other sacred rites of the Church. It is also holy through its *tie with the Heavenly Church.*

The very *body of the Church* is holy: *If the firstfruit be holy, the lump is also holy; and if the root be holy, so are the branches* (Rom. 11:16). Those who believe in Christ are "temples of God," "temples of the Holy Spirit" (I Cor. 3:16; 6:19). In the true Church there have always been and there always are people of the highest spiritual purity and with special gifts of Grace—martyrs, virgins, ascetics, holy monks and nuns, hierarchs, righteous ones, blessed ones. The Church has an uncounted choir of departed ones of all times and peoples. It has manifestations of the extraordinary gifts of the Holy Spirit, both visible and hidden from the eyes of the world.

The Church is holy by its calling, or its purpose. It is holy also by its fruits: *Ye have your fruit unto holiness, and the end everlasting life* (Rom. 6:22), as the Apostle Paul instructs us.

The Church is holy likewise through its pure, infallible *teaching of faith: The Church of the living God* is, according to the word of God, *the pillar and ground of the truth* (I Tim. 3:15). The Patriarchs of the Eastern Churches, concerning the infallibility of the Church in its teaching, express themselves thus: "In saying that the teaching of the Church is infallible, we do not affirm anything else than this, that it is unchanging, that it is the same as was given to it in the beginning as the teaching of God."

The sanctity of the Church is not darkened by the intrusion of the world into the Church, or by the sinfulness of men. Everything sinful and worldly which intrudes into the Church's sphere remains foreign to it and is destined to be sifted out and destroyed, like weed seeds at sowing time. The opinion that the Church consists only of righteous and holy people without sin does not agree with the direct teaching of Christ and His Apostles. The Saviour compares His Church with a field on which the wheat grows together with the tares, and again, with a net which draws out of the water both good fish and bad. In the Church there are both good servants and bad ones (Matt. 18:23–35), wise virgins and foolish (Matt. 25:1–13). "We believe," states the "Encyclical of the Eastern Patriarchs," "that the members of the Catholic Church are all the faithful, and only the faithful, that is, those who undoubtingly confess the pure faith in the Saviour Christ (the faith which we have received from Christ Himself, from the Apostles, and from the Holy Ecumenical Councils), even though certain of them might have submitted to various sins.... The Church judges them, calls them to repentance, and leads them on the path of the saving commandments. And therefore, despite the fact that they are subject to sins, they remain and are acknowledged as members of the Catholic Church as long as they do not become apostates and as long as they hold to the Catholic and Orthodox faith" (par. 11).

But there is a boundary, which if sinners go past, they, like dead members, are cut off from the body of the Church, either by a *visible* act of the Church authority or by the *invisible* act of God's judgment. Thus, those do not belong to the Church who are atheists or apostates from the Christian faith, and those who are sinners characterized by a conscious stubbornness and lack of repentance for their sins, as it says in the Catechism (ninth article).[3] Also among those who do not belong

---

[3] St. Philaret, Metropolitan of Moscow, *The Longer Catechism of the Orthodox, Catholic, Eastern Church.* English trans., p. 50.—3RD ED.

to the Church are heretics who have corrupted the fundamental dogmas of the faith, and schismatics who out of self-will have separated themselves from the Church (the 33rd Canon of the Council of Laodicea forbids prayer with schismatics). St. Basil the Great explains: "The ancients distinguished between heresy, schism, and an arbitrary assembly. They called *heretics* those who have completely cut themselves off and have become foreigners in the faith itself; they called *schismatics* those who have separated themselves in their opinions about certain ecclesiastical subjects and in questions which allow of treatment and healing; and they called *arbitrary assemblies* those gatherings composed of disobedient priests or bishops and uninstructed people."

The sanctity of the Church is *irreconcilable* with false teachings and heresies. Therefore the Church strictly guards the purity of the truth and herself excludes heretics from her midst.

The Catholicity of the Church

In the Greek text of the Nicaeo-Constantinopolitan Symbol of Faith (the Creed), the Church is called "catholic" (in the Slavonic translation, *sobornaya*). What is the significance of this Greek word?

The word *catholikos* in ancient Greek, pre-Christian literature is encountered very rarely. However, the Christian Church from antiquity chose this word to signify one of the principal attributes of the Church, namely, to express its universal character. Even though it had at its disposal such words as *cosmos* (the world), or *oikoumene* (the inhabited earth), evidently these latter words were insufficient to express a certain new concept which is present only to the Christian consciousness. In the ancient Symbols of Faith, wherever the word "Church" appears, it is unfailingly with the definition "catholic." Thus, in the Jerusalem Symbol of Faith we read: "And in one, holy, catholic Church"; in the Symbol of Rome: "In the holy, catholic Church, the communion of the Saints"; etc. In ancient Christian literature, this term is encountered several times in St. Ignatius the God-bearer, an Apostolic Father, for example when he says, "Where Jesus Christ is, there is the catholic Church." This term is constantly to be found in the Acts of all the Ecumenical Councils. In the direct translation of the word, it signifies the highest degree of all-embracingness, wholeness, fullness (being derived from *cath ola,* meaning "throughout the whole").

Side by side with this term there was also used, with the meaning of "universal," the word *oikoumenikos.* These two terms were not mixed. The Ecumenical Councils received the title *Oikoumenike Synodos,* from *oikoumenikos,* meaning from all the inhabited earth—in actual fact, the land which belonged to Greco-Roman civilization.

The Church is catholic. This corresponds to the Apostolic words, *the fullness of Him that filleth all in all* (Eph. 1:23). This concept indicates that the whole human race is called to salvation, and therefore all men are intended to be members of the Church of Christ, even though not all do belong to her in fact. *The Longer Catechism,* answering the question, "Why is the Church called catholic, or, which is the same thing, universal?" replies: "Because she is not limited to any place, nor time, nor people, but contains true believers of all places, times, and peoples."[4]

The Church is not limited by place. It embraces in itself all people who believe in the Orthodox way, wherever they might live on the earth. On the other hand it is essential to have in mind that the Church was catholic even when it was composed of a limited number of communities, and also when, on the day of Pentecost, its bounds were not extended beyond the upper room of Zion and Jerusalem.

The Church is not limited by time: it is foreordained to bring people to faith "unto the end of the world." *I am with you alway, even unto the end of the world* (Matt. 28:20). The Spirit, the Comforter, *will abide with you forever* (John 14:16). The Mystery of the Eucharist will be performed until the Lord comes again to earth (I Cor. 11:26).

The Church is not bound up with any conditions of civil order which it would consider indispensable for itself, nor with any definite language or people.

---

[4] Ibid.—3RD ED.

The Apostolic Church

The Church is called "Apostolic" because the Apostles placed the *historical* beginning of the Church. They spread Christianity to the ends of the earth, and almost all of them sealed their preaching with a martyr's death. The seeds of Christianity were sown in the world by their word and watered with their blood. The unquenched flame of faith in the world they lit by the power of their personal faith.

The Apostles preserved and transmitted to the Church the Christian *teaching of faith and life* in the form in which they had received it from their Master and Lord. Giving in themselves the example of the fulfillment of the commandments of the Gospel, they handed down to the faithful the teaching of Christ by word of mouth and in the Sacred Scriptures so that it might be preserved, confessed, and lived.

The Apostles established, according to the commandment of the Lord, the Church's *sacred rites.* They placed the beginning of the performance of the Holy Mysteries of the Body and Blood of Christ, of baptism, and of ordination.

The Apostles established in the Church the Grace-given *succession of the episcopate,* and through it the succession of the whole Grace-given ministry of the Church hierarchy, which is called to be *stewards of the Mysteries of God,* in accordance with I Corinthians 4:1.

The Apostles established the beginning of the *canonical structure* of the Church's life, being concerned that everything should be done *decently and in order* (I Cor. 14:40); an example of this is given in the fourteenth chapter of the First Epistle to the Corinthians, which contains directions for the assemblies where Church services are celebrated.

Everything we have said here concerns the historical aspect. But besides this there is another, *inward* aspect which gives to the Church an Apostolic quality. The Apostles were not only historically in the Church of Christ; they *remain* in it and are in it now. They were in the earthly Church, and they are now in the Heavenly Church, continuing to be in communion with believers on earth. Being the historical nucleus of the Church, they continue to be the spiritually living, although invisible, nucleus of the Church, both now and forever, in its constant existence. The Apostle John the Theologian writes: ... *Declare we unto you, that ye also may have fellowship with us; and truly our fellowship is with the Father, and with His Son Jesus Christ* (I John 1:3). These words have for us the same force as they had for the contemporaries of the Apostle: they contain an exhortation to us to be in *communion* with the ranks of Apostles, for the nearness of the Apostles to the Holy Trinity is greater than ours.

Thus, both for reasons of an historical character and for reasons of an inward character, the Apostles are the *foundations* of the Church. Therefore it is said of the Church: It is *built upon the foundation of the Apostles and Prophets, Jesus Christ Himself being the chief cornerstone* (Eph. 2:20). The naming of the Church as "apostolic" indicates that it is established not on a single Apostle (as the Roman Church later taught), but upon all twelve; otherwise it would have to bear the name of Peter, or John, or some other. The Church as it were ahead of time warned us against thinking according to a "fleshly" principle (I Cor. 1:12): "I am of Apollos, I am of Cephas." In the Apocalypse, concerning the city coming down from heaven it is said: *And the wall of the city had twelve foundations, and in them the names of the twelve Apostles of the Lamb* (Apoc. 21:14).

The attributes of the Church indicated in the Symbol of Faith, "one, holy, catholic, and apostolic," refer to the militant Church. However, they receive their full significance with the awareness of the oneness of this Church with the Heavenly Church in the one Body of Christ: the Church is one, with a unity that is both heavenly and earthly; it is holy with a heavenly-earthly holiness; it is catholic and apostolic by its unbroken tie with the Apostles and all the saints.

The Orthodox teaching of the Church, which in itself is quite clear and rests upon Sacred Scripture and Sacred Tradition, is to be contrasted with another concept which is widespread in the contemporary Protestant world and has penetrated even into Orthodox circles. According to this different concept, all the various existing Christian organizations, the so-called "confessions" and "sects," even though they are separated from each other, still comprise a single "invisible

Church," inasmuch as each of them confesses Christ as Son of God and accepts His Gospel. The dissemination of such a view is aided by the fact that side by side with the Orthodox Church there exists outside of her a number of Christians that exceeds by several times the number of members of the Orthodox Church. Often we can observe in this Christian world outside the Church a religious fervor and faith, a worthy moral life, a conviction—all the way to fanaticism—of one's correctness, an organization and a broad charitable activity. What is the relation of all of them to the Church of Christ?

Of course, there is no reason to view these confessions and sects as on the same level with non-Christian religions. One cannot deny that the reading of the word of God has a beneficial influence upon everyone who seeks in it instruction and strengthening of faith, and that devout reflection on God the Creator, the Provider and Saviour, has an elevating power there among Protestants also. We cannot say that their prayers are totally fruitless if they come from a pure heart, for *in every nation he that feareth Him ... is accepted with Him* (Acts 10:35). The Omnipresent Good Provider God is over them, and they are not deprived of God's mercies. They help to restrain moral looseness, vices, and crimes; and they oppose the spread of atheism.

But all this does not give us grounds to consider them as belonging to the Church. Already the fact that one part of this broad Christian world outside the Church, namely the whole of Protestantism, denies the bond with the heavenly Church, that is, the veneration in prayer of the Mother of God and the saints, and likewise prayer for the dead, indicates that they themselves have destroyed the bond with the one Body of Christ which unites in itself the heavenly and the earthly. Further, it is a fact that these non-Orthodox confessions have "broken" in one form or another, directly or indirectly, with the Orthodox Church, with the Church in its historical form; they themselves have cut the bond, they have "departed" from her. Neither we nor they have the right to close our eyes to this fact. The teachings of the non-Orthodox confessions contain heresies which were decisively rejected and condemned by the Church at her Ecumenical Councils. In these numerous branches of Christianity there is no unity, either outward or inward—either with the Orthodox Church of Christ or between themselves. The supra-confessional unification (the "ecumenical movement") which is now to be observed does not enter into the depths of the life of these confessions, but has an outward character. The term "invisible" can refer only to the Heavenly Church. The Church on earth, even though it has its invisible side, like a ship a part of which is hidden in the water and is invisible to the eyes, still remains visible, because it consists of people and has visible forms of organization and sacred activity.[5]

Therefore it is quite natural to affirm that these religious organizations are societies which are "near," or "next to," or "close to," or perhaps even "adjoining" the Church, but sometimes "against" it; but they are all *"outside"* the one Church of Christ. Some of them have cut themselves off, others have gone far away. Some, in going away, all the same have historical ties of blood with her; others have lost all kinship, and in them the very spirit and foundations of Christianity have been distorted. None of them find themselves under the activity of the Grace which is present in the Church, and especially the Grace which is given in the Mysteries of the Church. They are not nourished by that mystical table which leads up along the steps of spiritual perfection.

The tendency in contemporary cultural society to place all confessions on one level is not limited to Christianity; on this same all-equalling level are placed also the non-Christian religions, on the grounds that they all "lead to God," and besides, taken all together, they far surpass the Christian world in the number of members who belong to them.

All of such "uniting" and "equalizing" views indicate a forgetfulness of the principle that there can be many teachings and opinions, but there is only *one truth.* And authentic Christian unity—unity in the Church—can be based only upon oneness of mind, and not upon differences of mind. The Church is *the pillar and ground of the Truth* (I Tim. 3:15).

---

[5] Fr. Michael wrote a separate article on this subject. See Protopresbyter Michael Pomazansky, "Is There an Invisible Church?" *The Orthodox Word,* no. 97 (1981), pp. 82–87. Translated from his collected articles in Russian: *Life, Faith, and the Church* (Jordanville, N.Y.: Holy Trinity Monastery, 1976), pp. 198–207.—3RD ED.

THE CHURCH HIERARCHY

All the members of the Church of Christ comprise a single flock of God. All are equal before the judgment of God. However, just as the parts of the body have different functions in the life of the organism, and as in a house building each part has its own use, so also in the Church there exist various ministries. The highest ministry in the Church as an organization is borne by the hierarchy, which is distinct from the ordinary members.

The hierarchy was established by the Lord Jesus Christ. *He gave some, apostles; and some, prophets; and some, evangelists; and some, pastors and teachers; for the perfecting of the saints, for the work of the ministry, for the edifying of the Body of Christ: till we all come in the unity of the faith, and of the knowledge of the Son of God, unto a perfect man, unto the measure of the stature of the fullness of Christ* (Eph. 4:11–13).

No one in the Church can take upon himself the hierarchical ministry, but only one who is called and lawfully placed through the Mystery of Ordination. *No man taketh this honor unto himself, but he that is called of God, as was Aaron* (Heb. 5:4). No matter how high a moral life a man might lead, he cannot fulfill the hierarchical ministry without a special consecration. It is not possible, therefore, to draw a parallel between the degree of one's moral level and the degree of one's level in the hierarchy. Here a perfect correspondence is desirable but is not always attainable.

Apostles

The Lord Jesus Christ during His earthly ministry chose from among His followers twelve disciples—the Apostles (those "sent forth")—giving to them special spiritual gifts and a special authority. Appearing to them after His Resurrection, He said to them, *As My Father hath sent Me, even so send I you. And when He had said this, He breathed on them, and saith unto them, Receive ye the Holy Spirit.*

Whosesoever sins ye remit, they are remitted unto them; and whosesoever sins ye retain, they are retained (John 20:21–23). These words mean that it is essential to be sent from above in order to fulfill the Apostolic ministry, as well as the pastoral ministry that follows after it. The scope of these ministries is expressed in the final words of the Lord to His disciples before His Ascension: *Go ye therefore, and teach all nations, baptizing them in the name of the Father, and of the Son, and of the Holy Spirit, teaching them to observe all things whatsoever I have commanded you. And, lo, I am with you alway, even unto the end of the world. Amen* (Matt. 28:19–20). In these final words the Saviour indicates the triple ministry of the Apostles in their mission: (1) to teach, (2) to perform sacred functions (baptize), and (3) to govern ("teaching them to *observe* all things"). And in the words "I am with you alway, even unto the end of the world," He blessed the pastoral work of their successors for all times to the end of the ages, until the existence of the earthly Church itself should come to an end. The words of the Lord cited before this, "Receive ye the Holy Spirit" (John 20:21), testify that this authority of pastorship is inseparably united with special gifts of the Grace of the Holy Spirit. The three hierarchical ministries are united in a single concept of *pastorship,* in accordance with the expression of the Lord Himself: *Feed My lambs, feed My sheep* (the words to the Apostle Peter in John 21:15, 17), and of the Apostles: *Feed the flock of God* (I Peter 5:2).

The Apostles were always citing the idea of the *Divine institution* of the hierarchy. It was by a special rite that the Apostle Matthias was joined to the rank of the twelve in place of Judas who had fallen away (Acts 1). This rite was the choosing of worthy persons, followed by prayer and the drawing of lots. The Apostles themselves chose successors for themselves through *ordination.* These successors were the *bishops.*

Bishops

The Apostle Paul writes to Timothy, *Neglect not the gift that is in thee, which was given thee by prophecy, with the laying on of the hands of the presbytery* (I Tim. 4:14). And in another place the Apostle writes to him, *I put thee in remembrance, that thou stir up the gift of God, which is in thee by the putting on of my hands* (II Tim. 1:6). To Timothy and Titus, Bishops of Ephesus and Crete, is given the right to make priests: *For this cause I left thee in Crete, that thou shouldest set in order the things that are wanting and ordain presbyters in every city, as I had appointed thee* (Titus 1:5). Likewise they are given the right to give awards to presbyters: *Let the presbyters that rule well be counted worthy of double honor, especially they who labor in the word and doctrine. For the Scripture saith, Thou shalt not muzzle the ox that treadeth out the corn. And, The laborer is worthy of his reward* (I Tim. 5:17–18). Likewise, they have the right to examine accusations against presbyters: *Against a presbyter receive not an accusation, but before two or three witnesses* (I Tim. 5:19).

Thus the Apostles—those precisely among them who were called to the highest ministry in the Church by the Lord Himself—placed *bishops* as their immediate successors and continuers, and *presbyters* as their own helpers and as helpers of the bishops, as the "hands" of the bishops, placing the further matter of the ordination of presbyters with the bishops.

Presbyters (Priests)

Presbyters (literally "elders") were both in Apostolic times and in all subsequent times—and are today—the second degree of the hierarchy. The Apostles Paul and Barnabas, as the book of Acts relates, going through Lystra, Antioch, and Iconium, ordained presbyters in each Church (Acts 14:23). For the resolution of the question about circumcision, an embassy was sent to Jerusalem, to the Apostles and the presbyters at Jerusalem (Acts 15:2). At the Council of the Apostles, the presbyters occupied a place together with the Apostles (Acts 15:6).

Further, the Apostle James instructs: *Is any sick among you? Let him call for the elders (presbyters) of the Church, and let them pray over him, anointing him with oil in the name of the Lord* (James 5:14). From the instruction of the Apostle James we see that (1) presbyters perform the Church's sacred rites, and (2) in the early Church there could be several presbyters in each community, whereas only one bishop was appointed for a city and the region around it.

In the twenty-first chapter of the book of Acts, it is related that when the Apostle Paul returned to Jerusalem after his third Apostolic journey and visited the Apostle James, all the presbyters came, signifying that they made up a special Church rank. They repeated in the hearing of Paul the decree of the Apostolic Council concerning the noncircumcision of the pagans; but they asked him to perform the rite of his own purification, so as to avoid the reproach that he had renounced the name of Jew.

In the Apostolic writings the two names of "bishop" and "presbyter" are not always distinguished. Thus, according to the book of Acts the Apostle Paul called to himself in Miletus the "presbyters of the Church" from Ephesus (Acts 20:17), and instructing them he said, *Take heed therefore unto yourselves, and to all the flock, over which the Holy Spirit hath made you bishops (overseers), to feed the Church of God, which He hath purchased with His own blood* (Acts 20:28). However, from these and similar expressions one cannot conclude that in the age of the Apostles the two ranks—bishop and presbyter—were joined into one. This shows only that in the first century church terminology was not yet as standardized as it became later, and the word "bishop" was used in two meanings: sometimes in the special meaning of the highest hierarchical degree, and sometimes in the usual and general meaning of "overseer," in accordance with the Greek usage of that time. In our everyday terminology in Russia also, for example, the word "to inspect" is far from signifying that one necessarily has the rank of inspector.[6]

Deacons

The third hierarchical degree in the Church is the *deacons*. Deacons, seven in number, were chosen by the community of Jerusalem and ordained by the Apostles, as we read in the sixth chapter of the

---

[6] An "inspector" is the official in charge of overseeing the general good order in Orthodox seminaries.

book of Acts. Their first assignment was to help the Apostles in a practical, secondary activity: they were entrusted to "serve tables"—to give out food, and be concerned for the widows. These seven men were later called deacons, although in the sixth chapter of Acts this name is not yet used.

From the pastoral epistles it is apparent that the deacons were appointed by bishops (I Tim. 3:8–13). According to the book of Acts, for the ministry of deacon there were chosen people "filled with the Holy Spirit and wisdom" (Acts 6:3). They took part in preaching, as did St. Stephen, who sealed his preaching of Christ with his martyr's blood; and like St. Philip, who performed the Baptism of the eunuch (Acts 8:5 and 38). In the Epistle to the Philippians, the Apostle Paul sends greetings to "the bishops and deacons" (1:1), as bearers of the Grace-given hierarchical ministry, helpers of the bishops.

St. Justin the Martyr writes: "Those called deacons among us give to each of those present communion of the Bread upon which has been performed the Thanksgiving (Eucharist) and of the Wine and the Water, and they carry them out to those who are absent." This means that they distributed and carried out to the believers not only food in general, but also the Eucharistic gifts. Their ministry itself, therefore, was bound up in the ancient Church, as it is now, with the Divine services and the giving of Grace.

At the Council of Neo-Caesarea in 314, it was decreed that the number of deacons in a community, even in a large city, should not exceed seven, citing the passage in the book of Acts. In ancient Church literature, sometimes bishops and deacons are named without mention of presbyters, apparently in view of the fact that bishops themselves were the representatives of the communities in the cities, while the presbyters were given the ministry of the communities outside the cities.

The Three Degrees of the Hierarchy

Thus the Church hierarchy is composed of three degrees. None of the three stages can be seized solely by one's personal desire; they are given by the Church, and the appointment to them is performed by the blessing of God through the ordination of a bishop.

All three degrees of the priesthood are indispensable for the Church. Even though a small community may have as representatives of the hierarchy only one or two of the degrees (priest, a priest and a deacon, two priests, etc.), still, in the Church as a whole, and even in the local Church, it is essential that there be the fullness of the hierarchy. The Apostolic Father, St. Ignatius, expresses in his epistles the testimony of the ancient Church concerning this. He writes, "It is essential, as indeed you are acting, to do nothing without the bishop. Likewise obey the presbytery as apostles of Jesus Christ—our hope, in Whom may God grant that we live. And everyone should cooperate in every way with the deacons that serve the ministers of the Mysteries of Jesus Christ, for they are not ministers of food and drink, but servants of the Church of God." "All of you should revere the deacons, as a commandment of Jesus Christ, and the bishop as Jesus Christ, the Son of God the Father, and the presbyters as the assembly of God, as the choir of the Apostles. Without them there is no Church" (St. Ignatius the God-bearer, Epistle to the *Trallians,* par. 2; To the *Smyrneans,* par. 8).

The bishops comprise the highest rank of the hierarchy. In general, everywhere in life there is the principle of headship, and the highest degree of the hierarchy, which rules over presbyters and deacons, is dictated by the very logic of life itself. The same thing is clear from ancient Church literature. The same St. Ignatius writes: "Where the bishop is, there should the people also be, just as also where Jesus Christ is, there is the catholic Church" (Epistle to the *Smyrneans,* par. 8). In the expression of Tertullian, "Without bishops there is no Church" (Tertullian, *Against Marcion* 4.5).

Among the bishops there are some who are leaders by their *position,* but not by their hierarchical, Grace-given dignity. Thus it was also among the Apostles themselves. Although among the Apostles there were those who were specially venerated and renowned, revered as pillars (cf. Gal. 2:2, 9), still all were equal essentially, in their apostolic degree. *I suppose I was not a whit behind the very chiefest Apostles* (II Cor.

11:5, 12:11), the Apostle Paul declares twice, adding: *though I be nothing.* The mutual relations of the Apostles were built upon the foundation of hierarchical equality. Touching on his journey to Jerusalem to meet the most renowned Apostles, James, Peter and John, the Apostle Paul explains that he went "by revelation" (Gal. 2:2), testing himself by the catholic consciousness of the Apostles, but not by the personal view of any one among the most renowned. *But of these who seemed to be somewhat (whatsoever they were, it maketh no matter to me: God accepteth no man's person)* (Gal. 2:6). As for separate persons, the Apostle Paul writes: *When Peter was come to Antioch, I withstood him to the face, because he was to be blamed* for his attitude to the uncircumcised Christians (Gal. 2:11). The same mutual relations according to the principle of hierarchical Grace-given equality remain forever in the Church among the successors of the Apostles—the bishops.

The Councils of the Church

When among the Apostles there appeared a need to appeal to a higher authoritative voice or judgment—this was in connection with the important misunderstandings that arose in Antioch with regard to the application of the ritual law of Moses—the Apostles gathered in a Council at Jerusalem (Acts 15), and the decrees of this Council were acknowledged as obligatory for the whole Church (Acts 16:4). By this the Apostles gave an example of the conciliar resolution of the most important questions in the Church for all times.

Thus the highest *organ of authority* in the Church, and the highest authority in general, is a *council of bishops:* for a local Church it is a council of its local bishops, and for the Ecumenical Church, a council of the bishops of the whole Church.

The Succession and the Uninterruptedness of the Episcopate in the Church

The succession from the Apostles and the uninterruptedness of the episcopacy comprise one of the essential sides of the Church. And, on the contrary: the absence of the succession of the episcopacy in one or another Christian denomination deprives it of an attribute of the true Church, even if in it there is present an undistorted dogmatic teaching. Such an understanding was present in the Church from its beginning. From the Church History of Eusebius of Caesarea we know that all the local ancient Christian Churches preserved lists of their bishops in their uninterrupted succession.

St. Irenaeus of Lyons writes: "We can enumerate those who were appointed as bishops in the Churches by the Apostles, and their successors, even to our time." And, in fact, he enumerates in order the succession of the bishops of the Roman Church almost to the end of the 2nd century (*Against Heresies* 3.3).

The same view of the importance of the succession is expressed by Tertullian. He wrote concerning the heretics of his time: "Let them show the beginnings of their churches, and reveal the series of their bishops who might continue in succession so that their first bishop might have as his cause or predecessor one of the Apostles or an Apostolic Father who was for a long time with the Apostles. For the Apostolic Churches keep the lists (of bishops) precisely in this way. The Church of Smyrna, for example, presents Polycarp, who was appointed by John; the Roman Church presents Clement, who was ordained by Peter; and likewise the other Churches also point to those men whom, as being raised to the episcopacy by the Apostles themselves, they had as their own sprouts from the Apostolic seed" (Tertullian, "Concerning the Prescriptions" against the heretics).

The Position of Pastorship in the Church

I Cor. 4:1–4: *Let a man so account of us, as of the ministers of Christ, and stewards of the mysteries of God.... With me it is a very small thing that I should be judged of you, or of man's judgment.... But He that judgeth me is the Lord.*

I Peter 5:1–3: *The elders (presbyters) which are among you I exhort, who am also an elder, and a witness of the sufferings of Christ, and also a partaker of the glory that shall be revealed: Feed the flock of God which is among you, taking the oversight thereof, not by constraint, but willingly;*

not for filthy lucre, but of a ready mind; neither as being lords over God's heritage, but being examples to the flock.

Hebrews 13:7: *Remember them which have the rule over you, who have spoken unto you the word of God: whose faith follow, considering the end of their conversation (manner of life).*

Hebrews 13:17: *Obey them that have the rule over you, and submit yourselves: for they watch for your souls, as they that must give account, that they may do it with joy, and not with grief: for that is unprofitable for you.*

Chapter 8

The Holy Mysteries (Sacraments)

THE LIFE OF THE CHURCH IN THE HOLY SPIRIT

THE NEW LIFE

THE Church is surrounded by the sinful, unenlightened world; however, it itself is a new creation, and it creates a new life. And every member of it is called to receive and to create in himself this new life. This new life should be preceded by a break on the part of the future member of the Church with the life of "the world." However, when one speaks of the break with "the world," this does not mean to go away totally from life on earth, from the midst of the rest of mankind, which is often unbelieving and corrupt; *for then,* writes the Apostle Paul, *must ye needs go out of the world* (I Cor. 5:10). However, in order to enter the Church one must depart from the power of the devil and become in this sinful world *strangers and pilgrims* (I Peter 2:11). One must place a decisive boundary between oneself and "the world," and for this one must openly and straightforwardly renounce the devil; for one cannot serve two masters. One must cleanse in oneself the old leaven, so as to be a new dough (I Cor. 5:7).

Therefore, from the deepest Christian antiquity the moment of entrance into the Church has been preceded by a special "renunciation of the devil," after which there follows further the Baptism with the cleansing away of sinful defilement. Concerning this we read in detail in the *Catechetical Lectures* of St. Cyril of Jerusalem. In these

Homilies to the Catechumens we see that the "prayers of exorcism," signifying the banishment of the devil, which are in the present Orthodox service of Baptism, and the very "renunciation of Satan" by the person coming for Baptism, are very near in content to the ancient Christian rite. After this there is opened the entrance into the Kingdom of Grace, the birth into a new life "by water and the Spirit," concerning which the Saviour taught in the conversation with Nicodemus (John 3:5–6).

As to how the growth in this new life subsequently occurs, we know this also from the words of the Saviour Himself: *So is the Kingdom of God as if a man should cast seed into the ground, and should sleep, and rise night and day, and the seed should spring and grow up, he knoweth not how. For the earth bringeth forth fruit of herself; first the blade, then the ear, after that the full corn in the ear* (Mark 4:26–28). Thus all this new life—if only it is received inwardly, if a man sincerely desires to remain in it, if on his part he applies efforts to preserve it—acts in him with the *mystical power* of the Holy Spirit, although this invisible process can be almost unfelt by him.

The whole life of the Church is penetrated by the mystical actions of the Holy Spirit. "The cause of all preservation lieth in the Holy Spirit. If He think fit to blow upon a man, He taketh him up above the things of the earth, maketh him grow, and settleth him on high" (Sunday Antiphons from Matins, Tone 6). Therefore, every Church prayer, whether public or private, begins with the prayer to the Holy Spirit: "O Heavenly King, Comforter, the Spirit of Truth, Who art everywhere present and fillest all things, Treasury of good things and Giver of life, come and abide in us...." Just as rain and dew, falling upon the earth, vivify and nourish and give growth to every kind of growing thing, so do the powers of the Holy Spirit act in the Church.

In the Apostolic epistles, the actions of the Holy Spirit are called *excellency of power* (lit., "superabundant power," II Cor. 4:7), *Divine power* (II Peter 1:3), or "by the Holy Spirit." But most frequently of all they are signified by the word "Grace." Those who enter the Church have entered into the Kingdom of Grace, and they are invited to *come boldly unto the throne of Grace, that we may obtain mercy, and find Grace to help in time of need* (Heb. 4:16; see also Heb., chaps. 10–13).

GRACE

The word "Grace" is used in Sacred Scripture with various meanings.

Sometimes it signifies in general the mercy of God: God is *the God of all Grace* (I Peter 5:10). In this, its broadest meaning, Grace is God's goodwill to men of worthy life in all ages of humanity, and particularly to the righteous ones of the Old Testament like Abel, Enoch, Noah, Abraham, the Prophet Moses, and the later Prophets.

In the more precise meaning, the concept of Grace refers to the New Testament. Here in the New Testament we distinguish two fundamental meanings of this concept. First, by the Grace of God, the Grace of Christ, is to be understood the whole economy of our salvation, performed by the coming of the Son of God to earth, by His earthly life, His death on the Cross, His Resurrection, and His Ascension into heaven: *For by Grace are ye saved through faith; and that not of yourselves: it is the gift of God, not of works, lest any man should boast* (Eph. 2:8–9). Secondly, Grace is the name applied to the gifts of the Holy Spirit which have been sent down and are being sent down to the Church of Christ for the sanctification of its members, for their spiritual growth, and for the attainment by them of the Kingdom of Heaven.

In this second New Testament meaning of the word, Grace is a power sent down from on high, the power of God which is in the Church of Christ, which gives birth, gives life, perfects, and brings the believing and virtuous Christian to the appropriation of the salvation which has been brought by the Lord Jesus Christ.[1]

The Apostles, therefore, in their writings often used the Greek

---

[1] As mentioned above (p. 126, note 12), in Orthodox theology "Grace" most commonly refers to the Uncreated Energy, Power, or Operation of God, which is distinct yet inseparable from God's Essence. Thus, St. Gregory Palamas affirms that "This resplendence and deifying Energy of God, that deifies those who participate in

word *charis*, "Grace," as identical in meaning with the word *dynamis*, "power."[2] The term "Grace" in the sense of "power" given from above for holy life is found in many places of the Apostolic epistles (II Peter 1:3, Rom. 5:2, Rom. 16:20, I Peter 5:12, II Peter 3:18, II Tim. 2:1, I Cor. 16:23, II Cor. 13:14, Gal. 6:18, Eph. 6:24, and other places). The Apostle Paul writes: The Lord *said unto me, My Grace is sufficient for thee; for my strength is made perfect in weakness* (II Cor. 12:9).

The distinction between these two meanings of the word "Grace," and the predominant understanding of it in the Sacred Scripture of the New Testament as a Divine power, are important to keep in mind, because in Protestantism a teaching has become established about Grace only in its general significance of the great work of our redemption from sin through the Saviour's exploit on the Cross, after which—as the Protestants think—a man who has come to believe and has received the remission of sins is already among the saved. However, the Apostles teach us that a Christian, having justification as a gift in accordance with the general Grace of redemption, is in this life as an individual only "being saved" (I Cor. 1:18),[3] and needs the support of Grace-given powers. *We have access by faith into this Grace wherein we stand* (Rom. 5:2); *we are saved by hope* (Rom. 8:24).

---

it, constitutes Divine Grace, but it is not the Essence of God" (*Philokalia*, vol. 4, p. 390).

Only God is Uncreated; therefore, to say that Grace is Uncreated is to say that it is God Himself—or, as Vladimir Lossky puts it, it is "a mode of existence of the Trinity which is outside of Its inaccessible Essence" (*Mystical Theology*, p. 73). St. Basil the Great writes: "The Energies of God come down to us, but the Essence remains inaccessible" (Letter 234). Quoting these words of St. Basil, St. Gregory Palamas observes: "Thus it is impossible to participate in God's Essence, even for those who are deified by Divine Grace. It is, however, possible to participate in the Divine Energy" (*Philokalia*, vol. 4, p. 397).—3RD ED.

[2] In the Holy Scriptures the word *dynamis* ("power"; sometimes translated in the KJV as "virtue"), like the word *charis* ("Grace"), is often used to denote the Uncreated Energy of God. For example, *For there went virtue (dynamis) out of Him and healed them all* (Luke 6:19); *Somebody hath touched me, for I perceive that virtue (dynamis) is gone out of me* (Luke 8:46).—3RD ED.

[3] The King James Version translation of this verse, "unto us which are saved," is imprecise; the Greek text has the present participle: "who are being saved."

How, then, does the saving Grace of God act?

Both the spiritual birth and the further spiritual growth of a man occur through the mutual action of two principles. One of these is the Grace of the Holy Spirit; the other, man's opening of his heart for the reception of it, a thirst for it, the desire to receive it, as the thirsty, dry earth receives the moisture of rain—in other words, personal effort for the reception, preservation, and activity in the soul of the Divine gifts.

Concerning this cooperation of these two principles, the Apostle Peter says: *According as His Divine power hath given unto us all things that pertain unto life and godliness ...* (do you) *giving all diligence, add to your faith virtue; and to virtue knowledge; and to knowledge temperance; and to temperance patience; and to patience godliness; and to godliness brotherly kindness; and to brotherly kindness charity. For if these things be in you, and abound, they make you that ye shall neither be barren nor unfruitful in the knowledge of our Lord Jesus Christ. But he that lacketh these things is blind, and cannot see afar off, and hath forgotten that he was purged from his old sins* (II Peter 1:3–9). We read concerning the same thing in the Apostle Paul: *Work out your own salvation with fear and trembling: for it is God Who worketh in you both to will and to do of His good pleasure* (Phil. 2:12–13); that is, you yourselves cooperate, but remember that everything is given you by the Grace of God. "Except the Lord build the house of virtues, we labor in vain" (Hymn of Degrees of Sunday Matins, Tone 3; cf. Ps. 126:1).

In accordance with this sacred teaching, the Council of Carthage in the 3rd century decreed: "Whosoever should say that the Grace of God, by which a man is justified through Jesus Christ our Lord, avails only for the remission of past sins, and not for assistance against committing sins in the future, let him be anathema. For the Grace of Christ not only gives the knowledge of our duty, but also inspires us with a desire that we may be able to accomplish what we know" (Canons 125, also 126 and 127; for English text see *Seven Ecumenical Councils,* NPNF, p. 497—Canons 111 and 112 of the "African Code").

The experience of Orthodox ascetics inspires them to call Christians with all power to the humble acknowledgment of one's own infirmity, so that the saving Grace of God might act. Very expressive in this case are the expressions of St. Symeon the New Theologian (10th century):

"If the thought comes to you, instilled by the devil, that your salvation is accomplished not by the power of your God, but by your own wisdom and your own power, and if your soul agrees with such a thought, Grace departs from it. The struggle against such a powerful and most difficult battle which arises in the soul must be undertaken by the soul until our last breath. The soul must, together with the blessed Apostle Paul, call out in a loud voice, in the hearing of angels and men: 'Not I, but the Grace of God which is with me.' The Apostles and prophets, martyrs and hierarchs, holy monastics and righteous ones—all have confessed this Grace of the Holy Spirit, and for the sake of such a confession and with its help they struggled with a good struggle and finished their course" (*Homilies* of St. Symeon the New Theologian, Homily 4).

He who bears the name of Christian, we read in the same Holy Father, "if he does not bear in his heart the conviction that the Grace of God, given for faith, is the mercy of God ... if he does not labor with the aim of receiving the Grace of God, first of all through Baptism, or if he had it and it departed by reason of his sin, to cause it to return again through repentance, confession, and a self-belittling life; and if, in giving alms, fasting, performing vigils, prayers, and the rest, he thinks that he is performing glorious virtues and good deeds valuable in themselves—then he labors and exhausts himself in vain" (Homily 2).

What, then, is the significance of ascetic struggle? It is a weapon against *the lust of the flesh, and the lust of the eyes, and the pride of life* (I John 2:16). It is the cleaning of the field of the soul from stones, overgrown weeds, and swampy places, in preparation for a sacred sowing, which will be moistened from above by the Grace of God.

The Providence of God and Grace

From what has been set forth, it follows that there is a difference between the concepts of God's Providence and Grace. *Providence* is what we call God's power in the world that supports the existence of the world, its life, including the existence and life of mankind and of each man; while *Grace* is the power of the Holy Spirit that penetrates the inward being of man, leading to his spiritual perfection and salvation.

THE MYSTERIES (SACRAMENTS)

The inward life of the Church is *mystical* (or sacramental).[4] It does not at all coincide with the *history* of the Church, which shows us only the outward facts of the Church's existence, and especially its coming into conflict with the life of the world and the passions of the world. The inward life of the Church is the mystical cooperation of Christ as the Head, with the Church as His Body, in the Holy Spirit, by means of all mutually strengthening ties: *This is a great mystery: but I speak concerning Christ and the Church,* instructs the Apostle (Eph. 5:32).

Therefore, when the Apostles called themselves "stewards of the mysteries of God," saying, *Let a man so account of us, as of the ministers of Christ and stewards of the mysteries of God* (I Cor. 4:1, in Greek, *oikonomous mysterion Theou*), they have in mind various forms of their ministry and stewardship, as for example: (*a*) preaching, (*b*) the Baptism of those who have come to believe, (*c*) the bringing down of the Holy

---

[4] The word "mysteries" (Greek: *mysteria*) is the term used in the Orthodox East; "sacraments" (Latin: *sacramenta*), the term used in the Latin West. Since the latter term was used in the West before the schism of the Roman Church, there is nothing wrong with its usage by Orthodox Christians of the West, especially since few people around them are familiar with the word "mysteries"; but Orthodox people often prefer to use the Greek term. The adjectival form "mystical," used in the East, has of course a rather different and more inward connotation than the Western adjective "sacramental," which refers more specifically to the outward rites of the Mysteries.

Spirit through ordination, (*d*) the strengthening of the unity of the faithful with Christ through the Mystery of the Eucharist, and (*e*) the further deepening of the hearts of the faithful in the mysteries of the Kingdom of God, the deepening of the more perfect among them in *the wisdom of God in a mystery, even the hidden wisdom* (I Cor. 2:6–7).

Thus the activity of the Apostles was full of mystical elements (*mysterion*). Among them the central or culminating place was occupied by *sacred rites*. Therefore it is entirely natural that in the Church's life the series of special and most important moments of Grace-given ministry, the series of sacred rites, gradually acquired preeminently the name of "mysteries." St. Ignatius the God-bearer, an immediate disciple of the Apostles, writes concerning deacons that they likewise are "servants of the *mysteries* of Jesus Christ" (Epistle to the Trallians, par. 2). These words of St. Ignatius overturn the assertion of Protestant historians that in the ancient Church the concept of "mysteries" or "sacraments" was supposedly never applied to the Church's sacred rites.

The sacred rites called "mysteries" are, as it were, peaks in a long mountain range composed of the remaining rites and prayers of the Divine services.

In the Mysteries, prayers are joined with blessings in one form or another, and with special acts. The words of blessing accompanied by outward sacred acts are, as it were, spiritual vessels by which the Grace of the Holy Spirit is scooped up and given to the members of the Church who are sincere believers.

Thus, *a mystery (sacrament) is a sacred act which under a visible aspect communicates to the soul of a believer the invisible Grace of God.*

The name of "mystery" has become established in the Church as referring to seven rites:[5] Baptism, Chrismation, Communion (the Eu-

---

[5] In the Orthodox East, one may say, seven is not regarded as the "absolute" number of the Mysteries, as it tends to be regarded in the Latin West. Most commonly, it is true, only seven Mysteries are spoken of; but certain other sacred rites, such as the monastic tonsure, might also be considered, informally, as "Mysteries."

charist), Repentance, Priesthood, Matrimony, and Unction. *The Longer Catechism* thus defines the essence of each Mystery:

"In Baptism man is mystically born into spiritual life. In Chrismation he receives Grace which gives growth and strengthens. In Communion he is spiritually nourished. In Repentance he is healed of spiritual diseases (sins). In Priesthood he receives the Grace spiritually to regenerate and nurture others, by means of teaching, prayer, and the Mysteries. In Matrimony he receives Grace which sanctifies marriage and the natural birth-giving and upbringing of children. In Unction he is healed of diseases of the body by means of a healing of spiritual diseases."[6]

For the life of the Church itself as a whole, both as Body of Christ and as the "courtyard of the flock of Christ," the following are especially important and stand in the chief place: (*a*) the Mystery of the Body and Blood of Christ, or the Eucharist; (*b*) the Mystery of the sanctification of chosen persons to the service of the Church in the degrees of the hierarchy, or ordination, which gives the indispensable structure of the Church; and together with these, (*c*) the Mystery of Baptism, which sees to the increase of the numbers of the Church. But the other Mysteries also, which are appointed for the giving of Grace to individual believers, are indispensable for the fullness of the life and sanctity of the Church itself.

One must distinguish the "efficacy" of the Mystery (that is, that in itself it is an authentic Grace-giving power) from the "effectiveness" of the Mystery (that is, the extent to which one who receives the Mystery is vouchsafed its Grace-giving power). The Mysteries are "means which unfailingly act by Grace upon those who come to them," as is said in the "Encyclical of the Eastern Patriarchs" (par. 15). However, the fruitfulness of their reception by believers—their renewing and saving power—depends upon whether a man approaches the Mystery worthily. An unworthy reception of it can draw upon oneself not justification, but condemnation. Grace does not interfere with the freedom of

---

[6] St. Philaret, Metropolitan of Moscow, *The Longer Catechism of the Orthodox, Catholic, Eastern Church.* English trans., p. 53.—3RD ED.

man; it does not act upon him irresistibly. Often people, making use of the Mysteries of faith, do not receive from them that which they could give; for their hearts are not open to receive Grace, or else they have not preserved the gifts of God which they have received. This is why it happens that baptized people not only do not fulfill the vows given by them or by their sponsors at Baptism, and not only are deprived of the Grace of God already given to them, but often, to their own spiritual perdition, they become the enemies of God, deniers, unbelievers, "apostates."

By these facts of life the dignity of the Mysteries is by no means decreased. The great attainments of sanctity and righteousness seen among the ranks of martyrs for the faith, confessors, ascetics and wonderworkers, who even on earth became "earthly angels and heavenly men"—attainments unheard of outside of true Christianity—are the action of the invisible Grace of God, received in Baptism and Chrismation, kept warm through repentance and Communion of the Holy Mysteries, and preserved in the humble and trembling awareness that in every Christian "Christ is the One Who fights and conquers, and He is the One Who calls on God and prays and gives thanks and is reverent, and seeks with entreaty and humility. All this Christ does, rejoicing and being glad when He sees that in each Christian there is and remains the conviction that Christ is He Who does all of this" (St. Symeon the New Theologian, Homily 4).

THE MYSTERY (SACRAMENT) OF BAPTISM

The Establishment of the Mystery of Baptism

In the first place in the series of Mysteries of the Holy Church stands the Mystery of Baptism. It serves as the door leading into the Kingdom of Grace, or the Church, and it grants access to participation in the other Mysteries. Even before the establishment of the Mystery of Baptism, the Lord Jesus Christ in His conversation with Nicodemus indicated the absolute necessity of it for salvation: *Verily, verily, I say unto thee, except a man be born again, he cannot see the Kingdom of God.* When Nicodemus expressed his perplexity, *How can a man be born when he is old?* the Saviour replied that the new birth would be accomplished by water and the Spirit: *Verily, verily, I say unto thee, except a man be born of water and the Spirit, he cannot enter into the Kingdom of God. That which is born of the flesh is flesh, and that which is born of the Spirit is spirit* (John 3:3–6).

The establishment of this Grace-giving Mystery occurred after the Resurrection of Christ. Having appeared to His disciples, the Lord said to them that He had received from His Father all authority in heaven and on earth, and He continued: *Go ye therefore, and teach all nations, baptizing them in the name of the Father, and of the Son, and of the Holy Spirit, teaching them to observe all things whatsoever I have commanded you. And lo, I am with you alway, even unto the end of the world* (Matt. 28:19–20). And to this He added: *He that believeth and is baptized shall be saved; but he that believeth not shall be damned* (Mark 16:16). On the day of the descent of the Holy Spirit upon the Apostles, when after the speech of the Apostle Peter his listeners asked what they should do, the Apostle Peter said to them: *Repent, and be baptized every one of you in the name of Jesus Christ for the remission of sins, and ye shall receive the gift of the Holy Spirit* (Acts 2:37–38). In the same book of Acts are recorded several instances of Baptism performed by the Apostles. Thus, the Apostle Peter baptized Cornelius (chap. 10), the Apostle Paul baptized Lydia and those of her household (chap. 16), as well as the guard of the prison with his whole household (chap. 16).

The Meaning of the Mystery

The mystical, Grace-given aspect of Baptism is indicated in the above-cited passages of Sacred Scripture; Baptism is a "new birth," and it is performed for the salvation of men (Mark 16:16).[7] Moreover, setting forth the Grace-given significance of Baptism, the Apostles in

---

[7] As related earlier (pp. 207–8, note 20), in Baptism the new believer receives the Grace of God within him, united with his soul, as Adam had it before the fall.

St. Symeon the New Theologian writes concerning the saving fruits of this Mystery: "There has come another birth, or rebirth, which regenerates man through

their Epistles indicate that in it we are "sanctified," "cleansed," "justi-fied"; that in Baptism we "die to sin" so as to walk in renewed life; we are "buried with Christ," and we arise with Him. *Christ loved the Church, and gave Himself for it, that He might sanctify and cleanse it with the washing of water by the word* (that is, Baptism with the utter-ance of the words instituted to accompany it; Eph. 5:25–26). *Ye are washed, ye are sanctified, ye are justified in the name of the Lord Jesus and by the Spirit of our God* (I Cor. 6:11). *We are buried with Him by Bap-tism into death, that like as Christ was raised up from the dead by the glory of the Father, even so we also should walk in newness of life* (Rom. 6:4). Baptism is called *the washing of regeneration* (Titus 3:5). As for the sub-jective side—the state of soul of the person being baptized—it is indi-cated by the Apostle Peter, who calls Baptism the promise of *a good conscience toward God* (I Peter 3:21). Through Baptism at the same time one is joined to the Church.

The Means of the Performance of the Mystery

The comparison of Baptism with a washing by water, with the grave, and other such things indicates that this Mystery is to be per-formed through immersion. The Greek word *baptizo* itself signifies "to immerse." Concerning the Baptism of the eunuch by Philip we read in the book of Acts: *They went down both into the water, both Philip and the eunuch, and he baptized him. And when they were come*

Holy Baptism by the Holy Spirit, again unites him with the Divine Nature as it was when he was created by the hands of God, restores all the powers of his soul, renews them and brings them to the condition in which they were before the transgression of first-created Adam; in this way it leads him into the Kingdom of God, into which no one unbaptized can enter, and enlightens him with its light and grants him to taste its joys. Thus each one who is baptized becomes again such as Adam was before the transgression, and is led into the noetic Paradise and receives the commandment to work it and keep it—to work it by fulfillment of the commandments of Jesus Christ Who has recreated him, and to keep it by the keeping of the Grace of the Holy Spirit which was given to him through Holy Baptism, confessing that the power of this Grace which dwells in him fulfills together with him the command-ments of Christ" (*First-Created Man*, p. 71).—3RD ED.

up out of the water, the Spirit of the Lord caught away Philip (Acts 8:38). As an exception, the Church acknowledges the Christian martyrdom of the unbaptized as a "Baptism of blood." Baptism by sprinkling the Church acknowledges but does not approve, as being not canonical.

The immersion in water is done three times with the pronunciation of the words: "The servant of God (name) is baptized in the name of the Father, and of the Son, and of the Holy Spirit," in accordance with the commandment given by Christ Himself (Matt. 28:19). Thus was it performed in the ancient Church. The Epistle of the Apostle Barnabas already mentions this, and Tertullian directly indicates that "the manner of Baptism is prescribed," indicating the words of the Saviour concerning Baptism; Tertullian also testifies to the triple immersion and likewise indicates one particularity: that the one being baptized is asked to renounce Satan and his angels, and then to confess the Faith.

In certain passages of Sacred Scripture there is mentioned a Baptism in the name of the Lord Jesus (Acts 2:38; 8:16; 10:48). According to the interpretation of the ancient Fathers, the expression "in the name of the Lord Jesus" means "according to the command and tradition of Christ," or as a testimony of one's faith in Christ. By this expression there is not denied the fact of Baptism "in the name of the Father, of the Son, and of the Holy Spirit," as it has seemed to certain historians of Christianity who are of the rationalistic school. It is entirely natural that the writer of the book of Acts, the Apostle Luke, and the Apostle Paul also (Rom. 6:3; Gal. 3:27; I Cor. 1:13), when speaking of Baptism "in Christ" have in mind to distinguish this Baptism from the baptism of John or anything similar to it, as the *Baptism into Christianity.* Thus even now there is sung at Baptism, "As many as have been baptized into Christ have put on Christ" (Gal. 3:27).

The Indispensability of Baptism

Since in Baptism a man receives, in place of the old existence he had, a new existence and life, and becomes a child of God, a member of the Body of Christ or the Church, an inheritor of eternal life, it is therefore evident that Baptism is indispensable for all, including infants, so that growing in body and spirit they might grow in Christ. In the Apostolic Scriptures many times there is mention of the Baptism of whole families (the house of Lydia, the house of the prison guard,[8] the house of Stephanas—I Cor. 1:16), and nowhere is it mentioned that infants were excluded from this. The Fathers of the Church in their instructions to the faithful insist upon the Baptism of children. St. Gregory the Theologian, addressing Christian mothers, says: "Do you have an infant? Do not give time for harm to increase. Let him be sanctified in infancy, and from youth dedicated to the Spirit. Do you fear the seal because of the weakness of nature, as someone fainthearted and small in faith? But Anna even before giving birth promised Samuel to God, and after his birth she quickly dedicated him and raised him for the sacred garment, without fearing human weakness, but believing in God."

However, it is indispensable in this matter that the persons who offer the infant for Baptism should recognize all their responsibility for the raising up of the baptized infant in Christian faith and virtue. We read an instruction concerning this, for example, in the work *On the Ecclesiastical Hierarchy,* known under the name of St. Dionysius the Areopagite, which has always been highly respected by the Church: "It was pleasing to our divine instructors to allow infants also to be baptized, under the sacred condition that the natural parents of the child should entrust him to someone among the faithful who would instruct him well in divine subjects and then take care for the child as a father, given from above, and as a guard of his eternal salvation. This man, when he gives the promise to guide the child in pious life, is compelled by the bishop to utter the renunciations and the sacred confession."

How important for us is this instruction which comes from the ancient Christian Church! From it we see what responsibility the sponsor or godfather of the baptized person takes upon himself. How careful the parents of the child must be in choosing a sponsor! Of course, in a

---

[8] See p. 270 above.—3RD ED.

normal Christian family the parents themselves usually teach their children the truths of faith and their moral duty. But the contemporary breakup of the foundations of social life compel one to be on guard so that the child will not remain without Christian guidance. And even under favorable conditions a sponsor should keep close spiritual contact with his godchild and be ready at any needful moment to come to him with heartfelt Christian help.

The tenth paragraph of the Symbol of Faith reads: "I confess one Baptism for the remission of sins." This signifies that Baptism in the Orthodox Church, as a spiritual birth, if it has been performed as a sacred rite correctly through triple immersion in the name of the Father, and of the Son, and of the Holy Spirit, cannot be repeated.

Baptism: the Door to the Reception of Other Grace-giving Gifts

As we see from the above-cited statements of the Holy Apostles, and likewise from the whole teaching of the Church, Baptism is not only a symbol of cleansing and washing away the defilement of the soul, but in itself is the beginning and source of the Divine gifts which cleanse and annihilate all the sinful defilements and communicate a new life. All sins are forgiven, both original sin and personal sins; the way is opened for a new life; opened is the possibility to receive the gifts of God. Further spiritual growth depends upon the free will of man. But since temptation is capable of finding sympathy in the nature of man, who from the day of his first fall into sin has had an inclination to sin, therefore spiritual perfection cannot be accomplished without battle. A man finds help for this inward battle in the whole Grace-given life of the Church. The Holy Church opens up further Grace-given help to the newly baptized in the Mystery of Chrismation.

THE MYSTERY (SACRAMENT) OF CHRISMATION

The Mystery of Chrismation is performed usually immediately after the Mystery of Baptism, comprising together with it a single

Church rite. The performer of the Mystery, the bishop or priest, "anoints the one who has been baptized with Holy Myrrh, making the sign of the Cross on the brow and eyes, the nostrils, the lips, both ears, the breast, and the hands and feet" (from the *Book of Needs*); while signing each part of the body he pronounces the words, "The seal of the gift of the Holy Spirit." This Mystery is also performed on those who are united to the Church from heretical communities as one of the means of their being united to the Church. The words by which the Mystery is performed, "the seal of the gift of the Holy Spirit," indicate its significance and effect. It is (*a*) the culminating act of *being united* to the Church, the confirmation or seal of union; and (*b*) *the seal of the Grace-given powers* which are bestowed in it for strengthening and growth in spiritual life.

St. Cyprian writes: "Those baptized in the Church are sealed by *the seal of the Lord* after the example of the baptized Samaritans who were received by the Apostles Peter and John through laying on of hands and prayer (Acts 8:14–17).... That which was lacking in them, Peter and John accomplished.... Thus is it also with us.... They are made perfect by the seal of the Lord." In other Fathers of the Church also, Chrismation is called a "seal" (Clement of Alexandria, St. Cyril of Jerusalem), "the spiritual seal" (St. Ambrose of Milan), "the seal of eternal life" (St. Leo the Great), "the confirmation" (The Apostolic Constitutions), "the perfection" or "culmination" (Clement of Alexandria, St. Ambrose). St. Ephraim the Syrian writes: "By the seal of the Holy Spirit are sealed all the entrances into your soul; by the seal of the anointing all your members are sealed." St. Basil the Great asks: "How will your angel dispute over you, how will he seize you from the enemy, if he does not know the seal?... Or do you not know that the destroyer passed over the houses of those who were sealed, and killed the firstborn in the houses of those who were unsealed? An unsealed treasure is easily stolen by thieves; an unmarked sheep may safely be taken away."

This Mystery is likewise called the "gift of the Spirit" (St. Isidore of Pelusium), "the mystery of the Spirit" (Tertullian and St. Hilary), "the symbol of the Spirit" (St. Cyril of Jerusalem). St. Cyprian testifies that the ancients, speaking of the words of the Lord concerning the birth by water and the Spirit, understood the birth by water to be Baptism in the strict sense, and the birth by the Spirit to be Chrismation.

The Original Means of the Performance of this Mystery

These gifts of the Holy Spirit were originally given in the earliest Church through the laying on of hands.

Concerning this we read in the book of Acts (8:14–17), where it is related that the Apostles who were in Jerusalem, having heard that the Samaritans had received the word of God, sent to them Peter and John, who came and prayed for them so that they might receive the Holy Spirit: *For as yet He was fallen upon none of them, only they were baptized in the name of the Lord Jesus. Then laid they their hands on them and they received the Holy Spirit.* Likewise in Acts 19:2–6 we read about the Apostle Paul, that when Paul met disciples in Ephesus who had been baptized only with the baptism of John, *when they heard this, they were baptized in the name of the Lord Jesus; and when Paul had laid his hands upon them, the Holy Spirit came on them.* From these accounts in the book of Acts we see that in certain cases the Grace-giving actions of the Mysteries of Baptism and its seal, the laying on of hands, were expressed by immediate visible manifestations of the illumination of the Holy Spirit, joined to the spiritual joy of the newly converted, that they had been joined to the holy community, and that for them there had begun a new Grace-giving life.

In what way did the Grace-giving laying on of hands become the Grace-giving anointment with oil? Concerning this we may make a twofold supposition: Either the Apostles, in giving the Holy Spirit to believers through the laying on of hands, at the same time inseparably used also a different sign, anointing, concerning which the book of Acts, however, is silent; or, what is more probable, they themselves changed the visible sign of the Mystery (the laying on of hands), perhaps in the beginning in cases where they themselves were absent, replacing it with another visible sacred act (the anointment of the newly baptized with myrrh which had been received from the hands of the Apostles). But however it may have been, anointment undoubtedly comes from the Apostles, and for them it had its foundation in instructions from their Divine Teacher. The Apostle Paul writes: *Now He Who stablisheth us with you in Christ, and hath anointed us, is God; Who hath also sealed us, and given the earnest of the Spirit in our hearts* (II Cor. 1:21–22). The very words which perform the Sacrament, "the seal of the gift of the Holy Spirit," are closely bound up with this expression of the Apostle. The Apostle writes: *Grieve not the Holy Spirit of God, whereby ye are signed unto the day of redemption* (Eph. 4:30). The "day of redemption" in Sacred Scripture indicates Baptism. By the sign of the Holy Spirit, evidently, is to be understood the "seal of the Holy Spirit," which immediately follows Baptism.

Likewise, in the Epistle of the Apostle John we read: *But ye have an unction from the Holy One, and ye know all things.* And further, *The anointing which ye have received of Him abideth in you, and ye need not that any man teach you. But as the same anointing teacheth you of all things, and is truth, and is no lie, and even as it hath taught you, ye shall abide in Him* (I John 2:20, 27). In the words quoted from the Apostles Paul and John the term "anointing" indicates the communication to the faithful of a *spiritual gift.* But it is evident that the term "anointing" could be used in the spiritual significance precisely because Christians had before their eyes a material anointing.

The Holy Fathers of the Church place the very word "Christian" in a close bond with "Chrismation." *Chrisma* and *Christos* in Greek signify "anointment" and "the Anointed One." "Having become participants of Christ," says St. Cyril of Jerusalem, "you are worthily called 'Christians,' that is, 'anointed ones'; and concerning you God has said, *Touch not Mine anointed ones*" (Ps. 104:15).

In the account of the eighth chapter of the Acts of the Apostles we learn (*a*) that after the preaching of the Deacon, Apostle Philip, in Samaria, many persons, both men and women, were baptized; and (*b*) that then the Apostles who were in Jerusalem, having heard that the Samaritans had received the word of God, sent to the Samaritans Peter and John specifically in order to place their hands upon the baptized so that they might receive the Holy Spirit (Acts 8:12–17). This allows us to conclude that apart from the profoundly mystical side of the sending down of the gifts of the Spirit, this laying on of hands (and the Chrismation that later took its place) was at the same time *a confirmation of the correctness* of the Baptism and the seal of the *uniting* of baptized persons to the Church. In view of the facts that (1) the baptism with water had been performed long before this as a baptism of repentance, and (2) quite apart from this, at that time, as throughout the course of Church history, there were heretical baptisms, this second Mystery was performed by the Apostles themselves and their successors the bishops, as overseers of the members of the Church, whereas even the performance of the Eucharist had always been given to presbyters also.

With the extraordinary spreading of the holy faith, when people began to turn to Christ in all the countries of the world, the Apostles and their immediate successors, the bishops, could not personally be everywhere so as immediately after Baptism to bring down the Holy Spirit upon all the baptized through the laying on of hands. It may be that this is why it was "pleasing to the Holy Spirit" Who dwelt in the Apostles to replace the laying on of hands by the act of Chrismation, with the rule that the sanctification of the chrism should be performed by the Apostles and bishops themselves, while the anointment of the baptized with the sanctified chrism was left to presbyters. Chrism (myrrh) and no other kind of material was chosen in this case because in the Old Testament the anointment with myrrh was performed for the sending down upon people of special spiritual gifts (see Ex. 28:41; I Kings [I Sam.] 16:13; III [I] Kings 1:39). Tertullian writes: "After coming up from the font, we are anointed with blessed oil, according to the ancient rite, as of old it was the custom to anoint to the priesthood with oil from a horn." The Sixth Canon of the Council of Carthage only forbids presbyters to *sanctify* the Chrism.

Chrism and Its Sanctification

Just as it was the *Apostles* who were sent to the baptized Samaritans in order to bring down upon them the Holy Spirit, so also in the Mystery of Chrismation, the myrrh which is used, according to the decree of the Church, must be sanctified by a *bishop,* as the highest successor of the Apostles. The sanctification of myrrh occurs in a special solemn sacred rite, with the participation, when possible, of other bishops of the Church.[9]

In the West, the separation of Chrismation from Baptism occurred in about the 13th century. Moreover, at the present time in the Roman Church the anointment (which is called "confirmation") is performed only on the brow, whereas in the Orthodox Church the anointment with myrrh is made upon the brow, the eyes, the nostrils, the lips, the ears, the breast, the hands and feet. It is given in the Roman Church to those who have become seven years of age,[10] and it is performed by a bishop.

Apart from the Mystery of Chrismation, the myrrh is used also in exceptional circumstances. Thus, at the sanctification of a church there is performed the signing with the holy myrrh of the holy altar-table, upon which the Mystery of the holy Body and Blood of Christ will be performed, and likewise of the walls of the church. As a special rite, the anointment with myrrh is also performed at the accession to the royal throne of Orthodox kings.

THE MYSTERY (SACRAMENT) OF THE EUCHARIST

The Eucharist (literally "thanksgiving") is the Mystery in which the bread and wine of offering are changed by the Holy Spirit into the true Body and true Blood of our Lord Jesus Christ, and then the believers receive communion of them for a most intimate union with

---

[9] The Patriarch or chief Metropolitan consecrates the chrism for the whole of his local Church.

[10] Seven is the mininum age; Roman Catholics are usually confirmed between the ages of twelve and sixteen.—3RD ED.

Christ and eternal life. This Mystery is composed, thus, of two separate moments: (1) the changing or transformation of the bread and wine into the Body and Blood of the Lord, and (2) the Communion of these Holy Gifts. It is called "the Eucharist," "the Lord's Supper," "the Mystery of the Body and Blood of Christ." The Body and Blood of Christ in this Mystery are called the "Bread of heaven and the Cup of life" or the "Cup of salvation"; they are called the "Holy Mysteries," "the Bloodless Sacrifice." The Eucharist is the greatest Christian Mystery (Sacrament).

The Saviour's Words before the Establishment of the Mystery

Before the first performance of this Mystery at the Mystical Supper (the Last Supper), Christ promised it in His conversation concerning the Bread of Life on the occasion of the feeding of the five thousand men with five loaves. The Lord taught, *I am the living Bread which came down from heaven: If any man eat of this Bread, he shall live forever; and the Bread which I will give is My Flesh, which I will give for the life of the world* (John 6:51). The Jews evidently understood the words of Christ literally. They began to say to each other, *How can this man give us His flesh to eat?* (John 6:52). And the Lord did not tell the Jews that they had understood Him incorrectly, but only with greater force and clarity He continued to speak with the same meaning: *Verily, verily, I say unto you, except ye eat the Flesh of the Son of Man, and drink His Blood, ye have no life in you. Whoso eateth My Flesh, and drinketh My Blood, hath eternal life, and I will raise him up at the last day. For My Flesh is meat indeed, and My Blood is drink indeed. He that eateth My Flesh, and drinketh My Blood dwelleth in Me, and I in him* (John 6:53–56).

His disciples also understood the words of Christ literally: *This is a hard saying; who can hear it?* (John 6:60), they said. The Saviour, so as to convince them of the possibility of such a miraculous eating, indicated another miracle, the miracle of His future Ascension into heaven: *Doth this offend you? What and if ye shall see the Son of Man ascend up where He was before?* (John 6:61–62). Further, Christ adds, *It is the Spirit that quickeneth; the flesh profiteth nothing. The words I speak unto you, they are Spirit, and they are life* (John 6:63). By this remark Christ does not ask that His words about the Bread of Life be understood in any "metaphorical" meaning. *There are some of you that believe not,* He added immediately (John 6:64). By these words the Saviour Himself indicates that His words are difficult for faith: How is it that believers will eat His Body and drink His Blood? But He confirms that He speaks of His actual Body. His words concerning His Body and Blood are "Spirit and life." They testify (*a*) that he who partakes of them will have eternal life, and will be resurrected for the Kingdom of glory in the last day; and (*b*) that he who partakes of them will enter into the most intimate communion with Christ. His words speak not of life in the flesh, but of life in the Spirit. "The Bread of Heaven and the Cup of Life; taste and see that the Lord is good"—these are words we hear at the Liturgy of the Presanctified Gifts. This Communion of His Body and Blood is not important for the quenching of physical hunger, as was the feeding with manna in the desert, or the feeding of the five thousand—but it is important for eternal life.

The Establishment of the Mystery and Its Performance in Apostolic Times

Whereas the pre-indication of the Saviour concerning the future establishment of the Mystery of the Eucharist was given in the Gospel of John, the very establishment of the Mystery is set forth in three Evangelists—the Synoptics Matthew, Mark, and Luke—and then is repeated by the Apostle Paul.

In the Gospel of St. Matthew, in the twenty-sixth chapter, it is said: *As they were eating, Jesus took bread, and blessed it, and brake it, and gave it to the disciples, and said, Take, eat; this is My Body. And He took the cup, and gave thanks, and gave to them, saying, Drink ye all from it; for this is My Blood of the New Testament, which is shed for many for the remission of sins* (Matt. 26:26–28).

The same thing is said in the Gospel of Mark in the fourteenth chapter.

In the Gospel of Luke, the twenty-second chapter, we read: *And He took bread, and gave thanks, and brake it, and gave unto them, saying, This is My Body which is given for you: this do in remembrance of Me. Likewise also the cup after supper, saying, This cup is the New Testament in My Blood, which is shed for you* (Luke 22:19–20).

The same thing that the Evangelist Luke says we read in the First Epistle of St. Paul to the Corinthians, in the eleventh chapter, only with the prefatory words, *For I have received of the Lord that which also I delivered unto you, that the Lord Jesus, the same night in which He was betrayed, took bread, and when He had given thanks, He brake it, and said* ... (I Cor. 11:23–24).

The words of the Saviour at the Mystical Supper, *This is My Body, which is broken for you; this is My Blood of the New Testament, which is shed for many for the remission of sins,*[11] are completely clear and definite, and do not allow any other interpretation apart from the most direct one, namely, that to the disciples were given the true Body and the true Blood of Christ. And this is completely in accordance with the promise given by the Saviour in the sixth chapter of the Gospel of John concerning His Body and Blood.

Having given communion to the disciples, the Lord commanded: *This do in remembrance of Me.* This Sacrifice must be performed *till He come* (I Cor. 11:25–26), as the Apostle Paul instructs, that is, until the Second Coming of the Lord. This follows also from the words of the Saviour: *Except ye eat the flesh of the Son of Man, and drink His blood, ye have no life in you.* And indeed, the Eucharist was received by the Church from the first days as the greatest mystery; the institution of it is preserved with the greatest care and reverence; and it is performed and will be performed until the end of the world.

Concerning the performance of the Mystery of the Eucharist in Apostolic times in the Church of Christ, we may read in the Acts of the Apostles (2:42, 46; 20:7), and in the Apostle Paul in the tenth and eleventh chapters of the First Epistle to the Corinthians. The Apostle Paul writes: *The cup of blessing which we bless, is it not the com-*

---

[11] Quoting from I Cor. 11:24 and Matt. 26:28.—3rd Ed.

munion of the Blood of Christ? The bread which we break, is it not the communion of the Body of Christ? For we being many are one bread, and one body: for we are all partakers of that one Bread (I Cor. 10:16–17). And again: For as often as ye eat this bread, and drink this cup, ye do show the Lord's death till He come. Wherefore whosoever shall eat this Bread, and drink this Cup of the Lord unworthily shall be guilty of the Body and Blood of the Lord. But let a man examine himself, and so let him eat of that Bread, and drink of that Cup. For he that eateth and drinketh unworthily, eateth and drinketh damnation to himself, not discerning the Lord's Body. For this cause many are weak and sickly among you, and many sleep (I Cor. 11:26–30). In the quoted words the Apostle instructs us with what reverence and preparatory self-testing a Christian must approach the Eucharist, and he states that this is not simple food and drink, but the reception of the true Body and Blood of Christ.

Being united with Christ in the Eucharist, believers who receive Communion are united also with each other: We, being many, are one body, for we are all partakers of that one Bread.

The Changing of the Bread and Wine in the Mystery of the Eucharist

In the Mystery of the Eucharist, at the time when the priest, invoking the Holy Spirit upon the offered Gifts, blesses them with the prayer to God the Father: "Make this bread the precious Body of Thy Christ; and that which is in this cup, the precious Blood of Thy Christ; changing them by Thy Holy Spirit"—the bread and wine actually are changed into the Body and Blood by the coming down of the Holy Spirit.[12] After this moment, although our eyes see bread and wine on the Holy Table, in their very essence, invisibly for sensual eyes, this is

---

[12] This moment of the Invocation of the Holy Spirit is called the *Epiclesis*. Bishop Kallistos Ware writes: "According to Orthodox theology, the act of consecration is not complete until the end of *Epiclesis*.... Orthodox, however, do not teach that consecration is effected *solely* by the *Epiclesis*, nor do they regard the Words of Institution ['Take, eat, This is My Body …' 'Drink of it, all of you, This is My Blood …'] as incidental and unimportant. On the contrary, they look on the entire

the true Body and true Blood of the Lord Jesus, only under the "forms" of bread and wine.

Thus the sanctified Gifts (1) are not only signs or symbols, reminding the faithful of the redemption, as the reformer Zwingli taught; and likewise, (2) it is not only by His "activity and power" ("dynamically") that Jesus Christ is present in them, as Calvin taught; and finally, (3) He is not present in the meaning only of "penetration," as the Lutherans teach (who recognize the co-presence of Christ "with the bread, under the form of bread, in the bread"); but the sanctified Gifts in the Mystery are *changed* or (a later term) "transubstantiated"[13] into the true Body and true Blood of Christ, as the Saviour said: *For My flesh is meat indeed, and My Blood is drink indeed* (John 6:55).

This truth is expressed in the "Encyclical of the Eastern Patriarchs" in the following words: "We believe that in this sacred rite our Lord Jesus Christ is present not symbolically (*typikos*), not figuratively (*eikonikos*), not by an abundance of Grace, as in the other Mysteries, not by a simple descent, as certain Fathers say about Baptism, and not through a 'penetration' of the bread, so that the Divinity of the Word should 'enter' into the bread offered for the Eucharist, as the followers of Luther explain it rather awkwardly and unworthily—but truly and actually, so that after the sanctification of the bread and wine, the bread is changed, transubstantiated, converted, transformed, into the actual *true* Body of the Lord, which was born in Bethlehem of the

---

Eucharistic Prayer as forming a single and indivisible whole, so that the three main sections of the Prayer—Thanksgiving [culminating in the Words of Institution], *Anamnesis* [the act of 'calling to mind' and offering], *Epiclesis*—all form an integral part of the one act of consecration. But this of course means that if we are to single out a 'moment of consecration,' such a moment cannot come until the *Amen* of the *Epiclesis*" (*The Orthodox Church*, p. 283).—3RD ED.

[13] The term "transubstantiation" comes from medieval Latin scholasticism: following the Aristotelian philosophical categories, "transubstantiation" is a change of the "substance" or underlying reality of the Holy Gifts without changing the "accidents" or appearance of bread and wine. Orthodox theology, however, does not try to "define" this Mystery in terms of philosophical categories, and thus prefers the simple word "change."

Ever-Virgin, was baptized in the Jordan, suffered, was buried, resurrected, ascended, sits at the right hand of God the Father, and is to appear in the clouds of heaven; and the wine is changed and transubstantiated into the actual *true* Blood of the Lord, which at the time of His suffering on the Cross was shed for the life of the world. Yet again, we believe that after the sanctification of the bread and wine there remains no longer the bread and wine themselves, but the very Body and Blood of the Lord, under the appearance and form of bread and wine" (par. 17).

Such a teaching of the holy Mystery of Communion may be found in all the Holy Fathers, beginning from the most ancient ones, such as St. Ignatius the God-bearer, and other ancient Church writers such as St. Justin the Philosopher. However, in several of the ancient writers, this teaching is not expressed in completely precise terms, and in some expressions there seems to be almost a symbolical interpretation (something which the Protestants point out). However, this means of expression in part is to be explained by the polemical aims which these writers had in mind: for example, Origen was writing against a crudely sensual attitude to the Mystery; Tertullian was combatting the heresy of Marcion; and the apologists were defending the general Christian truths against the pagans, but without leading them into the depths of the Mysteries.

The Fathers who participated in the First Ecumenical Council confessed: "At the Divine Table we should not see simply the bread and the cup which have been offered, but raising our minds on high, we should with faith understand that on the sacred Table lies the Lamb of God Who takes away the sins of the world, Who is offered as a Sacrifice by the priests; and truly receiving His Precious Body and Blood, we should believe that this is a sign of our Resurrection."

In order to show and explain the possibility of such a transformation of the bread and wine by the power of God into the Body and Blood of Christ, the ancient pastors indicated the almightiness of the Creator and the special deeds of His almightiness: the creation of the world out of nothing, the mystery of the Incarnation, the miracles recorded in the holy books, and in particular the transformation of water into wine (St. John Chrysostom, St. Ambrose, St. Cyril of Jerusalem, St. John Damascene, and others). They also indicated how in us as well the bread and wine or water taken by us as food are converted, in a way unknown to us, into our own body and blood (St. John Damascene).

Some Observations on the Manner in Which the Lord Jesus Christ Remains in the Holy Gifts

1. Although the bread and wine are transformed in the Mystery into the Body and Blood of the Lord, He is present in this Mystery *with all His being,* that is, with His soul and with His very Divinity, which is inseparably united to His humanity.

2. Although, further, the Body and Blood of the Lord are broken in the Mystery of Communion and distributed, still we believe that *in every part*—even in the smallest particle—of the Holy Mysteries, those who receive Communion receive the entire Christ in His being, that is, in His soul and Divinity, as perfect God and perfect man. This faith the Holy Church expresses in the words of the priest at the breaking of the Holy Lamb: "Broken and divided is the Lamb of God, which is broken, though not disunited, which is ever eaten, though never consumed, but sanctifieth those that partake thereof."

3. Although at one and the same time there are many holy Liturgies in the universe, still there are not many Bodies of Christ, but one and the same Christ is present and is given in His body *in all the churches of the faithful.*

4. The bread of offering, which is prepared separately in all churches, after its sanctification and offering becomes *one and the same with the Body which is in the heavens.*

5. After the transformation of the bread and wine in the Mystery of the Eucharist into the Body and Blood, they no longer return to their former nature, but remain *the Body and Blood of the Lord forever,* whether or not they are consumed by the faithful. Therefore the Orthodox Church from antiquity has had the custom of performing on certain days the Liturgy of the *Presanctified* Gifts, believing that these

Gifts, sanctified at a preceding Liturgy, remain the true Body and Blood of Christ. There has likewise been from antiquity the custom of preserving the sanctified Gifts in sacred vessels in order to give Holy Communion to the dying. It is well known that in the ancient Church there existed the custom of sending out the sanctified Gifts through deacons to Christians who were not able to receive Communion of the Holy Gifts in church, for example to confessors, to those in prison, and to penitents. Often in antiquity believers brought the Holy Gifts with reverence from the churches to their own houses, and ascetics took Them with themselves to the desert to receive Communion.

6. Since to the God-Man Christ it is fitting to offer a single inseparable Divine worship, both according to His Divinity and His humanity, as a consequence of their inseparable union, therefore also to the Holy Mysteries of the Eucharist there should be given *the same honor and worship* which we are obliged to give to the Lord Jesus Christ Himself.

The Relation of the Eucharist to the Sacrifice on Golgotha

The Eucharistic sacrifice *is not a repetition* of the Saviour's sacrifice on the Cross, but it is an offering of the sacrificed Body and Blood once offered by our Redeemer on the Cross, by Him Who "is ever eaten, though never consumed." The sacrifice on Golgotha and the sacrifice of the Eucharist are inseparable, comprising a single sacrifice; but at the same time they are to be distinguished one from the other. They are inseparable: they are one and the same Grace-giving tree of life planted by God on Golgotha, but filling with its mystical branches the whole Church of God, and to the end of the ages nourishing by its saving fruits all those who seek eternal life. But they are also to be distinguished: the sacrifice offered in the Eucharist is called "bloodless" and "passionless," since it is performed after the Resurrection of the Saviour, Who *being raised from the dead, dieth no more; death hath no more dominion over Him* (Rom. 6:9). It is offered *without suffering,* without the shedding of blood, without death, although it is performed in remembrance of the sufferings and death of the Divine Lamb.[14]

The Significance of the Eucharist as a Sacrifice

It is a sacrifice of *praise and thanksgiving*. The priest who performs the Bloodless Sacrifice according to the rite of the Liturgies of St. Basil the Great and St. John Chrysostom, before the sanctification of the Gifts remembers in his secret prayer the great works of God; he glorifies and gives thanks to God in the Holy Trinity for calling man out of nonexistence, for His great and varied care for him after his fall, and for the economy of His salvation through the Lord Jesus Christ. Likewise all Christians present in church in these holy moments, glorifying God, cry out to Him: "We hymn Thee, we bless Thee, we give thanks to Thee, O Lord...."

The Eucharist is likewise a *propitiatory* sacrifice for all members of the Church. Giving to His disciples His Body, the Lord said of It: "Which is broken for you"; and giving His Blood He added, "Which is

---

[14] The Orthodox Church confesses that the sacrifice of the Eucharist is a real sacrifice, and at the same time that Christ was sacrificed once only, for all time, when He was crucified on Golgotha *to bear the sins of many* (Heb. 9:28). St. Nicholas Cabasilas explains this seeming paradox as follows:

"The sacrificing of a sheep consists in a changing of its state; it is changed from an unsacrificed sheep to a sacrificed one. The same is true here; [during the Divine Liturgy] the bread is changed from unsacrificed bread into the very Body of Christ which was truly sacrificed. Through this transformation the sacrifice is truly accomplished, just as that of the sheep was when it was changed from one state to another. For there has been in the sacrifice a transformation not in symbol but in reality; a transformation into the sacrificed Body of the Lord....

"Now it is clear that, under these conditions, it is not necessary that there should be numerous oblations of the Lord's body. Since the sacrifice [of the Eucharist] consists, not in the real and bloody immolation of the Lamb, but in the transformation of the bread into the sacrificed Lamb, it is obvious that the transformation takes place without the bloody immolation. Thus, though that which is changed is many, and the transformation takes place many times, yet nothing prevents the reality into which it is transformed from being one and the same thing always—a single Body, and the unique sacrifice of that Body" (*A Commentary on the Divine Liturgy*, pp. 81–82).—3RD ED.

shed for you and for many for the remission of sins." Therefore, from the beginning of Christianity the Bloodless Sacrifice was offered for the remembrance of both the living and the dead and for the remission of their sins. This is evident from the texts of all the Liturgies, beginning with the Liturgy of the Holy Apostle James, and this sacrifice itself is often directly called in these texts the sacrifice of propitiation.

The Eucharist is a sacrifice which in the most intimate fashion *unites all the faithful* in one body in Christ. Therefore, after the transformation of the Holy Gifts as also earlier at the proskomedia,[15] the priest remembers the Most Holy Lady Theotokos and all the saints, adding, "By their prayers visit us, O God"; and then he goes over to the commemoration of the living and the dead—the whole Church of Christ.

The Eucharist is also a sacrifice of *entreaty:* for the peace of the churches, for the good condition of the world, for authorities, for those in infirmities and labors, for all who ask for help—"and for all men and women."

Conclusions of a Liturgical Character

From the accounts in the Gospels and in the writings of the Apostles, and from the practice of the ancient Church, one must make the following conclusions:

a) In the Eucharist, as the Apostles were given at the Mystical Supper, so also all the faithful should be given not only the Body of Christ, but also the Blood of Christ. *Drink ye all from it,* the Saviour commanded (Matt. 26:27). *Let a man examine himself, and so let him eat of the bread, and drink of that cup* (I Cor. 11:28). (This is not observed in the Latin church, where laymen are deprived of the cup.)[16]

b) We are all partakers of that one Bread (I Cor. 10:17), writes the Apostle. In the ancient Church every community partook of one single bread, and in the Orthodox Liturgy there is blessed and broken

---

[15] *Proskomedia:* service of preparation for the Divine Liturgy.—3RD ED.

[16] While this was the universal Roman Catholic practice when the present book was written, since the Second Vatican Council of 1963 the cup has been made available to laymen in some Roman churches.—3RD ED.

one bread, just as one cup is blessed. (The blessing of the "one" bread was also violated by the Latin church in the second millennium.)

c) In all the passages of Holy Scripture where the bread of the Eucharist is mentioned, the bread is called *artos* in Greek (John, chap. 6; the Gospels of Matthew, Mark, Luke; in the Apostle Paul and the Acts of the Apostles). *Artos* usually signifies wheat bread which has risen through the use of leaven ("unleavened" is expressed in Greek by the adjective *azymos*). It is known that in Apostolic times—that is, from the very beginning, from its institution—the Eucharist was performed during the whole year, weekly, when the Jews did not prepare unleavened bread; this means that it was performed, even in the Jewish-Christian communities, with leavened bread. All the more may this be said of the communities of Christian converts from paganism, to whom the law regarding unleavened bread was entirely foreign. In the Church of the first Christians the material for the Mystery of the Eucharist, as is well known, was usually taken from the offerings of the people, who, without any doubt, brought to church from their homes the usual, leavened bread; it was also meant to be used, at the same time, for the love-feasts (*agape*) and for helping the poor.

The Necessity and Saving Nature of Communion of the Holy Mysteries

To receive communion of the Body and Blood of the Lord is the essential, necessary, saving, and consoling obligation of every Christian. This is evident from the words of the Saviour which He uttered when giving the promise regarding the Mystery of the Eucharist: *Verily, verily, I say unto you, except ye eat the Flesh of the Son of Man, and drink His Blood, ye have no life in you. Whoso eateth My Flesh, and drinketh My Blood, hath eternal life* (John 6:53–54).

The saving fruits or effects of the Mystery of the Eucharist, if only we commune worthily, are the following:

It unites us in the most intimate fashion with the Lord: *He that eateth My Flesh, and drinketh My Blood, dwelleth in Me, and I in him* (John 6:56).

It nourishes our soul and body and aids our strengthening, increase, and growth in spiritual life: *He that eateth Me, even he shall live by Me* (John 6:57).

Being received worthily, it serves for us as a pledge of the future resurrection and the eternally blessed life: *He that eateth of this Bread shall live forever* (John 6:58).

However, one should remember that the Eucharist offers these saving fruits only to those who approach it with faith and repentance; but an unworthy partaking of the Body and Blood of Christ brings all the more condemnation: *For he that eateth and drinketh unworthily, eateth and drinketh damnation to himself, not discerning the Lord's Body* (I Cor. 11:29).

THE MYSTERY (SACRAMENT) OF REPENTANCE

The Mystery of Repentance is a Grace-giving sacred rite in which, after the faithful offer repentance of their sins, the remission of sins is bestowed by the mercy of God through the intermediary of a pastor of the Church, in accordance with the Saviour's promise.

In the Mystery of Repentance the spiritual afflictions of a man are treated, impurities of soul are removed, and a Christian, having received forgiveness of sins, again becomes innocent and sanctified, just as he came out of the waters of Baptism. Therefore, the Mystery of Repentance is called a "spiritual medicine." A man's sins—which draw him downward; which dull his mind, heart, and conscience; which blind his spiritual gaze; which make powerless his Christian will—are annihilated, and his living bond with the Church and with the Lord God is restored. Being relieved of the burden of sins, he again comes to life spiritually and is able to strengthen himself and become perfected in the good Christian path.

The Mystery of Repentance consists of two basic actions: (1) the confession of his sins before a pastor of the Church by the person coming to the Mystery, and (2) the prayer of forgiving and remitting them, pronounced by the priest.

This Mystery is also called the *Mystery of Confession* (even though the confession of sins comprises only the first, preliminary part of it), and this indicates the importance of the sincere revelation of one's soul and the manifestation of one's sins.

Confession—that is, pronouncing aloud—is the expression of *inward repentance,* its result, its indicator. And what is repentance? Repentance is not only *awareness* of one's sinfulness or a simple *acknowledgment* of oneself as unworthy; it is not even contrition or *regret* (although all these aspects should enter into repentance). Rather, it is an act of one's *will for correction,* a desire and firm intention, a resolve, to battle against evil inclinations; and this condition of soul is united with a petition for God's help in the battle against one's evil inclinations. Such a heartfelt and sincere repentance is necessary not only so that the effect of this Mystery might extend to the *removal* of sins, but also so that there might enter the opened soul a Grace-giving *healing,* which does not allow the soul again to become immersed in the filth of sin.[17]

The very uttering aloud of one's spiritual afflictions and falls before a spiritual father—the confession of sins—has the significance that by means of it there are overcome (*a*) pride, the chief source of sins, and (*b*) the despondency of hopelessness in one's correction and salvation. The manifestation of the sin brings one already near to casting it away from oneself.

Those who approach the Mystery of Repentance prepare themselves for it by an effort of prayer, fasting, and entering deeply within themselves, with the aim of uncovering and acknowledging their sinfulness.

The mercy of God goes out to meet the repenting Christian, testifying, through the lips of the spiritual father, that the Heavenly Father does not reject one who comes to Him, just as He did not reject the prodigal son and the repentant publican. This testimony consists in the words of the special prayer and the special words of remission which are pronounced by the priest.

---

[17] The Greek word for repentance is *metanoia,* which literally means to "change the *nous.*" (On the *nous,* see p. 136, note 17 above.)—3RD ED.

The Institution of the Mystery

The Lord instituted the Mystery of Repentance after His Resurrection, when, having appeared to His disciples who, except for Thomas, were gathered together, He solemnly said to them: *Peace be unto you.…* *And when He had said this, He breathed on them, and saith unto them: Receive ye the Holy Spirit. Whosoever sins ye remit, they are remitted unto them; and whosoever sins ye retain, they are retained* (John 20:21–23). Moreover, even before this, Christ the Saviour twice uttered a promise about this Mystery. The first time He said to the Apostle Peter, when Peter, on behalf of all the Apostles, had confessed Him to be the Son of God: *I will give unto thee the keys of the Kingdom of Heaven: and whatsoever thou shalt bind on earth shall be bound in heaven; and whatsoever thou shalt loose on earth shall be loosed in heaven* (Matt. 16:19). The second time He testified to all the Apostles: *If he neglect to hear the Church, let him be unto thee as a heathen man and a publican. Verily I say unto you: whatsoever ye shall bind on earth shall be bound in heaven; and whatsoever ye shall loose on earth shall be loosed in heaven* (Matt. 18:17–18).

Priests are only the visible instruments at the performance of the Mystery, which is performed invisibly through them by God Himself.

St. John Chrysostom, having in mind the Divine institution of the authority of the pastors of the Church to loose and bind, says: "The priests decree below, God confirms above, and the Master agrees with the opinion of His slaves." The priest is here the instrument of God's mercy and remits sins not on his own authority, but in the name of the Holy Trinity.

The invisible effects of Grace in the Mystery of Repentance, in their breadth and power, extend to all the lawless deeds of men, and there is no sin that cannot be forgiven men if only they sincerely repent of it and confess it with lively faith in the Lord Jesus and hope in His mercy. *I am not come to call the righteous, but sinners to repentance* (Matt. 9:13), said the Saviour; and as great as was the sin of the Apostle Peter, He forgave him when he sincerely repented. It is known that the Holy Apostle Peter called to repentance even the Jews who crucified the true Messiah (Acts 2:38), and later he called Simon the sorcerer, the ancestor of all heretics (Acts 8:22); the Apostle Paul gave remission to the incestuous man who repented, subjecting him first to a temporary excommunication (II Cor. 2:7).

On the other hand, it is essential to remember that the remission of sins in the Mystery is an act of mercy, not of irrational pity. It is given for a man's spiritual profit, *for edification, and not for destruction* (II Cor. 10:8). This lays a great responsibility upon the one who performs the Mystery.

Holy Scripture speaks of cases or conditions when sins are *not* forgiven. In the word of God there is mention of the blasphemy against the Holy Spirit, which *shall not be forgiven unto men... neither in this world, neither in the world to come* (Matt. 12:31–32). Likewise, it speaks of the *sin unto death,* for the forgiveness of which it is not commanded even to pray (I John 5:16). Finally, the Apostle Paul instructs that *it is impossible for those who were once enlightened, and have tasted of the heavenly gift, and were made partakers of the Holy Spirit, and have tasted the good word of God, and the powers of the world to come, if they shall fall away, to renew them again unto repentance, seeing they crucify to themselves the Son of God afresh, and put Him to an open shame* (Heb. 6:4–6).

In all these cases, the reason why the forgiveness of sins is not possible is to be found in the sinners themselves, and not in the will of God; more precisely, it lies in the lack of repentance of the sinners. How can a sin be forgiven by the Grace of the Holy Spirit, when blasphemy is spewed forth against this very Grace? But one must believe that, even in these sins, the sinners, if they offer sincere repentance and weep over their sins, will be forgiven. "For," says St. John Chrysostom about the blasphemy against the Holy Spirit, "even this guilt will be remitted to those who repent. Many of those who have spewed forth blasphemies against the Spirit have subsequently come to believe, and everything was remitted to them" (*Homilies on the Gospel of St. Matthew*). Further, the Fathers of the Seventh Ecumenical Council speak of the possibility of forgiveness for deadly sins: "The sin unto death is when certain ones, after sinning, do not correct themselves.... In such ones the Lord Jesus does not abide, unless they humble themselves and recover from their fall into sin. It is fitting for them once more to approach God and with contrite heart to ask for the remission of this sin and forgiveness, and not to become vainglorious over an unrighteous deed. For *the Lord is nigh unto them that are of a contrite heart* (Ps. 33:18)."

The permission and even the direct demand to repeat the Mystery of Repentance is clear from the words of the Gospel: *Joy shall be in heaven over one sinner that repenteth, more than over ninety and nine just persons, which need no repentance* (Luke 15:7). In the Apocalypse of St. John the Theologian we read: *Unto the angel of the Church of Ephesus write: ... I will come unto thee quickly, and will remove thy candlestick out of his place, except thou repent* (Apoc. 2:1, 5).

Epitimia (Penance)

By *epitimia* is to be understood an interdiction or punishment (II Cor. 2:6) which, according to Church canons, the priest as a spiritual physician decrees for certain repenting Christians in order to treat their moral diseases. Such penances, for example, are: a special fast, above that which is set for everyone; prayers of repentance together with a definite number of prostrations; and others. The basic form of *epitimia* which existed in the practice of the ancient Church was excommunication from Communion of the Holy Mysteries for a greater or lesser period.

In the ancient Church there existed a rite of public repentance for the "fallen," and in particular for those who had not held firm in the faith during the persecutions. According to this rite, the penitents were divided into four classes:[18] (*a*) the "weepers," who did not have the right to be present at the public Divine services and, stretching out their hands off the church porch, with weeping would beg those who entered the church to pray for them; (*b*) the "hearers," for whom it was permitted to be in the narthex of the church all the way to the end of

---

[18] According to Canon 11 of the First Ecumenical Council (and its commentaries). See *The Seven Ecumenical Councils*, NPNF, pp. 24–27.

the liturgy of the Catechumens; (c) the "prostrators," who entered the church itself but also did not participate in the Liturgy of the Faithful (after the Liturgy, on bended knees, they were vouchsafed the pastoral blessing); and (d) the class of those who "stood together" with the faithful for the whole Liturgy, but could not receive Communion of the Holy Mysteries.

Penances are given not to everyone, but only to certain repenting Christians: to those who, either from the seriousness or the quality of their sins, or because of the character of their repentance, have need of these spiritual treatments. Such an interdiction was laid by the Apostle Paul upon the Corinthian Christian who had committed incest, when in order to treat him he commanded that he be excommunicated from the Church and from contact with the faithful and that he be *deliver(ed) unto Satan for the destruction of the flesh, that the spirit may be saved* (I Cor. 5:1–5). And then, after his sincere contrition, he commanded him again to be received into Church communion (II Cor. 2:6–8).

Penances have the character of punishments, but not in the strict sense and not for the sake of "satisfaction for sins," as the Roman theologians teach. They are acts which are corrective, healing, pedagogical. Their purpose is to increase sorrow for the sins performed and to support the resolve of the will to be corrected. The Apostle says: *Godly sorrow worketh repentance to salvation not to be repented of: but the sorrow of the world worketh death* (II Cor. 7:10). That is, sorrow for the sake of God produces an unchanging repentance unto salvation.

The canons of the holy Councils and the Holy Fathers affirm that penances in antiquity were considered a means of spiritual healing; that the ancient pastors, placing them upon sinners, were not concerned merely to punish justly, one more and another less, in accordance with the crimes of each, for the proper satisfaction of God's justice for sins, but that they had in mind the good influence of these punishments upon the sinner. Therefore, if they saw a need for it they would lessen them, shorten the time of the interdiction, or even remove them completely. A canon of the Sixth Ecumenical Council says: "It behooves those who have received from God the power to loose and bind, to consider the quality of the sin and the readiness of the sinner for conversion, and to apply medicine suitable for the disease, lest if he is injudicious in each of these respects he should fail in regard to the healing of the sick man. For the disease of sin is not simple, but various and multiform, and it germinates many mischievous offshoots, from which much evil is diffused, and it proceeds further until it is checked by the power of the physician."[19]

The Roman Catholic View

From this is apparent the unacceptability of the Roman Catholic view of penances, which proceeds from legal concepts according to which (*a*) every sin or sum of sins must have an *ecclesiastical* punishment (apart from the fact that often misfortunes—for example, illnesses—are a natural recompense for sin, so that often the sinner himself can see in his fate a Divine punishment for sins); (*b*) this punishment can be removed by an "indulgence," which can be given even in advance, for example, on the occasion of jubilee celebrations;[20] c) the Church, that is, its head, the Bishop of Rome (the Pope), in giving indulgences, applies to persons who are subject to penance the "merits of the saints," taking them from the so-called "treasury of supererogatory works."[21]

If among certain Western teachers of the ancient Church, pen-

---

[19] Canon 102 of the Quinisext Council (considered as part of the Sixth Ecumenical Council); *Seven Ecumenical Councils,* NPNF, p. 408.

[20] For example, the "holy year" proclaimed by Pope Paul VI in 1975.

[21] Roman Catholic theologians divide good works into two aspects: *merit* (which is personal and nontransferrable), and *satisfaction* (expiation); the latter aspect can be transferred to others who are lacking in "satisfaction." The "satisfaction" of all saints (and first of all, of Christ Himself) make up a "treasury" which the Pope distributes to the faithful by means of "indulgences," formally defined as "a remission of the temporal punishment due to sin, the guilt of which has been forgiven." "Supererogatory works," or "works of supererogation," are the "excess" satisfactions of saints, not required for their salvation, which enter into the above-mentioned "treasury." (See the *Catholic Encyclopedia,* 1913 ed., article "Indulgences.") All these ideas were developed in 13th-century scholasticism and are totally foreign to Orthodox thinking.

ances were called "satisfactions," they were called this only in the moral sense, as a means for deepening the awareness of sinfulness in the sinner, this being "satisfactory" for the aim of edification, but not as a legal justification.

Spiritual Guidance

One must distinguish from the Mystery of Confession the moral guidance of a spiritual father, something widespread in antiquity and now in use especially among monastics. Often this is fulfilled by persons who are not consecrated, that is, who do not have the priestly rank, when upon them lies the duty of guiding their spiritual children. The confession of one's thoughts and acts before a spiritual guide has an immense psychological significance in the sense of moral upbringing, for the correction of evil inclinations and habits, the overcoming of doubts and waverings, and so forth. But such spiritual guidance does not have the significance of a Mystery of a Grace-giving sacred action.

THE MYSTERY (SACRAMENT) OF PRIESTHOOD

Concerning the pastoral ministry in the Church we have spoken already in the section on the Church hierarchy (chap. 7). It was shown there that the hierarchy was established in the Church by the Lord Jesus Christ Himself, that it has been with the Church from its very beginning, and that in the Apostolic period it received an organization in three degrees (bishop–priest–deacon).

But the hierarchical ministry in the Church, especially that of bishop and priest, is a special ministry, an exceptional one: it is a ministry of *Grace*. Here we find the shepherding of the flock of God, the highest example of which was given by the Lord in His earthly ministry. *I am the good shepherd, and know My sheep, and am known of Mine. The good shepherd giveth his life for the sheep* (John 10:14, 11). Here we find a standing before the Lord in prayer not only for oneself, but also for the people. Here we find the guidance of the souls of men on the path to their attainment of the Kingdom of Heaven. The clergy, on behalf of the whole people, offer the Bloodless Sacrifice in the Divine Liturgy. And if in every good work we ask the blessing of God and the help of God, can we imagine entering upon such an exalted and responsible pastoral ministry—entering upon it for one's whole life—without the invocation of God's Grace which blesses this labor, which cooperates with it and strengthens the future pastor? This blessing does indeed take place. It is brought down upon the one who approaches with sacred trembling to the reception of the gift of sacred ministry in the *Mystery of Priesthood,* through the laying on of hands by a bishop who himself bears by succession the Grace of the priesthood, accompanied by the prayer of the entire congregation of clergy and people who are present at the Divine service. It is called likewise the Mystery of *Cheirotonia.*

The Sacred Scripture gives direct and clear indications that the placing in the rank of priesthood is the communication of a special Grace-giving mystical gift, without which this ministry cannot be fulfilled.

Cheirotonia in the Ancient Church

According to the expression of the Acts of the Apostles, when the Apostles, who acted in everything according to the instruction of Christ and the inspiration of the Holy Spirit, found it necessary to place deacons in the Church in order to serve tables—first ordinary tables, and later also the Lord's Table—in order to lighten the services of the Apostles themselves, they first of all offered to the gathering of their disciples to choose from amongst themselves seven tested men filled with the Holy Spirit and wisdom. And when they had been chosen and placed before them, *when they had prayed, they laid their hands on them* (Acts 6:2–6). Here with absolute clarity and distinctiveness are set apart from each other, as two distinct acts, the election of certain persons for the ministry of deacon and the laying on of hands over them with prayer. The election is something merely human, while the laying on of hands is a sacred action especially intended for this aim, and an act of Divine Grace.

In the same book of the Acts of the Apostles we find an indication of the laying on of hands as a sacred act by means of which *presbyters* also were ordained in the early Church. Speaking of how the Apostles Paul and Barnabas went preaching through the cities of Asia Minor—Derbe, Lystra, Iconium, and Antioch—increasing in them the number of Christians, the writer of the book, the Holy Apostle Luke, informs us: *And when they had ordained (cheirotonisantes) for them elders (presbyters) in every church, and had prayed with fasting, they commended them to the Lord* (Acts 14:23). Here the laying on of hands is presented, on the one hand, as a sacred act known to all, by means of which presbyters were ordained for one church or another, and on the other hand as a sacred act which had a special importance, as is apparent from the fact that it was performed by the Apostles Paul and Barnabas themselves. It is clear from this that this ordination was not merely a rite or a sign, but was the communication of a special gift. And this is precisely testified to later with full emphasis by the same Apostle Paul, when in his farewell conversation with the presbyters of the Church of Ephesus he thus expresses himself concerning them: *Take heed therefore unto yourselves, and to all the flock, over which the Holy Spirit hath made you overseers (bishops), to feed the Church of God, which He hath purchased with His own blood* (Acts 20:28). That this placing by the Holy Spirit was through the apostolic laying on of hands or ordination is evident from the above-cited text (Acts 14:23).

Finally, in the epistles of the Apostle Paul to Timothy we have a direct and clear indication of ordination as a Grace-giving sacred action through which *bishops* were appointed. Thus, in the first epistle to Timothy, who was bishop of the Church of Ephesus, the Apostle writes: *Neglect not the gift that is in thee, which was given thee by prophecy, with the laying on of the hands of the presbytery* (I Tim. 4:14). In his other epistle to him he writes: *I put thee in remembrance, that thou stir up the gift of God, which is in thee by the putting on of my hands* (II Tim. 1:6). By putting together these two passages, we see that Timothy was ordained by the *presbytery* and by the Apostle Paul himself, or what is the same thing, by an assembly of the eldest clergy under the presidency of the Apostle Paul; and likewise, that in this sacred action there was communicated to Timothy the gift of God, and this gift of God is to remain with him forever as his inheritance. Of him is demanded only one thing: not to neglect it, but to keep it warm. That the laying on of hands here means nothing else than episcopal ordination is entirely confirmed by the further instructions to Timothy: from them it is evident that he was clothed with the authority to ordain others (I Tim. 5:22), to have supervision over those presbyters who were in his jurisdiction (I Tim. 5:17, 19), and in general to be a builder *in the House of God, which is the Church of the living God* (I Tim. 3:15).

"Election" and "Ordination" in the Ancient Church

What has been said brings one to the undoubted conclusion that the Apostles, by the authority of Christ, established three hierarchical degrees, and that for the raising up of selected persons into these degrees there was established ordination, which communicates to them the active Grace of God which is indispensable for their ministry. It goes without saying that the successors of the Apostles, the bishops, had to fulfill precisely what had been decreed by the Apostles: that is, ordination through laying on of hands, joining to it the same exalted meaning and the same significance that were given by the Apostles.

And so it has been in actual fact in the Church in later times.

Although in the early Church ordination to the rank of priesthood occurred after a general election, with the agreement of the church community or the local church, this "ordination" itself was an act totally separate and distinct from the agreement or election, and it was performed by persons equal in their authority to the Apostles, and who were their successors: the bishops. So it has remained up to our days. Among the earliest testimonies of this we may indicate the homily of St. Irenaeus of Lyons (2nd century), which says: "One must follow those presbyters (in the sense of the 'eldest' in the Church, that is, bishops) who are in the Church and who, as we have indicated, have the succession from the Apostles, and who, together with the succession of the episcopacy, by the good disposition of the Father, have received the reliable gift of the truth." The expression, "with the succession of the episcopacy they have received the gift of the truth," speaks evidently of the gift of Grace received through their ordination. The same idea may be found also in Tertullian. In Clement of Alexandria (3rd century) there is already a definite indication that the "election" is not at all what is given by ordination through the laying on of hands, just as the election by Christ of the Apostles, among whose number was Judas, was not the same thing as the "ordination" which the Apostles subsequently received through the breathing of Christ (John 20:22). The election of certain persons for the priesthood is the work of men; but the ordination of them is not the work of men, but the work of God (Clement, *Stromata*).

The Apostolic Canons command: "Let a bishop be ordained by two or three bishops. Let a presbyter, deacon, and the rest of the clergy be ordained by one bishop" (Canons 1 and 2; *Seven Ecumenical Councils,* NPNF, p. 594). Here also is established the unrepeatability of the *Cheirotonia* (Ordination): "If any bishop, presbyter, or deacon shall receive from anyone a second ordination, let both the ordained and the ordainer be deposed; unless indeed it can be proved that he had his ordination from heretics" (68th Canon; *Seven Ecumenical Councils,* NPNF, p. 598). Thus the Grace given in the *Cheirotonia* of the priesthood is acknowledged to be just as unchanging and ineffaceable as the Grace given in Baptism. However, the Grace of *Cheirotonia* is special and distinct from the Grace which is given in Baptism and in the Mystery of Chrismation.

The Essence and Effectuating Words of the Mystery

Thus the Mystery of Priesthood is a sacred action which, through the prayerful laying on of the hands of a bishop upon the head of the chosen person, brings down upon this person the Divine Grace which sanctifies and ordains him to a certain rank of the Church hierarchy and later cooperates with him in his passing through the hierarchical obligations. The prayer of *Cheirotonia* is the following: "The Divine Grace which always healeth that which is infirm and completeth that which is wanting, elevateth (name) the most devout subdeacon, to be a deacon (or deacon, to be a priest). Wherefore, let us pray for him, that the Grace of the All-Holy Spirit may come upon him."

The Mystery of *Cheirotonia* is always included in the rite of the Divine Liturgy. Distinct from the Mystery of *Cheirotonia* is ordination by prayer to the lower ranks of the clergy (reader, subdeacon); this is called *Cheirothesia* (from a Greek word that has a purely Christian ecclesiastical meaning and came into use relatively late).

The Celibacy of Bishops

For a bishop there exists the obligation of celibacy. In the first centuries of Christianity such a demand was not obligatory, but even in apostolic times it was allowed for bishops to avoid marriage for the sake of the ascetic struggle of continence. This custom became strengthened, and the Sixth Ecumenical Council made it a canon. As regards priests and deacons, the Church regarded that such a burden should not be laid upon them as obligatory, and that the ancient canon should be followed which forbids clergy, after receiving ordination, to enter into marriage, but which allows to the Mystery of Priesthood persons who are already bound by marriage, even regarding this as natural and normal. A second marriage, as well as having a wife who has been married before, are hindrances to ordination. In the Roman Church in the 4th to 6th centuries, celibacy began to be introduced likewise for priests and deacons. This innovation was rejected by the Sixth Ecumenical Council;[22] but this prohibition was not heeded by the Roman popes.

The Protestants have rejected the priesthood as a "sacrament."

---

[22] That is, the Roman practice of *mandatory* celibacy for priests and deacons was rejected. See Canon 13 of the Quinisext Council (as mentioned on p. 42, note 23 above, the decrees of this Council are accepted by the Orthodox Church as a continuation of those of the Sixth Ecumenical Council), in *Seven Ecumenical Councils,* NPNF, p. 371).—3RD ED.

Their pastors are only elected and appointed by the people, but do not receive any kind of special consecration, and in this sense they are not to be distinguished from the ordinary members of their communities. Historically this is explained by opposition to the abuses of their rights by the Latin clergy at the end of the Middle Ages. The Protestants made as their theoretical justification the opinion that ordination to the priesthood began to be called by the fixed name of "sacrament" only in more recent times. But of course such a justification has no value whatsoever. We see from the teaching and practice of the Apostles, and from the constant belief of the Church, that *Cheirotonia* from the beginning was a sacramental, Grace-giving sacred action, and therefore the fact that in a later period it began to be called a "sacrament" did not introduce anything new, but only expressed its essence more precisely in a single word. In a similar way, for example, the term *homoousios,* accepted at the First Ecumenical Council, did not introduce anything new into the ancient Church teaching of the Divinity of the Son of God, but only defined it more precisely and confirmed it. Unfortunately, Protestant scholars, defending the false position of Protestantism, continue stubbornly, but without proof, to deduce the very concept of the Christian Mysteries from the practice of the pagan mysteries.

THE MYSTERY (SACRAMENT) OF MARRIAGE

The Purpose of the Christian Family

The family, as is well known, comprises the fundamental cell of the organism of society, being the nucleus and foundation of society. Thus also in the militant Church of Christ, it is a basic unit of the Church body. Therefore the Christian family in itself is called in the writings of the Apostles a "church": *Greet Priscilla and Aquila, my helpers in Christ Jesus ... and the church that is in their house* (Rom. 16:3, 5); *Salute ... Nymphas and the church which is in his house* (Col. 4:15). From this it is understandable what great attention should be given to the family from the point of view of the Church, so that the family might fulfill its purpose of being a small "church."

There is yet another way of personal life which is blessed in Christianity: virginity or celibacy. Celibacy for the sake of Christ has created another kind of Christian social unit: monasticism. The Church places it above married life, and in actuality, in the history of the Church it has been a leading, guiding element, a support of the Church, bringing into realization to the greatest degree the moral law of the Gospel, and preserving the dogmas, the Divine services, and other foundations of the Church.

However, not all can take upon themselves the vow of virginity in the name of Christ and the Church. Therefore, while blessing virginity as a chosen and a perfect form of life, the Church blesses also married life for the sake of those exalted, and at the same time difficult, aims which are placed before the Christian family, and this blessing is acknowledged as a Mystery.

The Significance of the Mystery

In the Mystery of Marriage the Church invokes the help of God on those being married, that they might understand, fulfill, and attain the aims set before them; namely, to be a "house church," to establish within the family truly Christian relationships, to raise children in faith and life according to the Gospel, to be an example of piety for those around one, and to bear with patience and humility the unavoidable sorrows and, often, sufferings which visit family life.

The Central Moment of the Mystery

The beginning moment in the existence of the Christian family is the sacred action of Marriage. The chief part in the rite of the Mystery of Marriage is the placing of the crowns upon those being married with the words: "The servant of God (name) is married to the handmaid of God (name) in the name of the Father and of the Son and of the Holy Spirit," and then the common blessing of both with the thrice-repeated short prayer, "O Lord our God, crown them with glory and honor."

Marriage as a Divine Institution

That marriage has the blessing of God upon it is said many times in the Holy Scripture. Thus, in Genesis 1:27–28 we read: *So God created man in His own image, in the image of God created He him; male and female created He them. And God blessed them, and God said unto them, Be fruitful, and multiply, and replenish the earth.* Likewise, in Genesis 2:18–24, the writer of Genesis, having spoken of the creation of the woman from the rib of Adam and of how she was led to the man, adds: *Therefore shall a man leave his father and his mother, and shall cleave unto his wife: and they shall be one flesh.*

The Saviour Himself, commanding that faithfulness be preserved in marriage and forbidding divorce, mentions these words of the book of Genesis and instructs: *What therefore God hath joined together, let not man put asunder* (Matt. 19:4–6). These words of the Lord clearly testify to the moral dignity of marriage. The Lord Jesus Christ sanctified marriage by His presence at the marriage in Cana of Galilee, and here He performed His first miracle.

The Apostle Paul compares the mystical character of the Church with marriage in these words: *Husbands, love your wives even as Christ also loved the Church, and gave Himself for it;* and further: *For this cause shall a man leave his father and mother, and shall be joined unto his wife, and they two shall be one flesh. This is a great mystery, but I speak concerning Christ and the Church* (Eph. 5:25, 31–32). The Apostle Paul speaks more in detail about marriage and virginity in I Corinthians, the seventh chapter. Placing virginity above marriage, he does not condemn marriage, commanding that it be preserved and advising that one not be divorced even from an unbeliever, in hope of converting the other one to the faith. Having indicated the highest impulses for remaining in virginity, in conclusion he says the following: *Such* (those who marry) *shall have trouble in the flesh; but I spare you* (I Cor. 7:28).

Having in mind the Christian purpose of marriage, the Church forbids entering into marriage with heretics (canons of the Fourth and Sixth Councils), and likewise with those of other religions.[23]

The Indissolubility of Marriage

The Church only in exceptional circumstances agrees to the dissolving of a marriage, chiefly when it has been defiled by adultery, or when it has been destroyed by conditions of life (for example, long absence of one spouse, without word). The entrance into a second marriage after the death of a husband or wife, or in general the loss of one spouse by the other, is allowed by the Church, although in the prayers for those being married the second time, forgiveness is asked for the sin of a second marriage. A third marriage is tolerated only as a lesser evil to avoid a greater evil—immoral life (as St. Basil the Great explains).

THE MYSTERY (SACRAMENT) OF UNCTION

The Essence of the Mystery

The Mystery of Unction is a sacred action in which, while the body is anointed with oil, the Grace of God which heals infirmities of soul and body is called down upon a sick person (*Longer Catechism*, p.

---

[23] See Canon 14 of the Council of Chalcedon, and Canon 72 of Quinisext (*Seven Ecumenical Councils*, NPNF, pp. 278–79 and 397). The Orthodox Church in modern times has not been quite so strict. The present rule of the Russian Church Outside of Russia, for example, allows marriage with the non-Orthodox who are closest in faith to Orthodoxy: Roman Catholics, Armenians, Episcopalians, Lutherans, Presbyterians. Other Orthodox Churches today have similar rules. Canon 72 of the Quinisext Council also allows Orthodox converts to remain with their spouses after conversion, for as St. Paul says: *The unbelieving husband is sanctified by the wife, and the unbelieving wife is sanctified by the husband* (I Cor. 7:14). In actual practice, "mixed marriages" are not conducive to the formation of a "house church" or to the preservation of fervent Orthodoxy in the children of such unions, and the conversion to Orthodoxy of the non-Orthodox spouse is much to be preferred.

65). It is performed by a gathering of presbyters, ideally seven in number; however, it can be performed by a lesser number and even by a single priest.

The Divine Institution of the Mystery

Even in Old Testament times, oil signified Grace, joy, a softening, a bringing to life. Anointment of the sick with oil was done by the Apostles, as we read in the Evangelist Mark (6:13): They *anointed with oil many that were sick, and healed them.*

The clearest testimony of the Mystery of Unction is to be found in the Apostle James (5:14–15): *Is any sick among you? Let him call for the elders (presbyters) of the Church, and let them pray over him, anointing him with oil in the name of the Lord. And the prayer of faith shall save the sick, and the Lord shall raise him up; and if he have committed sins, they shall be forgiven him.* The Apostle speaks here not of a special "gift" of healing; rather he prescribes the sacred action in a definite form, which was to enter into the custom of the Church: the performance of it by the presbyters of the Church, prayers, anointment; and he joins to this, as its consequence, the easing of bodily illness and the forgiveness of sins.

One cannot understand the words of the Apostle James about anointment with oil as referring to a usual healing method of those times, since oil, with all its beneficial attributes, is not a means of healing against every disease. The Apostles did not introduce anything of themselves, but they taught only what the Lord Jesus Christ had commanded them, and what the Holy Spirit had inspired in them; and they called themselves not the "institutors" of the Mysteries of God, but only the "stewards" of the Mysteries and the "servants of Christ." Consequently, Unction also, which is commanded here by the Apostle James, has a Divine institution.

In ancient Christian literature one may find indirect testimonies of the Mystery of Unction in St. Irenaeus of Lyons and in Origen. Later there are clear testimonies of it in Sts. Basil the Great and John Chrysostom, who have left prayers for the healing of the infirm which entered later into the rite of Unction; and likewise in St. Cyril of Alexandria. In the fifth century, Pope Innocent I answered a series of questions concerning the Mystery of Unction, indicating in his answers that (*a*) it should be performed "upon believers who are sick"; (*b*) it may be performed also by a bishop, since one should not see in the words of the Apostle, *let him call for the presbyters,* any prohibition for a bishop to participate in the sacred action; (*c*) this anointment may not be performed "on those undergoing ecclesiastical penance," because it is a "Mystery," and "to those who are forbidden the other Mysteries, how can one allow only one?"

This Mystery is performed on the sick who are capable of receiving it consciously and participating in prayer for themselves; however, it may also be performed on children. The place of this sacred action may be either the church or the dwelling where the sick person is. The Mystery of Unction is usually preceded by Confession and is usually concluded with the Mystery of Communion.

The visible side of the Mystery comprises seven anointings of the sick person with oil by the participating priests in order; this is done in the form of a cross on the forehead, the nostrils, the cheeks, the lips, the chest, and both sides of the hands, accompanied by prayers and by the reading of specific passages in the Epistles and the Gospels. During the anointing itself, seven times this prayer is pronounced: "O Holy Father, Physician of souls and bodies, Who didst send Thine only begotten Son, our Lord Jesus Christ, Who healeth every infirmity and delivereth from death: Heal also Thy servant (name)," and so forth.

The rite of Unction begins with the singing of troparia and a canon; the final prayer in the rite is a prayer of remission of sins. A whole assembly of servants of the Lord stand before Him on behalf of the sick person, and by the prayer of faith on behalf of the whole Church entreat Him, the Most Merciful One, to grant to the infirm one the remission of transgressions and to purify his conscience from every defilement. There is also kept in mind the fact that a person who has grown weak in body and soul is not always capable of offering the proper confession of his sins. This lightening of the conscience of the one who receives the Mystery of Unction opens the way also for a

Grace-giving healing of his bodily infirmity through the prayer of faith.

There is allowed and sometimes practiced a special rite of Unction, which is performed in church on many persons at the same time, on a special day assigned for this, for the general healing of infirmities of soul and body; but this rite is not precisely identical to the Mystery of Unction.[24]

Unction Among Protestants and Roman Catholics

The Protestants have rejected the Mystery of Unction, although Luther, at least in the beginning, was not against allowing it in church practice. The Roman Church up to now has given Unction only to sick persons who were already near death, as a form of preparation for death, which is why this Mystery is called among Roman Catholics "Extreme Unction," the Sacrament of the dying. Such a teaching appeared in the Roman Church beginning in the 12th century and is in clear contradiction to the words of the Apostle James.

From ancient times in the Church, the dying were given, as a preparation for death, Holy Communion of the Body and Blood of Christ.[25]

---

[24] In this rite, usually performed in the evening of Passion Wednesday, as if in preparation for our Lord's death and burial, all present come forward to be anointed by each of the seven (or fewer) priests. The rite is identical to that of the Mystery of Unction, except that if there are many people (and seven priests), the anointings may be performed all together at the end of the service, instead of after each reading of the Gospel, to the accompaniment of a repeated refrain to a special Lenten melody: "Hearken to us, O Lord; hearken to us, O Master; hearken to us, O Holy One."

[25] This, of course, does not mean that the Mystery of Unction is not performed also on the dying; those dying of a long illness may even receive Unction several times in the course of their illness. However, Unction is a separate Mystery, for the healing of the sick, and is not a necessary part of the rites administered to the dying, which usually include Confession, Holy Communion, and the Prayers for the Departure of the Soul (when death seems close). If the sick person dies, the consecrated oil left from Unction is, according to ancient tradition, poured cross-form over his body in the coffin at the end of the funeral service.

Chapter 9

Prayer
as the Expression of the
Inward Life of the Church

THE SPIRITUAL BOND OF THE
MEMBERS OF THE CHURCH IN PRAYER

PRAYER is the manifestation of the Church's life and the spiritual bond of its members with God in the Holy Trinity, and of all with each other. It is so inseparable from faith that it may be called the atmosphere of the Church or the breathing of the Church. Prayers are the threads of the living fabric of the Church body, and they go in all directions. The bond of prayer penetrates the whole body of the Church, leading each part of it into the common life of the body, animating each part and helping it by nourishing, by cleansing, and by other forms of mutual help (Eph. 4:16). It unites each member of the Church with the Heavenly Father, the members of the earthly Church with each other, and the earthly members with the heavenly members. It does not cease, but yet more increases and is exalted in the Heavenly Kingdom.

Through the whole Sacred Scripture of the New Testament there goes the commandment of ceaseless prayer: *Pray without ceasing* (I Thess. 5:17); *praying always with all prayer and supplication in the Spirit* (Eph. 6:18); *and He spake a parable unto them to this end, that men ought always to pray, and not to faint* (Luke 18:1).

The perfect example of personal prayer was given to us by the Lord Jesus Christ Himself. He left as an example the prayer "Our Father"—the Lord's Prayer. Prayer is (*a*) the form of the Church's life,

311

(*b*) an instrument or means of its activity, and (*c*) its power of over-coming.

Prayer is of two kinds: public and private. There is prayer which is of words, and in particular sung, and there is mental prayer, that is, in-ward prayer, or the prayer of the mind in the heart.[1] The content of prayer is (*a*) praise or glory; (*b*) thanksgiving; (*c*) repentance; (*d*) en-treaty for the mercy of God, for the forgiveness of sins, for the giving of good things of soul and body, both heavenly and earthly. Repentance before God sometimes has the form of a conversation with one's own soul—as, for example, often occurs in the canons.[2]

Prayer may be for oneself or for others. Prayer for each other ex-

---

[1] Mental (noetic) prayer, inward prayer, and prayer of the mind in the heart are usually associated with the Jesus Prayer: "Lord Jesus Christ, Son of God, have mercy on me, a sinner"; or, in its shorter form, "Lord Jesus Christ, have mercy on me." Holy ascetics of the Church have reached great heights of inward prayer with the aid of the Jesus Prayer; however, this Prayer is not reserved for such ascetics only. Saying the Jesus Prayer is a fundamental practice of Orthodox spiritual life, which should be undertaken by all Orthodox Christians, both monastic and lay.

Archimandrite Sophrony (Sakharov) indicates a sequence in the practice of the Jesus Prayer: "First it is a verbal matter: we say the prayer with our lips while trying to concentrate our attention on the Name and the words. Next, we no longer move our lips but pronounce the Name of Jesus Christ, and what follows after, in our minds, mentally. In the third stage mind and heart combine to act together: the attention of the mind is centered in the heart and the prayer is said there. Fourthly, the prayer be-comes self-propelling. This happens when the prayer is confirmed in the heart and, with no especial effort on our part, continues there, where the mind is concentrated. Finally, the prayer, so full of blessing, starts to act like a gentle flame within us, as in-spiration from on High, rejoicing the heart with a sensation of Divine love and de-lighting the mind in spiritual contemplation. This last state is sometimes accompanied by a vision of Light.

"A gradual ascent to prayer is the most trustworthy. The beginner who would embark on the struggle is usually recommended to start with the first step, verbal prayer, until body, tongue, brain and heart assimilate it. The time that this takes var-ies. The more earnest the repentance, the shorter the road" (*His Life Is Mine,* p. 113).—3RD ED.

[2] Not, of course, the canons or rules of councils, but the canons, usually com-posed of nine canticles or odes, which are a regular part of the services of Matins and Compline, or may be read or sung privately.

presses the mutual love between members of the Church. Since, according to the Apostle, *love never faileth* (I Cor. 13:8), the earthly members of the Church not only pray for each other, but also, according to the law of Christian love, they pray for those who are departed (the heavenly members); and the heavenly members likewise pray for those on earth, as well as for the repose of their brethren who are in need of the help of prayer. Finally, we ourselves appeal to those in heaven with the entreaty to pray for us and for our brethren. Upon this bond of the heavenly with the earthly is founded also the concern of the angels over us and our prayers to them.

The power of prayer for others is constantly affirmed by the word of God. The Saviour said to the Apostle Peter: *I have prayed for thee, that thy faith fail not* (Luke 22:32). The Holy Apostle Paul often entreats Christians to pray for him: *I trust that through your prayers I shall be given unto you* (Philemon, v. 22). *Brethren, pray for us, that the word of the Lord might have free course and be glorified, even as it is with you* (II Thes. 3:1). Being far away, the Apostle is joined with his spiritual brethren in common prayer: *Now I beseech you, brethren, for the Lord Jesus Christ's sake, and for the love of the Spirit, that ye strive together with me in your prayers to God for me* (Rom. 15:30). The Apostle James instructs: *Pray one for another, that ye may be healed. The effectual fervent prayer of a righteous man availeth much* (James 5:16). St. John the Theologian saw in revelation how in the heavens twenty-four elders, standing at the throne of God, fell down before the Lamb, and everyone had harps and vials filled with incense, *which are the prayers of saints* (Apoc. 5:8); that is, they raised up the prayers of the saints on earth to the Heavenly Throne.

Prayer for the Dead

Pray one for another (James 5:16).
Whether we live ... or die, we are the Lord's (Rom. 14:8).
Love never faileth (I Cor. 13:8).
Whatsoever ye shall ask in My name, that will I do, that the Father may be glorified in the Son (John 14:13).

313

In God all are alive. Church life is penetrated by a living awareness and feeling that our dead ones continue to live after death, only in a different form than on earth, and that they are not deprived of spiritual nearness to those who remain on earth. Therefore, the bond of prayer with them on the part of the pilgrim Church (on earth) does not cease. *Neither death nor life ... shall be able to separate us from the love of God, which is in Christ Jesus our Lord* (Rom. 8:38–39). The departed need only one kind of help from their brethren: prayer and petition for the remission of their sins.

And this is the confidence that we have in Him (the Son of God), *that, if we ask anything according to His will, He heareth us. And if we know that He hear us, whatsoever we ask, we know that we have the petitions that we desired of Him. If any man see his brother sin a sin which is not unto death, he shall ask, and He shall give him life for them that sin not unto death. There is a sin unto death: I do not say that he shall pray for it* (I John 5:14–16).

Corresponding to this instruction of the Apostle, the Church prays for all its children who have died with true repentance. Praying for them as for those who are alive, the Church follows the words of the Apostle: *Whether we live, therefore, or die, we are the Lord's. For to this end Christ both died and rose, and revived, that He might be Lord both of the dead and living* (Rom. 14:8–9). Those, however, who have died in unrepented sins, outside the communion of the Church, are not even vouchsafed the Church's prayers, as follows from the above-mentioned words of the Apostle John: *I do not say that he should pray for it.*[3]

In the Old Testament Church also there existed the custom of praying for the dead. Concerning this there is the testimony of sacred history. Thus, in the days of the pious leader of the Jews Judas Maccabeus, when, after an inspection of those who had fallen on the field of battle, there was found in their garments plunder from the gifts offered to idols, all the Jews *blessed the ways of the Lord, the righteous Judge, Who reveals the things that are hidden; and they turned to prayer, beseeching that the sin which had been committed might be wholly blotted*

---

[3] See pp. 294–95 above.—3RD ED.

out. And Judas Maccabeus himself sent to Jerusalem *to provide for a sin offering. In doing this he acted very well and honorably, taking account of the resurrection* (II Mac. 12:39–45).

That the remission of sins for those who have sinned not unto death can be given both in the present life and after death is naturally to be concluded from the words of the Lord Himself: *Whosoever speaketh a word against the Son of Man, it shall be forgiven him; but whosoever speaketh against the Holy Spirit, it shall not be forgiven him, neither in this world, neither in the world to come* (Matt. 12:32). Similarly, from the word of God we know that the Lord Jesus has *the keys of hell and of death* (Apoc. 1:18); consequently, He has power to open the gates of hell by the prayers of the Church and by power of the propitiatory Bloodless Sacrifice which is offered for the dead.

In the Christian Church all the ancient Liturgies, both of East and West, testify to the Church's remembrance in prayer of the dead. Such Liturgies are known under the names of the Holy Apostle James, the brother of the Lord; St. Basil the Great; St. John Chrysostom; and St. Gregory the Dialogist. Similar references are to be found in the Roman, Spanish, and Gallican Liturgies, and finally, in the ancient Liturgies of the groups that separated from Orthodoxy: the Jacobites, Copts, Armenians, Ethiopians, Syrians, and others. For all their numbers, there is not a single one of these Liturgies where there is no prayer for the dead. The testimony of the Fathers and teachers of the Church speaks of the same thing.

Concerning the good effect of prayerful communion in the name of the Lord Jesus Christ between those living on earth and the dead, St. Ephraim the Syrian, for example, reasons thus: "For the dead, the remembrance performed by the saints during their lifetime is beneficial. We see an example of this in a number of the works of God. For example, in a vineyard there are the ripening grapes in the field, and the wine already squeezed out into vessels; when the grapes ripen on the grapevine, then the wine which stands unmoving in the house begins to froth and be agitated, as if desiring to escape. The same thing happens, it seems, with another plant, the onion; for as soon as the onion which has been sown in the field begins to ripen, the onion which is in the house also begins to give sprouts. And so, if even growing things have between themselves such a fellow-feeling, will not the petitions of prayer be all the more felt by the dead? And when you will sensibly agree that this occurs in accordance with the nature of creatures, then just imagine that you are the first of the creatures of God."

In praying for the dead, the Church intercedes for them just as for the living, not in its own name, but in the name of the Lord Jesus Christ (John 14:13–14), and by the power of His Sacrifice on the Cross, which was offered for the deliverance of all. These fervent prayers help the seeds of new life which our departed ones have taken with them—if these seeds have been unable to open up sufficiently here on earth—to gradually open up and develop under the influence of prayers and with the mercy of God, just as a good seed is developed in the earth under the life-giving rays of the sun, with favorable weather. But nothing can revive rotten seeds which have lost the very principle of vegetative life. Similarly, powerless would be prayers for the dead who have died in impiety and without repentance, who have quenched in themselves the Spirit of Christ (I Thes. 5:19). It is precisely concerning such sinners that one must remember the words of the Saviour in the parable of the rich man and Lazarus: that there is no deliverance for them from the deepest parts of hell, and no transference for them into the bosom of Abraham (Luke 16:26). And indeed, such people usually do not leave behind them on earth people who might pray sincerely for them to God; likewise, they have not acquired for themselves friends in heaven among the saints, who, when they fail (that is, die), might receive them into everlasting habitations—that is, might pray for them (Luke 16:9).

Of course, on the earth it is not known to what lot each has been subjected after his death. But the prayer of love can never be profitless. If our dead ones who are dear to us have been vouchsafed the Kingdom of Heaven, they reply to prayer for them with an answering prayer for us. And if our prayers are powerless to help them, in any case they are not harmful to us, according to the word of the Psalmist: *My prayer shall return to my bosom* (Ps. 34:16), and according to the word of the Saviour: *Let your peace return to you* (Matt. 10:13). But they are indeed profitable for us. St. John Damascene remarks: "If anyone wishes to anoint a sick man with myrrh or some other sacred oil, first he becomes a partaker of the anointing himself and then he anoints the sick one. So also, everyone who struggles for the salvation of his neighbor, first receives benefit himself, and then offers it to his neighbor; for God is not unjust, so as to forget the works, according to the word of the Divine Apostle."

Communion in Prayer with the Saints

The Church prays for all who have died in the faith, asking forgiveness for their sins. For there is no man without sin, *if he have lived even a single day upon earth* (Job 14:5, Septuagint). *If we say that we have no sin, we deceive ourselves, and the truth is not in us* (I John 1:8). Therefore, no matter how righteous a man might be, when he departs from this world, the Church accompanies his departure with prayer for him to the Lord. *Brethren, pray for us,* the Holy Apostle Paul asks his spiritual children (I Thes. 5:25).

At the same time, when the common voice of the Church testifies to the righteousness of the reposed person, Christians, apart from prayer for him, are taught by the good example of his life and place him as an example to be imitated.

And when, further, the common conviction of the sanctity of the reposed person is confirmed by special testimonies, such as martyrdom, fearless confession, self-sacrificing service to the Church, the gift of healing, and especially when the Lord confirms the sanctity of the reposed person by miracles after his death when he is remembered in prayer—then the Church *glorifies* him in a special way. How can the Church not glorify those whom the Lord Himself calls His "friends"? *Ye are my friends.... I have called you friends* (John 15:14–15), whom He has received in His heavenly mansions in fulfillment of the words: *Where I am, there ye may be also* (John 14:3). When this happens, prayers for the forgiveness of the sins of the departed one and for his repose cease; they give way to other forms of Church communion with him, namely: (*a*) the praising of his struggles in Christ, since *neither do men light a candle and put it under a bushel, but on a candlestick; and it*

317

giveth light unto all that are in the house (Matt. 5:15); (*b*) petitions to him that he might pray for us, for the remission of our sins, for our moral advancement, and that he might help us in our spiritual needs and in our sorrows.

It is said: *Blessed are the dead who die in the Lord from henceforth* (Apoc. 14:13); and we indeed bless them.

It is said: *And the glory which Thou gavest Me, I have given them* (John 17:22); and we indeed give to them this glory, according to the Saviour's commandment.

Likewise the Saviour said: *He that receiveth a prophet in the name of a prophet shall receive a prophet's reward; and he that receiveth a righteous man in the name of a righteous man shall receive a righteous man's reward* (Matt. 10:41). *Whosoever shall do the will of My Father Who is in heaven, the same is My brother, and sister, and mother* (Matt. 12:50). Therefore, we also should receive a righteous man as a righteous man. If he is a brother for the Lord, then he should be such for us also. The saints are our spiritual brothers, sisters, mothers, fathers; and our love for them is expressed by communion in prayer with them.

The Apostle John wrote to the Christians: *That which we have seen and heard declare we unto you, that ye also may have fellowship with us: and truly our fellowship is with the Father, and with His Son Jesus Christ* (I John 1:3). And in the Church this fellowship with the Apostles is not interrupted; it goes over with them into the other realm of their existence, the heavenly realm.

The nearness of the saints to the Throne of the Lamb and the raising up by them of prayers for the Church on earth are depicted in the Apocalypse of St. John the Theologian: *And I beheld, and I heard the voice of many angels round about the Throne, and the beasts, and the elders; and the number of them was ten thousand times ten thousand, and thousands of thousands,* who praised the Lord (Apoc. 5:11).

Communion in prayer with the saints is the realization in actual fact of the bond between Christians on earth and the Heavenly Church of which the Apostle speaks: *Ye are come unto Mount Zion, and unto the city of the living God, the Heavenly Jerusalem, and to an innumerable company of angels, to the general assembly and the Church of the firstborn, who are written in heaven, and to God the Judge of all, and to the spirits of just men made perfect* (Heb. 12:22–23).

The Sacred Scripture presents numerous examples of the fact that the righteous, while still living on earth, can see and hear and know much that is inaccessible to the ordinary understanding. All the more are these gifts present with them when they have put off the flesh and are in heaven. The Holy Apostle Peter saw into the heart of Ananias, according to the book of Acts (5:3). To Elisha was revealed the lawless act of the servant Gehazi (IV Kings, chap. 4; II Kings in KJV); and what is even more remarkable, to him was revealed all the secret intentions of the Syrian court, which he then communicated to the King of Israel (IV Kings 6:12). The saints, when still on earth, penetrated in spirit into the world above. Some of them saw choirs of angels, others were vouchsafed to behold the image of God (Isaiah, Ezekiel), and still others were exalted to the third heaven and heard there mystical, unutterable words, as for example, the Holy Apostle Paul. All the more when they are in heaven, are they capable of knowing what is happening on earth and of hearing those who appeal to them, since the saints in heaven *are equal unto the angels* (Luke 20:36).

From the parable of the Lord about the rich man and Lazarus (Luke 16:19–31), we know that Abraham, being in heaven, could hear the cry of the rich man who was suffering in hell, despite the "great gulf" that separates them. The words of Abraham about the rich man's brethren, *They have Moses and the prophets; let them hear them* (Luke 16:29), clearly indicate that Abraham knows the life of the Hebrew people which has occurred after his death; he knows of Moses and the Law, of the prophets and their writings. The spiritual vision of the souls of the righteous in heaven, without any doubt, is greater than it was on earth. The Apostle writes: *Now we see through a glass, darkly, but then face to face; now I know in part, but then shall I know even as also I am known* (I Cor. 13:12).

The Holy Church has always held the teaching of the invocation of the saints, being fully convinced that they intercede for us before God in heaven. This we see from the ancient Liturgies. In the Liturgy of the Holy Apostle James it is said: "Especially we perform the memorial of the Holy and Glorious Ever-Virgin, the Blessed Theotokos. Remember her, O Lord God, and by her pure and holy prayers spare and have mercy on us." St. Cyril of Jerusalem, explaining the Liturgy of the Church of Jerusalem, remarks: "Then we also commemorate (in offering the Bloodless Sacrifice) those who have previously departed: first of all, patriarchs, prophets, apostles, martyrs, so that by their prayers and intercession God might receive our petition."

Numerous are the testimonies of the Fathers and teachers of the Church, especially from the 4th century onwards, concerning the Church's veneration of the saints. But already from the beginning of the 2nd century there are direct indications in ancient Christian literature concerning faith in the prayer of the saints in heaven for their earthly brethren. The witnesses of the martyric death of St. Ignatius the God-bearer (beginning of the 2nd century) say: "Having returned home with tears, we had the all-night vigil.... Then, after sleeping a little, some of us suddenly saw blessed Ignatius standing and embracing us, and others likewise saw him praying for us." Similar records, mentioning the prayers and intercession for us of the martyrs, are to be found in other accounts from the epoch of persecutions against Christians.

THE OUTWARD SIDE OF PRAYER
(PHYSICAL)

Prayer is *the offering of the mind and heart to God*. However, while we are living in the body upon earth, our prayer naturally is expressed in various outward forms: bows and prostrations, the sign of the Cross, the lifting up of the hands, the use of various objects in the Divine services, and all the outward actions of the public Divine services of Orthodox Christians.

The Christian worship of God, in its highest state, is worship *in spirit and in truth* (John 4:23–24). The Christian Divine services are incomparably more exalted than the Old Testament ones. Although the Old Testament services were instituted according to the command of God Himself (Exodus 25:40), still they served only as *the example and shadow of heavenly things* (Heb. 8:5). They were done away with as "decayed and grown old" and near to "vanishing away" (Heb. 8:13) with the institution of the New Testament, which was sanctified by the holy Blood of the Lord Jesus Christ. The Divine services of the New Testament consist not in constant sacrifices of calves and rams, but in the prayer of praise, thanksgiving, and petition, in the offering of the Bloodless Sacrifice of the Body and Blood of Christ, and in the bestowing of Grace in the Holy Mysteries.

However, Christian prayer has also various outward actions. The Lord Jesus Christ Himself did not avoid the outward manifestations of prayer and sacrifice actions: He bowed the knee, fell on His face, and prayed; He raised His hands and blessed; He breathed and said to His disciples, Peace be to you; He used outward actions when healing; He visited the Temple in Jerusalem and called it "the house of My Father": *My house shall be called the house of prayer* (Matt. 21:13). The Apostles also did all these things.

Spiritual worship must be accompanied by bodily worship, as a result of the close bond and mutual influence of soul and body. *What? know ye not that your body is the temple of the Holy Spirit Who is in you, Whom ye have of God, and ye are not your own? For ye are bought with a price; therefore glorify God in your body, and in your spirit, which are God's* (I Cor. 6:19–20).

A Christian is not only called to glorify God with his soul and in his body, but everything surrounding him he must also direct to the glorification of the Lord. *Whether therefore ye eat, or drink, or whatsoever ye do, do all to the glory of God* (I Cor. 10:31). One should sanctify by prayer not only oneself but also that which one makes use of: *For every creature of God is good, and nothing to be refused, if it be received with thanksgiving: for it is sanctified by the word of God and prayer* (I Tim. 4:4–5). The Christian is called consciously to aid towards the end that around him, in his hands, and in his consciousness there might be realized the call of the Psalm: *Let every thing that hath breath praise the Lord* (Ps. 150:5). This is done by the Orthodox Christian Divine services, taken in their wholeness.

The Veneration of Icons

One of the outward forms of the worship of God and the veneration of the saints is the use of sacred images and the respect shown to them.

Among the various gifts of man which distinguish him from other creatures is the gift of art, or of depictions in line and color. This is a noble and high gift, and it is worthy to be used to glorify God. With all the pure and high means available to us we must glorify God according to the call of the Psalmist: *Bless the Lord, O my soul, and all that is within me bless His holy name* (Ps. 102:1). "All that is within me" refers to all the capabilities of the soul. And truly, the capability of art is a gift from God. Of old under Moses *the Lord hath called by name Bezaleel, the son of Uri, the son of Hur, of the tribe of Judah; and He hath filled him with the spirit of God, in wisdom, in understanding, and in knowledge, and in all manner of workmanship; and to devise skilled works, to work in gold, and in silver, and in brass, and in the cutting of stones, to set them, and in carving of wood, to make any manner of cunning work. And He hath put in his heart that he may teach* (others).... *Them hath He filled with wisdom of heart, to work all manner of work, of the engraver, and of the cunning workman, and of the embroiderer* (Ex. 35:30–35).

The material objects made by the skilled work of artists for the tabernacle of Moses, as also subsequently for the Temple of Solomon, were all sacred. However, while some of them served more as sacred adornments, others were especially revered and became exceptional places of God's glory. For example, there was the "Ark of the Covenant," the very touching of which without special reverence could cause death (II Kings [II Sam.] 6:6–7—the incident with Uzzah at the time of the transferral of the Ark under David, when Uzzah was struck dead because he touched the Ark with his hand). There were also the "Cherubim of glory" over the Ark, in the midst of which God deigned to reveal Himself and to give His commands to Moses. *There I will meet with thee, and I will commune with thee from above the mercy seat, from between the two Cherubim which are upon the ark of the testimony, of all things which I will give thee in commandment unto the children of Israel* (Ex. 25:18–22). These were "the visible image of the Invisible God" (in the expression of Metropolitan Macarius in his *Orthodox Dogmatic Theology*).

Among the numerous depictions on the walls and curtains of the Old Testament Temple, there were no depictions of the departed righteous ones, such as exist in the Christian Church. They were not there because the righteous ones themselves were awaiting their deliverance, waiting to be brought up out of hell; this was accomplished by the descent into hell and the Resurrection of Christ. According to the Apostle, *they without us should not be made perfect* (Heb. 11:40); they were glorified *as saints* only in the New Testament.

If in the Sacred Scripture there are strict prohibitions against the erection of idols and the worship of them, one cannot at all transfer these prohibitions to Christian icons. Idols are the images of false gods, and the worship of them was a worship of demons, or else of imaginary beings that have no existence; and thus, in essence, it is a worship of the lifeless objects themselves—wood, gold, or stone. But the Sacred Scripture strictly instructs us to *put a difference between holy and unholy, and between unclean and clean* (Lev. 10:10). He who is unable to see the difference between sacred images and idols blasphemes and defiles the icons; he commits sacrilege and is subject to the condemnation of Sacred Scripture, which warns: *Thou that abhorrest idols, dost thou commit sacrilege?* (Rom. 2:22).

The discoveries of ecclesiastical archeology show that in the ancient Christian Church there existed sacred images in the catacombs and in other places of assembly for prayer, and subsequently in Christian churches. If in certain cases Christian writers have expressed themselves against the existence of statues and similar images, they have in mind the pagan worship (the Council of Elvira in Spain, 305). Sometimes, however, such expressions and prohibitions were evoked by the special conditions of the time—for example, the necessity to hide one's holy things from the pagan persecutors and from the non-Christian masses who had a hostile attitude toward Christianity.

It is natural to suppose that in the earliest period in the history of

Christianity the first need was that people be drawn away from pagan idol-worship, and only later could there be brought into being the idea of the fullness of the forms for glorifying God and His saints; and among these forms there is a place for a glorification in colors, in sacred images.

The Seventh Ecumenical Council in the following words expressed the dogma of the veneration of sacred icons: "We therefore … define with all certitude and accuracy that just as the figure of the precious and life-giving Cross, so also the venerable and holy images … should be set forth in the holy churches of God (for veneration)…. For by so much more frequently as they are seen in artistic representation (that is, the Lord Jesus Christ, the Theotokos, the angels and saints who are depicted in the icons), by so much more readily are men lifted up to the memory of their prototypes, and to a longing after them. And to these should be given due salutation and honorable reverence (Greek: *timitiki proskynisis*), not indeed that true worship of faith (Greek: *latreia*) which pertains alone to the Divine Nature; but to these … incense and lights may be offered…. For the honor which is paid to the image passes on to that which the image represents" (*Seven Ecumenical Councils,* NPNF, p. 550).[4]

---

[4] This distinction between the "worship" of God and the "reverence" or "veneration" shown for icons was set forth first by St. John Damascene in his treatises on the icons. See his *On the Divine Images,* translated by David Anderson (Crestwood, N.Y.: St. Vladimir's Seminary Press, 1980), pp. 82–88, and the introduction, pp. 10–11.

Nothing is said in the Orthodox canons regarding the veneration of statues, such as came to be used in the religious art of the West in the Middle Ages and later centuries. However, the virtually universal tradition of the Orthodox Church of both East and West in the early centuries, and of the Eastern Church in later centuries, has been to allow as religious art two-dimensional depictions and bas-reliefs, but not statues in the round. The reason for this seems to lie in the realism that is inevitable in three-dimensional depictions, making them suitable for representing the things of this world of earth (for example, the statues of emperors), but not those of the heavenly world into which our earthly thinking and realism cannot penetrate. Two-dimensional icons, on the other hand, are like "windows to heaven" which are much more capable of raising the mind and heart to heavenly realities.

The Veneration of Holy Relics

In giving veneration to the saints of God who have departed with their souls into heaven, the Holy Church at the same time honors the relics or bodies of the saints of God which remain on earth.

In the Old Testament there was no veneration of the bodies of the righteous, for the righteous themselves were still awaiting their deliverance. Then also the flesh (of the dead) in itself was considered unclean.

In the New Testament, after the Incarnation of the Saviour, there was an elevation not only of the concept of man in Christ, but also of the concept of the body as the dwelling place of the Holy Spirit. The Lord Himself, the Word of God, was incarnate and took upon Himself a human body. Christians are called to this: that not only their souls but also their bodies, sanctified by holy Baptism, sanctified by the reception of the Most Pure Body and Blood of Christ, might become true temples of the Holy Spirit. *Know ye not that your body is the temple of the Holy Spirit, Who is in you?* (I Cor. 6:19). And therefore the bodies of Christians who have lived a righteous life, or who have become holy through receiving a martyr's death, are worthy of special veneration and honor.

The Holy Church in all times, following Sacred Tradition, has shown honor to holy relics. This honor has been expressed (*a*) in the reverent collection and preservation of the remains of the saints of God, as is known from accounts even of the 2nd century, and then from the testimonies of later times; (*b*) in the solemn uncovering and translation of holy relics; (*c*) in the building over them of churches and altars; (*d*) in the establishment of feasts in memory of their uncovering or translation; (*e*) in pilgrimages to holy tombs, and in adorning them; and (*f*) in the constant rule of the Church to place relics of holy martyrs at the dedication of altars, or to place holy relics in the holy antimension upon which is performed the Divine Liturgy.

This very natural honor given to the holy relics and other remains of the saints of God has a firm foundation in the fact that God Himself has deigned to honor and glorify them by innumerable signs and miracles—something for which there is testimony throughout the whole course of the Church's history.

Even in the Old Testament, when saints were not venerated with a special glorification after death, there were signs from the bodies of the righteous. Thus, the body of a certain dead man, after being touched to the bones of the Prophet Elisha in his tomb, immediately came to life, and the dead man arose (IV [II] Kings 13:21). The body of the Holy Prophet Elijah was raised up alive into heaven, and the mantle of Elijah, which was left by him to Elisha, parted by its touch the waters of the Jordan for the crossing of the river by Elisha.

Going over to the New Testament, we read in the book of the Acts of the Apostles that handkerchiefs and belts ("aprons") from the body of the Apostle Paul were placed upon the sick, and the diseases of the sick were cured, and evil spirits departed from them (Acts 19:12). The Holy Fathers and teachers of the Church have testified before their hearers and readers of the miracles occurring from the remains of the saints, and often they have called their contemporaries to be witnesses of the truth of their words. For example, St. Ambrose says in his homily at the uncovering of the relics of Sts. Gervasius and Protasius: "You have known and even seen yourselves many who have been delivered from demons, and even more of those who had no sooner touched the garments of the saints with their hands than immediately they were healed of their infirmities. The miracles of antiquity have been renewed from the time when, through the coming of the Lord Jesus, there has been poured out upon the earth a most abundant Grace! You see many who have been healed as if by the shadow of the saints. How many cloths have been handed from hand to hand! How many garments, laid upon the sacred remains and from the mere touching become a source of healing, do believers entreat from each other! All strive at least a little to touch (them), and the one who touches becomes well." Similar testimonies may be read in St. Gregory the Theologian, St. Ephraim the Syrian, St. John Chrysostom, Blessed Augustine, and others.

Already from the beginning of the 2nd century there is information on the honor given by Christians to the remains of saints. Thus, after describing the martyr's death of St. Ignatius the God-bearer, Bishop of Antioch, a person who witnessed this death states that "Of what remained from his body (he was torn to pieces by beasts in the circus), only the firmest parts were taken away to Antioch and placed in a linen as an invaluable treasure of the Grace which dwelt in the martyr, a treasure left to the Holy Church." The residents of the cities, beginning with Rome, received these remains in succession at that time, and carried them on their shoulders, as St. John Chrysostom later testified, "to the present city (Antioch), praising the crowned victor and glorifying the struggler." Likewise, after the martyr's death of St. Polycarp, Bishop of Smyrna, and the burning of his body by the Proconsul, the Christians "gathered the bones of St. Polycarp as a treasure more precious than precious stones and purer than gold, and placed them ... for the celebration of the day of his martyric birth, and for the instruction and confirmation of future Christians."

The remains of the saints (in Greek, *ta leipsana;* in Latin, *reliquiae,* both meaning what is "left") are revered whether or not they are incorrupt, out of respect for the holy life or the martyric death of the saint, and all the more when there are evident and confirmed signs of healing by prayer to the saints for their intercession before God. The Church Councils many times (for example, the Moscow Council of 1667) have forbidden the recognition of the reposed as saints solely by the sign of the incorruption of their bodies. But of course the incorruption of the bodies of the righteous is accepted as one of the Divine signs of their sanctity.[5]

Here let us note that the Slavonic word *moshchi,* "relics," refers not only to the bodies of saints: in Church Slavonic this word signifies in general the bodies of the reposed. Thus, in the Rite of Burial in the *Book of Needs* we read: "And taking the relics of the reposed, we go out of the Church," etc. The ancient Slavonic *moshchi* (from the root *mog*) is apparently kin to the word *mogila,* "grave."

---

[5] One might say that the incorruption of a dead body is no *guarantee* of sanctity: examples can be given of Oriental swamis whose bodies were incorrupt long after death (whether by some natural means related to their ascetic life, or by a demonic counterfeit); and of some great Orthodox saints (for example, St. Seraphim of Sarov, St. Herman of Alaska) there remain only bones. The relics of St. Nectarios of Pentapolis (†1920) were incorrupt for several years, and then quickly decayed (in the ground), leaving only fragrant bones.

Revering holy relics, we believe not in the power or the might of the remains of the saints in themselves, but rather in the prayerful intercession of the saints whose holy relics are before us.

THE PATH OF THE CHRISTIAN

THE CROSS OF CHRIST: THE PATH, THE POWER, AND THE BANNER OF THE CHURCH

The dogmatic teaching of the Church has the most intimate connection with the whole moral order of Christian life; it gives to it a true direction. Any kind of departure from the dogmatic truths leads to an incorrect understanding of the moral duty of the Christian. Faith demands a life that corresponds to faith.

The Saviour has defined the moral duty of man briefly in the two commandments of the law: the commandment to love God with one's whole heart, soul, mind, and understanding; and the commandment to love one's neighbor as oneself. But at the same time the Saviour taught that the authentic fulfillment of these commandments is impossible without some degree of self-renunciation, self-sacrifice: it demands *struggle*.[6]

And where does the believer find strength for struggle? He receives it through communion with Christ, through love for Christ which inspires him to *follow after Him*. This struggle of following Him Christ called His "yoke": *Take My yoke upon you.... For My yoke is easy, and My burden is light* (Matt. 11:29–30). He called it also a *cross*. Long before the day of His crucifixion, the Lord taught: *If any man will come after Me, let him deny himself, and take up his cross, and follow Me* (Matt. 16:24). *He that taketh not his cross, and followeth after Me, is not worthy of Me* (Matt. 10:38).

---

[6] The Russian word *podvig* most commonly means "struggle," but sometimes must be translated more specifically as "asceticism" or "ascetic exploit."

The Orthodox path of the Christian is *the path of the cross and of struggle*. In other words, it is the path of patience; of the bearing of sorrows, persecutions for the name of Christ, and dangers from the enemies of Christ; of despising the goods of the world for the sake of Christ; of battling against one's passions and lusts.

Such a path of following Christ was taken by His Apostles. *I am crucified with Christ*, writes the Apostle Paul (Gal. 2:20). *God forbid that I should glory, save in the Cross of our Lord Jesus Christ, by Whom the world is crucified unto me, and I unto the world* (Gal. 6:14). Following the path of Christ, the Apostles finished the struggle of their life with a martyr's death.

All believers are called to struggle according to their strength: *They that are Christ's have crucified the flesh with the passions and lusts* (Gal. 5:24). The moral life cannot exist without inward battle, without self-restraint. The Apostle writes: *For many walk, of whom I have told you often, and now tell you even weeping, that they are the enemies of the Cross of Christ; whose end is destruction, whose god is their belly, and whose glory is in their shame, who mind earthly things* (Phil. 3:18–19).

The whole history of the Church has been built on struggles: at first the sufferings of the martyrs in the earliest Christian age; then the self-sacrificing labors of the pillars of the Church, the hierarchs; and then the personal ascetic struggles, spiritual attainments in the battle with the flesh, on the part of the desert dwellers and other strugglers—"earthly angels and heavenly men," the righteous ones who have lived in the world without being defiled by the world. And thus up to now Christianity is adorned with confessors and martyrs for faith in Christ. And the Holy Church supports in believers this duty of self-restraint and spiritual cleansing by means of instructions and examples from the Gospel and the whole Sacred Scripture, by the examples of the saints, by the rules of the Church typicon, by vigils, fasts, and appeals to repentance.

Such is the lot not only of each separate Christian but of the Church herself as a whole: to be persecuted for the Cross of Christ, as was shown in the visions to the Holy Apostle John the Theologian in the Apocalypse. The Church in many periods of her history has endured totally open sorrows and persecutions and the martyr's death of her best servants—what one contemporary priest and Church writer has called the "harvest of God"—while in other periods, even in periods of outward prosperity, she has endured sorrows from inward enemies, from the unworthy manner of life of her members, and in particular of the people who are assigned to serve her.

Thus is defined the dogma of the Cross. The Cross is the path of the Christian and the Church.

At the same time it is also *the power of the Church.* Looking with his mental eyes *unto Jesus the Author and Finisher of our faith* (Heb. 12:2), the Christian finds spiritual strength in the awareness that after the Lord's death on the Cross there followed the Resurrection; that by the Cross the world has been conquered; that if we die with the Lord we shall reign with Him, and shall rejoice and triumph in the manifestation of His glory (I Peter 4:13).

The Cross, finally, is the *banner* of the Church. From the day when the Saviour bore the Cross on His shoulders to Golgotha and was crucified on the material Cross, the Cross became the visible sign and banner of Christianity, of the Church, of everyone who believes in Christ.

Not everyone who belongs to Christianity "in general" has such an understanding of the Gospel. Certain large Christian societies deny the Cross as a visible banner, considering that it has remained what it was, an instrument of reproach. The Apostle Paul already warned against such an "offense of the Cross" (Gal. 5:11), *lest the Cross of Christ should be made of none effect. For the preaching of the Cross is to them that perish foolishness; but unto us which are being saved, it is the power of God* (I Cor. 1:17–18). He exhorted men not to be ashamed of the Cross as a sign of reproach: *Let us go forth therefore unto Him without the camp, bearing His reproach,* he teaches (Heb. 13:13–14). For the reproach on the Cross led to the Resurrection in glory, and the Cross became the implement of salvation and the path to glory.

Having always before oneself the image of the Cross, making on oneself the sign of the Cross, the Christian first of all brings to his mind that he is called to follow the steps of Christ, bearing in the name of Christ sorrows and deprivations for his faith. Secondly, he is strengthened by the power of the Cross of Christ for battle against the evil in himself and in the world. And thirdly, he confesses that he awaits the manifestation of the glory of Christ, the Second Coming of the Lord, which itself will be preceded by the manifestation in heaven of the *sign of the Son of Man,* according to the Divine words of the Lord Himself (Matt. 24:30). This sign, according to the unanimous understanding of the Fathers of the Church, will be a magnificent manifestation of the Cross in the sky.

The sign of the Cross that we place upon ourselves or depict on ourselves by the movement of the hand is made in silence, but at the same time it is said loudly, because it is an open confession of our faith.

Thus, with the Cross is bound up the whole grandeur of our redemption, which reminds us of the necessity of personal struggle for the Christian. In the representation of the Cross, even in its name, is summed up the whole history of the Gospel, as also the history of martyrdom and the confession of Christianity in all ages.[7]

Reflecting deeply on the wealth of thoughts bound up with the Cross, the Church hymns the power of the Cross: "O invincible and incomprehensible and Divine power of the precious and life-giving Cross, forsake not us sinners."

---

[7] In explaining why Christians venerate the Cross, St. John Damascene sums up what has been accomplished through the Cross, which, as he says, is a term denoting the death of Christ: "Every action of Christ and all His working of miracles were truly very great and Divine and wonderful, but of all things the most wonderful is His honorable Cross. For by nothing else except the Cross of our Lord Jesus Christ has death been brought low, the sin of our first parent destroyed, hell plundered, resurrection bestowed, the power given us to despise the things of this world and even death itself, the road back to the former blessedness made smooth, the gates of Paradise opened, our nature seated at the right hand of God, and we made children and heirs of God. By the Cross all things have been set aright. For *as many of us as were baptized into Jesus Christ,* says the Apostle, *were baptized into His death* (Rom. 6:3), and *as many of you as have been baptized into Christ have put on Christ* (Gal. 3:27); moreover, *Christ is the power and wisdom of God* (I Cor. 1:24). See how the death of Christ, the Cross, that is to say, has clothed us with the subsistent wisdom and power of God!" (*Exact Exposition* 4.11; FC, pp. 349–50).—3RD ED.

331

Chapter 10

Christian Eschatology

THE FUTURE FATE OF THE WORLD AND MANKIND

*Yet once, and I will shake the heavens
and the earth* (Haggai 2:6).

THE Nicaeo-Constantinopolitan Symbol of Faith (the Creed), in the seventh, eleventh, and twelfth paragraphs, contains the Orthodox Christian confession of faith in the future coming of the Son of God to earth, the General (Last) Judgment, and the future eternal life.

Paragraph 7: *And He is coming again with glory to judge the living and the dead; and His Kingdom will have no end.*

Paragraph 11: *I look for the resurrection of the dead.*

Paragraph 12: *And the life of the age to come. Amen.*

In the Divine economy there is a plan for the future until the end of the ages. And an inseparable part of Christian teaching is composed of what the word of God tells us about the events of the end of time: the Second Coming of the Lord, the resurrection of the dead, and the end of the world; and then about the beginning of the Kingdom of Glory and eternal life. The last part of Dogmatic Theology thus speaks about the culmination of the great process whose beginning is set forth in the first page of the book of Genesis.

THE PARTICULAR JUDGMENT: THE FATE OF MAN AFTER DEATH UNTIL THE GENERAL JUDGMENT

Death is the common lot of men. But for man it is not an annihilation, but only the separation of the soul from the body. The truth of the immortality of the human soul is one of the fundamental truths of Christianity. *God is not a God of the dead, but of the living; for all live unto Him* (Matt. 22:32; Luke 20:38). In the New Testament Sacred Scripture, death is called "the decease (departure) of the soul" (*I will endeavor that ye may be able after my decease to have these things always in remembrance,* II Peter 1:15). It is called the deliverance of the soul from prison (II Cor. 5:1–4); the putting off of the body (*knowing that shortly I must put off this my tabernacle,* II Peter 1:14); a departure (*having a desire to depart, and to be with Christ, which is far better,* Phil. 1:23; *the time of my departure is at hand,* II Tim. 4:6); a sleep (*David fell asleep,* Acts 13:36).

The state of the soul after death, according to the clear testimony of the word of God, is not unconscious but conscious (for example, according to the parable of the rich man and Lazarus, Luke 16:19–31). After death man is subjected to a judgment which is called "particular" to distinguish it from the general Last Judgment. It is easy in the sight of the Lord to reward a man *on the day of death according to his conduct,* says the most wise son of Sirach (11:26). The same thought is expressed by the Apostle Paul: *It is appointed unto men once to die, but after this the judgment* (Heb. 9:27). The Apostle presents the judgment as something which follows immediately after the death of a man, and evidently he understands this not as the General Judgment, but as the Particular Judgment, as the Holy Fathers of the Church have interpreted this passage. *Today shalt thou be with Me in Paradise* (Luke 23:43), the Lord uttered to the repentant thief.

In Sacred Scripture it is not given us to know how the Particular Judgment occurs after a man's death. We can judge of this only in part from separate expressions which are found in the word of God. Thus, it is natural to think that in the Particular Judgment also a large part in the fate of a man after death is taken both by good and by evil angels: the former are implements of God's mercy, and the latter—by God's allowance—are implements of God's justice. In the parable of the rich man and Lazarus, it is said that Lazarus *was carried by the angels into Abraham's bosom* (Luke 16:22). In the parable of the foolish rich man, he is told: *Thou fool, this night thy soul shall be required of thee* (lit.:

"they shall take," Luke 12:20); evidently it is evil powers who will "take it" (St. John Chrysostom). For, on the one hand, the angels of these "little ones," in the Lord's own words, always behold the face of the Heavenly Father (Matt. 18:10), and likewise at the end of the world the Lord will send His angels, who will *sever the wicked from among the just, and shall cast them into the furnace of fire* (Matt. 13:49); and on the other hand, our *adversary the devil, as a roaring lion, walketh about, seeking whom he may devour* (I Peter 5:8), and the air, as it were, is filled with the spirits of evil under the heavens, and their prince is called the "prince of the power of the air" (Eph. 6:12, 2:2).

Based on these indications of Sacred Scripture, from antiquity the Holy Fathers of the Church have depicted the path of the soul after its separation from the body as a path through such spiritual expanses, where the dark powers seek to devour those who are weak spiritually, and where therefore one is in special need of being defended by the heavenly angels and supported by prayer on the part of the living members of the Church. Among the ancient Fathers the following speak of this: Sts. Ephraim the Syrian, Athanasius the Great, Macarius the Great, Basil the Great, John Chrysostom, and others.

The most detailed development of these ideas is made by St. Cyril of Alexandria in his "Homily on the Departure of the Soul," which is usually printed in the Sequential Psalter (the Psalter with additions from the Divine services). A pictorial depiction of this path is presented in the Life of St. Basil the New (March 26), where the departed blessed Theodora, in a vision during sleep communicated to the disciple of Basil, tells what she has seen and experienced after the separation of her soul from the body and during the ascent of the soul into the heavenly mansions.

The path of the soul after its departure from the body is customarily called the "toll-houses." With regard to the images in the accounts of the toll-houses, Metropolitan Macarius in his *Orthodox Dogmatic Theology* remarks: "One must firmly remember the instruction which the angel made to St. Macarius of Alexandria when he had just begun telling him of the toll-houses: 'Accept earthly things here as the weakest kind of depiction of heavenly things.' One must picture the toll-houses as far as possible in a spiritual sense, which is hidden under the more or less sensuous and anthropomorphic features."[1]

Concerning the state of the soul after the Particular Judgment, the Orthodox Church teaches thus: "We believe that the souls of the dead are in a state of blessedness or torment according to their deeds. After being separated from the body, they immediately pass over either into joy or into sorrow and grief; however, they do not feel either complete blessedness or complete torment. For complete blessedness or complete torment each one receives after the General Resurrection, when the soul is reunited with the body in which it lived in virtue or in vice" ("Encyclical of the Eastern Patriarchs on the Orthodox Faith," par. 18). Thus the Orthodox Church distinguishes two different conditions after the Particular Judgment: one for the righteous, another for sinners; in other words, paradise and hell. The Church does not recognize the Roman Catholic teaching of three conditions: (1) blessedness, (2) purgatory, and (3) gehenna (hell). The very name "gehenna" the Fathers of the Church usually refer to the condition *after* the Last Judgment, when both death and hell will be cast into the "lake of fire" (Apoc. 20:14–15). The Fathers of the Church, basing themselves on the word of God, suppose that the torments of sinners before the Last Judgment have a preparatory character. These torments can be eased and even taken away by the prayers of the Church ("Encyclical of the Eastern Patriarchs," par. 18). Likewise, the fallen spirits are *reserved in everlasting chains under darkness* (in hell) *until the judgment of the great day* (Jude, v. 6; II Peter 2:4).

THE SIGNS OF THE NEARNESS OF THE DAY OF THE SECOND COMING OF THE LORD AND THE LAST JUDGMENT
(Matthew, chapter 24)

It was not pleasing to the Lord—for our own moral benefit—to reveal to us the time of the "last day" of the present heaven and earth, the

---

[1] For a more detailed account of the Orthodox understanding of the toll-houses, see *The Soul After Death* (Platina, Calif.: St. Herman of Alaska Brotherhood, 1980), pp. 73–96. [Fourth edition, 2004, pp. 64–87].

day of the Coming of the Son of Man, "the Day of the Lord." *Of that day and hour knoweth no man, no, not the angels of heaven, but My Father only* (Matt. 24:36). *It is not for you to know the times or the seasons, which the Father hath put in His own power* (Acts 1:7). The fact that the time is unknown should arouse Christians to a constant spiritual vigilance: *Take ye heed, watch and pray, for ye know not when the time is.... And what I say unto you I say unto all, Watch* (Mark 13:33, 37).

However, the unknowability of the time of the Lord should not prevent Christians from reflecting deeply on the course of historical events and discerning in them the *signs* of the approach of the time of the "last day." The Lord taught: *Now learn a parable of the fig tree: When his branch is yet tender, and putteth forth leaves, ye know that summer is nigh. So likewise ye, when ye shall see all these things, know that it is near, even at the doors* (Matt. 24:32–33).

Here are some of the signs indicated in the word of God:

a) The spread of the Gospel to the whole world: *And this Gospel of the Kingdom shall be preached in all the world for a witness unto all nations; and then shall the end come* (Matt. 24:14).

b) On the other hand, there will be an extraordinary manifestation of the powers of evil: *Because iniquity shall abound, the love of many shall wax cold* (Matt. 24:12). The Apostle Paul says: *In the last days perilous times shall come. For men shall be lovers of their own selves, covetous, boasters, proud, blasphemers ... lovers of pleasures more than lovers of God, having a form of godliness, but denying the power thereof* (II Tim. 3:1–5). Faith in general will grow weak: *When the Son of Man cometh, shall He find faith on the earth?* (Luke 18:8).

c) The devil will raise up warfare against the Kingdom of Christ through his instrument, Antichrist. The name "Antichrist" is used in Sacred Scripture in two meanings. In a broad, general sense it indicates every enemy of Christ; this is the meaning when "antichrists" are spoken of in the First and Second Epistles of St. John the Theologian. But in a particular sense, "Antichrist" signifies a definite person—the adversary of Christ who is to appear before the end of the world. Concerning the qualities and actions of this Antichrist we read in the Apostle Paul: *Let no man deceive you by any means: for that day shall not come, except there come a falling away first, and that man of sin be revealed, the son of perdition, who opposeth and exalteth himself above all that is called God, or that is worshipped, so that he as God sitteth in the temple of God, showing himself that he is God.… For the mystery of iniquity doth already work: only he who now letteth will let, until he be taken out of the way. And then shall that Wicked be revealed, whom the Lord shall consume with the spirit of His mouth, and shall destroy by the brightness of His Coming: even him, whose coming is after the working of Satan with all power and signs and lying wonders, and with all deceivableness of unrighteousness in them that perish; because they received not the love of the truth, that they might be saved. And for this cause God shall send them strong delusion, that they should believe a lie* (II Thes. 2:3–11).

The image of this adversary of God is presented also in the Prophet Daniel (chapters 7 and 11), and in the New Testament in the Apocalypse of St. John the Theologian (chapters 11–13). The activity of Antichrist will continue until the very day of Judgment (II Thes. 2:8). The character of the person of Antichrist and a description of his activities are depicted hypothetically, but in detail, by St. Cyril of Jerusalem in his *Catechetical Lectures* (the fifteenth), and by St. Ephraim the Syrian in his "Homily on the Coming of the Lord and Antichrist."[2]

d) In the Apocalypse of St. John the Theologian there is indicated the appearance of "two witnesses" during the period of the Antichrist's activity; they will prophesy of the truth and perform miracles, and when they finish their testimony they will be killed, and then after "three days and a half" will be resurrected and ascend into heaven (Apoc. 11:3–12).[3]

---

[2] See, in the NPNF translation of St. Cyril's *Catechetical Lectures,* pp. 106–10. St. Ephraim's homily, "Concerning the Coming of the Lord, the End of the World, and the Coming of Antichrist," has been translated into English in *Orthodox Life,* 1970, no. 3.

[3] According to the universal interpretation of the Holy Fathers, these "two witnesses" (mentioned also in Zachariah, chap. 3) are the Old Testament righteous ones Enoch and Elijah, who never died but were carried up alive into heaven, and endure their earthly death only during the reign of Antichrist.

THE SECOND COMING OF THE SON OF MAN
(Matthew, chapter 25)

The spiritual gaze of mankind which believes in Christ, beginning with the time of the Ascension from earth to heaven of the Son of God, has been directed to the greatest future event of world history: His Second Coming to earth.

Testimony to the reality of this expected Coming was given quite definitely many times by the Lord Jesus Christ Himself, together with a whole series of details regarding it (Matt. 16:27 and chap. 24; Mark 8:38; Luke 12:40 and 17:24; John 14:3). The angels declared it at the Lord's Ascension (Acts 1:11). The Apostles often mention it: the Apostle Jude (vv. 14–15); the Apostle John (I John 2:28); the Apostle Peter (I Peter 4:13); and the Apostle Paul many times (I Cor. 4:5; I Thes. 5:2–6; and other places).

The Lord Himself described to His disciples the manner of His Coming in the following characteristics:

It will be sudden and obvious to everyone: *For as the lightning cometh out of the east and shineth even unto the west, so shall also the Coming of the Son of Man be* (Matt. 24:27).

First of all, there *shall appear the sign of the Son of Man in heaven; and then shall all the tribes of the earth mourn* (Matt. 24:30). This, according to the universal interpretation of the Holy Fathers of the Church, will be the sign of the life-giving Cross of the Lord.

The Lord will come surrounded by innumerable choirs of angels, in all His glory: *And they shall see the Son of Man coming in the clouds of heaven with power and great glory* (Matt. 24:30), *with the holy angels* (Mark 8:38). *He shall sit on the throne of His glory* (Matt. 25:31). Thus, the Second Coming will be different from the first when the Lord *humbled Himself, and became obedient unto death, even the death of the Cross* (Phil. 2:8).

He will come to *judge the world in righteousness* (Acts 17:31) and to *reward every man according to his works* (Matt. 16:27). In this the purpose of His Second Coming into the world is to be distinguished in essence from the purpose of His first Coming, when He came *not to judge the world, but that the world through Him might be saved* (John 3:17); He came *to give His life* (as) *a ransom for many* (Matt. 20:28).

THE RESURRECTION OF THE DEAD
(I Corinthians, chapter 15)

In the great day of the Coming of the Son of Man there will be accomplished the universal resurrection of the dead in a transfigured appearance. Concerning the resurrection of the dead the Lord says: *The hour is coming, in the which all that are in the graves shall hear His* (the Son of God's) *voice, and shall come forth: they that have done good, unto the resurrection of life; and they that have done evil, unto the resurrection of damnation* (John 5:28–29). When the Sadducees expressed unbelief in the possibility of the resurrection, the Lord reproached them: *Ye do err, not knowing the Scriptures, nor the power* (that is, the Almightiness) *of God* (Matt. 22:29).

The certainty of the truth of the resurrection and the importance of the belief in the resurrection were expressed by the Apostle Paul in the following words: *If there be no resurrection of the dead, then is Christ not risen; and if Christ be not risen, then is our preaching vain, and your faith is also vain. Yea, and we are found false witnesses of God, because we have testified of God that He raised up Christ: Whom He raised not up, if so be that the dead rise not.... But now is Christ risen from the dead, and become the firstfruits of them that slept.... For as in Adam all die, even so in Christ shall all be made alive* (I Cor. 15:13–15, 20, 22).

The resurrection of the dead will be universal and simultaneous, both of the righteous and of sinners. All the dead *shall come forth: they that have done good, unto the resurrection of life; and they that have done evil, unto the resurrection of damnation* (John 5:29). *There shall be a resurrection of the dead, both of the just and unjust* (Acts 24:15; these are the words of the Apostle Paul before the governor Felix). If the same Apostle in another place (I Cor., chap. 15, likewise I Thes., chap. 4), speaking of the resurrection of the dead in Christ, does not mention the resurrection of sinners, this is evidently because his direct purpose is to strengthen the faith of the Christians themselves in *their* future resurrection in Christ. However, there is no doubt that the appearance or form of the resurrected righteous will be different from that of resurrected sinners: *Then shall the righteous shine forth as the sun in the Kingdom of their Father*—are words spoken by the Lord only of the righteous (Matt. 13:43). "Some will resemble light, and others darkness," reflects St. Ephraim the Syrian on this passage (Homily "On the Fear of God and the Last Judgment").

From the word of God one must conclude that the resurrected bodies will be *essentially* the same ones that belonged to their souls in this earthly life: *THIS corruptible must put on incorruption, and THIS mortal must put on immortality* (I Cor. 15:53). But at the same time they will be transfigured, and first of all, the bodies of the righteous will be incorrupt and immortal, as is evident from the same words of the Apostle. They will be completely free from weakness and from the infirmities of the present life. They will be spiritual, heavenly, not having earthly, bodily needs. Life after the resurrection will be like the life of the fleshless spirits, the angels, according to the word of the Lord (Luke 20:36). As for sinners, their bodies also without any doubt will rise in a new form, but while receiving an incorrupt and spiritual nature, at the same time they will express in themselves the condition of their souls.[4]

With the aim of making faith in the future transfiguration of bod-

---

[4] Thus, St. Nicholas Cabasilas writes: "The resurrection is the restoration of our human nature. Such things God gives freely, for just as He forms us without us willing it, so He forms us anew though we have contributed nothing to it. On the other hand, the Kingdom and vision of God and union with Christ are privileges which depend on willingness. They are possible only for those who have been willing to receive them and have loved them and longed for them. For such it is fitting that they should enjoy the presence of the things for which they longed; for the unwilling it is impossible.... One need not therefore marvel that while all will live in immortality, it is not all who will live in blessedness. All equally enjoy God's Providence for our nature, but it is only those who are devout towards God who enjoy the gifts which adorn their willingness" (*The Life in Christ*, pp. 81–82).—3RD ED.

ies easier, the Apostle compares the future resurrection with sowing, a symbol of resurrection given by nature: *Some man will say, How are the dead raised up? and with what body do they come? Thou fool, that which thou sowest is not quickened, except it die; and that which thou sowest, thou sowest not that body that shall be, but bare grain, it may chance of wheat, or of some other grain; but God giveth it a body as it hath pleased Him, and to every seed his own body* (I Cor. 15:35–38).

With the same aim the Fathers of the Church have indicated that in the world in general nothing is annihilated and disappears, and that God is powerful to restore that which He Himself has created. Turning to nature, they found in it similarities to the resurrection, such as: the sprouting of plants from a seed which is thrown in the earth and rots away; the yearly renewal of nature in springtime; the renewal of the day; the awakening from sleep; the original formation of man from the dust of the earth; and other manifestations.

The universal resurrection and the events that follow after it are realities which we are incapable of representing fully with our imagination, since we have never experienced them in their authentic future form; nor can we fully understand them with our rational thought, nor resolve those numerous questions which arise before the curious mind in connection with them. Therefore, both these questions themselves and those personal conceptions which have been expressed in answer to them—often in various forms—in the writings of the Fathers and teachers of the Church, do not enter immediately into the subject of dogmatic theology, the duty of which is to sketch the precise truths of faith founded upon Sacred Scripture.

The Error of Chiliasm

Very widespread at the present time is the teaching about a thousand-year kingdom of Christ on earth before the universal or last judgment; this teaching is known by the name of "chiliasm" (from the Greek *chiliasmos*, a thousand years). The essence of this teaching is as follows:

Long before the end of the world, Christ will come again to earth to overcome Antichrist and resurrect only the righteous, to establish a new kingdom on earth in which the righteous, as a reward for their struggles and sufferings, will reign together with Him for the course of one thousand years, taking enjoyment of all the good things of temporal life. After this there will follow a second, universal resurrection of the dead, the universal judgment, and the universal and eternal giving of rewards. Such are the ideas of the chiliasts. The defenders of this teaching found themselves on the visions of the seer of mysteries (St. John the Theologian) in the twentieth chapter of the Apocalypse. There it is said that an angel descended from heaven and bound Satan for a thousand years, and that the souls of those *beheaded for the witness of Jesus and for the word of God* came to life and reigned with Christ for a thousand years. *This is the first resurrection* (Apoc. 20:4–5). *And when the thousand years are expired, Satan shall be loosed out of his prison, and shall go out to deceive the nations* (Apoc. 20:7–8). Soon there follows the judgment of the devil and of those who were deceived by him. The dead will be raised up and judged according to their deeds. *And whosoever was not found written in the book of life was cast into the lake of fire.... This is the second death* (Apoc. 20:15, 14). Upon those who have been resurrected in the first resurrection, however, the second death will have no power.

Chiliastic views were spread in antiquity chiefly among heretics. However, they are also to be encountered in certain ancient Christian writers of the universal Church (for example Papias of Hierapolis, St. Justin the Martyr, St. Irenaeus of Lyons). In more recent times these views were resurrected in the Protestant sects; and finally, we see attempts in certain modernist theologians of our times to introduce chiliastic ideas also into Orthodox theological thought.

As has been indicated, in this teaching there are supposed to be two future judgments, one for the resurrected righteous ones, and then a second, universal one; there are two future resurrections, first one of the righteous, and then another of sinners; there are two future comings of the Saviour in glory; there is a future, purely earthly—even though blessed—reign of Christ with the righteous ones as a definite historical epoch. Formally, this teaching is based on an incorrect understanding of the expression "the first resurrection"; while inwardly, its cause is rooted in the loss, among the masses of contemporary sectarianism, of faith in life after death, in the blessedness of the righteous in heaven (with whom they have no communion in prayer); and another cause, in certain sects, is to be found in utopian dreams for society hidden behind religious ideas and inserted into the mysterious images of the Apocalyse.

It is not difficult to see the error of the chiliastic interpretation of the twentieth chapter of the Apocalypse. Parallel passages in Sacred Scripture clearly indicate that the "first resurrection" signifies spiritual rebirth into eternal life in Christ through Baptism, a resurrection through faith in Christ, according to the words, *Awake thou that sleepest, and arise from the dead, and Christ shall give thee light* (Eph. 5:14). *Ye are risen with Christ,* we read many times in the Apostles (Col. 3:1 and 2:12; Eph. 2:5–6). Proceeding from this, by the thousand-year reign one must understand the period of time from the very beginning of the Kingdom of Grace of the Church of Christ, and in particular of the triumphant Church of heaven, until the end of the world. The Church which is militant upon earth in essence also is triumphant in the victory performed by the Saviour, but it is still undergoing battle with the "prince of this world," a battle which will end with the defeat of Satan and the final casting of him into the lake of fire.

The "second death" is the judgment of sinners at the Last Judgment. It will not touch those who *have part in the first resurrection* (Apoc. 20:6); this means that those who are spiritually reborn in Christ and purified by the Grace of God in the Church will not be subjected to judgment, but will enter into the blessed life of the Kingdom of Christ.

If it was at one time possible to express chiliastic ideas as private opinions, this was only until the Ecumenical Church expressed its judgment about this. But when the Second Ecumenical Council (381), in condemning all the errors of the heretic Apollinarius, condemned also his teaching of the thousand-year reign of Christ and introduced into the very Symbol of Faith the words concerning Christ:

And His Kingdom will have no end—it became no longer permissible at all for an Orthodox Christian to hold these opinions.[5]

THE END OF THE WORLD
(II Peter, chapter 3)

As a result of the fall of man, the whole creation has been unwillingly subjected to *the bondage of corruption* and *groaneth and travaileth in pain together* with us (Rom. 8:21–22).[6] The time will come when the whole material and human world must be purified from human sin and renewed, just as the spiritual world must be purified from the sin in the angelic world. This renewal of the material world must be accomplished on the "last day," the day when the last judgment of the world will be accomplished; and it will occur by means of fire. Man-

---

[5] One of the leading Fathers of the early Church who combatted the heresy of chiliasm was Blessed Augustine; see his discussion of this in *The City of God* 20.7–9. He connects the "binding" of the devil for a thousand years (Apoc. 20:2) with the "binding" of the "strong man" in Mark 3:27 (see also John 12:31, the words of Christ just before His Passion: *Now shall the prince of this world be cast out*), and states that "the binding of the devil is his being prevented from the exercise of his whole power to seduce men." Orthodox Christians who have experienced the life of Grace in the Church can well understand what Protestants cannot: that the "thousand years" (the whole period) of Christ's reign with His saints and the limited power of the devil is *now*.

A related error, widespread among contemporary Protestants, is that of the "rapture." Unheard of before the 19th century, this belief has it that during the "great tribulation" near the end of the world (either before or after the "millennium," according to various versions), true Christians will be "raptured" into the air to escape the sufferings of those who remain on earth. It is based on a misinterpretation of I Thes. 4:17, which teaches that *at the very end of the world* believers will be "caught up in the clouds," together with the resurrected dead, "to meet the Lord" Who is coming for judgment and the opening of the eternal Kingdom of Heaven. The Scripture is quite clear that even the elect will suffer on earth during the "tribulation" period, and that for their sake this period will be shortened (Matt. 24:21–22).

[6] St. Symeon the New Theologian teaches: "Do you see that this whole creation in the beginning was incorrupt and was created by God in the manner of Paradise? But later it was subjected by God to corruption, and submitted to the vanity of men" (*First-Created Man*, p. 103).—3RD ED.

kind before the Flood perished by being drowned in water, but the Apostle Peter instructs us that *the heavens and the earth which are now, by the same word are kept in store, reserved unto fire against the day of judgment and perdition of ungodly men* (II Peter 3:7). *The day of the Lord will come as a thief in the night, in the which the heavens shall pass away with a great noise and the elements shall melt with fervent heat, the earth also and the works that are therein shall be burned up....* Nevertheless we, according to His promise, look for new heavens and a new earth, wherein dwelleth righteousness* (II Peter 3:10, 13).

That the present world is not eternal was prophesied even by the Psalmist when he cried out to God: *In the beginning, O Lord, Thou didst lay the foundation of the earth, and the heavens are the works of Thy hands. They shall perish, but Thou abidest; and all like a garment shall grow old, and as a vesture shalt Thou fold them, and they shall be changed* (Ps. 101:25–27). And the Lord Jesus Christ said: *Heaven and earth shall pass away* (Matt. 24:35).

The end of the world will consist not in its total destruction and annihilation, but in a complete change and renewal of it.[7] The Fifth Ecumenical Council, in refuting various false teachings of the

---

[7] St. Symeon the New Theologian describes this transformation and renewal of creation as follows: "You should know likewise what is to be the glory and the brightly shining state of the creation in the future age. For when it will be renewed, it will not again be the same as it was when it was created in the beginning. But it will be such as, according to the word of the divine Paul, our body will also be. Concerning our body the Apostle says: *It is sown a natural body, but is raised ... a spiritual body* (I Cor. 15:44) and unchanging, such as was the body of our Lord Jesus Christ, the second Adam, after the Resurrection.... In the same way also the whole creation, according to the commandment of God, is to be, after the General Resurrection, not such as it was created, material and sensuous, but it is to be re-created and to become a certain immaterial and spiritual dwelling, surpassing every sense, and as the Apostle says of us, *We shall not sleep, but we shall all be changed, in a moment, in the twinkling of an eye* (I Cor. 15:51). Thus also the whole creation, after it shall burn up in the Divine fire, is to be changed....

"The heaven will become incomparably more brilliant and bright than it appears now; it will become completely new. The earth will receive a new, unutterable beauty, being clothed in many-formed, unfading flowers, bright and spiritual.... The whole world will become more perfect than any word can describe. Having become

Origenists, solemnly condemned also their false teaching that the material world would not merely be transformed, but would be totally annihilated.

As for those men whom the coming of the Lord will find alive on earth, according to the word of the Apostle they will be instantly changed, exactly in the same way that the resurrected dead will be changed: *We shall not all sleep, but we shall all be changed in a moment, in a twinkling of an eye, at the last trump; for the trumpet shall sound, and the dead shall be raised incorruptible, and we shall be changed. For this corruptible must put on incorruption, and this mortal must put on immortality* (I Cor. 15:51–53).

THE UNIVERSAL JUDGMENT
(Apocalypse, chapters 21 and 22)

There are numerous testimonies in Sacred Scripture of the actuality and indisputability of the future Universal Judgment: John 5:22, 27–29; Matt. 16:27; 7:21–23; 11:22, 24; 12:36, 41–42; 13:37–43; 19:28–30; 24:30; 25:31–46; Acts 17:31; Jude, vv. 14–15; II Cor. 5:10; Rom. 2:5–7; 14:10; I Cor. 4:5; Eph. 6:8; Col. 3:24–25; II Thes. 1:6–10; II Tim. 4:1; Apoc. 20:11–15. Of these testimonies the most complete picture of this Last Judgment by the Saviour is given in Matthew 25:31–46 (*When the Son of Man shall come in His glory ...*). In accordance with this picture we may draw conclusions regarding the characteristics of the Judgment. It will be:

universal, that is, extending to all men living and dead, good and evil, and according to other indications given in the word of God, even to the fallen angels themselves (II Peter 2:4; Jude, v. 6);

solemn and open, for the Judge will appear in all His glory with all His holy angels before the face of the whole world;

---

spiritual and divine, it will become united with the noetic world; it will be a certain mental Paradise, a heavenly Jerusalem, the inalienable inheritance of the sons of God. Such an earth has not been inherited as yet by a single man; we are all strangers and foreigners. But when the earthly will be united with the heavenly, then also the righteous will inherit that already-renewed earth whose inheritors are to be those meek ones who are blessed by the Lord" (*First-Created Man,* pp. 103–5).—3RD ED.

strict and terrible, performed in all the justice of God—it will be *a day of wrath and revelation of the righteous judgment of God* (Rom. 2:5).

final and definitive, determining for all eternity the fate of each one who is judged. The result of the Judgment will be eternal reward—blessedness for the righteous and torment for the evil who are condemned.

Depicting in the brightest and most joyful features the eternal life of the righteous after the Universal Judgment, the word of God speaks with the same positiveness and certainty concerning the eternal torments of evil men. *Depart from Me, ye cursed, into everlasting fire,* the Son of Man will say on the day of judgment; *and these shall go away into everlasting punishment, but the righteous into life eternal* (Matt. 25:41, 46). This condition of torment is presented in Sacred Scripture as a place of torment, and it is called gehenna. (The image of the fiery gehenna is taken from the Valley of Hinnom outside Jerusalem, where at one time executions were performed, and likewise every kind of unclean thing was dumped, as a result of which a fire was constantly burning there to guard against infection.) The Lord said: *If thy hand offend thee, cut it off; it is better for thee to enter into life maimed, than having two hands to go into hell (gehenna), into the fire that never shall be quenched, where their worm dieth not, and the fire is not quenched* (Mark 9:43–44, likewise 45–48). *There shall be weeping and gnashing of teeth,* the Saviour repeated many times concerning gehenna (Matt. 8:12 and other places). In the Apocalypse of St. John the Theologian this place or condition is called *a lake of fire* (Apoc. 19:20). And in the Apostle Paul we read: *In flaming fire taking vengeance on them that know not God, and that obey not the Gospel of our Lord Jesus Christ* (II Thes. 1:8). The images of the "worm that dieth not" and the "fire that is not quenched" are evidently symbolical and indicate the severity of the torments.[8] St. John Damascene remarks: "Sinners will be given over to everlasting fire, which will not be a material fire such as we are

---

[8] By "symbolical" our contemporary, rationalistic language usually understands "not real, no more than an image"—a definition which would give a very misleading idea of the life of the future age. With regard to the images in which future blessedness and future torment are described, one might repeat the words of the angel to St.

accustomed to, but a fire such as God might know" (*Exact Exposition* 4.27; FC, p. 406).

"I know," writes St. John Chrysostom, "that many are terrified only of gehenna; but I think that the deprivation of that glory (of the Kingdom of God) is a torment more cruel than gehenna" (Homily 23 on Matthew). "This deprivation of good things," he reflects in a different place, "will cause such torment, such sorrow and oppression, that even if no punishment awaited those who sin here, it in itself (this deprivation) could torment and disturb our souls more powerfully than the torments of gehenna.... Many foolish people desire only to be delivered from gehenna; but I consider much more tormenting than gehenna the punishment of not being in that glory. And I think that he who is deprived of it should weep not so much over the torments of gehenna as over being deprived of the good things of heaven, for this alone is the cruelest of all punishments" (Homily 1, to Theodore).

We may read a similar explanation in St. Irenaeus of Lyons (*Against Heresies* 5.27).

St. Gregory the Theologian teaches: "Acknowledge the resurrection, the judgment, and the awarding of the righteous by the Judgment of God. And this awarding for those who have been purified in heart will be light, that is, God visible and known according to the degree of one's purity, which we also call the Kingdom of Heaven. But for those who are blinded in mind, that is, for those who have become estranged from God, according to the degree of their present nearsightedness, there will be darkness" (Homily 40, On Holy Baptism).

Macarius of Alexandria on the toll-houses (quoted in the text above): "Accept earthly things here as the weakest kind of depiction of heavenly things"; but such images as the "worm" and the "fire" certainly correspond to a reality that is frightful beyond imagination—and a reality which, while not "material" according to our experience of earthly matter, is still somehow "bodily," corresponding to the resurrected spiritual body that will experience them. One may read of the frightfully "real" experience of the "worm that dieth not" by a spiritual son of St. Seraphim of Sarov ("Are There Tortures in Hell?" in *Orthodox Life*, 1970, no. 5) in order to gain an insight into the nature of the future torments of gehenna.

The Church, basing itself on the word of God, acknowledges the torments of gehenna to be eternal and unending, and therefore it condemned at the Fifth Ecumenical Council the false teaching of the Origenists that the demons and impious people would suffer in hell only for a certain definite time, and then would be restored to their original condition of innocence (*apokatastasis* in Greek).[9] The condemnation at the Universal Judgment is called in the Apocalypse of St. John the Theologian the "second death" (Apoc. 20:14).

An attempt to understand the torments of gehenna in a relative sense, to understand eternity as some kind of age or period—perhaps a long one, but one still having an end—was made in antiquity, just as it is made today; this view in general denies the reality of these torments. In this attempt there are brought forward conceptions of a logical kind: the disharmony between such torments and the goodness of God is pointed out, as is the seeming disproportion between crimes that are temporal and the eternity of the punishments for sin, as well as the disharmony between these eternal punishments and the final aim of the creation of man, which is blessedness in God.

But it is not for us to define the boundaries between the unutterable mercy of God and His justice or righteousness. We know that the Lord *will have all men to be saved, and to come unto the knowledge of the truth* (I Tim. 2:4); but man is capable, through his own evil will, of rejecting the mercy of God and the means of salvation. Chrysostom, in

---

[9] The teaching of a restoration (*apokatastasis*) of creation at the Second Coming of Christ is found in Acts 3:19–21: *Repent ye, therefore, and be converted, that your sins may be blotted out, when the times of refreshing shall come from the presence of the Lord; and He shall send Jesus Christ, Who was before preached unto you: Whom the heaven must receive until the times of restitution (apokatastaseos) of all things....* Here *apokatastasis* is to be understood as the change, renewal and transfiguration of man and the cosmos at the time of the General Resurrection, as outlined in the present chapter. It is not to be understood as "universal salvation," that is, the heretical Origenist notion that *all* human beings and even all the demons will ultimately enter into everlasting blessedness. The Orthodox understanding of *apokatastasis* is presented in the *Ambigua* of St. Maximus the Confessor, which contain both a refutation and a correction of Origenism. (See St. Maximus the Confessor, *On the Cosmic Mystery of Jesus Christ*, p. 56.)—3RD ED.

interpreting the depiction of the Last Judgment, remarks: "When He (the Lord) spoke about the Kingdom, after saying, *Come, ye blessed of My Father, inherit the Kingdom,* He added: which is *prepared for you from the foundation of the world* (Matt. 25:34); but when speaking about the fire, He did not speak thus, but He added: which is *prepared for the devil and his angels* (Matt. 25:41). For I have prepared for you a Kingdom, but the fire I have prepared not for you but for the devil and his angels. But since you have cast your own selves into the fire, therefore accuse yourself for this" (Homily 70 on Matthew).

We have no right to understand the words of the Lord only conditionally, as a threat or as a certain pedagogical means applied by the Saviour. If we understand it this way we err, since the Saviour does not instill in us any such understanding, and we subject ourselves to God's wrath according to the word of the Psalmist: *Why hath the ungodly one provoked God? For he hath said in his heart: He will not make enquiry* (Ps. 9:34).

Moreover, the very concept of "anger" in relation to God is conditional and anthropomorphic, as we learn from the teaching of St. Anthony the Great, who says: "God is good, dispassionate and immutable. Now someone who thinks it reasonable and true to affirm that God does not change, may well ask how, in that case, it is possible to speak of God as rejoicing over those who are good and showing mercy to those who honor Him, while turning away from the wicked and being angry with sinners. To this it must be answered that God neither rejoices nor grows angry, for to rejoice and to be offended are passions; nor is He won over by the gifts of those who honor Him, for that would mean He is swayed by pleasure.... He is good, and He only bestows blessings and never does harm, remaining always the same. We men, on the other hand, if we remain good through resembling God, are united to Him; but if we become evil through not resembling God, we are separated from Him. By living in holiness, we cleave to God; but by becoming wicked we make Him our enemy. It is not that He grows angry with us in an arbitrary way, but it is our own sins that prevent God from shining within us, and expose us to the demons who punish us. And if through prayer and acts of compassion we gain release from our sins, this does not mean that we have won God over and made Him change, but that through our actions and our turning to God we have cured our wickedness and so once more have enjoyment of God's goodness. Thus to say that God turns away from the wicked is like saying that the sun hides itself from the blind" (*Philokalia,* vol. 1, p. 352).

Worthy of attention likewise is the simple comment in this regard of Bishop Theophan the Recluse: "The righteous will go into eternal life, but the satanized sinners into eternal torments, in communion with demons. Will these torments end? If satanism and becoming like Satan should end, then the torments also can end. But is there an end to satanism and becoming like Satan? We will behold and see this then. But until then we shall believe that just as eternal life will have no end, so also the eternal torment that threatens sinners will have no end. No conjectures can show the possibility of the end of satanism. What did Satan not see after his fall! How much of the powers of God was revealed! How he himself was struck by the power of the Lord's Cross! How up to now all his cunningness and malice are defeated by this power! But still he is incorrigible, he constantly opposes; and the farther he goes, the more stubborn he becomes. No, there is no hope at all for him to be corrected! And if there is no hope for him, then there is no hope either for men who become satanized by his influence. This means that there must be hell with eternal torments."[10]

The writings of the holy Christian ascetics indicate that the higher one's moral awareness is raised, the more acute become the feeling of moral responsibility, the fear of offending God, and the awareness of the unavoidability of punishment for deviating from the commandment of God. But to just the same degree does hope in God's mercy grow. To hope in it and ask for it from the Lord is for each of us a duty and a consolation.

---

[10] St. John Damascene writes: "One should note that the fall of the angels is just what death is to men. For, just as there is no repentance for men after their death, so is there none for angels after their fall" (*Exact Exposition* 2.4; FC, p. 210).—3RD ED.

THE KINGDOM OF GLORY

With the end of this age and the transformation of the world into a new and better world, there is revealed the eternal Kingdom of God, the Kingdom of Glory.

Then will come to an end the Kingdom of Grace, the existence of the Church on earth, the militant Church; it will enter into this Kingdom of Glory and will merge with the heavenly Church. *Then cometh the end, when He shall have delivered up the Kingdom to God, even the Father; when He shall have put down all rule and all authority and power. For He must reign, till He hath put all enemies under His feet. The last enemy that shall be destroyed is death.... And when all things shall be subdued unto Him* (the Father), *then shall the Son also Himself be subject unto Him that put all things under Him, that God may be all in all* (I Cor. 15:24–26, 28). These words concerning the end of the Kingdom of Christ must be understood as the fulfillment of the Son's mission, which He accepted from the Father, and which consists of the conducting of mankind to God through the Church. Then the Son will reign in the Kingdom of Glory together with the Father and the Holy Spirit, and *of His Kingdom there shall be no end,* as the Archangel announced to the Virgin Mary (Luke 1:33), and as we read in the Symbol of Faith: "And His Kingdom will have no end." St. Cyril of Jerusalem says of this: "For will not He who reigned before overthrowing his enemies, reign all the more after He has conquered them?" (*Catechetical Lectures*).

Death will have no power in the Kingdom of Glory. *The last enemy that shall be destroyed is death.... Then shall be brought to pass the saying that is written, Death is swallowed up in victory* (I Cor. 15:26, 54). *There shall be time no longer* (Apoc. 10:6).

The eternal blessed life is presented vividly in the twenty-first chapter of the Apocalypse: *And I saw a new heaven and a new earth, for the first heaven and the first earth were passed away: and there was no more sea* (Apoc. 21:1). In the future kingdom everything will be spiritualized, immortal, and holy.

But the chief thing is that those who attain the future blessed life and become *partakers of the Divine Nature* (II Peter 1:4) will be participants in that most perfect life, whose source is in God alone.[11] In particular, the future members of the Kingdom of God will be vouchsafed, like the angels, to *see God* (Matt. 5:8), to behold His glory not as through a dark glass, not by means of conjectures, but face to face. And not only will they behold this glory, but they themselves will be *partakers* of it, shining like *the sun in the Kingdom of their Father* (Matt. 13:43), being "fellow heirs" with Christ, sitting with Christ on a throne and sharing with Him the royal grandeur (Apoc. 3:21, Rom. 8:17, II Tim. 2:11–12).

As is symbolically depicted in the Apocalypse, *they shall hunger no more, neither thirst any more; neither shall the sun light on them, nor any heat. For the Lamb which is in the midst of the throne shall feed them, and shall lead them unto living fountains of waters; and God shall wipe away all tears from their eyes* (Apoc. 7:16–17). As the Apostle Paul says, drawing from the words of the Prophet Isaiah: *Eye hath not seen, nor ear heard, neither have entered into the heart of man, the things which God hath prepared for them that love Him* (I Cor. 2:9, cf. Is. 64:4).

Blessedness in God will be all the more desirable in that it will be eternal, without end: *The righteous (shall go) into life eternal* (Matt. 25:46).

However, this glory in God, in the thought of the Holy Fathers of the Church, will have its degrees, corresponding to the moral dignity of each one. One may conclude this also from the words of Sacred Scripture: *In My Father's house are many mansions* (John 14:2); *He shall reward every man according to his works* (Matt. 16:27); *every man shall receive his own reward according to his own labor* (I Cor. 3:8); *one star differeth from another star in glory* (I Cor. 15:41).

St. Ephraim the Syrian says: "Just as everyone takes enjoyment of

---

[11] This, as indicated earlier (p. 221, note 27), is the ultimate state of man's deification: a state, however, which is not static but which is characterized by a never-ending progress toward God. By the words *partakers of the Divine Nature,* we are not of course to understand that we can become God by nature, but rather that we can partake of God's Nature through participation in His Grace (Energies).—3RD ED.

the rays of the sensual sun according to the purity of his power of seeing and of the impressions that are given, and just as in a single lamp which illumines a house each ray has its place, while the light is not divided into many lamps; so also in the future age all the righteous will dwell inseparably in a single joy, but each in his own degree will be illuminated by the single mental sun, and to the degree of his worth he will draw in joy and rejoicing as if in a single atmosphere and place, and no one will see the degrees that are higher and lower, lest looking on the surpassing Grace of another and upon his own deprivation, he will thereby have some cause in himself for sorrow and disturbance. May this not be there, where there is neither sorrow nor sighing; but everyone according to the Grace proper to him in his measure will rejoice inwardly, while outwardly all will have a single contemplation and a single joy" (St. Ephraim the Syrian, "On the Heavenly Mansions").

Let us conclude this exposition of the truths of the Orthodox Christian faith with the words of Metropolitan Macarius of Moscow at the end of his long course in dogmatic theology: "Grant to us, O Lord, to all of us always, the living and undying memory of Thy future glorious Coming, Thy final terrible judgment upon us, Thy most righteous and eternal giving of rewards to the righteous and to sinners—that in its light and with the help of Thy Grace *we should live soberly and righteously and godly in this present world* (Titus 2:12), and thus we might attain finally to the eternal blessed life in heaven, so that with all our being we might glorify Thee, together with Thine Unoriginate Father, and Thy Most Holy and Good and Life-giving Spirit, unto the ages of ages" (*Orthodox Dogmatic Theology*, vol. 2, p. 674).

APPENDIX I

ON THE NEW CURRENTS IN RUSSIAN PHILOSOPHICO-THEOLOGICAL THOUGHT, from the Point of View of the Dogmas of the Orthodox Christian Faith

By Protopresbyter Michael Pomazansky

1. THE QUESTION OF DOGMATIC DEVELOPMENT

The question of dogmatic development has long been a subject of discussion in theological literature: Can one accept, from the Church's point of view, the idea of the development of dogmas? In the majority of cases this is essentially a dispute over words; a difference occurs because the word "development" is understood in different ways: Does one understand "development" as the uncovering of something already given, or as a new revelation?

In general, the view of theological thought is this: The Church's consciousness from the Apostles down to the end of the Church's life, being guided by the Holy Spirit, in its essence is one and the same. Christian teaching and the scope of Divine Revelation are unchanging. The Church's teaching of faith does not develop, and the Church's awareness of itself, with the course of the centuries, does not become higher, deeper, and broader than it was among the Apostles. There is nothing to add to the teaching of faith handed down by the Apostles. Although the Church is always guided by the Holy Spirit, still we do not see in the history of the Church, and we do not expect, new dogmatic revelations.

Such a view on the question of dogmatic development was present, in particular, in the Russian theological thought of the 19th century. The seeming difference in the opinions of various persons on this question was a matter of the circumstances under which it was discussed. In discussions with Protestants it was natural to defend the right of the Church to "develop" dogmas, meaning by this the right of Councils to establish and sanction dogmatic propositions. In discussions with Roman Catholics, on the other hand, it was necessary to oppose the arbitrary dogmatic innovations made by the Roman Church in modern times, and thus to oppose the principle of the creation of new dogmas which have not been handed down by the ancient Church. In particular, the question of the Old Catholics in the second half of the 19th century—including the attempt to draw the Old Catholics nearer to Orthodoxy, with both sides rejecting the Vatican dogma of papal infallibility—strengthened in Russian theological thought the conservative point of view on the question of dogmatic development, the view which does not approve of the establishment of new dogmatic definitions.

In the 1880s we see a different approach to this question. V. S. Soloviev, who supported the union of Orthodoxy with the Roman Church, desiring to justify the dogmatic development of the Roman Church defended the idea of the development of the Church's dogmatic consciousness. He argued thus: "The Body of Christ changes and is perfected" like every organism; the original "basis" of faith is uncovered and clarified in the history of Christianity; "Orthodoxy stands not merely by antiquity, but by the eternally living Spirit of God."

Soloviev was inspired to defend the point of view of "development" not only by his sympathies for the Roman Church, but also by his own religio-philosophical outlook—his ideas on Sophia, the Wisdom of God; on God-Manhood as a historical process; etc. Carried along by his own metaphysical system, Soloviev in the 1890s began to put forth the teaching of the "eternal feminine," which, he said, "is not merely an inactive image in God's mind, but a living spiritual being which possesses all the fullness of power and action. The whole process of the world and history is the process of its realization and incarnation in a great multiplicity of forms and degrees.... The heavenly object of our love is only one, and it is always and for everyone one and the same, the eternal Femininity of God."[1]

Thus, a whole series of new concepts began to enter Russian religious thought. These concepts did not evoke any special resistance in Russian theological circles, since they were expressed more as philosophy than as theology.

Soloviev by his literary works and speeches was able to inspire an interest in religious problems among a wide circle of Russian educated

---

[1] Soloviev's ideas might be superficially compared to the "women's liberation" movement of today, whose latest attempt in religious circles has been to "desex" the Bible and remove all references to the "masculine" nature of God. Today's movement, however, does not really touch on philosophy or theology, remaining primarily a movement of social "liberation"; whereas Soloviev's thought is more serious, being a kind of resurrection of ancient Gnostic philosophy. Both of them, however, are equally outlandish in the forms their ideas take, and both are agreed in seeing a necessity to change traditional Christian dogmas and expressions.

[Since Fr. Seraphim Rose wrote the above paragraph (in 1981), the modern feminist movement has entered more deeply into the realm of theology, and has naturally drawn ideas from the "sophiology" of V. S. Soloviev. From within many mainline Christian churches (Protestant and Roman Catholic), there has grown a strong and determined movement to "re-imagine" the Christian faith: to replace traditional Christian dogmas with radical feminist theology, pantheism, and Gnosticism, and to incorporate worship of "Sophia" as a goddess. In 1993 the first "Re-imagining" conference was held in Minneapolis, Minnesota, in conjunction with the World Council of Churches' Ecumenical Decade of Churches in Solidarity with Women. The participants took part in a "liturgy" wherein milk and honey were used rather than bread and wine, and the goddess "Sophia" was worshipped rather than Jesus Christ. At a later Re-imagining conference held in 1998, Sophia-worshipping participants also shared biting into large red apples to express their solidarity with Eve, whom they regard as a heroine for having partaken of the forbidden fruit.

Although conservative Christians have spoken out against the conferences, the Re-imagining community remains influential within mainline churches, holding interdenominational caucuses to discuss strategies for expansion. As recently as June 2004, during the Presbyterian General Assembly in Richmond, Virginia, a "Voices of Sophia" meeting was held in which Sophia was invoked as a goddess.

More significantly, feminist theology has become the most prominent trend on mainline seminary campuses today, and is a driving force behind the ecumenical movement. The main coordinator of the 1993 Re-imagining conference, Mary Ann Lundy, is now the Deputy Director of the World Council of Churches.]

society. However, this interest was joined to a deviation from the authentic Orthodox way of thinking. This was expressed, for example, in the Petersburg "religio-philosophical meetings" of 1901–1903. At these meetings, such questions as the following were raised: "Can one consider the dogmatic teaching of the Church already completed? Are we not to expect new revelations? In what way can a new religious creativity be expressed in Christianity, and how can it be harmonized with Sacred Scripture and the Tradition of the Church, with the decrees of the Ecumenical Councils, and the teachings of the Holy Fathers?" Especially symptomatic were the disputes concerning "dogmatic development."

In Russian religious and social thought, at the beginning of the present [20th] century there appeared an expectation of the awakening of a "new religious consciousness" on Orthodox soil. The idea began to be expressed that theology should not fear new revelations, that dogmatics should use a more broadly rational basis, that it cannot entirely ignore the personal prophetic inspiration of the present day, that there should be a broadening of the circle of fundamental dogmatic problems, so that dogmatics itself might present a complete philosophico-theological worldview. The eccentric ideas expressed by Soloviev received further development and changes, and the first place among them was given to the problem of sophiology. The most outstanding representatives of the new current were Priest Paul Florensky (*The Pillar and Foundation of the Church* and other works) and Sergei N. Bulgakov, who was later an Archpriest (his later sophiological writings include *The Unsetting Light, The Unburnt Bush, Person and Personality, The Friend of the Bridegroom, The Lamb of God, The Comforter,* and *The Revelation of John*).

In connection with these questions it is natural for us to ask: Does dogmatic theology, in its usual form, satisfy the need of the Christian to have a whole world outlook? Does not dogmatics, if it refuses to acknowledge the principle of development, remain a lifeless collection of separate dogmas?

With all assurance one must say that the sphere of revealed truths which enter into the accepted systems of dogmatic theology gives every opportunity for the formation of an exalted and at the same time clear and simple worldview. Dogmatic theology, built on the foundation of firm dogmatic truths, speaks of a Personal God Who is inexpressibly near to us, Who does not need intermediaries between Himself and the creation: it speaks of God in the Holy Trinity *Who is above all, and through all, and in you all* (Eph. 4:6), of God Who loves His creation, Who is a lover of mankind and condescending to our infirmities, but does not deprive His creatures of freedom; it speaks of each man and of mankind, of man's high purpose and exalted spiritual possibilities, and at the same time of his sad moral level at the present time, of his fall; it presents ways and means for the return to the lost Paradise, revealed by the Incarnation and the death on the Cross of the Son of God, and the way to acquire the eternal blessed life. All these are vitally necessary truths. Here faith and love, knowledge, and its application in action, are inseparable.

Dogmatic theology does not pretend to satisfy on all points the curiosity of the human mind. There is no doubt that to our spiritual gaze Divine Revelation has revealed only a small part of the knowledge of God and of the spiritual world. We see, in the Apostle's words, *through a glass darkly* (I Cor. 13:12). An innumerable number of God's mysteries remain closed for us.

But one must state that the attempts to broaden the boundaries of theology, whether on a mystical or on a rational foundation, which have appeared both in ancient and modern times, do not lead to a more complete knowledge of God and the world. These systems lead into the thickets of refined mental speculations and place the mind before new difficulties. The chief thing, however, is this: nebulous opinions about the inner life in God, such as are to be seen in certain theologians who have entered the path of philosophizing in theology, do not harmonize with the immediate feeling of reverence, with the awareness and feeling of God's closeness and sanctity, and indeed, they stifle this feeling.

However, by these considerations we do not at all deny every kind of development in the sphere of dogma. What, then, is subject to development in dogmatics?

The history of the Church shows that the *quantity* of dogmas, in the narrow sense of the word, has gradually increased. It is not that dogmas have developed, but that the sphere of dogma in the history of the Church has broadened until it has come to its own limit, given by Sacred Scripture. In other words, the increase has been in the quantity of the truths of faith that have received a precise formulation at the Ecumenical Councils, or in general have been confirmed by Ecumenical Councils. The work of the Church in this direction has consisted in the precise definition of dogmatic statements, in their clarification, in showing their basis in the word of God, in finding their confirmation in Church Tradition, in declaring them obligatory for all the faithful. In this work of the Church, the scope of dogmatic truths always remains in essence one and the same; but in view of the irruption of unorthodox opinions and teachings, the Church sanctions some dogmatic statements which are Orthodox and rejects others which are heretical. One cannot deny that thanks to such dogmatic definitions the content of faith has become more clear in the awareness of the people of the Church and in the Church hierarchy itself.

Further, theological learning itself is subject to development. Dogmatic theology can use various methods; it can be supplemented by material for further study; it can make a greater or lesser use of the facts of exegesis (the interpretation of the text of Sacred Scripture), of Biblical philology, of Church history, of Patristic writings, and likewise of rational concepts; it can respond more fully or more timidly to heresies, false teachings, and various currents of contemporary religious thought. But theological learning (as opposed to theology proper) is an outward subject in relation to the spiritual life of the Church. It only studies the work of the Church and its dogmatic and other decrees. Dogmatic theology as a branch of learning can develop, but it cannot develop and perfect the teaching of the Church. (One may see an approximate analogy of this in the study of any writer: Pushkinology, for example, can grow, but from this the sum of the thoughts and images placed into his work by the poet himself is not increased.) The flowering or decline of theological learning can coincide or fail to coincide with the general level, with the rise or decline of spiritual life in the Church at one or another historical period. The development of theological learning can be impeded without loss to the essence of spiritual life. Theological learning is not called to guide the Church in its entirety; it is proper for it to seek out and to keep strictly to the guidance of the Church's consciousness.

It is given to us to know what is necessary for the good of our souls. The knowledge of God, of Divine life and Divine Providence, is given to men in the degree to which it has an immediate application in life. The Apostle teaches us this when he writes: *According as His Divine power hath given unto us all things that pertain unto life and godliness … giving all diligence, add to your faith virtue, and to virtue knowledge, and to knowledge temperance, and to temperance patience, and to patience godliness, and to godliness brotherly kindness, and to brotherly kindness charity* (II Peter 1:3–7).

2. PHILOSOPHY AND THEOLOGY

Into contemporary theological thought there has penetrated the view that Christian dogmatic theology should be supplemented, made "fruitful," enlightened by a philosophical foundation, and that it should accept philosophical conceptions into itself.

"To justify the faith of our Fathers, to raise it to a new degree of rational awareness"—this is the way V. S. Soloviev defines his aim in the first lines of one of his works, *The History and Future of Theocracy.* In the aim thus formulated there would be nothing essentially worthy of blame. However, one must be careful not to mix together two spheres—dogmatic learning and philosophy. Such a mixture is liable to lead one into confusion and to the eclipsing of their purpose, their content, and their methods.

In the first centuries of Christianity the Church writers and Fathers of the Church responded broadly to the philosophical ideas of their time, and they themselves used the concepts which had been worked out by philosophy. Why? By this they threw out a bridge from

Greek philosophy to Christian philosophy. Christianity stepped forth as a worldview which was to replace the philosophical views of the ancient world, as standing above them. Then, having become in the 4th century the official religion of the state, it was called by the state itself to take the place of all systems of worldviews which had existed up to that time. This is the reason why, at the First Ecumenical Council in the presence of the Emperor, there occurred a debate of the Christian teachers of faith with a "philosopher."

But there had to be not simply a substitution (of Christian philosophy for pagan). Christian apologetics took upon itself the aim of taking possession of pagan philosophical thought and directing its concepts into the channel of Christianity. The ideas of Plato stood before Christian writers as a preparatory stage in paganism for Divine Revelation. Apart from this, in the course of things, Orthodoxy had to fight Arianism, not so much on the basis of Sacred Scripture as by means of philosophy, since Arianism had taken from Greek philosophy its fundamental error—namely, the teaching of the Logos as an intermediary principle between God and the world, standing below the Divinity itself. But even with all this, the general direction of the whole of Patristic thought was to base all the truths of the Christian faith on the foundation of Divine Revelation and not on rational, abstract deductions. St. Basil the Great, in his treatise, "What Benefit Can Be Drawn from Pagan Works," gives examples of how to use the instructive material contained in these writings. With the universal spread of Christian conceptions, the interest in Greek philosophy gradually died out in Patristic writings.

And this was natural. Theology and philosophy are distinguished first of all by their *content*. The preaching of the Saviour on earth declared to men not abstract ideas, but a new life for the Kingdom of God; the preaching of the Apostles was the preaching of salvation in Christ. Therefore, Christian dogmatic theology has as its chief object the thorough examination of the teaching of salvation, its necessity, and the way to it. In its basic content, theology is soteriological (from the Greek *soteria*, "salvation"). Questions of ontology (the nature of existence), of God in Himself, of the essence of the world and the nature of man, are treated by dogmatic theology in a very limited way. This is not only because they are given to us in Sacred Scripture in such a limited form (and, with regard to God, in a hidden form), but also for psychological reasons. Silence concerning the inward in God is an expression of the living feeling of God's omnipresence, a reverence before God, a fear of God. In the Old Testament this feeling led to a fear of even naming the name of God. Only in the exaltation of reverent feeling is the thought of the Fathers of the Church in some few moments raised up to beholding the life within God. The chief area of their contemplation was the truth of the Holy Trinity revealed in the New Testament, and Orthodox Christian theology as a whole has followed this path.

Philosophy goes on a different path. It is chiefly interested precisely in questions of ontology: the essence of existence, the oneness of existence, the relation between the absolute principle and the world in its concrete manifestations, and so forth. Philosophy by its nature comes from *skepsis*, from doubt over what our conceptions tell us; and even when coming to faith in God (in idealistic philosophy), it reasons about God "objectively," as of an object of cold knowledge, an object which is subject to rational examination and definition, to an explanation of its essence and of its relationship as absolute existence to the world of manifestations.

These two spheres—dogmatic theology and philosophy—are likewise to be distinguished by their *methods* and their *sources*.

The source of theologizing is Divine Revelation, which is contained in Sacred Scripture and Sacred Tradition. The fundamental character of Sacred Scripture and Tradition depends on our faith in their truth. Theology gathers and studies the material which is to be found in these sources, systematizes this material, and divides it into appropriate categories, using in this work the same means which the experimental sciences use.

Philosophy is rational and abstract. It proceeds not from faith, like theology, but seeks to base itself either on the indisputable fundamental axioms of reason, deducing from them further conclusions, or upon the facts of science or general human knowledge.

Therefore one can simply not say that philosophy is able to raise the religion of the Fathers to the degree of knowledge.

However, by the distinctions mentioned above, one should not deny entirely the cooperation of these two spheres. Philosophy itself comes to the conclusion that there are boundaries which human thought by its very nature is not capable of crossing. The very fact that the history of philosophy for almost its whole duration has had two currents—idealistic and materialistic—shows that its systems depend upon a personal predisposition of mind and heart; in other words, that they are based upon something which lies beyond the boundaries of proof. That which lies beyond the boundaries of proof is the sphere of faith, a faith which can be negative and unreligious, or positive and religious. For religious thought, what "is above" is the sphere of Divine Revelation.

In this point there appears the possibility of a union of the two spheres of knowledge—theology and philosophy. Thus is religious philosophy created; and in Christianity, this means Christian philosophy.

But Christian religious philosophy has a difficult path: to bring together freedom of thought, as a principle of philosophy, with faithfulness to the dogmas and the whole teaching of the Church. "Go by the free way, wherever the free mind draws you," says the duty of the thinker; "be faithful to Divine Truth," whispers to him the duty of the Christian. Therefore, one might always expect that in practical realization the compilers of the systems of Christian philosophy will be forced to sacrifice, willingly or unwillingly, the principles of one sphere in favor of the other. The Church consciousness welcomes sincere attempts at creating a harmonious, philosophical Christian worldview; but the Church views them as private, personal creations, and does not sanction them with its authority. In any case, it is essential there be a precise distinction between dogmatic theology and Christian philosophy, and every attempt to turn dogmatics into Christian philosophy must be decisively rejected.[2]

---

[2] Probably the most successful attempt, from the Orthodox point of view, at the creation of a true Christian philosophy in 19th-century Russia, is to be found in the

3. REMARKS ON THE RELIGIO-PHILOSOPHICAL SYSTEM OF V. S. SOLOVIEV

The impulse for the new currents of Russian philosophical thought was given, as was said, by Vladimir S. Soloviev, who set as his aim "to justify the faith of the Fathers" before the reason of his contemporaries. Unfortunately, he made a whole series of direct deviations from the Orthodox Christian way of thinking, many of which were accepted and even developed by his successors.

Here are a series of points in Soloviev's philosophy which are most evidently distinct from, and even directly depart from, the teaching of faith confessed by the Church:

1. Christianity is presented by him as the highest stage in the gradual development of religions. According to Soloviev, all religions are true, but one-sided; Christianity synthesizes the positive aspects of the preceding religions. He writes: "Just as outward nature is only gradually revealed to the mind of man and to mankind, and as a result of this we must also speak of the development of experimental or natural science, so also the Divine Principle is gradually revealed to the consciousness of man, and we must speak of the development of religious experience and religious thinking.... Religious development is a positive and objective process, a real mutual relationship between God and man—the process of God-Manhood. It is clear that ... not a single one of its stages, or a single moment of the religious process, can in itself be a lie or an error. 'False religion' is a contradiction in terms."

---

philosophical essays of I. V. Kireyevsky (†1856), a spiritual son of Elder Macarius of Optina who also helped the Elder in the Optina translations of the works of the Holy Fathers. Unfortunately, Russian religious thought in the second half of the 19th century did not follow his lead; if it had, Russian Orthodoxy might have been spared the neo-Gnostic speculations of Soloviev and such followers of his as Bulgakov and Berdyaev, whose influence continues in "liberal" Orthodox circles even to this day. Kireyevsky's philosophy might well be considered the Orthodox answer to these speculations. (See Fr. Alexey Young, *A Man Is His Faith* [London: St. George Information Service, 1980].)

2. The teaching of the salvation of the world, in the form in which it is given by the Apostles, is put aside. According to Soloviev, Christ came to earth not in order to "save the human race." Rather, He came so as to raise it to a higher degree in the gradual manifestation of the Divine Principle in the world—the process of the ascent and deification of mankind and the world.[3] Christ is the highest link in a series of theophanies, and He crowns all the previous theophanies.

3. The attention of theology according to Soloviev is directed to the ontological side of existence, that is, to the life of God in Himself, and because of the lack of evidence for this in Sacred Scripture, his thought hastens to arbitrary constructions which are rationalistic or based upon imagination.

4. In the Divine life there is introduced an essence which stands at the boundary between the Divine and the created world; this is called Sophia.

5. In the Divine life there is introduced a distinction of masculine and feminine principles. In Soloviev this is a little weak. Fr. Paul Florensky, following Soloviev, presents Sophia thus: "This is a great Royal and Feminine Being which, being neither God nor the eternal Son of God, nor an angel, nor a holy man, receives veneration both from the Culminator of the Old Testament and from the Founder of the New" (*The Pillar and Foundation of the Truth*).

6. In the Divine life there is introduced an elemental principle of striving, which compels God the Logos Himself to participate in a definite process and subordinate Himself to this process, which is to lead the world out of a condition of pure materiality and inertia into a higher, more perfect form of existence.

7. God, as the Absolute, as God the Father, is presented as far

---

[3] Orthodox theology also teaches that man is called to deification, and that this deification has been made possible by Jesus Christ. However, the Orthodox understanding of the deification of a Christian (i.e., deification not by nature but by Grace), is fundamentally different from Soloviev's heretical understanding of it (i.e., the uniting of the Divine and human natures in a Christian, as in Christ Himself). Fr. Michael describes the latter more fully in point no. 8 below. See also p. 146, note 2; p. 202, note 14; p. 222, note 28; and p. 353, note 11 above.—3RD ED.

away and inaccessible to the world and to man. He goes away from the world, in contradiction of the word of God, into an unapproachable sphere of existence which, as absolute existence, has no contact with relative existence, with the world of phenomena. Therefore, according to Soloviev, there is necessary an Intermediary between the Absolute and the world. This Intermediary is called the "Logos," who was incarnate in Christ.

8. According to Soloviev, the first Adam united in himself the Divine and human natures, in a way similar to their mutual relationship in the God-Manhood of the incarnate Word; however, he violated this mutual relationship. If this is so, then the deification of man is not only a Grace-given sanctification of man, but is a restoration in him of this very God-Manhood, a restoration of the two natures. But this is not in accordance with the whole teaching of the Church—a teaching that understands deification only as a receiving of Grace. St. John Damascene writes: "There was not and there will never be another man composed of both Divinity and humanity," apart from Jesus Christ.

9. Soloviev writes: "God is the Almighty Creator and Pantocrator, but not the ruler of the earth and the creation which proceeds from it." "The Divinity ... is incommensurable with earthly creatures and can have a practical and moral relationship (authority, dominion, governance) only through the mediation of man, who as a being both divine and earthly is commensurable both with Divinity and with material nature. Thus, man is the indispensable subject of the true dominion of God" (*The History and Future of Theocracy*). This affirmation is unacceptable from the point of view of the glory and power of God and, as has been said, it contradicts the word of God. Indeed, it does not even correspond to simple observation. Man subjects nature to himself not in the name of God, as an intermediary between God and the world, but for his own purposes and egotistic needs.

The few points here noted of divergence between the views of Soloviev and the teaching of the Church indicate the unacceptability of the religious system of Soloviev as a whole for the Orthodox consciousness.

4. THE TEACHING OF THE WISDOM OF GOD
IN HOLY SCRIPTURE

The word *sophia*, "wisdom," is encountered in the sacred books of both the Old Testament (in the Greek translation) and the New Testament.

In the New Testament Sacred Scripture it is used in three meanings:

1. In the usual broad meaning of wisdom, understanding: *Jesus increased in wisdom and stature* (Luke 2:52); *But wisdom is justified of all her children* (Luke 7:35).

2. In the meaning of the wise economy of God expressed in the creation of the world, in His Providence over the world, and in the salvation of the world from sin: *O the depth of the riches both of the wisdom and knowledge of God!... For who hath known the mind of the Lord, or who hath been His counselor?* (Rom. 11:33–34). *We speak the wisdom of God in a mystery, even the hidden wisdom, which God ordained before the world unto our glory* (I Cor. 2:7).

3. In relation to the Son of God as the Hypostatical Wisdom of God: *But we preach Christ crucified ... Christ the power of God, and the wisdom of God* (I Cor. 1:23–24); *Who of God is made unto us wisdom* (I Cor. 1:30).

In the Old Testament Sacred Scripture we find in many places statements concerning wisdom. Here also there are the same three meanings for this term. In particular, wisdom is spoken of in the book of Proverbs and in two of the Apocryphal books: the Wisdom of Solomon and the Wisdom of Joshua, Son of Sirach.

a) In the majority of cases, human wisdom is presented here as a gift of God which one must hold exceptionally dear. The very titles of the books, the "Wisdom" of Solomon and the "Wisdom" of Joshua, Son of Sirach, indicate in what sense—namely, in the sense of human wisdom—one must understand this word here. In other Old Testament books separate episodes are cited which specially depict human wisdom—for example, the famous judgment of Solomon.

The above-named books introduce us to the direction of thought of the God-inspired teachers of the Jewish people. These teachers inspire the people to be guided by reason, not to give way to blind inclinations and passions, and to hold firmly in their actions to the commands of prudence, correct judgment, the moral law, and the firm foundations of duty in personal, family, and public life.

A large part of the ideas in the book of Proverbs is devoted to this subject. The title of this book, "Proverbs," forewarns the reader that he will find in it a figurative, metaphorical, and allegorical means of exposition. In the introduction to the book, after indicating the theme of it, which is "understanding, wisdom, and instruction," the author expresses the assurance that *a wise man ... will understand a parable, and a dark speech, the sayings of the wise also, and riddles* (Prov. 1:5–6, Septuagint)—that is, he will understand its figurativeness, its allegoricalness, its "hard saying" (Prov. 1:3), without taking all the images in a literal sense.

And indeed, in the further reasoning of the book, there is revealed an abundance of images and personifications in the application of the wisdom that man can possess. *Acquire wisdom, acquire understanding.... Say unto wisdom, thou art my sister; and call understanding thy kinswoman* (Prov. 4:5, 7:4). *Forsake it not, and it shall cleave to thee; love it, and it shall keep thee.... Secure it, and it shall exalt thee; honor it, that it may embrace thee; that it may give unto thy head a crown of graces, and may cover thee with a crown of delight* (Prov. 4:6, 8–9, Septuagint). *For she sits by the gates of princes, and sings in the entrances* (Prov. 8:3, Septuagint). The same kind of thinking about human wisdom is contained in the Wisdom of Solomon.

It is clear that all these sayings about wisdom in no way can be understood as a teaching of a personal Wisdom, the soul of the world, in the sophiological sense. A man possesses it, obtains it, loses it; it serves him; its beginning is called "the fear of the Lord"; and side by side with wisdom there are also named "understanding" and "instruction" and "knowledge."

b) And where does wisdom come from? Like everything else in the world, it has a single source: God. *For the Lord gives wisdom, and*

from His presence come knowledge and understanding (Prov. 2:6). God is
the Guide even of wisdom and the Corrector of the wise (Wisdom of Solomon 7:15).

A second group of utterances in Holy Scripture refer to this wisdom of God, which is *the wisdom in God Himself.* Ideas of the wisdom
in God are interspersed with ideas of the wisdom in man.

If the dignity of understanding and wisdom in man are so exalted,
then how majestic they are in God Himself! The writer uses the most
majestic expressions possible in order to present the power and grandeur of the *Divine wisdom.* Here also he makes broad use of personifi-
cation. He speaks of the grandeur of the Divine plans which, according
to our human conceptions, seem to have preceded the creation; because the wisdom of God lies at the foundation of all that exists, therefore it is before everything, earlier than everything that exists. *The Lord
made me the beginning of His ways for His works. He established me before time was in the beginning, before He made the earth, even before He
made the depths.... Before all hills, He begets me.... When He prepared
the heaven, I was present with Him* (Prov. 8:22–25, 27, Septuagint).
The author speaks of the beauty of the world, expressing in images
what was said of the creation in the book of Genesis (it was very good).
He says on behalf of wisdom: *I was by Him ... I was that wherein He
took delight; and daily I rejoiced in His presence continually* (Prov. 8:30).

In all the above-cited images of wisdom, and other similar ones,
there are no grounds for seeing in a direct sense any personal spiritual
being, distinct from God Himself, a soul of the world or idea of the
world. This does not correspond to the images given here: an ideal "essence of the world" could not be called "present" at the creation of the
world (see the Wisdom of Solomon 9:9); only something extraneous
to both the Creator and the creation could be "present." Likewise, it
could not be an "implement" of the creation itself if it itself is the soul
of the created world. Therefore, in the above-cited expressions it is natural to see personifications (a literary device), even though they are so
expressive as to be near being made into hypostases or actual persons.

c) Finally, the writer of the book of Proverbs is prophetically
exalted in thought to the prefiguration of the *New Testament economy*

of God, which is to be revealed in the preaching of the Saviour of the world, in the salvation of the world and of mankind, and in the creation of the New Testament Church. This prefiguration is to be found in the first verses of the ninth chapter of Proverbs: *Wisdom has built a house for herself, and set up seven pillars. She has killed her beasts; she has mingled her wine in a bowl …* (Prov. 9:1–6, Septuagint). This magnificent image is equal in power to the prophecies of the Saviour in the Old Testament prophets.

Since the economy of salvation was performed by the Son of God, the Holy Fathers of the Church, and following them the Orthodox interpreters of the book of Proverbs in general, refer the name "wisdom of God," which essentially belongs to the Holy Trinity as a whole, to the Second Person of the Holy Trinity, the Son of God, as the Fulfiller of the Counsel of the Holy Trinity.

By analogy with this prophetic passage, the images in the book of Proverbs which were indicated above as referring to the wisdom in God (in chapter 8) are also interpreted as applying to the Son of God. When the Old Testament writers, to whom the mystery of the Most Holy Trinity was not entirely revealed, say, *In wisdom hath He made them all* (Ps. 103:26)—for a New Testament believer, a Christian, in the name "Word" and in the name "Wisdom" is revealed the Second Person of the Holy Trinity, the Son of God.

The Son of God, as a Hypostasis of the Holy Trinity, contains in Himself all the Divine attributes in the same fullness as do the Father and the Holy Spirit. However, as having manifested these attributes to the world in its creation and its salvation, He is called the Hypostatic Wisdom of God. On the same grounds, the Son of God can also be called the Hypostatic Love (see St. Symeon the New Theologian, Homily 53); the Hypostatic Light (*walk* [in the light] *while ye have the light*—John 12:35); the Hypostatic Life ("Thou hast given birth to the Hypostatic Life"—Canon of the Annunciation, Canticle 8); and the Hypostatic Power of God (*We preach … Christ the power of God*—I Cor. 1:23–24).

APPENDIX II

THE ECUMENICAL COUNCILS
and the Heresies That Have Attacked the Church's Teaching

Compiled by Hieromonk Seraphim Rose

The **First Ecumenical Council** (the first of Nicaea). Called in 325 over the Arian heresy; under St. Metrophanes, Archbishop of Constantinople; St. Sylvester, Pope of Rome; and Emperor St. Constantine the Great. Number of fathers (bishops): 318.

The **Second Ecumenical Council** (the first of Constantinople). Called in 381 over the heresy of Macedonius; under St. Gregory the Theologian, Archbishop of Constantinople; Damasus, Pope of Rome; and Emperor St. Theodosius the Great. Number of fathers: 150.

The **Third Ecumenical Council** (of Ephesus). Called in 431 over the Nestorian heresy (the heresy of Theodore, Bishop of Mopsuestia, supported by Nestorius, Archbishop of Constantinople); under St. Cyril, Archbishop of Alexandria; St. Celestine, Pope of Rome; and Emperor Theodosius the Younger. Number of fathers: 200.

The **Fourth Ecumenical Council** (of Chalcedon). Called in 451 over the Monophysite heresy (the heresy held by Archimandrite Eutyches of Constantinople, Archbishop Dioscorus of Alexandria, and others); under St. Anatolius, Patriarch of Constantinople; St. Leo the Great, Pope of Rome; and Emperor Marcian. Number of fathers: 630.

The **Fifth Ecumenical Council** (the second of Constantinople). Called in 553 over the question of the "Three Chapters" which were bound up with the heresy of Theodore of Mopsuestia and Nestorius (the heresy condemned at the Third Ecumenical Council); under St.

Eutychius, Archbishop of Constantinople; Virgilius, Pope of Rome; and Emperor St. Justinian the Great. Number of fathers: 165.

The Sixth Ecumenical Council (the third of Constantinople). Called in 680 over the Monothelite heresy; under St. George, Patriarch of Constantinople, St. Agatho, Pope of Rome, and Emperor Constantine Pogonatus. Number of fathers: 170.

The Seventh Ecumenical Council (the second of Nicaea). Called in 787 over the Iconoclast heresy; under St. Tarasius, Patriarch of Constantinople; Adrian, Pope of Rome; Emperor Constantine and Empress Irene. Number of fathers: 367.

THE HERESIES WHICH DISTURBED THE CHURCH IN THE FIRST MILLENNIUM

(according to *The History of the Christian Church* by Eugraph Smirnov)

Even the briefest survey of the heretical movements in Christianity from the first days of the Church's existence is profitable in that it shows, side by side with the common teaching of the universal Church, the "rule of faith," how various were the deviations from the truth and how very often they assumed a sharply aggressive character and evoked a bitter battle within the Church. In the first three centuries of Christianity the heresies spread their influence over a comparatively small territory; but from the 4th century certain heresies seized about half the (Roman) Empire and caused an immense exertion of the Church's strength to do battle with them; and at the same time, when certain heresies gradually died down, others arose in their place. And if the Church had remained indifferent to these deviations from the truth, what—speaking according to human reasoning—would have happened to Christian truth? But the Church—with the help of the epistles of bishops, the exhortations and excommunications of local and regional councils (and, beginning with the 4th century, of Ecumenical Councils), sometimes with the cooperation and sometimes with the opposition of the governmental authorities—brought the "rule of faith" unshaken out of the battle and preserved Orthodoxy un-harmed. Thus it was in the first thousand years.

The second millennium has not changed this situation. In these years the deviations from Christian truth, the divisions and sects, have been many more than in the first millennium. Certain currents hostile to Orthodoxy are no less passionate in their proselytism and hostility to Orthodoxy than was the case in the epoch of the Ecumenical Coun-cils. This means that it is essential to be vigilant in preserving Ortho-doxy. A special vigilance in defending dogmas is required now because of a false path which has come from Christian circles outside the Church; this false path, while it seeks to attain a seemingly good aim, is unacceptable for the Orthodox Church: It is disdainful with regard to the dogmatic side of Christian faith in its striving to realize the unity of the whole Christian world.[1]

THE FIRST TO THIRD CENTURIES

Judaizers

The **Ebionites** (from the name of the heretic Ebion or from the Hebrew word *ebion,* "poor"). They considered Jesus Christ to be a prophet like Moses; they demanded of all Christians the strict fulfill-ment of the law of Moses; they looked on the Christian teaching as a supplement to the law of Moses.

The **Nazarites.** They believed in the Divinity of Jesus Christ, but insisted on the fulfillment of the law of Moses by Christians who were Jews, without demanding this of the non-Jewish Christians (moderate Ebionites).

The **Ebionite-Gnostics.** Their teaching was composed of the teaching of the Jewish sect of the **Essenes,** who lived on the Dead Sea (Qumran excavations, the "Dead Sea Scrolls"), joined to the elements

---

[1] See Fr. Michael's comments on this "ecumenical movement" on p. 250 above; see also his article "The Church of Christ and the Contemporary Movement for Uni-fication in Christianity," in Protopresbyter Michael Pomazansky, *Selected Essays* (Jordanville, N.Y.: Holy Trinity Monastery, 1996), pp. 210–31.—3RD ED.

of Christianity and Gnosticism. The Essenes considered themselves the preservers of the pure religion revealed to Adam but later obscured in Judaism. The Ebionite-Gnostics recognized the restoration of this religion by Christ, as the bearer of the Divine Spirit; the Gnostic element was expressed in their view on matter as being an evil principle, and in the preaching of severe asceticism.

Gnosticism

The foundation of the Gnostic systems is the idea of the creation of a higher religio-philosophical knowledge (*gnosis*) by uniting Greek philosophy and the philosophy of the learned Alexandrian Jew Philo with the Eastern religions, especially the religion of Zoroaster. In this way the Gnostics worked out diverse systems which set forth an absolute resolution of all questions of existence. To the metaphysical constructions made on this foundation were added fantasy-like symbolical forms. Having become acquainted with Christianity and even having accepted Christianity, the Gnostics did not abandon their fantastic constructions, but strove to unite them with Christianity. Thus arose the numerous Gnostic heresies in the midst of Christianity.

Gnostics of Apostolic Times

Simon Magus (the Sorcerer). Using the devices of sorcery, he gave himself out as "some great one" (Acts 8:9), a "higher Eon" in the Gnostic sense. He is considered the first ancestor of all heretics.[2]

Cerinthus the Alexandrian. His teaching is a mixture of Gnosticism and Ebionitism. He lived for some time in Ephesus when the Apostle John the Theologian was there.[3]

The **Docetists.** They considered the human nature in Christ to be only a phantom, since they considered flesh and matter in general to be evil. St. John the Theologian directed accusations against them in his epistles (for example, I John 4:2–3).

---

[2] For details of his life and contests with the Apostle Peter, see the Life of the latter (Lives of Saints, June 29).

[3] See the Life of St. John the Theologian in *Orthodox Life*, 1980, no. 3.

The **Nicolaitans** (Apoc. 2:5–16). Starting from the Gnostic demands for the mortification of the flesh, they ended by allowing immorality.

In Post-Apostolic Times

The **Alexandrian Gnostics** (the Syrian Basilides and the Jew Valentinus and their followers). Starting from dualism, or the acknowledgment of two fundamental principles of existence, they considered matter to be an inactive, inert, dead, negative principle, while—

The **Syrian Gnostics,** accepting the same dualism, acknowledged matter as the active principle of evil (in the religion of Zoroaster, "Ahriman"). To this current, among others belonged Tatian, who had been a disciple of St. Justin the Philosopher and who preached a strict asceticism. The **Antinomians** were an offshoot of the Syrian Gnostics; they permitted immorality for the purpose of weakening and mortifying the principle of evil—the flesh, matter.

The **Marcionites** (from Marcion, the son of a Syrian bishop who excommunicated his son for Gnosticism). The founder of the heresy, Marcion, taught that the world was governed on the one hand by a good God, the spiritual principle, and on the other hand by a demiurge, the creator of and sovereign over matter. In Jesus Christ, according to the teaching of Marcion, the good God Himself came down to earth and assumed a phantom body. The Marcionites taught the impossibility of the knowledge of God.[4] This heresy survived until the 6th century.

Carpocrates and his followers lessened the Divinity of Jesus Christ. His sect is one of the numerous "antinomian" sects (deniers of the moral law—in Greek, *nomos*, "law"—as limiting the free spirit).

---

[4] The Marcionite heresy was also known for its complete rejection of the Old Testament. Of the New Testament Gospels, Marcion only accepted the Gospel according to St. Luke, and that only in a form which had been mutilated to conform to his own ideas.—3RD ED.

Manichaeism

The Manichaean heresy, like Gnosticism, was a mixture of elements of Christianity with the principles of the religion of Zoroaster. In the teaching of Manes, who founded this heresy, the battle in the world between the principles of spirit and matter, good and evil, light and darkness, comprises the history of heaven and earth, in which is manifested the activity of (*a*) the life-giving spirit; (*b*) the passionless Jesus; and (*c*) the suffering Jesus, "the Soul of the world." The passionless Jesus, descending to earth, assumed only the appearance of man (Docetism), taught men, and promised the coming of the Comforter. The promised Comforter was manifested in the person of Manes, who purified the teaching of Jesus which had been corrupted by men, and opened the Kingdom of God. Manes preached a strict asceticism. Accused of distorting the religion of Zoroaster, Manes was killed in Persia. This heresy was spread primarily in the Western half of the Roman Empire and was especially strong in the 4th and 5th centuries.

Antitrinitarianism

This heresy, which was also called Monarchianism, arose on a basis of philosophical rationalism; the heretics did not acknowledge the teaching of Three Persons in God. The heresy had two branches: the Dynamists and the Modalists.

1) The **Dynamists** falsely taught that the Son of God and the Spirit of God were Divine **Powers** (to this group belonged Paul of Samosata, a bishop in Antioch in the 3rd century).

2) The **Modalists**, in place of the teaching of a Trinity of Persons, falsely taught of the revelation of God in three successive **forms;** they were also called Patripassians, since they set forth the idea that God the Father was subject to sufferings. A leading representative of this heresy was Sabellius, who had been a presbyter in Ptolemais of Egypt.

Montanism

This heresy received its name from Montanus, an unlearned man who imagined himself to be the Paraclete (the Comforter); he lived in the 2nd century. As opposed to the Antitrinitarians, the Montanists demanded the complete submission of reason to the commands of faith. Their other distinguishing features were the strictness of their asceticism and the rejection of those who had "fallen" in the persecutions. The ascetic spirit of the Montanists disposed to them the learned presbyter of Carthage, Tertullian, who joined them, although he ended his life a little apart from this heresy. The Roman bishops Eleutherius and Victor were also disposed towards Montanism. The Montanists accepted the teaching of the thousand-year earthly Kingdom of Christ (Chiliasm).

(The heresy of **Chiliasm** was held, apart from the Montanists, by several other heresies as well—for example, the Ebionites. Before the Second Ecumenical Council, when Chiliasm was condemned, certain teachers of the Church were also sympathetic to this teaching.)

THE FOURTH TO NINTH CENTURIES

Arianism

The Arian heresy, which disturbed the Church greatly for a long-time, had as its originator the Alexandrian presbyter Arius. Arius was born in Libya and had been a student in the theological school of Antioch, which avoided every kind of abstraction in interpreting the dogmas of faith (as opposed to the contemplative spirit and mystical inclination of the Alexandrian school). He interpreted the dogma of the Incarnation in a purely rational way, relying on a concept of the oneness of God, and began to teach falsely of the inequality of the Son of God with the Father, and of the created nature of the Son. His heresy seized the Eastern half of the empire, and despite its condemnation at the First Ecumenical Council, it survived almost to the end of the

4th century. After the First Ecumenical Council Arianism was continued and developed by:

The **Anomoeans,** or strict Arians;

Aetius, who had been a deacon in the Church of Alexandria; and

Eunomius, who before his excommunication had been Bishop of Cyzicus.

Aetius and Eunomius brought Arianism to its final heretical conclusions by developing the teaching that the nature of the Son of God is different from and unlike the nature of the Father.

Apollinarianism

Apollinarius the Younger was a learned man who had been Bishop of Laodicea (from 362). He taught that in the God-Manhood of Christ the human nature was incomplete; accepting the tripartite composition of human nature—spirit, irrational soul, and body—he affirmed that in Christ only the body and soul were human, but His mind was Divine. This heresy did not spread very far.

The Heresy of Macedonius

Macedonius, Bishop of Constantinople (about 342), taught falsely of the Holy Spirit in an Arian sense, namely, that the Holy Spirit is a ministering creature. His heresy was condemned at the Second Ecumenical Council, which was called because of this heresy.

(At the Second Ecumenical Council other heresies were also given over to anathema: the heresies of the Eunomians, Anomoeans, Eudocians (Arians), Semi-Arians (or Spirit-fighters), Sabellians, and others.)

Pelagianism

Pelagius, a layman and ascetic from Britain (beginning of the 5th century), and Celestius the presbyter denied the inheritance of the sin of Adam by his descendents, considering that each man is born innocent, and only thanks to moral freedom does he easily fall into sin.

Pelagianism was condemned at the Third Ecumenical Council together with Nestorianism.

Nestorianism

This heresy takes its name from Nestorius, who had been Archbishop of Constantinople. Predecessors of Nestorius in this false teaching were Diodore, teacher of the theological school of Antioch, and Theodore, Bishop of Mopsuestia (died in 429), whose disciple was Nestorius. Thus, this heresy came from the school of Antioch. Theodore of Mopsuestia taught the "contiguity" of the two natures of Christ, but not their union from the time of the conception of the Word. These heretics called the Most Holy Virgin Mary "Christotokos," but not "Theotokos" (as having given birth to Christ but not to God). The heresy was condemned at the Third Ecumenical Council.

Monophysitism (the Heresy of Eutyches)

The heresy of the Monophysites arose among the monks of Alexandria and was a reaction against Nestorianism, which had lessened the Divine Nature of the Saviour. The Monophysites considered that the human nature of the Saviour had been absorbed by His Divine Nature, and therefore they acknowledged in Christ only *one nature*.

In addition to the aged archimandrite of Constantinople, Eutyches, who gave the beginning to this unorthodox teaching, it was also defended by Dioscorus, Archbishop of Alexandria, who imposed this heresy by force at a council of bishops, thanks to which the council itself received the name of "robber council." The heresy was condemned at the Fourth Ecumenical Council.

Monothelitism

Monothelitism was a softened form of Monophysitism. While acknowledging two natures in Christ, the Monothelites taught that in Christ there was only one will—namely, the Divine will. Adherents of this teaching included several patriarchs of Constantinople who were later excommunicated (Pyrrhus, Paul, Theodore). It was also supported by Honorius, Pope of Rome. This teaching was rejected as false at the Sixth Ecumenical Council.

Iconoclasm

Iconoclasm was one of the most powerful and prolonged heretical movements. The Iconoclast heresy began in the first half of the 7th century and continued to disturb the Church for more than a hundred years. Directed against the veneration of icons, it touched also on other aspects of the faith and Church order (for example, the veneration of saints). The seriousness of this heresy was increased by the fact that a whole series of Byzantine emperors acted energetically in its favor for reasons of internal and external politics; these emperors were also hostilely disposed to monasticism. The heresy was condemned at the Seventh Ecumenical Council in 787, and the final triumph of Orthodoxy occurred in 842 under St. Methodius, Patriarch of Constantinople; at that time there was established the feast of the "Triumph of Orthodoxy," which is observed by the Church up to now (on the first Sunday of Lent).

APPENDIX III

FATHERS AND TEACHERS OF THE CHURCH
and Church Writers Mentioned in the Text of
Orthodox Dogmatic Theology
(Arranged by date of death)

By Hieromonk Seraphim Rose

A. Before the Council of Nicaea

St. DIONYSIUS the Areopagite   A.D. 96

A disciple of the Apostle Paul (Acts 17:34), first Bishop of Athens, martyred in Paris; commemorated October 3. To him have been attributed a number of works (*Mystical Theology, The Divine Names, The Heavenly Hierarchy, The Ecclesiastical Hierarchy*) which formulated the basic Orthodox teaching on these subjects and inspired later Orthodox theologians from the time of St. Maximus the Confessor (7th century). Because his works seem to have been unknown in the first Christian centuries, and in a style and content seem to be later in date, it is generally accepted that in their present form they are of the 5th century. Modern scholars therefore call the author "Pseudo-Dionysius," but in the Orthodox world, where the concept of "authorship" is not so restricted, there is no difficulty in seeing these works as in the *tradition* of St. Dionysius—and through him, of St. Paul.

St. CLEMENT, fourth Bishop of Rome   101

A disciple of Apostles Peter and Paul, ordained by St. Peter, commemorated as a hieromartyr on November 25. His one surviving work

(*The Epistle to the Corinthians*) is one of the earliest works of Christian literature after the New Testament and is an important source for early Christian dogma, liturgy, history, and Church hierarchy.

St. IGNATIUS the God-bearer   107

The second Bishop of Antioch; according to tradition he was the very child our Lord took into His arms (Mark 9:36–37)—one reason for his title of "God-bearer"; commemorated on December 20 and January 29. Martyred in Rome; on his way there he wrote seven epistles to Christian communities and to St. Polycarp, which contain a wealth of information on early Church dogma, liturgy, and organization, and which speak of his readiness for martyrdom.

St. POLYCARP, Bishop of Smyrna   156

A disciple of St. John the Theologian, he was placed in his see by the Apostles; commemorated February 23. His martyrdom is set forth in the earliest detailed account of a single martyr,[1] giving an excellent picture of his noble Christian character. His *Epistle to the Philippians* describes the doctrine, organization, and Christian charity of the Church in about A.D. 130.

PAPIAS of Hieropolis   Mid–2nd century

He was a disciple of St. John the Theologian and a friend of St. Polycarp; the fragments of his works that survive relate some of the oral teaching of the disciples of the Apostles. Unfortunately, he was led astray by an earthly understanding of the thousand-year reign of Christ (Apoc. 20:4), and led others astray into this heresy of chiliasm.

St. JUSTIN the Philosopher   165

The leading Christian apologist of the 2nd century; his writings depict the conversion of the best representatives of the pagan world to Christ. He wrote two *Apologies* against the pagans and the *Dialogue*

---

[1] That is, outside the New Testament.—3RD ED.

with the Jew Trypho. An early account of his martyrdom (the official court proceedings) has survived; he is commemorated on June 1.

TATIAN the Syrian   After 172

A pupil of St. Justin, he was also converted from paganism; but while Justin respected Greek philosophy and tried to lead it up to Christianity, Tatian went to an extreme in rejecting pagan thought, which finally led him to found the Gnostic sect of Encratites ("Abstinents"), which rejected matrimony, the use of meat and wine, etc.

ATHENAGORAS of Athens   After 177

An eloquent Christian apologist, his attitude to pagan literature was similar to St. Justin's. He wrote a *Supplication for the Christians* to Emperor Marcus Aurelius, defending from reason the Christian idea of the resurrection of the body.

St. THEOPHILUS of Antioch[2]   After 180

The sixth Bishop of Antioch, he was converted in mature years from paganism and wrote apologetic works defending Christianity against pagan objections. He used the New Testament Scriptures much more than earlier apologists, and was the first to speak clearly of their Divine inspiration.

St. IRENAEUS of Lyons   202

A disciple of St. Polycarp of Smyrna, he heard through him of St. John the Theologian, and thus was directly linked to the Apostolic age. Coming to the West, he succeeded St. Photinus as Bishop of Lyons and gained a reputation as a peacemaker in the Church. His chief work is *Against Heresies,* a defense of Orthodox Christianity against the Gnostics, using both human reason and Sacred Scripture and Tradition. Although this book is marred by his chiliastic teaching, it is the

---

[2] He is absent from the Greek *Synaxaria* but is commemorated as a saint in the Slav collections. His memory is celebrated on December 6.—3RD ED.

most important Orthodox theological work of the 2nd century and is an important witness of the Church traditions of that time. He is commemorated as a hieromartyr on August 23.

CLEMENT of Alexandria   c. 223

A convert from paganism, he traveled through many lands seeking instruction from Christian teachers. He finally became the disciple of the Christian philosopher Pantaenus in Alexandria and succeeded him as head of the school of catechumens there, being ordained presbyter. Together, they were the founders of the "Alexandrian" school of Christian theology, which emphasized a speculative and allegorical investigation of the Christian revelation. As distinct from earlier Christian writers, whose aim was chiefly to defend and justify Christianity, Clement was the first to try to systematize Christian knowledge and define its relation to ancient pagan culture, which he knew well. His chief work is a trilogy: *Exhortation to the Greeks* (aimed at converting pagans), *The Tutor* (giving instruction in Christian life), and the *Stromata* (discussing mainly the relation of Christianity to secular learning).

TERTULLIAN of Carthage   c. 223

A pagan lawyer in Rome, after his conversion he used his talents to defend Christian faith, rites, and life against heretics (especially the Gnostics) and pagans. His early writings contain much information on early Christian teaching and practices, including the only detailed pre-Nicaean work on a Christian sacrament (*On Baptism*). He was very passionate by temperament, and all his writings are polemical in nature; he had little tolerance for pagan culture ("What has Athens to do with Jerusalem?") and does not use it in defending the faith ("I believe because it is absurd"). In his later years (after 207) he joined the Montanist heresy, which followed "spirit-filled prophets" rather than the Church hierarchy, and became extremely rigoristic and "sectarian" in his views (no forgiveness for sins after Baptism, against art, against remarriage, etc.). He also taught the chiliastic heresy.

ORIGEN of Alexandria   253

The son of Christian parents, he headed the catechetical school in Alexandria at the age of 18; in his last twenty years he founded and presided over the school of theology in Caesarea of Palestine. He suffered in the persecutions of Decius shortly before his death. A brilliant thinker who attracted many by his philosophy, he strove to harmonize Christian teaching with pagan Greek thought; the influence of Plato over him (especially in his teachings on the preexistence of human souls and universal salvation), together with his allegorical interpretations of Scripture, led to heated controversies over his teaching, ending in the condemnation of his errors by the Church in the 6th century. Sts. Basil the Great and Gregory the Theologian made an anthology of some of his Orthodox writings, but because of his errors many of his works have not survived.

St. CYPRIAN, Bishop of Carthage   258

A convert from paganism, he was elected Bishop of Carthage shortly before the persecution of Decius (250), when he fled from Carthage. He died a martyr, being beheaded for the faith in 258, and is commemorated on August 31. The chief influence on his theology was the Orthodox writings of Tertullian. His own writings are all on practical subjects of Christian life and discipline: prayer, almsgiving, his own conversion, how to reconcile to the Church those who fell away during the persecutions, an *Exhortation to Martyrdom, On the Unity of the Church.* He is one of the most authoritative of the early Fathers of the Church.

St. DIONYSIUS (the Great) of Alexandria   265

A convert from paganism and a disciple of Origen, he became Bishop of Alexandria and head of the catechetical school there. He suffered exile for the faith and had great influence as a defender of Orthodoxy; commemorated as a hieromartyr on October 5. Only a few of his many writings survive, including a Canonical Letter which is accepted as part of the canons of the Orthodox Church (*Seven Ecumenical Councils,* NPNF, p. 600); they are important for the history of the Church in his times.

St. GREGORY the Wonderworker c. 270

A disciple of Origen at Caesarea, he became Bishop of Neocaesarea—where he converted almost the whole city—and founder of the Church in Cappadocia. He astonished his contemporaries by his many miracles; commemorated November 17. Of his writings there remain chiefly a Creed (preserved by St. Gregory of Nyssa in his Life of this Saint) and a Canonical Letter (*Seven Ecumenical Councils*, NPNF, p. 602).

St. METHODIUS, Bishop of Olympus (or Patara) 311

He died a martyr; commemorated June 20. A highly educated theologian, he refuted Origen's teaching of the preexistence of souls and his spiritualistic concept of the resurrection of the body. His chief remaining works are dialogues: *The Banquet* (on virginity) and *On the Resurrection* (against Origen).

LACTANTIUS After 317

A native of Africa, he became a Christian and an apologist for the faith, and was called in his old age (317) by Emperor Constantine to be the tutor of his son in Gaul. His *Divine Institutes* is the first Latin attempt at a summary of Christian teaching.

B. The Fourth and Fifth Centuries

1. In the East

St. ALEXANDER, Bishop of Alexandria 328

Bishop of Alexandria from 312; commemorated May 29. It was during his episcopate that the Arian controversy arose. He first tried fatherly persuasion on Arius, then called a council (318), where the heresy was condemned. His epistles were the only written protests against Arianism before the First Ecumenical Council (325), where he took a leading part. He died after many struggles in defending Orthodoxy.

EUSEBIUS Pamphili, Bishop of Caesarea 340

The first Church historian. His *Church History* is a rich collection of historical facts, documents, and writings from the first three centuries. He also wrote a *Life of Constantine* and apologetic works. Thinking to find a compromise with Arianism, he himself fell into Arian views.

St. ANTHONY the Great 356

The founder of anchoretic monasticism; commemorated January 17. His Letters (which he dictated, since he himself was unable to read or write) set forth the principles of the ascetic and spiritual life and warn against Arianism. St. Athanasius' *Life of St. Anthony* presents him as the model of ascetic perfection.

St. EPHRAIM the Syrian 372

Repenting for the sins of his youth, he led a life of true Christian asceticism and love. He was ordained deacon by St. Basil the Great, but refused the rank of priest and (later) of bishop. Commemorated January 28. Praised by the Fathers of the 4th century for his erudition and wisdom, he was renowned especially for his commentaries on the Scripture, his writings against heresies, his Church hymns, and above all for his writings on repentance, which (together with his famous Lenten prayer) are read in Orthodox churches during Great Lent.

St. ATHANASIUS the Great 373

After a pious childhood, he was ordained deacon in 319 and accompanied St. Alexander to the Council of Nicaea in 325, succeeding him as Bishop of Alexandria in 328. He was the great defender of the faith of Nicaea against the Arians, suffering exile five times for this. Commemorated January 18 and May 2. Besides his many anti-Arian writings, he wrote a classic exposition of the Christian doctrine of redemption (*The Incarnation of the Word*) and a *Life of St. Anthony* that not only began a new genre of Christian literature, but was also a primary inspiration for the spread of the monastic ideal in the West as well as the East.

St. BASIL the Great   379

After receiving a brilliant classical education in Athens, he was baptized at about thirty years of age and then traveled to the East to see the monastic way of life. Returning to his home in Asia Minor, he retired to the desert and hoped to live there quietly. However, he was made Archbishop of Caesarea, where he became known for his works of charity, and was placed in the center of the battle against Arianism and other heresies, suffering exile for his Orthodoxy. Commemorated on January 1 and (together with St. Gregory the Theologian and St. John Chrysostom) as one of the great "Three Hierarchs" of the Church on January 30. His writings include monastic rules and other ascetic texts, refutations of Arianism, homilies on Genesis (the *Hexaemeron*) and other books of Scripture, numerous letters, and the text of the Liturgy used even up to now in the Orthodox Church (together with the shortened version of it made by St. John Chrysostom).

St. CYRIL, Bishop of Jerusalem   386

Banished from his see three times for his confession of Orthodoxy against the Arians, he took an honored part in the Second Ecumenical Council (381). Commemorated March 18. He is chiefly known for his *Catechetical Lectures*, setting forth the Orthodox faith for catechumens, and the *Mystagogical Lectures,* concerning the Holy Mysteries.

St. GREGORY the Theologian (of Nazianzus)   390

A fellow student of St. Basil in Athens and his lifelong friend, he used his broad learning in the service of theology. He was one of the leaders in the Orthodox battle against Arianism, especially in the years he served as Archbishop of Constantinople (379–381), culminating in the Second Ecumenical Council (381), over part of which he presided. His *Five Theological Orations* delivered in these years gained him the title of "Theologian." His other works include orations on feast days and saints, poems, and letters. With St. Basil and St. Gregory of Nyssa, he is one of the three great Cappadocian Fathers. Commemorated on January 25 and 30.

St. MACARIUS the Great 390

One of the great Egyptian desert fathers at the dawn of monasticism, he was famous for his spiritual wisdom as well as his many miracles. His *Fifty Spiritual Homilies* are a basic textbook of the principles of Orthodox spiritual and ascetic life. Commemorated January 19.

DIODORE, Bishop of Tarsus 393

A native of Antioch, he obtained an excellent classical education in Athens before returning to Antioch to head a monastic community and teach at its school, where St. John Chrysostom was among his pupils. He defended the Nicene faith against pagans (especially Julian the Apostate) and heretics (Manichaeans and others), and had an honored place at the Second Ecumenical Council. After his death he was suspected of being an inspirer of Nestorianism, which is why few of his works (chiefly Biblical commentaries and apologetic works) have survived.

St. AMPHILOCIUS, Bishop of Iconium After 394

A close friend of the three Cappadocian Fathers, he was with them in their defense of Orthodoxy against the Arians. He was a leading hierarch at the Second Ecumenical Council (381) and presided at a council in Side (390) which condemned the Messalian heresy. Few of his writings have survived. Commemorated November 23.

St. GREGORY, Bishop of Nyssa 395

The younger brother of St. Basil the Great, he was educated chiefly by him and joined him in his monastery after giving up a worldly career. He took a prominent part in the Second Ecumenical Council. Commemorated January 10. He wrote dogmatic works (the *Great Catechism*), commentaries on Scripture (*The Making of Man, The Life of Moses*, etc.), ascetic treatises, apologetic works against the Arians and others, a *Life of Macrina* (his sister), orations, and letters. Known as a speculative theologian, he erred in accepting Origen's teaching of universal salvation (while rejecting Origen's other errors).

St. EPIPHANIUS of Cyprus   403

An enthusiastic supporter of monasticism, he founded a monastery near Gaza where he was abbot for thirty years, until being elected Metropolitan of Cyprus (367). He was suspicious of classical learning and was a special enemy of Origen. His chief works, *Ancoratus* (*The Firmly Anchored Man*) and *Panarion* (*The Medicine Chest*), are directed against heresies and contain the most detailed early description of them. Commemorated May 12.

St. JOHN CHRYSOSTOM   407

Born of Christian parents in Antioch, he received a good religious upbringing and secular education and began life as a lawyer. Being drawn by the monastic life (which he led for two years in a cave in the desert), he soon plunged into the study of Holy Scripture. After being ordained a priest, he attracted multitudes to hear his eloquent and inspired sermons, which gained for him the title of "Golden-mouth" (Chrysostom). In 398 he was raised to the post of Archbishop of Constantinople, where he was a zealous preacher of Orthodoxy and an accuser of the vices of those in high places, which led to his fall from imperial favor. On the way to his second place of exile he died. Commemorated November 13 and January 27 and 30. The largest part of his writings are sermons on Scripture, most notably the epistles of St. Paul; his other works include *On the Priesthood*, writings on the ascetic and monastic life, and homilies on saints and feast days.

St. ISIDORE of Pelusium   c. 435

A priest of Pelusium in Egypt and a disciple of St. John Chrysostom, he was renowned for his piety, monastic life, and knowledge of Holy Scripture. He has left two thousand letters, which reveal him as a teacher of the ascetic and moral life and a defender of Orthodoxy against Arianism. Commemorated February 4.

St. CYRIL of Alexandria   444

Patriarch of Alexandria from 412, he was the leader in the defense of Orthodoxy and the title of "Theotokos" for the Virgin Mary against the Nestorian heresy at the Third Ecumenical Council (431) and in many writings. He also wrote works against the Arians and pagans, many commentaries on Scripture, and sermons and letters. Commemorated January 18 and June 9.

Blessed THEODORET   458

Bishop of Cyrus near Antioch, he received his education in Syrian monasteries. Involved in controversy because for a long time he refused to condemn Nestorius (fearing to go to an extreme), he later became a confessor of Orthodoxy against the heresy of Eutyches (Monophysitism) at the Fourth Ecumenical Council (451). His writings are quite various and include, apart from his polemical works, commentaries on Scripture, the last great refutation of paganism (which reveals his broad knowledge of pagan literature), a *Church History* that continues Eusebius' narrative to 428, a *History of the Lovers of God* (the Lives of thirty Syrian ascetics known to him), and many letters.

2. In the West

St. HILARY, Bishop of Poitiers   368

A native of Gaul and a convert from paganism, he was one of the chief defenders of Orthodoxy in the West against the Arian heresy, for which he suffered exile. His chief work is *On the Trinity*. Commemorated January 13.

St. AMBROSE, Bishop of Milan   397

When still a provincial governor and catechumen, he was raised by popular acclaim in eight days to the rank of bishop. He was a leader in the West of the battle against Arianism and paganism. Commemorated December 7. One of the greatest Fathers of the Church, he wrote many commentaries on Scripture, dogmatic works, books on the sacraments and the duties of the clergy, and writings on monastic and moral life. He introduced antiphonal singing and other liturgical influences from the East into the West, and himself wrote hymns.

Blessed JEROME   **419**

After being educated in Rome, he visited the East, where he met St. Gregory the Theologian and lived in monasteries. He returned to Rome as a priest and took part in church affairs, inspiring many of the noble Roman ladies to abandon the world. In 385 he retired to Bethlehem, where he ended his life in scholarly studies. Commemorated June 15. He translated the whole Bible into Latin (the "Vulgate"), wrote commentaries on many of its books, defended the monastic life and wrote Lives of desert fathers, and compiled brief biographies of the Christian teachers of the first four centuries.

Blessed AUGUSTINE, Bishop of Hippo   **430**

After a sinful youth, he was baptized after meeting St. Ambrose and became the most renowned Christian teacher in the West. An inspired preacher, he brought many to repentance. In the East he is respected more for his piety and moral writings than for his theology, where, especially in his teaching on Grace, his exaggerations have given rise to controversy. His writings include the *City of God* (against the pagans), the *Confessions, Soliloquies,* numerous sermons and letters, and polemical works against the Manichaeans, Donatists, and Pelagians. Commemorated June 15.

St. JOHN CASSIAN, presbyter of Marseilles   **435**

A Westerner, he received a monastic formation in Egypt and Palestine and heard the sermons of St. John Chrysostom in Constantinople. He returned to the West and gave the first systematic presentation of the principles of Eastern monasticism in the West in his *Institutes* and *Conferences;* he also founded monasteries for men and women in Marseilles, and wrote a book *Against Nestorius.* Commemorated February 29.

St. VINCENT of Lerins   **c. 450**

A zealous defender of Orthodoxy against the Nestorian heresy, he also fearlessly defended his Christian flock by persuading Attila the Hun not to attack Rome. His letter against the heresy of Eutyches was read and approved at the Fourth Ecumenical Council (451) (*Seven Ecumenical Councils*, NPNF, pp. 254–58). He left many sermons and letters on moral life and discipline. Commemorated February 18.

C. Later Fathers and Teachers

St. GREGORY the Dialogist, Pope of Rome[3]   604

A wealthy prefect of Rome, he early renounced the world and gave his fortune for the building of monasteries. As a deacon he traveled to Constantinople and studied the rites and customs of the Eastern Church. As Pope he sent the mission of St. Augustine of Canterbury to England and reorganized the Roman Church services on the Eastern model, handing down the simple "Gregorian Chant" to the West. The Liturgy of the Presanctified Gifts still bears his name in the Orthodox Church. He wrote the celebrated *Dialogues* on the monastic saints of Italy (including the first Life of St. Benedict), a *Pastoral Rule* for clergy, commentaries on Scripture, and numerous letters. Commemorated March 12.

St. MAXIMUS the Confessor   662

Born of a noble family of Constantinople, he was secretary of Emperor Heraclius. Seeing the heresy of Monothelitism taught at court, he left the world, became a monk, and engaged in an energetic battle against the heresy, gaining its condemnation at a council in Rome.[4] For his confession of Orthodoxy his tongue was cut out and his hand cut off. Commemorated January 21 and August 13. His chief writings are on spiritual life (*Four Centuries on Charity* and others); his other works include explanations of the Liturgy and the books of St. Dionysius the Areopagite, and polemical writings against the Monothelites and Monophysites.[5]

---

[3] Also known as St. Gregory the Great.—3RD ED.

[4] The Lateran Council of 649.—3RD ED.

[5] A large part of St. Maximus' writings is also devoted to combatting and correcting the errors of Origenism.—3RD ED.

St. ANASTASIUS the Sinaite   686

Presbyter and abbot of Mt. Sinai, he is chiefly known for his battle against the heresy of the "Acephalites" (Monophysites). His works include a *Guide* (against the Monophysites) and *Answers to Questions* (on more general subjects). Commemorated April 20.

St. JOHN DAMASCENE   750

A minister under the caliph in Damascus, he wrote three letters in defense of the holy icons, for which he was slandered before the caliph and his hand was cut off. After his miraculous healing by the Mother of God, he abandoned the world and retired to St. Sabbas's monastery near Jerusalem, where he wrote many books. His most famous work is the *Exact Exposition of the Orthodox Faith*, which is the best summary of the teachings of the early Church Fathers. He also wrote polemical works against various heresies (most notably the three letters against the Iconoclasts) and sermons on feast days. He is renowned as the writer of many feast-day hymns and canons (including the service of Pascha), and as the compiler of the *Octoechos*, whose verses (especially the dogmatika) are a summing up of Orthodox teaching. Commemorated December 4.

St. PHOTIUS the Great   891

Of noble birth and a relative of martyrs and confessors, he occupied a high place at the Byzantine court when he was elected Patriarch of Constantinople, even though he was still a layman. He suffered much from the political intrigues of the court, but while he was Patriarch he was able to state clearly the Orthodox position against the pretensions to universal rule of the Pope of Rome and against the Western error of the *Filioque*. He also did much for the conversion of the Slavs, sending the mission of Sts. Cyril and Methodius. He wrote on the Procession of the Holy Spirit, against the Paulicians (a new Manichaean sect), dogmatic works, sermons, letters; he made an important collection of the Church's canons, and in his *Library* made an excellent critical compilation of a number of both Christian and pagan works. Commemorated February 6.

St. SYMEON the New Theologian 1022

Raised in the imperial court of Constantinople, he early attended the Studite monastery where, under the direction of Symeon the Devout, he labored in the strictest ascetic life. Elected abbot of the monastery of St. Mamas, he renewed it spiritually with his teachings. He suffered much from monks who did not desire such strict teaching, as well as over the veneration of his own spiritual father after the latter's death. Commemorated March 12 and October 12. His homilies on spiritual life, on the highest as well as a common level, have an honored place in the *Philokalia*, and are so profound that they have earned him the title of "New Theologian."

Blessed THEOPHYLACTUS of Bulgaria c. 1110

A native of Constantinople, he received a good classical education and became Bishop of Ohrid in Bulgaria when it was still under Byzantine rule. He is mainly known for his commentaries on almost all the books of the New Testament, where he followed closely the commentaries of St. John Chrysostom. He wrote also homilies, letters, and an accusation against the errors of the Latins which, while mild in tone, emphasizes the impossibility of accepting the *Filioque*.

St. GREGORY Palamas 1359

A learned monk of Mt. Athos of exalted spiritual life; later he became Archbishop of Thessaloniki. He fought the heresy of the Latinizer Barlaam of Calabria, who rose against the contemplative life of the hesychast monks (those living in silence) and taught that the light of Mt. Tabor and the Grace of God in general is something created. St. Gregory, in his many treatises on this subject, distinguishes between the Essence and the Energies of God, both being equally uncreated; through the uncreated Energies man can have true communion with God, which would not be the case if Barlaam's opinions were correct. Commemorated November 14 and on the Second Sunday of Lent—the latter feast a special recognition of his importance in the defense of Orthodoxy.

St. MARK of Ephesus   1444

A learned man and devout monk, he was ordained Metropolitan of
Ephesus and accompanied the Byzantine Emperor to the false union
council of Florence (1439), where he alone defended the fullness of
Orthodox teaching against the concessions to Latin doctrine which the
Pope demanded. His addresses at the council against the Latin doctrines of purgatory and the *Filioque* remain a model of Orthodox
teaching, and his epistles after the council were instrumental in causing
the Orthodox Church to reject the union. Commemorated January
19.

St. NICODEMUS the Hagiorite   1809

A monk of various sketes of Mt. Athos, he was a leader (together
with St. Macarius of Corinth in Greece and Blessed Paisius
Velichkovsky[6] for Russia) of the 18th-century Orthodox movement of
return to the sources of the Church's faith and piety. He combined the
strictest ascetic life with an immense labor of writing. His works are all
directed to the practical benefit of Orthodox Christians; they include
Lives of all the major saints of the Church (*Great Synaxaristis*) and of
the new martyrs of Greece, the *Evergetinos* (sayings of the desert fathers), a *Handbook of Counsel* on spiritual life, *Unseen Warfare*, commentaries especially on the epistles of St. Paul, the *Rudder* (a collection
of the Church's canons), and many others. He was a zealous defender
of Orthodox teaching and practice against the innovations of the Latins. Commemorated July 14.

St. IGNATIUS Brianchaninov   1867

An offspring of the monastic tradition of Blessed Paisius
Velichkovsky, he was a leading apologist in Russia for Orthodox monasticism and Patristic Orthodoxy against the errors of modern secular
"enlightenment." He was an especially keen critic of wrong approaches
in spiritual life and exposed the many forms of spiritual deception

---

6 Canonized by the Russian Orthodox Church Outside of Russia in 1982, and
by the Russian Orthodox Church (Moscow Patriarchate) in 1988.—3RD ED.

(*prelest*). His works include *The Arena* (addressed to the monastics of the last times), *On the Prayer of Jesus*, and numerous homilies on aspects of the spiritual life.

St. THEOPHAN the Recluse   1894
After retiring from his bishopric in 1866, he conducted a work of Orthodox enlightenment in Russia similar to that of St. Nicodemus in Greece. He translated into Russian the *Philokalia, Unseen Warfare*, and many homilies of St. Symeon the New Theologian; he wrote detailed commentaries on the epistles of St. Paul, several basic textbooks of spiritual life (*The Path to Salvation, What the Spiritual Life Is*), and numerous letters on spiritual and moral life. Like Bishop Ignatius, he was especially concerned to preserve the purity of the Orthodox worldview against modern "enlightenment."

St. JOHN of Kronstadt   1908
A Russian parish priest who was a wonderworker in the spirit of the ancient saints of Orthodoxy, he revealed himself in his diaries and sermons as a defender of Patristic faith and piety against the errors of modern times. His *My Life in Christ* is a treasury of Orthodox attitudes and worldview. Commemorated October 19 and December 20.

St. NECTARIOS of Pentapolis   1920
Pious and humble from his childhood, he was ordained bishop in the Church of Alexandria, only to suffer deposition from the envy of his colleagues. The last thirty years of his life he spent as director of a seminary school and then as builder and spiritual father of a convent in Aegina. His numerous miracles after his death have revealed him as a wonderworker of our times. Always intent on the Orthodox enlightenment of himself and others, he wrote numerous works on aspects of Orthodox faith and piety, including a thorough refutation of the errors of Roman Catholicism; his aim was always to strengthen Christians in the simplicity, love, and self-sacrifice of genuine Orthodoxy. Commemorated November 9.

BIBLIOGRAPHY

Works in "The Fathers of the Church" series are indicated by the abbreviation "FC" in the main text and footnotes.

Works in "The Nicene and Post-Nicene Fathers" series are indicated by the abbreviation "NPNF" in the main text and footnotes. This series, together with "The Ante-Nicene Fathers" series, was originally published by T & T Clark, Edinburgh, Scotland, from 1867 to 1872. It was reprinted by the Christian Literature Publishing Company, New York, from 1886 to 1890; and by Wm. B. Eerdmans Publishing Company, Grand Rapids, Michigan, from 1952 to 1994. From 1994 to the present, it has been reprinted by Hendrickson Publishers, Peabody, Massachusetts.

All the sources in this bibliography are in English unless otherwise noted.

Athanasius the Great, St. *Four Discourses Against the Arians; Against the Heathen; Letters of Athanasius.* The Nicene and Post-Nicene Fathers, 2nd Series, vol. 4.

———. *On the Incarnation.* London: A. R. Mowbray & Co., 1953. Reprint. Crestwood, N.Y.: St. Vladimir's Seminary Press, 1993.

Augustine, Blessed. *The City of God.* The Nicene and Post-Nicene Fathers, 1st Series, vol. 2.

Basil Krivocheine, Archbishop. *In the Light of Christ.* Crestwood, N.Y.: St. Vladimir's Seminary Press, 1986.

Basil the Great, St. *Hexaemeron.* The Fathers of the Church, vol. 46. Washington, D.C.: The Catholic University of America Press, 1963.

———. *Hexaemeron.* The Nicene and Post-Nicene Fathers, 2nd Series, vol. 8.

———. *On the Holy Spirit.* The Nicene and Post-Nicene Fathers, 2nd Series, vol. 8.

Boosalis, Harry M. *Orthodox Spiritual Life according to St. Silouan the Athonite.* South Canaan, Pa.: St. Tikhon's Seminary Press, 2000.

Cyril of Alexandria, St. *Commentary on Romans* (in Greek, with Latin translation). *Patrologiae Cursus Completus, Series Graeca,* vol. 74. Edited by J. P. Migne. Paris, 1857–1866.

Cyril of Jerusalem, St. *Catechetical Lectures.* The Nicene and Post-Nicene Fathers, 2nd Series, vol. 7.

Damascene, Hieromonk. *Father Seraphim Rose: His Life and Works.* Platina, Calif.: St. Herman of Alaska Brotherhood, 2003.

Eusebius Pamphili, Bishop of Caesarea. *The History of the Church from Christ to Constantine.* Translated by G. A. Williamson. Baltimore, Md.: Penguin Books, 1965.

The Festal Menaion. Translated by Mother Mary and Archimandrite Kallistos Ware. London: Faber and Faber, 1969. Reprint. South Canaan, Pa.: St. Tikhon's Seminary Press, 1990.

George, Archimandrite. *Deification as the Purpose of Man's Life.* Mount Athos, Greece: Holy Monastery of St. Gregorios (Grigoriou Monastery), 1997.

Gregory (Nazianzen) the Theologian, St. Homily 28 (Second Theological Oration); Homily 31 (Fifth Theological Oration), "On the Holy Spirit"; Homily 33, "Against the Arians, and Concerning Himself." The Nicene and Post-Nicene Fathers, 2nd Series, vol. 7.

Gregory of Nyssa, St. "Homily on His Ordination." *Works of St. Gregory of Nyssa* (in Russian), vol. 4.

Gregory Palamas, St. *The Homilies of Saint Gregory Palamas,* vol. 1. Edited by Christopher Veniamin. South Canaan, Pa.: St. Tikhon's Seminary Press, 2002.

Isaac the Syrian, St. *Ascetical Homilies.* Boston, Mass.: Holy Transfiguration Monastery, 1984.

Irenaeus of Lyons, St. *Against Heresies.* The Ante-Nicene Fathers, vol. 1.

John Chrysostom. *Commentary on the Gospel of St. John.* Fathers of the Church, vol. 41 (Homilies 48–88). New York: Fathers of the Church, Inc., 1959.

———. *Homilies on Genesis.* The Fathers of the Church, vol. 74 (Homilies 1–17), vol. 82 (Homilies 17–45), and vol. 87 (Homilies 46–67). Washington, D.C.: The Catholic University of America Press, 1986, 1990, 1992.

———. *Homilies on the Gospel of St. Matthew.* The Nicene and Post-Nicene Fathers, 1st Series, vol. 10.

———. *Homilies on Romans.* The Nicene and Post-Nicene Fathers, 1st Series, vol. 11.

———. *Works of St. John Chrysostom* (in Russian), vols. 1, 4, 9 and 11. St. Petersburg: St. Petersburg Theological Academy, 1895, 1898, 1905.

John Damascene, St. *Exact Exposition of the Orthodox Faith.* The Fathers of the Church, vol. 37. New York: Fathers of the Church, Inc., 1958.

————. *Exact Exposition of the Orthodox Faith.* The Nicene and Post-Nicene Fathers, 2nd Series, vol. 9.

————. *On the Two Wills in Christ* (in Greek). *Clavis Patrum Graecorum.* Turnhout, Belgium: Brepols Publishers, 1974–1987.

John of Kronstadt, St. *My Life in Christ* (in Russian). Moscow, 1894.

John Maximovitch of Shanghai and San Francisco, St. *The Orthodox Veneration of the Mother of God.* Platina, Calif.: St. Herman of Alaska Brotherhood, 1978. Revised ed. *The Orthodox Veneration of Mary the Birthgiver of God,* 1994.

Lossky, Vladimir. *The Mystical Theology of the Eastern Church.* London: James Clarke & Co. Ltd. Reprint. Crestwood, N.Y.: St. Vladimir's Seminary Press, 1976.

Macarius of Moscow, Metropolitan. *Orthodox Dogmatic Theology* (in Russian). St. Petersburg, 1883.

Maximus the Confessor, St. *Selected Writings.* Mahwah, N.J.: Paulist Press, 1985.

————. *On the Cosmic Mystery of Jesus Christ.* Translated by Paul M. Blowers and Robert Louis Wilken. Crestwood, N.Y.: St. Vladimir's Seminary Press, 2003.

Nicholas Cabasilas, St. *A Commentary on the Divine Liturgy.* London: Society for Promoting Christian Knowledge, 1960. Reprint. Crestwood, N.Y.: St. Vladimir's Seminary Press, 1977.

————. *The Life in Christ.* Crestwood, N.Y.: St. Vladimir's Seminary Press, 1974.

On the Dormition of the Mother of God: Early Patristic Homilies. Translation and introduction by Brian E. Daley, S.J. Crestwood, N.Y.: St. Vladimir's Seminary Press, 1998.

Philaret, Metropolitan of Moscow [St.]. *The Longer Catechism of the Orthodox, Catholic, Eastern Church* (in Russian). Moscow, 1830. Revised ed. Moscow, 1839. English translation: *The Catechism of the Orthodox Church.* Willits, Calif.: Eastern Orthodox Books, 1971.

The Philokalia, vol. 1. Translated by G. E. H. Palmer, Philip Sherrard, and Archimandrite Kallistos Ware. London: Faber and Faber, 1979.

The Philokalia, vol. 3. London: Faber and Faber, 1984.

The Philokalia, vol. 4. London: Faber and Faber, 1995.

Seraphim Rose, Fr. *The Place of Blessed Augustine in the Orthodox Church.*

Platina, Calif.: St. Herman of Alaska Brotherhood, 1983. Revised edition, 1996.

The Seven Ecumenical Councils. The Nicene and Post-Nicene Fathers, 2nd Series, vol. 14.

Sophrony, Archimandrite. *His Life Is Mine.* Crestwood, N.Y.: St. Vladimir's Seminary Press, 1977.

Staniloae, Fr. Dumitru. *Orthodox Spirituality.* South Canaan, Pa.: St. Tikhon's Seminary Press, 2002.

Sylvester, Bishop. *An Essay in Orthodox Dogmatic Theology, with an Historical Exposition of the Dogmas* (in Russian), vol. 3. Kiev, 1892–1893.

Symeon the New Theologian, St. *The First-Created Man.* Platina, Calif.: St. Herman of Alaska Brotherhood, 1994.

———. *Homilies* (in Russian), vols. 1 and 2. Moscow: Athonite Russian Monastery of St. Panteleimon, 1890, 1892.

———. *On the Mystical Life: The Ethical Discourses,* vol. 1. Crestwood, N.Y.: St. Vladimir's Seminary Press, 1995.

Vincent of Lerins, St. *Commonitorium.* Fathers of the Church, vol. 7. New York: Fathers of the Church, Inc., 1949.

Ware, Timothy (Bishop Kallistos of Diokleia). *The Orthodox Church.* New York: Penguin Books, 1993.

Young, Fr. Alexey, ed. *Letters from Father Seraphim.* Richfield Springs, N.Y.: Nicodemos Orthodox Publication Society, 2001.

SCRIPTURAL INDEX

New Testament references follow the Kings James Version;
Old Testament references are taken from the Septuagint,
unless otherwise noted.

INDEX

fire of, 347–48, 348n, 350
Heraclius, Emperor, 394
heresies, 15, 26, 34, 47, 90, 95, 101, 163, 186, 243, 245, 249, 258, 360, 372–73, 388, 391–92, 394–95
heretics, 41, 58, 82–83, 294, 302, 307, 342, 385, 390
Herman of Alaska, St., 327n
hesychasm, 396
heterodoxy, 30
hierarchy, Church, 42, 213, 239–40, 265, 241, 243, 251–52, 255–57, 268, 383, 385, see also bishops; episcopate
  Divine institution of, 252, 298
  equality in, 256–57
  ministries of, 252
  succession of, see Apostles, Holy, succession from; episcopate, succession of
  three degrees of, 255
Hilary, Bishop of Poitiers, St., 83, 275, 392
holiness, 168n, 199, 243, 350, see also sanctity
Holy Fathers
  teaching of, 15–16, 20, 23–24, 26, 31, 39, 42–44, 42–43n, 47, 55n, 59, 62, 67, 69, 82, 86–88, 90–95, 111n, 117n, 122, 125, 126n, 133–35, 137, 139, 146, 150, 152, 163n, 166n, 180, 182, 184–85, 190n, 210n, 235, 277, 285, 296, 326, 333–34, 337n, 338, 353, 358, 365n, 371, see also Patristic theology/tradition
  commemoration of, 44
  consensus of, 43, 43n, 151
  mind of, 13
Holy Spirit, 78, 81–83, 94, 137n, 189, 192, 195, 203, 206, 216, 230, 254–55, 261, 265–67, 270, 294, 299–300, 303, 308, 315, 352, 379
  animates the Church, 240, 261
  as Sanctifier, 218
  as Spirit of Truth, 227, 261
  Christians as temples of, 243
  Church Councils inspired by, 41
  as Comforter, 79, 81, 86, 91, 101, 218, 227, 261
  coming down of, in the Eucharist, 283
  descent of, 174, 196, 223, 231, 270
  Divinity of, 228
  false teachings regarding, 100

gifts of, 101, 139, 228, 231, 243, 252, 276, 278
  as Giver of life, 78, 111, 261, 354
  guidance of the Church by, 40, 85, 355
  human body as the temple of, 211, 321, 325
  Old Testament references to, 80
  omnipresence of, 261
  one in Essence with the Father and the Son, 83–84, 87, 89, 91, 100–102
  participation in the act of creation of, 108
  as Perfecting Cause of the creation, 111, 116
  as personal, 89, 101
  prayer to, 261
  procession of, from the Father, 72, 77, 81, 85–87, 89–92, 395
  received in Baptism, 207–8n
  reception of the Grace of, 227–28, 251–52, 276, 278
  Sacred Scripture inspired by, 32
  sent down into the world, 86, 92–93, 227–28
  worship of, 101
Holy Trinity, 39, 49, 95, 248, 252, 263n, 272, 288, 311, 354, 359, 363, 371
  confession of, in the ancient Church, 82–83
  creation by, 111
  Divinity of, 87
  dogma of, 77–78, 82–83, 86
  eternalness of, 67, 86
  hypostatic attributes of the Persons of, 77
  incomprehensibility of, 58, 84
  love between Persons of, 78, 97
  New Testament revelation of, 80–82
  Old Testament indications of, 79–80, 87
  one worship of, 77, 81, 85, 93
  oneness of Essence in, 72, 74–75, 77, 79, 91, 93
  as personal, 84, 89
  Persons of, 72, 75, 77, 79, 84, 86, 102
  prayer to, 78
Holy Trinity Monastery/Seminary, Jordanville, New York, 11, 13–14, 16, 22
Honorius, Pope of Rome, 381
hope, 133, 161, 175–76, 213, 256, 263, 293
humility, 27, 53, 157, 218, 269, 305
hymns, Church, 26, 44, 83, 205, 208, 216, 236, 264, 331, 388, 392, 395

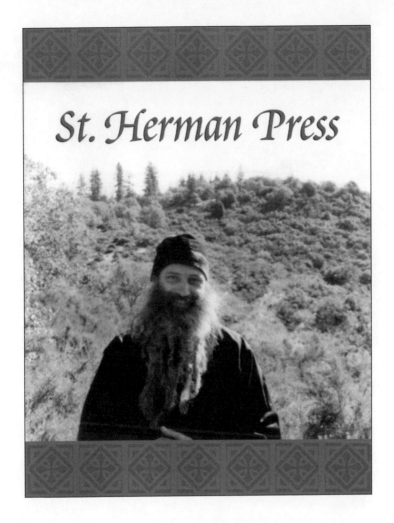

ST. HERMAN OF ALASKA BROTHERHOOD

Since 1965, the St. Herman Brotherhood has been publishing
works of Orthodox Christian spirituality.
Write for our free 88-page catalogue, featuring over sixty titles of
published and forthcoming books and periodicals.

St. Herman of Alaska Brotherhood
P. O. Box 70, Platina, CA 96076

You can also view our catalogue online, and order online, at
sainthermanpress.com

ORTHODOX DOGMATIC THEOLOGY

Typeset in Adobe Garamond.
Printed on fifty pound Glatfelter Offset paper
and Smyth-sewn bound at Thomson-Shore, Inc.,
Dexter, Michigan.